W0108050

AN INTRODUCTION TO
THE MAITHILI LANGUAGE
OF NORTH BIHAR

Owing to the antiquity and rarity of this book, certain pages are regrettably absent, and readability is compromised due to the blurring of the original text. If you possess any insights regarding the availability of these missing sections, kindly inform us. Your assistance is crucial in ensuring the completion of this significant work for the benefit of future generations.

AN INTRODUCTION TO THE MAITHILI LANGUAGE OF NORTH BIHAR:

CONTAINING A GRAMMAR, CHRESTOMATHY & VOCABULARY

GEORGE A. GRIERSON

IN TWO PARTS

PART - I

Published by

Gyan Publishing House
5, Ansari Road
Daryaganj, New Delhi-110002
Phone: 011-47034999, 9811692060
E-mail: books@gyanbooks.com

Distribution Network
gyanbooks.com
India, USA, Canada, UK, Australia

© **Publisher**

All rights reserved. No part of this work may be reproduced, stored, adapted, or transmitted in any form or by any means, electronic, mechanical, photocopying, micro-filming, recording or otherwise, or translated in any language, without the prior written permission of the copyright owner and the publisher.

ISBN: 978-93-7097-373-2 (Set)

978-93-7097-256-8 (PB)

First Published, 1882

2nd Impression 2025

Printed at: Gyan Press, Delhi.

The book is sold subject to the condition that it shall not, by way of trade or otherwise, be lent, resold, hired out, or otherwise circulated without the prior publisher's written consent.

**AN INTRODUCTION TO
THE MAITHILI LANGUAGE OF NORTH BIHAR** (PART - I)
Author: GEORGE A. GRIERSON

AN INTRODUCTION

TO THE

MAITHILÍ LANGUAGE

OF

NORTH BIHÁR

CONTAINING

A GRAMMAR, CHRESTOMATHY & VOCABULARY.

BY

GEORGE A. GRIERSON, B. C. S.

———•◆•———

PART I.

GRAMMAR.

1881.

PREFACE TO THE SECOND EDITION.

When I undertook the preparation of this second edition of my Maithilī Grammar, my intention was to do little more than to arrange a corrected reprint of the first edition published in 1881. I soon found that the necessary corrections were so heavy and so important that the whole work had to be recast. It has, in fact, been rewritten.

. When the first edition was prepared, the only specimens of literary Maithilī available were those then in my possession, and subsequently published in my Maithilī Chrestomathy. Since then more literary materials have been discovered and have been made available to students. These have all been carefully worked through by me, and, as a result, I have been able to give in the present edition of the Grammar a fairly complete set of examples of the manner in which the various forms are employed. The examples are not absolutely complete, for I have rigidly confined myself to passages taken from actually existing literature. With the exception of a few reproduced from the first edition, not a single example has been made up for the purpose of illustration.

The second edition has been prepared in England, and I have not had the advantage of further native assistance; but, on the other hand, I have fully utilized my notes which have been accumulating during the past twenty-five years. As compared with the former edition, the book represents a quarter of a century's progress in the study of an interesting and by no means easy dialect.

GEORGE A. GRIERSON.

CAMBERLEY,
June 11th, 1906.

CONTENTS.

—— o ——

PART III.

CONJUGATION.

PART IV.

INDECLINABLES.

INTRODUCTION.

In submitting the following somewhat full grammar of the Maithili dialect to the Asiatic Society of Bengal, I wish to explain the sources of my information.

They may be divided into two classes—

      1*st*—Forms obtained by translating into Maithili.

      2*nd*—Forms obtained by translating from Maithili.

The first I obtained as follows: I printed paradigms of all the forms in Hindī and Sanskrit Grammar and circulated them as widely as possible amongst the paṇḍits, village school masters, and educated native gentlemen of Northern Mithilā, with directions to give the exact translation of each of these forms in their own native language.

I was enabled, in this way, to collect some fifty most useful books of forms, supplied by representatives of all classes of society, from the village *guru*, who knew little more than the herd-boys he taught, to the most learned paṇḍits of Mithilā. I am glad to say that the utmost interest was taken in my design, for the people are proud of their language and were pleased at the idea of its being made a polite one by obtaining the honour of print. These books of paradigms formed the basis of this grammar. They were compared with each other; and where one was found wanting, another supplied the deficiency. At the same time, it must not be imagined that they showed many mutual discrepancies: on the contrary, considering the many varied sources from which they were derived, their unanimity was wonderful and justifies me in hoping that what I here publish will be found fairly accurate.

With regard to the forms obtained by translating from Maithili, they were obtained in various ways. In cutcherry I collected myself a large number of words from the mouths of the witnesses who came in from a distance. These I found very useful in checking the books of forms above referred to. I also collected a number of country songs, which afforded invaluable materials when properly sifted.

From these two sources, aided by the practical knowledge possessed by myself and one or two native friends, the following grammar has been compiled. I wish I could believe that it is thoroughly accurate ; all I can say is that we have done our best to make it as accurate as possible.

The above was what I said about the first edition. During the twenty-five years which have since elapsed, I have had frequent opportunities of checking my statements on the spot, and, when necessary, of correcting them. A large mass of notes on the language has also accumulated, and the results of all these have been incorporated in the present edition.

The *Chrestomathy*, published in Part II of the first edition, contained all the Maithilī literature then known to me. Its most important contents were the *Song of Salhēs*, the *Song of the Famine*, a collection of poems attributed to Vidyāpati Ṭhakkura, and another of poems by Harṣa Nātha. Since then the following Maithilī works have been published: *Twenty-one Vaishnava Hymns*, Manbōdh's *Haribans*, the *Gīt Dīnā Bhadrik* and the *Gīt Nebārak*, all edited by the present writer. An excellent *Rāmāyaṇa* and a translation into Maithilī of Vidyāpati's Sanskrit *Puruṣa Parīkṣā* have also been composed by Paṇḍit Chandra Jhā, and have been printed and published in Darbhanga. All these have been carefully worked through by me, and have furnished innumerable examples of the various forms given in the grammar.

Maithilī is one of the three dialects,—Maithilī, Magahī, and Bhojpurī—of the Bihārī language. Roughly speaking, we may say that Maithilī occupies North Bihār, east of the river Gaṇḍak, although towards the east it has crossed the Ganges and is spoken in parts of South Bihār. Magahī occupies South Bihār, east of the Sōn, and the northern of the two plateaux of Chota Nagpur. Bhojpurī occupies the southern plateau of Chota Nagpur and the the country north and south of the Ganges as far west as, say, Benares. Maithilī and Magahī are much more closely related to each other than either is to Bhojpurī. Indeed, the last named might almost be called a separate language. The approximate number of the speakers of each, each in its own habitat, are :—

Maithili	...	...	...	10,000,000
Magahi	...	...	...	6,240,000
Bhojpuri	...	...	...	20,000,000
			Total ...	36,240,000

Besides these there are speakers of the various Bihārī dialects scattered all over Northern India and even in the Deccan.

Turning more specially to Maithilī, the standard form of the language is that spoken in the Madhubani subdivision of the Darbhanga district, and in the adjoining portion of the district of Bhagalpur. It is this form which is described in the present grammar. The other forms of the dialect are described in the present writer's *Seven Grammars* quoted below.

The following account of the Maithilī dialect, as a whole, is taken from the Vol. V² of the Linguistic Survey of India:—

Maithilī or Tirᵃhutiyā is, properly speaking, the language of Mithilā or Tairabhukti (the ancient name of Tirhut). According to the Mithilā-māhātmya, a Sanskrit work of considerable repute in the territory which it describes, Mithilā is the country bounded on the north by the Himālaya, on the south by the Ganges, on the west by the river Gandak, and on the east by the river Kosi. It thus includes the British districts of Champaran, Muzaffarpur and Darbhanga, as well as the strip of the Nepal Tarai, which runs between these districts and the lower ranges of the Himālaya. The districts of Muzaffarpur and Darbhanga originally formed one district called Tirhut, and that name is still used as a convenient appellation for the country included in these two districts. At the present day, the language of the greater portion of Champaran is a form of Bhojpuri and not Maithilī, but, with that exception, Maithilī is spoken over the whole of this tract. It has also extended east of the river Kosi, and occupies the greater part of the district of Purnea. It has moreover crossed the Ganges, and is now spoken over the whole of the South-Gangetic portion of the Bhagalpur District, over the eastern portion of the South-Gangetic portion of the Monghyr District, and in the north and west of the Sonthal Parganas.

Maithilī is spoken in its greatest purity by the Brāhmaṇas of the north of the Darbhanga and Bhagalpur districts, and by

those of western Purnea. These men have a literature and tradi-
tions that retarded the corruption of the dialect. It is also
spoken with some purity, but with more signs of the wearing
away of inflexions, in the south of the Darbhanga District, and in
those portions of the Monghyr and Bhagalpur Districts which lie
on the northern bank of the Ganges. This may be called Southern
Standard Maithilī. To the east, in Purnea, it becomes more and
more infected with Bengali, till, in the east of that District it is
superseded by the Siripuriā dialect of that language which is a
border form of speech, Bengali in the main, but containing expressions borrowed from Maithilī, and written, not in the Bengali
character, but in the Kaithī of Bihār. The Maithilī spoken in
Purnea may be called Eastern Maithilī.

South of the Ganges, Maithilī is influenced more or less by
the Magahī spoken to its west, and, partly also by Bengali. The
result is a well-marked dialect, locally known as *Chikā-chiki bōlī*,
from its frequent use of the syllable '*chik*,' the base on which the
Verb Substantive is conjugated.

The Maithilī spoken in the Muzaffarpur District, and in a
strip of country on the western side of Darbhanga. is strongly
infected by the neighbouring Bhojpurī spoken in various forms
in the adjacent district of Saran and in the greater part of Champaran. So much is this the case, that, as spoken by some people,
it is difficult to say whether the dialect is Maithilī or Bhojpurī.
It may be called Western Maithilī.

The Musalmāns of Mithilā do not all speak Maithilī. In
Muzaffarpur and Champaran, they speak an altogether different
dialect, closely allied to the language of Oudh. It is locally
known as Shēkhaī or as Musalmānī, and is sometimes called
Jolahā Bōlī, after the caste which forms one of the most numerous
Musulmān tribes, according to popular opinion, of the locality.
The true Jolahā Bōlī, however, is the language spoken by the
Musalmāns of Darbhanga, which is a form of Maithilī, though
somewhat corrupted by the admission of Persian and Arabic
words to its vocabulary.

The number of people who speak each form of Maithilī is as
follows :—

Number of Sub-dialect.			Number of Speakers.
Standard	...	...	... 1,946,800
Southern Standard		...	... 2,300,000
Eastern	...	...	... 1,302,300
Chikā-chiki	...	...	... 1,719,781
Western	...	...	... 1,783,495
Jolahā	...	...	... 337,000

Total number of speakers of Maithili
in Maithili-speaking districts ... 9,389,376

These figures do not include the speakers of Maithili in the Nepal Tarai, concerning whom no figures are available. Under any circumstances, therefore, we shall be justified in assuming that at least ten million people speak Maithili in the country of which it is the vernacular.

The number of persons who speak Maithili in other parts is unknown. All that we can say is that, in Bengal and Assam, they have been estimated as amounting to about 275,000 people. They are not so numerous in other provinces.

Maithili is the only one of the Bihārī dialects which has a literary history. For centuries the pandits of Mithilā have been famous for their learning, and more than one Sanskrit work of authority has been written by them. One of the few learned women of India whose name has come down to us was Lakhimā Thakkurāṇi, who, according to tradition, lived at the end of the 14th century A.D. Nor was the field of vernacular literature neglected by them. The earliest vernacular writer, of whom we have any record, was the celebrated Vidyāpati Thakkura or Ṭhākur, who graced the court of Mahārājā S'iva Simha of Sugāonā, and who flourished in the middle of the 15th century. As a writer of Sanskrit works he was an author of considerable repute, and one of his works, translated into Bengali, is familiar as a text-book, under the name of the *Puruṣa-parīkṣā*, to every student of that language. But it is upon his dainty songs in the vernacular that his fame chiefly rests. He was the first of the old master-singers whose short religious poems, dealing principally with Rādhā and Kriṣṇa, exercised such an important influence on the religious

history of Eastern India. His songs were adopted and enthusiasti-
cally recited by the celebrated Hindu reformer Caitanya, who flourished at the beginning of the sixteenth century, and, through him,
became the house-poetry of the Lower Provinces. Numbers of
imitators sprung up, many of whom wrote in Vidyāpati's name,
so that it is now difficult to separate the genuine from the imita-
tions, especially as in the great collection of these Vaiṣṇava songs,
the *Pada-kalpa-taru*, which is the accepted authority in Bengal,
the former have been altered in the course of generations to suit
the Bengali idiom and metre. The *Pada-kalpa-taru* was the only
record that we had of the poet's vernacular works, till, in the
first edition of the *Maithilī Chrestomathy*, the present writer was
enabled to publish a collection of songs attributed to Vidyāpati,
which he collected in Mithilā itself, partly from the mouths of
itinerant singers and partly from manuscript collections in the
possession of local paṇḍits. That all the songs in this collection
are genuine is not a matter capable of proof, but there can be
little doubt that most of them are so, although the language has
been greatly modernised in the course of transition from mouth to
mouth during the past five centuries. A larger collection of these
songs has been made by Babu Nagēndra Nāth Gupta, and will, it
is believed, shortly be published.

Vidyāpati Ṭhakkura or, as he is called in the vernacular,
Bidyāpati Ṭhākur, had many imitators in Mithilā itself, of whom
we know nothing except the names of the most popular, and a few
stray verses. Amongst them may be mentioned Umāpati, Nandī-
pati, Mōda-narāyaṇa, Ramāpati, Mahīpati, Jayānanda, Caturbhuja,
Sarasa-rāma, Jayadēva, Kēśava, Bhañjana, Cakrapāṇi, Bhānunātha, and Harṣanātha or, in the vernacular, Harkh-nāth. The
last two were alive when the present writer was in Darbhanga
thirty years ago.

Amongst other writers in Maithili may be mentioned Manbōdh Jhā, who died about the year 1788 A.D. He composed a
Haribans, or poetical life of Kṛṣṇa, of which ten cantos are still
extant, and enjoy great popularity.

The drama has had several authors in Mithilā. The local
custom has been to write the body of a play in Sanskrit, but the
songs in the vernacular. The best known of these plays are as
follows. None of them has been published.

The *Pārijāta-harana*, and the *Rukmiṇi-pariṇaya*, both by Vidyāpati Thakkura.

The *Gaurī-pariṇaya* by Kavi-lāla.

The *Uṣā-harana* by Harṣanātha above mentioned.

The *Prabhāvati-harana* by Bhānunātha above mentioned.

Under the enlightened guidance of the late Mahārāja of Darbhanga, there has been a remarkable revival of Maithili literature during the past few years. At least one author deserving of special note has come to the front, Candra Jhā, who has shown remarkable literary powers. He has written a *Mithilā-bhāṣā Rāmāyaṇa*, and a translation, with an edition of the original Sanskrit text, of the *Puruṣa-parīkṣā* of Vidyāpati Thakkura, both of which will well repay the student by their perusal.

No translation of any part of the Bible into Maithili has been issued by the Bible Society, nor is that language included amongst those into which the Serampore missionaries translated the Scriptures. At the same time, if an article in the *Calcutta Review* is to be believed, the first translation of any portion of the Bible into any language of Northern India was that of the Gospels and Acts, made into the Chikā-chikī dialect of Maithili, by Father Antonio, at the end of the eighteenth century. The only other translations with which I am acquainted are versions of the Sermon on the Mount, and other short portions of Scripture, made about thirty years ago by Mr. John Christian, and published at Monghyr.

Authorities—

I.—EARLY REFERENCES.—The earliest reference which I can find to Maithili or Tirhutiyā is in Amaduzzi's preface to Beligatti's *Alphabetum Brammhanicum*, published in 1771. This contains a list of Indian languages amongst which is 'Tourutiana.'

Colebrooke in his famous essay on the Sanskrit and Prakrit languages written in the year 1801, is the first to describe Maithili [1] as a distinct dialect. He points out its affinity with Bengali, discusses the written character used by the Brāhmaṇs, and adds, 'as the dialect of Mithilā has no extensive use, and does not appear

---

[1] *Asiatic Researches*, Vol. VII (1801), pp. 199 ff. Reprinted in his *Essays*. Ed. 1873, p. 26.

to have been at any time cultivated by elegant poets, it is unnecessary to notice it any further in this place.' Since then,[1] like the
other dialects of Bihār, Maithili remained unnoticed and forgotten.
till Mr. Fallon gave a few specimens of it in the *Indian Antiquary*[2]
in the year 1875. In the preceding year, it is true, some examples
of the dialect were given in Sir George Campbell's *Specimens*,[3] but
they are there classed as some of many dialects of Hindī spoken in
Bihār. Indeed, at this time it was the general belief that, all
over Bihār, the language spoken was a corrupt form of Hindī,
whereas, as Colebrooke had long previously pointed out, it was
much more nearly allied to Bengali than to the Hindī of the North-
Western Provinces. Matters remained in this state, till the first
edition of the present Maithili grammar appeared in the year
1880-81.

II.—GRAMMARS—

Beside the present work, reference may be made to the
following : —

HOERNLE, A. F. R.,—*A Grammar of the Eastern Hindi compared
with the other Gaudian Languages.* London, 1880. In this
Grammar, Dr. Hoernle recognized Maithili as a dialect distinct
from Hindi. He was able to give some specimens of its
grammatical forms, but no published materials were then
available.

GRIERSON, G. A.;—*Seven Grammars of the Dialects and Sub-Dialects
of the Bihári Language.* Part I, *Introductory*, Calcutta, 1883 ;
Part IV, *Maithil-Bhojpúrí Dialect of Central and South
Muzoffarpur,* 1884; Part V, *South Maithili Dialect of South
Darbhangá, North Munger, and the Mudhepúrá Subdivision of
Bhagalpúr;* Part VI, *South Maithil-Mágadhí Dialect of South*

---

[1] Note, however, Aimé-Martin's *Lettres édifiantes et curieuses*, Paris,
1840. In Vol. II, p. 295, when describing the languages of India, he says,
' le *Marthila* (sic) se retrouve dans Neypal.'

[2] Vol. IV (1875), p. 340.

[3] *Specimens of Languages of India, including those of the Aboriginal Tribes
of Bengal, the Central Provinces and the Eastern Frontier,* Calcutta, 1874.
The specimens given are headed, ' Vernacular of West Tirhoot,' ' Vernacular
of East Tirhoot,' and ' Vernacular of West Purneah (Hindee),' respectively.
They will be found on pp. 60 ff.

Munger and Bárh Subdivision of Patna; Part VII, *South Maithili-Bengáli Dialect of South Bhagulpúr;* Part VIII, *Maithil-Bangáli Dialect of Central and Western Puraniyá.*

KELLOGG, The Rev. S. H.,—*A Grammar of the Hindí Language in which are treated . . . . the colloquial dialects of Maithila* (sic), *etc., with copious philological notes.* Second Edition, Revised and Enlarged. London, 1893. (The first edition does not deal with Maithilí).

The Maithilí portion of Dr. Kellogg's work is confessedly based on the grammars of the present writer.

III.—DICTIONARIES—

GRIERSON, G. A.,—Besides the vocabulary attached to the Maithilí Chrestomathy, there is one in the edition of Manbōdh's Haribans mentioned below.

HOERNLE, A. F. R., and GRIERSON, G. A.,—*A Comparative Dictionary of the Bihárí Language.* Part I, Calcutta, 1885 ; Part II, 1889. Only two parts issued.

IV.—GENERAL LITERATURE—

Regarding Vidyápati, see Beames, *The Early Vaishnava Poets of Bengal,* Indian Antiquary ii, 1873, p. 37, and the same author's *On the Age and Country of Bidyápati, ibid.* iv, 1875, p. 299. See also the Bengali Magazine entitled the *Banga-darśana,* Vol. iv, for Jaishṭha, 1282, Bg. san, pp. 75 and ff. Also the present writer's *Vidyápati 'and his Contemporaries,* in *Indian Antiquary,* Vol. xiv, 1885, p. 182 ; Eggeling, *Catalogue* of Sanskrit MSS. in the India Office Library, Part iv, No. 2864; and the present writer in the *Proceedings* of the Asiatic Society of Bengal, for August, 1895. Also the present writer *On Some Mediæval Kings of Mithilā,* in *Indian Antiquary,* Vol. xxviii, 1899, p. 57. Also Nagēndra Nāth Gupta, *Vidyápati Ṭhākur* in J.A.S.B., Vol. lxxiii, Pt. I, Extra No. 1904, pp. 20 ff., and the present writer in J.A.S.B. [N. S.], Vol. i (1905), p. 228. The following contain editions of the Bengali recension of the poet's works. *Vidyápati-kṛita-padávali,* edited by Akshaya Chandra Sarkār. Chinsurah, 1285, Bg. s. *Vidyápatir Padávali,* Edited with an Introduction by S'āradā Charaṇ Maitra. Second Edition, Calcutta, 1285, Bg. s. *Prāchīna Kāvya Saṁgraha,* Part I, Edited by Akshaya Chandra

Sarkār. Calcutta, 1291, Bg. s. Up to the date of writing the only edition of the Mithilā recension is that in the Maithilī Chrestomathy.

For the benefit of those who wish to study Maithilī, the following is a list of the principal works that have been published in the language.

Besides the text in the Maithilī Chrestomathy we have :—

Twenty-one Vaishnava Hymns. Edited and translated by the present writer. *Journal* of the Asiatic Society of Bengal, Vol. liii. 1884, Special Number, pp. 76 and ff.

Manbodh's Haribans. Edited and translated by the same. *Ibid.* Vol. li, 1882, pp. 129 and ff., and Vol. liii, 1884, Special Number, pp. 1 and ff.

Selected Specimens of the Bihārī Language, Part I, The Maithilī Dialect. The Gīt Dīnā Bhadrik, and the Gīt Nebārak. Edited and translated by the same. *Zeitschrift der Deutschen Morgenländischen Gesellschaft,* Vol. xxxix, 1885, pp. 617 and ff.

Vidyāpati's *Puruṣa-parīkṣā,* Edited, and translated in prose and verse into Maithilī, by Candra Jhā. Darbhangā, Rāj Press. Śākē 1810.

Mithilā-Bhāṣā Rāmāyaṇa, by Candra Jhā. A version of the story of the Rāmāyaṇa in Maithilī verse. Darbhangā, Union Press. San 1299 Faslī.

MAITHILĪ GRAMMAR.

PART I.

ALPHABET AND VOCABULARY.

CHAPTER I.

THE ALPHABET.

1. The Alphabets in use in Mithilā are three—The Dēvanāgarī, the Maithilī, and the Kaithī. The first is familiar to every reader of this, and need not be described here. In Mithilā it is not much used in common life, and seldom even in manuscripts.

2. The Maithilī is the character used by the Maithil Brāhmaṇs, both in the affairs of common life, and in their sacred books. Few of the Brāhmaṇs, who are not professed paṇḍits, can read the Dēva-nāgarī character. The Maithilī character is also affected by Maithil Kāyasthas, who pretend to be better educated than their fellows. The Maithilī character is nearly the same as that of Bengali, differing only in one or two letters.

3. The Kaithī character is that in general use throughout Mithilā by all educated persons who are not Brāhmaṇs. It is a corruption of the Dēva-nāgarī, and can be written much faster than the latter, even as fast as *shikasta* Urdū. There was a clerk in my office in Madhubani, who could write excellent Kaithī more quickly than even the most practised of the old "Persian" muharrirs. Besides the speed with which it can be written, it has the advantage of thorough legibility. It is the official character employed in Government offices throughout Bihār and Chutiā Nāgpur.

4. A lithographed comparative table, giving specimens of these three alphabets, will be found at the end of this Grammar.

Pronunciation.

(a) *Vowels.*

5. The vowels should be pronounced as in Sanskrit, with the following exceptions:—

6. The vowel *a* has four distinct sounds, not two, as in Sanskrit. In Sanskrit we have ब *a* and श्रा *ā*. In Maithilī each of these has developed into a pair, a short and a long. The sound of short ब *a* is peculiar. It is not so broad as that of the corresponding vowel in Bengali, but on the other hand it is broader than the neutral vowel in Hindī. We may describe it as something between the *o* in 'cob,' and the *u* in 'cub,' or as the short sound corresponding to the long *a* in the word 'all.' From this has developed a long sound almost exactly like that of the *å* in 'all.' This long sound is nearly confined to the termination of the second person in verbs, and is due to the influence of a *u* which once followed it, but has now disappeared. Thus, the termination ब्ह *åh* is derived from an older ब्हु *ahu*. The sound is not usually represented in native writing but is commonly written merely as ब *a*. When it is desired to show it in writing it is sometimes represented by the mark of length ऽ. above the line, and sometimes by the *visarga* : . Thus देखबऽह or देखबःह. I shall in these pages employ the former sign, and in transliteration, I shall adopt the sign *å*, which is the character used for this sound in the publications of the Assam Government, and has been borrowed from Swedish.

7. Just as a long ब *å* sound has been developed from ब, so a secondary short *a*-sound has been developed from श्रा *ā*. Ordinarily speaking, this letter is pronounced as the *a* in 'far.' Sometimes, according to the rule of the short antepenultimate to be described below (*see* § 32 and ff.), it has to be shortened, and is then pronounced like the *a* in 'farrier.' In native writing it is not customary to indicate this sound, an ordinary श्रा *ā* being usually written in its place. Some writers, however, use ब *a* for this sound, instead of ब्रा. In the following pages, I shall indicate it, in the

Dēva-nāgarī character, by the short mark ` written above the line. Thus मार्ले, I killed. In transliteration I shall indicate it by the sign ă. Native scribes would write this word either मारले or मरले. This short छा ă has a great tendency to be weakened to च a, and it may be taken as a general rule that, unless ambiguity would ensue it does usually become च a. Thus the long form of पानि *pānī.* water, is properly पानिया *păniyā,* but is usually पनिया *paniyā.* On the other hand, 'I killed,' is always pronounced मार्ले *mărᵃlai,* and never मरले *marᵃlai,* however it is written, because the latter pronunciation would lead to ambiguity, मरले *marᵃlai* properly meaning ' he died.'

8.   The rule for the pronunciation of a final *a* is the same as in Hindī. As a general rule, it is silent in prose as in गुण pronounced *guṇ.* not *guṇa ;* फल *phal,* not *phala.* In other terms these words are practically monosyllables, and the final silent *a* is not counted as a syllable in applying phonetic rules depending on the number of syllables in a word (*see* §§ 28 and ff., 32 and ff.). Similarly सफल *saphal* must be treated as a dissyllable, not as a trisyllable. and so on. In transliteration this final silent *a* will be omitted in the following pages in writing prose. In poetry it is pronounced and will therefore be represented in transliteration.

In a few cases a final *a* is pronounced even in prose. When there is any doubt, I shall indicate it in the Dēva-nāgarī character by the sign o, and in transliteration I shall, when so pronounced, always write it in full. The most important cases in which it is pronounced are :—

(i)   Original monosyllables, such as न *na.* not.

(ii)   Words in which the final *a* is necessary for enunciation. as in शास्त्र॰ *śāstra.* a holy book ; प्रिय॰ *priya,* dear ; ग्राह्य॰ *grāhya.* acceptable (see § 26).

(iii)   A few verbal forms, in which it is really *ā,* as in देखिहँ *dēkhihă.* be pleased to see ; देखि कँ *dēkhⁱ-kă.* having seen.

9.   When two words are compounded, the final *a* of the first member reappears and is pronounced very lightly. Thus फलदायक

(फल *phal* + दायक *dāyak*) is pronounced *phal^{a}dāyak*, in which the *a* is hardly audible, very like the Hebrew *sh^{a}wā mobile*.

The same imperfect *a* also occurs in many polysyllabic words in the syllable after the accent, when not final. Thus हमरा *hám^{a}rā*, me ; देखबैह *dékh^{a}bāh*, you will see (but देखब *dékhab* with the *a* fully pronounced as it is in the final syllable) ; देखल *dékhal* or देखलिऐ *dékh^{a}liai*, I saw. As above shown, I represent this imperfect vowel in transliteration by a small ^{a} above the line. I have not thought it necessary to indicate it in the Dēva-nāgarī character. Natives never do so.

In poetry, the final silent *a*, and this imperfect ^{a} are always fully pronounced. We thus have, in poetry, *guṇa, phala, saphala, phaladāyaka, hamarā, dekhabâh* (or, more usually, the older form *dekhabahu*), *dēkhaba, dēkhala* and *dekhaliai*.

10. The short vowels इ *i* and उ *u*, when final in prose are also, as a rule, only half-pronounced. They may then be compared, in this respect, to the 'compound *sh^{a}wās*' of Hebrew, which, however, occur at the beginning, not at the end, of a syllable. They are not absolutely silent, but (as in Sindhī, Kāśmīrī, and Dravidian languages) are barely audible. Natives make no attempt to indicate in writing the extreme shortness of these vowels. As the matter is of some importance, I shall in the following pages indicate the fact by the sign for *virāma* (੍) placed under the vowel-sign. In transliteration I shall indicate it by small letters above the line. Thus, अछि *ach^i*, he is ; देखथु *dēkhath^u*, let him see. As in the case of the final absolutely silent *a*, these imperfect ^{i} and ^{u} are not counted as forming syllables in applying the rule of the short antepenultimate (§ 32). For the purposes of that rule देखथु *dēkhath^u* is a word of two syllables.

There are exceptions in which a final *i* is pronounced as a full vowel. These are :—

(i) The final *i* of the plural termination ऩि ^{a}*ni*, as in लोकनि *lok^{a}ni* (not लोकनि *lōkan^i*) people, the plural of लोक *lōk*, a person.

(ii) The final *i* of masculine nouns, as in पानि *pāni*, water ; मानि *māni*, proud (not पानि *pān^i*, मानि *mān^i*).

(iii) A final *i* preceded by a vowel, as in इलुकाइ *halukāi*, lightness (not इलुकाइ *halukā*ⁱ).

These imperfect vowels are frequently nasalised by *anunāsika*. Thus देखितहिँ *dekhitah*ⁱ, immediately on seeing; देखलहुँ *dekhᵃlah*ᵘ, I saw.

In poetry these imperfect ⁱ and ᵘ are fully pronounced, thus *achi, dēkhathu*.

11. As in the case of आ *ā*, the vowel ए *ē* has two sounds, a short and a long. The long sound is the one with which we are familiar in Sanskrit, something like that of the *a* in 'mate.' The other is the corresponding short sound, something like that of the *e* in 'met.' Natives make no distinction between these two sounds in writing. In the following pages, the long sound will be represented by ए or, when non-initial, by ˜, and the short sound by ए or, when non-initial, by ‾. In transliteration I shall represent them by *ē* and *e* respectively.

It should be noted that ए *e* and इ *i* are freely interchangeable. Thus, we may either have पएताइ *paëtăh* or पएताइ *païtăh*, he will see. Northern Maithili, as a rule, prefers to use ए *e*.

12. In an exactly 'similar way, there is a pair of long and short *o* sounds. The long is the Sanskrit ओ *ō*, and is sounded like the second *o* in 'promote.' The short has the sound of the first *o* in the same word, and will be represented in the following pages by ओ or, when non-initial, by ो. The corresponding transliteration will be *ō* and *o*, respectively. Native writers make no distinction between these two sounds, representing both by ओ. As in the case of ए *e* and इ *i*, ओ *o* and उ *u* are freely interchangeable, ओ *o* being usually preferred in the north and उ *u* in the south. Thus, we have either पओलहुँ *paölah*ᵘ or पउलहुँ *paülah*ᵘ, I obtained.

13. In Sanskrit the vowels ऐ *ai* and औ *au* are really diphthongs made up of आ + इ *ā + i* and आ + उ *ā + u*, respectively. Their origin is therefore *āi* and *āu*, and the pronunciation is distinctly long. We may compare the pronunciation of the *ai* in the English word *aisle*, and of the *ou* in the English word 'our.' In Maithili these sounds only occur in words directly borrowed

from Sanskrit as in कँकेयी *Kaṅkēyī*, ौषष *auṣadh*. In Maithili
these letters invariably represent an older ष + र (or ष्) *a* (not *ā*) +
i (or *e*) and ष + ञ (or ो) *a* (not *ā*) + *u* (or *o*) respectively. In fact,
at the present day native writers sometimes write ॆ and ॊ and
sometimes षर or षष्, षञ or षषो. Thus they write the present
participle of the root ॆख *dēkh*, see, sometimes ॆॆखॆन (or in this book
ॆॆखॆन *dekhait*) and sometimes ॆखर (or in this book ॆॆखरॆन *dekhaït*).
I have even, on occasions, seen the word spelt ॆॆखयिन, in which
the य is merely a fulcrum for carrying the ॆ much as *alif* is employed in Hindōstānī. Again 'I shall obtain' is written पॆॆबॆ
(or in this book पॆॆबॆ *païbai*), परॆबॆ (or in this book पष्बॆ *paëbai*),
or ॆॆबॆ (or in this book ॆॆबॆ *paibai*). Similarly they indicate 'he will
obtain,' by पष्नाॆ (or in this book पष्नांॆ *paütăh*), पष्ोनाॆ (or
in this book पष्ोनांॆ *paötăh*) or ोनाॆ (or in this book ोनांॆ
pautăh). Native writers make no distinction between the Sanskrit
and Maithili *ai* and *au*. Both *ai* sounds they represent, in the
Sanskrit fashion by ॆ, and both *au* sounds by ॊ. As, however,
the Maithili sounds are shorter both by origin and in pronunciation,
I represent the short sounds by ॆ (or, when non-initial, by ॆ),
and by ॊ (or, when non-initial by ॆ), respectively. In transliteta-
tion, I represent the long sounds by *aī* and *aū*, and the short sounds
by *ai* and *au*.

It is important to note that the Maithili ॆ *ai* and ॊ *au* are
merely alternative graphic representations of षर *aï* or षष् *aë* and
षञ *aü* or षषो *aö*, respectively. This rule must be borne in mind in
counting syllables for applying the rule of the short antepenultimate (§ 33, ii) in which both ॆ *ai* and ॊ count each as *two* syllables.
Thus, the word ॆॆखॆन *dekhait*, seeing, must be considered as a word
of three syllables, *viz.*, ॆ *de* + ख *kha* + रन *it*, and not as one of
two.

As, whatever the method of writing employed may be, the

pronunciation of चर and ऐ and of चउ and औ is in each case identical, I shall in future make no distinction in transliteration.[1] I shall represent both चर and ऐ by *ai*, and both चउ and औ by *au*. अए will be represented by *ae* (pronounced, however, the same as *ai*). and अओ will be represented by *ao* (pronounced as *au*).

14. Native scribes are by no means uniform in their methods of representing vowel-sounds in writing. In the table below I give the system of spelling adopted for this grammar, and also the more usual scribal variations.

System of spelling adopted in this Grammar.	Variations often employed by native scribes.
र initial (र्च्छा, a wish, देइदत, seeing).	यि (यिच्छा), यौ (यौंच्छा), ए (देखएत)
र medial (लिखित, written).	ई (लौखीत) (very common).
ई initial (ईंटा, a brick).	यी (यींटा).
उ initial (उच्छा, a torch).	वु (वुच्छा), or वू (वूच्छा).
ऊ initial (ऊंच, high).	वू (वूंच), or व (वंच).
ऊ medial (भूठ, false).	उ (भुठ) (very common).
प्र ए } initial (प्रक, one).	ॱॅ (ॲक).
ऐ ए } initial (प्रेठ, twist).	ऐे (ऐंठ).
ऒ ओ } initial (ओर, direction).	वो (वोर).

NOTE.—All the above are only varieties of spelling, and have nothing to do with pronunciation.

[1] Whether the sound is really dipthongal, or whether the two elements are separately pronounced, it is difficult to say. Pronunciation varies in different mouths. In old Maithili the sound was certainly not dipthongal, and it seems to me that at the present day the vowels are beginning to coalesce, but that the custom has not yet been established.

15. The vowels ऋ *ṛ* ॠ *ṝ* and ऌ *ḷ* only occur in words borrowed direct from Sanskrit. When so met, they are pronounced like *ri*, *rī*, and *li*, respectively. They are never found in pure Maithili words.

16. The following is therefore a complete conspectus of all the Maithili vowels. Those which are only found in Sanskrit words are marked with the letter S.

Short.	Long.
अ *a*	ऍ *ằ*
अॊ *ă*	आ *ā*
इ *i*	ई *ī*
उ *u*	ऊ *ū*
ऋ *ṛ* (S.)	ॠ *ṝ* (S.)
ऌ *ḷ* (S.)	
ऍ *e*	य *ē*
ऍे *ai*	ऍे *ai* (S.)
ओ *o*	ओ *ō*.
औ *au*	औ *aū* (S.)

17. The Sanskrit *Visarga* (:) no longer exists in Maithili except in a few borrowed words. The character is, however, as stated above, sometimes, but rarely, employed to indicate the sound of the letter *å̇*.

18. *Anusvāra* (˙), when immutable, is also retained in a few words borrowed from Sanskrit. It is very commonly employed (like the changeable *anusvāra* of Sanskrit) as a *compendium scripturae* for ङ *ṅ*, ञ *ñ*, ण *ṇ*, न *n*, or म *m* before another consonant of the same class. Thus बुँदा instead बुन्दा *bundā*. It will hence be represented in transliteration by *ṅ*, *ñ*, *ṇ*, *n*, or *m*, according to circumstances. Native writers very commonly employ it instead of *anunāsika*.

19. *Anunāsika* (˙) is met extremely frequently. It indicates the nasal sound which we hear in the French word 'bon.'

It will be represented in transliteration by the mark ˜ placed over the nasalised vowel. Thus अंखियाँ *ākhiyā*, an eye. मँ *mã̀* or मँ *mẽ̃* in ; बाँहि *bā̃h*[i], an arm ; देखलङ्ड *dekh*[a]*lah*[u], I saw.

20. *Consonants.*

क *k*, ख *kh*, ग *g*, घ *gh*, ङ *n̄*, च *c*, छ *ch*, ज *j*, झ *jh*, ञ *ñ*, ट *t*, ठ *th*, ड *ḍ*, ढ *ḍh*, त *t*, थ *th*, द *d*, ध *dh*, न *n*, प *p*, फ *ph*, ब *b*, भ *bh*, म *m*, य *y*, र *r*, ल *l*, व *w*, श *ś*, स *s*, and ह *h* are usually pronounced as in Sanskrit.

21. When ड *ḍ* and ढ *ḍh* are not initial they become ड़ *r* and ढ़ *rh*. These cerebral *r*-sounds, are not so definitely cerebral as in Western Hindi. They are very frequently interchanged with र *r* and रह *rh* respectively, and, indeed the latter dental sounds more nearly approach the correct pronunciation. Thus, 'a horse' is either घोड़ *ghōr* or घोर *ghōr*, of which two the latter is the preferable spelling. Native custom as to writing these sounds fluctuates.

22. The pronunciation of ण *ṇ* is peculiar. The cerebral nature of its sound is much more marked than in the Sanskrit of Eastern India. It has more the sound of a muffled cerebral *r* followed by a cerebral *ṇ*; e.g., राबण is pronounced almost like *Rābarṇ*. the *r* in *rṇ* having a peculiar muffled sound, impossible to describe in writing. न *n* is occasionally substituted for ण *ṇ* and is then pronounced as *n*.

23. Original य *y* and व *w* always become ज *j* and ब *b* respectively, although the letters य and व are often retained in writing. In the following pages the spelling will strictly follow the pronunciation. Thus I shall write जौबन *jaūban*, not यौवन *yaūvan*, and बात *bāt*, not वात *wāt*. The only cases in which we find य *y* and व *w* with their proper pronunciations are when they are used euphonically,—like the *ya-śruti* of the Prakrit Grammarians,—as described in the following sections.

24. When two vowels, of which the latter is short or long *ā* come together, a euphonic य *y* or व *w* is often inserted to prevent

a hiatus. The insertion is generally optional, and is merely intended to facilitate utterance. This euphonic insertion takes place between ă and ă, between ĭ and ă, between ĕ and ă, between ŭ and ă, and between ŏ and ă.

(i) Between ă and ă the semi-vowel which is inserted is always *w*.[1] नेनआ *nenᵃ-ā* becomes नेनवा *nenᵃwā*, a boy. In this case the insertion is not optional, but is compulsory.

(ii) Between *i* or *e* and ă, the inserted letter is *y*. Thus मालिआ *măliā* or मालिया *măliyā*, a gardener. In this case the insertion of the *y* is quite optional, but careful writers generally insert it.

(iii) Between ĭ or ĕ and ă it is always *w* which is inserted, and the insertion is compulsory. Thus मालीवा *mălīwā* for मालीआ *mălīā*, a gardener. Here it must be explained, that the *w* was originally really between *a* and *ā*. Almost the only case in which ĭ immediately precedes *ā* is in the redundant form of nouns (§ 41). This form properly ends in इयवा *iyᵃwā*, thus—मालियवा *măliyᵃwā* —and the इय *iyᵃ* is liable to be contracted to ई *ī*, so that we get मालीवा *mălīwā*.

(iv) Between ŭ or ŏ and ă, the inserted vowel is always *w*. The insertion is quite optional, not compulsory, but careful writers usually omit it. We thus get आँसुआ *ăsuā* or आँसुवा *ăsuwā*, a tear.

In the following pages, I shall follow the usage of the most careful writers, and shall spell upon the principles indicated by the forms नेनवा *nenᵃwā*, मालिया *măliyā*, मालीवा *mălīwā*, and आँसुआ *ăsuā*.

The above are the only instances in which य़ *y* and व़ *w* really occur in Maithilī, and it will be seen that, as they are euphonic additions and only appear between contiguous vowels, they can never occur at the beginning of a word, except in the case of the incorrect native spellings indicated in § 14.

---

[1] In Western India, on the contrary, it is usually *y*.

It must, however, be mentioned that the diphthongs ऐ *ai* and औ *au* are often written अय *ay^a* and अव *aw^a* by some writers. This is only a question of spelling. Again the vowel ए *e* is often written य *ya*, and the vowel ओ *o* is often written व *wa*. Thus we find होएब *hōeb*, to be, written होयब ; केओ *keō*, any one, written क्यो *kyō*; and पाओल *pāōl*, I got, written पावल *pāwal*. This again is a mere matter of spelling. The pronunciation is not affected.

25. The sibilants श *ś* and ष *ṣ* only appear in words borrowed from Sanskrit. The only sibilant which Maithilī has of its own is the dental स *s*. श *ś* is pronounced as in Sanskrit; but ष *ṣ* when standing alone, and not compounded with another consonant is always pronounced like ख *kh*. Thus षष्ठ *ṣaṣṭh*, sixth, pronounced *khaṣṭh*. This pronunciation is universal : the vulgar even write such a ष *ṣ* phonetically ख *kh*. In the compound consonant र्ष *rṣ* ष *ṣ* is also always pronounced as ख *kh* ; e.g. आकर्षण *ākarṣaṇ* is pronounced *ākarkhaṇ* By some this ख *kh* sound of ष *ṣ* is pro- nounced as a guttural breathing, and not as a guttural check,— something, but not quite, like the Persian خ *kh*, or the *ch* in 'loch.' The compound letter क्ष *kṣ* is pronounced like च्छ *cch*, which is occasionally written for it by the vulgar ; *e.g.* लच्छी is so written, and is pronounced as *Lakṣmī* by purists, but is commonly written and pronounced लच्छमी *Lacch^amī*. The compound ष्प *ṣp* is peculiar. It is pronounced something like *hfp* ; e.g., पुष्प *puṣp*, a flower, is pronounced *puhfp*. This seems to be a relic of the old Sanskrit *upadhmānīya*.

Native scribes regularly write श *ś* for स *s* ; thus, they write शागर *śāgar*, instead of सागर *sāgar*, the sea. The pronunciation is, however, always that of a dental स *s*. In Māgadhī Prakrit every स *s* was pronounced as श *ś*. This pronunciation has long ceased to exist in Bihār, but the mode of writing has survived.

26. The letter ह *h*, when compound with य *y*, becomes ह्य *hy*, which, in words borrowed from Sanskrit, is pronounced in a

peculiar way. If *zh* be taken to represent the Persian ﮊ *zh*, the pronunciation of this compound can best be represented by *zhjy*; e.g., ग्राह्य॰, *fit to be accepted*, is pronounced *grăzhjya*, the final य a being retained in pronunciation, though usually inert, for the sake of euphony (§ 8).

27. The mute letters are divided into surds and sonants. Surds and sonants may each be aspirated or unaspirated. Thus—

SURDS.		SONANTS.	
Unaspirated.	Aspirated.	Unaspirated.	Aspirated.
क् *k.*	ख् *kh.*	ग् *g.*	घ् *gh.*
च् *c.*	छ् *ch.*	ज् *j.*	झ् *jh.*
ट् *ṭ.*	ठ् *ṭh.*	ड् *ḍ,* ड़् *r*	ढ् *ḍh,* ढ़् *rh.*
त् *t.*	थ् *th.*	द् *d.*	ध् *dh.*
प् *p.*	फ् *ph.*	ब् *b.*	भ् *bh.*

In connexion with the sonants, there is an important rule.

(i) When any unaspirated sonant is preceded by *anunāsika.*[1] the nasal of the corresponding class may be substituted for the two.

(ii) When an aspirated sonant is preceded by *anunāsika*, the nasal of the corresponding class aspirated by the addition of *h* may be substituted for the two.

Thus—

(i) ँग् ~ *g* may become ङ् *ṅ.* Thus. आँग *ā̃g* or आङ *āṅ* a limb.

ँज् ~ *j* may become ञ् *ñ.* This is, however, of very rare occurrence. Example, आँजू *ā̃jū* or आञू *āñū.* a tear.

---

[1] Traces of a somewhat similar change have been noted on Māgadhī Prakrit, e.g. *aññali* for *añjali.*

इ॒ ~ *r* may become ण् *ṇ*. Thus, भाँइ *bhār̃* or भाण *bhāṇ*, an earthen pot.

द॒ ~ *d* may become न् *n*. Thus, नीँद *nĩd* or नीन *nīn*, sleep.

ब॒ ~ *b* may become म॒. *m*. Thus, नीँब *nĩb* or नीम *nīm*, a *nīm*-tree.

(ii) घ॒ ~ *gh* may become ङ् *ṅh*. Thus. सीँघ *sĩgh* or सीङ *siṅh*, a lion.

झ॒ ~*jh* may become ञ् *ñh*. This, as in the case of ज॒ ~ *j*, is very rare. Example माँझ *mãjh* or माञ *māñh*, middle.

ढ॒ ~ *ṛh* may become ण् *ṇh*. Thus, कोँढ *kõṛh* or कोण *kōṇh*, a pumpkin.

ध॒ ~ *dh* may become न् *nh*. Thus बाँध *bãdh* or बान्ह *bānh*, bind. Compare as a reverse example कान्ह *kānh* or काँध *kãdh*, a name of *Kṛṣṇa*.

भ॒ ~ *bh* may become म् *mh*. Thus खाँभ *khãbh* or खाम्ह *khāmh*. a pillar.

All the above changes are quite optional. Those of इ॒ ~ *r*. ढ॒ ~ *ṛh*. द॒ ~ *d*, ध॒ ~ *dh*, ब॒ ~ *b*. भ॒ ~ *bh*, are very common. The others, especially those of ज॒ ~ *j* and झ॒ ~*jh*, are more rare.

There is one point to be noted. The aspirated nasals ङ् *ṅh*. ञ् *ñh*, ण् *ṇh*, न् *nh*, and म् *mh*. are never treated as compound letters, and do *not* make a preceding vowel long by position. They are treated exactly like aspirated mutes ख् *kh*, घ् *gh*, छ् *ch*, झ् *jh*, and so on. They might indeed be added as single letters to the alphabet. Thus :—

Gutturals. क् *k*. ख् *kh*. ग् *g*, घ् *gh*, ङ् *ṅ*, ङ् *ṅh*.

Palatals. च् *c*, छ् *ch*, ज् *j*. झ् *jh*, ञ् *ñ*, ञ् *ñh*.

Cerebrals, ट् *ṭ*, ठ् *ṭh*, ड् *ḍ*, ड़् *r*, ढ् *ḍh*, ढ़् *ṛh*, ण् *ṇ*, ण् *ṇh*.

Dentals, त् *t*, थ् *th*. द् *d*, ध् *dh*, न् *n*, न् *nh*.

Labials प् *p*, फ् *ph*, ब् *b*, भ् *bh*, म् *m*, म् *mh*.

ACCENTUATION.

28. The stress accent exists in Maithilī. but is not strongly pronounced. In counting syllables for fixing the place of an accent. the final silent *a* of words ending in a consonant, and a final imperfect *ᶦ* and *ᵘ* are not considered. On the other hand, the imperfect *ᵃ* in the middle of a word, corresponding to the Hebrew *shᵃwā mobile*, is counted as a syllable. For instance, in the word देखलड़ *dékhᵃlàhᵘ*, there are for our present purposes three syllables, *viz.*, दे *dé* + ख *khᵃ* + लड़ *làhᵘ*.

(i) If a word ends in a consonant (whether followed by imperfect *ᶦ* or *ᵘ* or not) preceded by a long vowel or a diphthong, the main accent is on the last syllable. Thus किसान *kisắn*, a cultivator: देखलहुन्हि *dèkhᵃlahúnhᶦ*, you saw; देखलिऐन्हि *dèkhᵃliáinhᶦ*, I saw.

(ii) If a word ends in a fully pronounced vowel, and if the penultimate is long, the accent falls on the penultimate. Thus पानि *pắni*, water; छोटक्का *chòṭákkā*, small.

(iii) In other cases (except in the case of words borrowed from Sanskrit) the accent falls on the antepenultimate. Thus हमरा *hámᵃrā*, me; लोकनि *lókᵃni*, people: खोपड़ी *khópᵃrī* a hut: देखलड़ *dékhᵃlàhᵘ*, I saw; तितलिया *titáliyā*, a butterfly.

If a word, which has the accent on the antepenultimate, takes a suffix, the antepenultimate becomes the syllable before the antepenultimate, and may optionally retain the accent. Thus, the word तितली *titᵃlí*, a butterfly, has the accent on *ti*. the antepenultimate. The long form of तितली *titᵃlí* is made by suffixing *ā*, and we get तितलिया *titaliyā*. This ordinarily has the accent on *tá*. the new antepenultimate, according to the above rule: thus *titáliyā*, but some people retain the accent on the *ti*. and say *títaliyā*. Pronunciation in this respect fluctuates much.

(iv) In words borrowed from Sanskrit. the accent may be thrown back as far as the syllable before the antepenultimate. provided the antepenultimate and the penultimate are both short. Here again pronunciation varies. कुटिलता, deceitfulness. may be either *kúṭilatā* or *kùṭilᵃtā*.

29. If the accent does not fall on the first syllable of a word. that syllable has a secondary accent, which I indicate by the sign, as in *kìsán, dèkhᵃlahū̃nhⁱ, dèkhᵃlidìnhⁱ, chòṭákkā, tìtáliyā* and *kùṭilᵃtā* given above.

30. If a word ends in imperfect ⁱ or ᵘ and if the last syllable has not the main accent of the word, then that syllable has a secondary accent, as in देखथि *dèkhàthⁱ*, he may see ; ककरङ्क *kákᵃràh²*, any one (accusative) ; देखलङ्क *dèkhᵃlàhⁿ*, I saw.

31. In compound words, the first member retains its own stress-accent as a secondary accent, the stress-accent of the second member being the stress-accent of the word. Thus मुख-चंद *mùkhᵃcánd*, the moon of a girl's face. Compound words borrowed directly from Sanskrit are often treated as simple words. Thus बिद्यापति *bìdyā-patⁱ*, which, according to the above rule, should be pronounced *bìdyā-pátⁱ* is always pronounced *bìdyápàtⁱ*. The word is the name of a famous poet of Mithilā.

RULE OF THE SHORT ANTEPENULTIMATE.

32. The following rules are most important. They are applied rigorously throughout the whole system of Maithili Grammar, and unless they are fully grasped, much of what is in the following pages will be found obscure.

(*i*) *The rules here given apply only to Maithili words. They do not apply to words borrowed direct from Sanskrit, which are not subject to change.*

(*ii*) *The genius of the whole Maithilī language is adverse to the existence of a long vowel in a Maithilī word, when it would occupy a position removed more than two syllables from the end of a word.*

Note.—In counting syllables neither the final silent *a*, nor a final imperfect ⁱ or ᵘ counts as a syllable; but the medial imperfect ᵃ, corresponding to the Hebrew *shᵃvā mobile* does so count. Thus घर *ghar*, a house, is a word of one syllable; देखब *dèkhab*, I shall see, चाओरि *āoⁱ*, and, सूतथु *sūtathᵘ* let him sleep, are words of two syllables; while सुतिहँ *sutihã*, sleep thou, and देखबे *dekhᵃbẽ*, you will see, are words of three syllables.

33. The practice of shortening a vowel is subject to the following rules :—

(i) Whenever the vowel आ *a* finds itself in the antepenultimate syllable, *i.e.*, in the third from the end of the word, it is shortened to आ *ă*. Thus, नांउआ *năuā* (or, contracted, नौआ *nauā*) long form of नाऊ *nāū*, a barber ; आंगिया *ăgiyā*, long form of आगि *āgi*, fire ; पांओलंह *păolăh* (or, contracted, पौलंह *paulăh*), 2nd plur. past of पाउब *pāeb*, to obtain ; मांरलक *mărᵃlak*, he struck, from मारब *mārab*, to strike ; बांतिया *bătiyā*, long form of बात *bāt*, a word.

There is a tendency to pronounce and write this shortened आं *ă* as if it were अ *a*, so that we sometimes hear, instead of the above ; नउआ *nauā* ; अगिया *agiyā* ; बतिया *batiyā*. But this is only in the case of nouns. आं *ă* does not often become अ *a* in verbs, as this would tend to give rise to ambiguity. Thus, the verb *mār*, means 'strike,' while, if we shortened it to *mar*, the root would mean ' die.' Sometimes, however, we find आ *ā* shortened to अ *a*, even in verbs. In this respect, the rule is that we may have अ *a* if no ambiguity occurs. Compare § 7.

(ii) Similarly, any other vowel finding itself in the antepenultimate, is shortened, provided a consonant which is not euphonic य *y* or व *w* follows it. Thus, सिखलक *sikhᵃlak*, he learnt, from √ सीख *sikh*, learn ; देखइत *dekhaït* (or, contracted) देखैत *dekhait*), seeing. On the other hand, चूअलांह *cūᵃlăh* or चूवलांह *cūwᵃlăh*, he dripped ; सीअलक *siᵃlak* or सीयलक *siyᵃlak*, he sewed ; from roots चू *cū* and सी *si* ; in which the long *ī* and the long *ū* are retained as they are followed by vowels or by euphonic *y* or *w*.

From the above it will be noted that the contraction of *a* and *i* to *ai* does not affect the shortening. In other words ऐ *ai* and औ *au*, for the purposes of these rules, count as two syllables each.

(iii) Any vowel whatever, finding itself removed more than three syllables from the end of the word is shortened, whether it is followed by a consonant or not. Thus चूदतथौंलि *cuit^athĭnhⁱ* (if) he had dripped, from root चू *cū* ; वोदबद *hoĭaï* (or, contracted वोद्दे *hoĭaĭ*), (if) I become, from root वो *hō*, become ; देखितिबउ *dekhitiaŭ* (or, contracted देखितिबौ *dekhitiau*) (if) I had seen you, from root देख *dĕkh*.

34. Amongst native writers of Maithili no fixed usage has as yet established itself regarding the graphic representation of the short antepenultimate. Though it is always pronounced short, it is often *written* long. Thus we find the words given above sometimes written नाउथा, बागिया, पाथोलद (or पौलद) मारलक, बातिया, सौललक, and चूदतथौंलि, and sometimes नउथा (or नौथा), बमिया, पथोलद, मरलक, बतिया, सिललक, and चूदतथौंलि देखदत and वोद्दे are, of course always written देखदत and वोदसे as the writers have no character for short *e, o,* or *ai.*

35. All the above examples have exhibited the shortening of vowels long by nature. Exactly the same principle is followed in the case of vowels long by position. When such vowels precede a compound consonant (usually a nasal plus a mute, or a double mute), the nasal is weakened to *anunāsika,* and the double consonant is simplified. Thus from the root बन्ध *bandh,* to bind we have बंधुआ *bādhuā* or बन्हुआ *banhuā* (see § 27, ii) not बन्धुआ *bandhuā,* a prisoner; and from the long form (see § 41) चोटक्का *choṭakkā,* small, we have the redundant form चोटकवा *choṭak^awā.*

——o——

CHAPTER II.

VOCABULARY.

36. In the preceding pages I have more than once made a distinction between Maithili words and Sanskrit words.

37. Maithili is an Indo-Aryan language, and though the statement is not strictly accurate, it may conveniently be said to be descended from Sanskrit. According to native belief it *is* so

3

descended.[1] In the course of its development it passed through various stages, the latest of which (before the birth of Maithilī) was that known as Māgadhi Prakrit, the colloquial language of the whole of Bihār, in various stages of development from, say, the time of Buddha (550 B.C.) down to about A.D. 1000.[2] From this Māgadhī Prakrit are directly descended not only Maithili and the other languages of Bihār, but also Bengali, Assamese, and Oṛiyā. For our present purposes it is sufficient to remember that the Maithilī Vocabulary is descended from Sanskrit through Māgadhī Prakrit.

38. In order to supply real or fancied deficiencies in this vocabulary, writers have borrowed words from other languages,— English, Persian, Arabic, and Sanskrit. The English, Persian, and Arabic importations are very few in number, but the case is different with Sanskrit. In the vocabulary compiled for this work, out of the first hundred words, about twenty-seven may claim to be more or less distorted forms of words borrowed direct from Sanskrit, without having passed through Māgadhī Prakrit. These borrowed Sanskrit words are just as foreign to the language as are Latin words borrowed at the present day by French or Italian. Natives are quite aware of the existence of these two classes of words, and have given each class a name. They call the words borrowed from Sanskrit *Tatsamas,* *i.e.,* 'the same as It' ('It' being Sanskrit), while the true Maithilī words, which have developed naturally through Māgadhi Prakrit they call '*Tadbhavas'* *i.e.,* 'sprung from It.'

39. The distinction between these two classes of words is of importance, for *Tatsamas,* like all borrowed words in all languages, are treated as foreigners and are not subject to the phonetic rules which govern *Tadbhavas.* For instance, the rule of the short antepenultimate does not apply to *Tatsamas.* Again *Tatsamas* cannot be conjugated (with one or two rare exceptions) as verbs. For instance दर्शन *darśan* is a *Tatsama* meaning 'seeing,' but we cannot

---

[1] Accurately speaking, it is descended from an ancient form of Indo-Aryan speech akin to, but not the same as, that which became fixed by ancient literary use in the form of Sanskrit.

[2] It must be understood that these limits are only approximate.

say द्र्शने-र्छि *darśanai-ach*[i], he sees. If we want to use the word we must compound it with another *Tadbhava* verb and say द्र्शन करे-र्छि *darśan karai-ach*[i], he does seeing. From this it follows that the class of *Tatsama* words is confined to nouns substantive or nouns adjective, and that, as a broad rule, no verb can be a *Tatsama*.

For the future, on the following pages, I shall employ these two words, *tatsama* and *tadbhava*, in the sense explained above.

PART II.

DECLENSION.

—◆◆◆—

CHAPTER I.

40.   Space will not permit us to go at any length into the
question of the formation of Maithili nouns.   It must suffice to say
that, with few exceptions, nouns are formed on the same principles
as in Western Hindi, and in other Indo-Aryan languages.   I shall
first deal with—

EQUIVALENT FORMS OF NOUNS.

41.   All nouns, whether substantives or adjectives, admit of
various equivalent forms, *i.e.*, of various forms which do not differ
appreciably in meaning.   These forms are the *short*, the *long*, and
the *redundant*.   The *short* form may be either *weak* or *strong*.
In practice every noun does not take all these four forms, only
experience can teach which of the short forms (the weak or strong)
is employed in the case of any particular noun ; but theoretically all
nouns, and in reality some few nouns, do take both.   All nouns
can, at option, take the long and redundant forms.

42.   The *short* form is the primary form by which the word is
generally known.   It is also, in most cases, the only one admissible
in good and literary language.

43.   Of its two varieties, the *weak* form is the shortest form of
the noun, generally ending in a consonant, a short *i*, or an imperfect

¹. Thus घोड़ *ghōṛ*, a horse; लोह *lōh*, iron; पानि *pāni*, water; मारि a beating; छोट *chōṭ*, small (masc.); छोटि *chōṭi*, small (fem.).

44. The *strong* form is simply the weak form (when such exists) strengthened by the addition of आ *ā*, or by the lengthening of the final vowel. When there is no weak form, the strong form always ends in a long vowel. Thus, घोड़ा *ghōṛā*, a horse; लोहा *lōhā*, iron; मारी *mārī*, a beating; छोटा *chōṭā*, small (masc.); छोटी *chōṭī*, small (fem.); आंसू *āsū* (no weak form), a tear; पोथी *pōthī* (no weak form), a book.

45. The *long* forms of *substantives* are made by adding one of the suffixes आ *ā*, या *yā*, or वा *wā* (sometimes vulgarly आँ *ā̃* or ई *ẽ̄*, याँ *yā̃* or यें *yẽ*, वाँ *wā̃* or वें *wẽ*) to the short form, the final vowels of which, if long, are shortened. Thus घोड़वा *ghoʳwā* (or -ʳwā̃,-ʳwẽ), a horse; मारिया *māriyā* or मारिआ *māriā*, a beating, पोथिया *pothiyā* or पोथिआ *pothiā*. a book; आंसुवा *āsuwā* or आंसुआ *āsuā*, a tear.

46. The *long* forms of *adjectives* are similarly made by adding one of the suffixes का *kā* or क्का *kkā* (fem. की *kī* or क्की *kī*) to the short forms. Thus, from बड़ *baṛ* or बड़ा *baṛā* (short forms), great, we have as long form बड़का *baʳkā*. So from छोट *chōṭ* or छोटा *chōṭā*, small, we have छोटका *choʳakā* or छोटक्का *choṭakkā*, and from भारि *bhāri* or भारी *bhārī*, heavy, भारिका *bhărikā* or भारिक्का *bhărikka*. For the long form of the feminine छोटि *chōṭi*, however, we must go back to the masculine छोट *chōṭ*, and form a new feminine from the long form. Thus, छोटकी *choʳakī* or छोटक्की *choṭakkī*. There is no such form as छोटिका *choṭikā* or छोटिक्का *choṭikkā* derived directly from छोटि *chōṭi*.

47. The *redundant* forms of substantives and adjectives are formed from their long forms precisely as long forms of substantives are formed from their short forms, *viz.*, by adding आ *ā*, या *yā*, or वा *wā*, to the long forms; but, once these additions are made

there are frequent contractions. We thus get the following table
exhibiting all the forms at one view.

Short form.		Long form.	Redundant form.
Weak.	Strong.		
घोड़ *ghōṛ*, a horse	घोड़ा *ghōṛā*	घोड़वा *ghoṛᵃwā*	घोड़ौबा *ghoṛauwā* (contracted from घोड़ववा *ghoṛᵃwᵃwā.*
घर *ghar*, a h o u s e (masc.)	none	घरवा *gharᵃwā*	घरौबा *gharauwā* (similarly contracted).
None	सभा *sabhā*, an assembly (fem.)	सभवा *sabhᵃwā*	सभौबा *sabhauwā.*
बात *bāt*, a word (fem.) (So all feminines ending in a consonant.)	none	बतिया *băṭiyā*	बतियवा *băṭiyᵃwā* (or contracted) बतौबा *băṭīwā.*
मारि *mārⁱ*, a beating. (So any noun ending in ⁱ.)	मारी *mārī*	मरिया *măriyā*	मरियवा *măriyᵃwā* or मरौबा *mari- wā.*
पानि *pāni*, water. (So any noun in *i*.)	none	पनिया *păniyā*	पनियवा *păniyᵃwā* or पनौबा *păni- wā.*
None.	पोथी *pōthī*, a book. (So any noun in *ī*.)	पोथिया *pothiyā*	पोथियवा *pothiyᵃ- wā* or पोथीबा *pothīwā.*

SHORT FORM.		Long form.	Redundant form.
Weak.	**Strong.**		
None	चाँसू *āsū*, a tear. So any noun in *ū*.	चाँसुआ *āsuā*	चाँसुअवा *āsuᵃwā* or चाँसुआ *āsūā*.
छोट *chŏṭ*, small So any mascu-line adjec-tive.	छोटा *chŏṭā*	{ छोटका *choṭᵃkā* { छोटक्का *choṭákkā*	छोटकवा *choṭᵃkawā* छोटक्वा *choṭák̇ᵃwā*.
छोटि *c h ŏ ṭ i*, small. So any feminine adjective.	छोटी *chŏṭī*	{ छोटकी *choṭᵃkī* { छोटक्की *choṭákkī*	छोटकिया *choṭᵃkiyā*. छोटक्किया *choṭákkiyā*.

48. With reference to the above table, attention must be called to the remarks in § 24 concerning the optional in-sertion or omission of euphonic य् *y* and व् *w*. For instance, in-stead of बतिया *bātiyā*, we may have बतिआ *batiā*, and instead of चाँसुआ *āsuā*, we may have चाँसुवा *āsuwā*. Attention is also to be called to the fact that natives very frequently substitute च *a* for चा *ā* in writing (this does not affect the pronunciation). So that, in native books, we should usually find forms like बतिया *batiyā*, बतीवा *batīwā*, पनिया *paniyā*, चाँसुआ *āsuā*, and so on. It will be noticed that the rule of the short antepenultimate (§§ 32 and ff.) comes into full force in these forms.

49. All these forms, the short weak, the short strong, the long, and the redundant, have, in theory, exactly the same mean-ing. The long form is, however, generally used in a non-honorific sense or to give definiteness. Thus नेनवा *nenᵃwā*, the boy (fami-liarly or contemptuously); घोड़वा *ghorᵃwā*, *the* horse. The long form in the feminine is frequently employed in the sense of a

diminutive. Thus नेनी *nēnī*, a girl, नेनिया *neniyā*, a little girl ; खाट *khāṭ*, a bed, खटिया *khaṭiyā*, a cot.

50. The redundant form is used in much the same sense as the long form, but only by the vulgar or in familiar language. The vulgar, indeed, employ both the long and the redundant forms as caprice dictates, in the sense of the short form. The use of the redundant form in this way is still more vulgar or familiar than that of the long form.

NOMINAL SUFFIXES.

51. In the following examples, as my object is here purely practical, I shall not attempt to distinguish between primary and secondary suffixes. It must be understood that अइ *ai* or अए *ae* and ऐ *ai* are always absolutely interchangeable, and so also अउ *au* or अओ *ao* and औ *au*. I have written, in each case, the forms which I have seen most frequently.

52. आ *ā* (Masculine). The strong short forms in आ *ā* correspond to the large class of Hindi nouns which end in आ *ā*, such as Hindi घोड़ा *ghōṛā*, a horse ; but many nouns, which in Hindi are only used in the strong form, in Maithilī prefer the weak form. Thus :—

Maithilī.	Hindī.
आन्ह *ānh*, blind	अाँधा *ā̃dhā*
ऊँच *ūc*, high	ऊँचा *ū̃cā*
कान *kān*, one-eyed	काना *kanā*
कान्ह *kānh*, the shoulder	काँधा *kā̃dhā*
गहीर *gahīr*, deep	गहिरा *gahirā*
गोर *gōr*, pale	गोरा *gūrā*
घोड़ *ghōṛ*, a horse	घोड़ा *ghōṛā*
चून *cūn*, lime	चूना *cūnā*
छूर *chūr*, a knife	छूरा *chūrā*
दहिन *dahin*, right (not left)	दहिना *dahinā*
बहीर *bahīr*, deaf	बहिरा *bahirā*

Maithilī.	*Hindī.*
मूस *mūs*, a rat	मूसा *mūsā*
लोह *lōh*, iron	लोहा *lōhā*
सार *sār*, a brother-in-law	साला *sālā*
सोन *sōn*, gold	सोना *sōnā*
So (weak form in *ⁱ*)	
मारि *mārⁱ*, a beating	मारी *mārī*

In some cases Maithilī has the strong, as well as the weak form. Thus, घोड़ा *ghōrā* as well as घोड़ *ghōr*, लोहा *lōhā* as well as लोह *lōh*, but in all the above, the weak form is the one customarily heard.

Weak nouns are of course very common in Hindī. But I think it is safe to say that they are much more common, both in the case of masculine and in that of feminine nouns, in Maithilī.

53. आ *ā* (**Feminine**). Nearly all the feminine words in आ *ā* are *tatsamas* borrowed directly from Sanskrit, such as सभा *sabhā*, an assembly. The only Maithilī *tadbhavas* which I have noted as ending in this letter are बुन्द *bund* or बुन्दा *bundā*, a drop, and the connected बुना *bunō*, zero, the figure 0.

54. आस *ās*, वास *wās*. These usually form desideratives as in Hindī, but are not so common as in that language. The only forms which I have met in Maithilī are :—

पिआस *piās*, thirst; hence पिआसल *piāsal*, thirsty.

तरास *tarās*, thirst; hence तरासल *tarāsal*, thirsty.

(This word is not to be confounded with तरास *tarās*, fear).

मुतवास *mutᵃwās*, desire to make water (Hindī मुतास *mutās*).

हगवास *hɪgᵒwās*, desire to stool (Hindī हगास *hagās*).

Other words with (in form) the same suffix, but not desideratives, are such as :—

झपास *jhapās*, a violent burst of rain (so Hindī for *jhapa-vāsā*, sudden rain).

गड़ांस *garā̃s*, a pole-axe (Hindī गड़ासा *gārāsā*).

The derivation of the suffix in the last two words is obscure.

55. आह *āh*. (*Fem.* आहि *ahⁱ*), weak form; आहा *āhā* (*Fem.*

āhi), **strong form.** This is a common adjectival termination in Maithilī. Thus :—

चधलाइ *adhᵃlāh,* bad.

पिछड़ाइ *pichᵃṛāh,* slippery.

बताइ *batāh* or बउराइ *baurāh,* mad.

बलुआइ *baluāh,* sandy.

The strong form is specially used in the following three cases :—

पछिमाहा *pachimāhā,* a man of the west.

दछिनाहा *dachināhā,* a man of the south.

उतराहा *utᵃrāhā,* a man of the north.

But पूबा *pūbā,* a man of the east.

56. As probably connected with these forms we may quote घोड़हिया *ghoṛahiyā,* a horse-dealer, which is the long form of घोड़ाही *ghoṛāhī,* a masculine noun which I have not met in the short form. Compare also बटोही *baṭohī,* a wayfarer, from बाट *bāṭ,* a road.

57. ि *i,* **weak short form ;** ी *ī,* **strong short form ;** िया *iyā,* **long form.**

The weak short form is mainly employed to make feminines from masculine weak short forms ending in a consonant ; as गोर *gōr,* fair, fem. गोरि *gōrᵢ.* It also forms feminine nouns generally, as in गोहि *gōhᵢ,* an iguana ; डारि *ḍārᵢ,* a line ; भुँइ *bhūi* (the final vowel fully pronounced being preceded by a vowel, see § 10) ; or भुइयाँ *bhuiyā̃* (long form), the ground ; लगति *laggatᵢ,* an assessment ; बाँहि *bā̃hᵢ,* an arm ; करुआरि *karuārᵢ,* an oar ; दूरि *dūrᵢ,* distance ; आगि *āgᵢ,* fire.

An important class falling under this head consists of feminine verbal nouns formed by adding ि *i* to the root, as in मारि *mārᵢ,* a beating ; भूलि *bhūlᵢ,* an error.

In Hindi most of the above end in long ी *ī,* as in गोरी *gōrī,* गोही *gōhī.* Sometimes in that language the final vowel is dropped, as in बाँह *bā̃h* (fem.), an arm ; दूर *dūr* (fem.), distance ; and in the case of Hindi verbal nouns the ₹ *i* may be either dropped or the strong form is used, as मार *mār* (fem.) or मारी *mārī*, a beating.

Masculine nouns of this class (when in the weak form) end in a fully pronounced ₹ *i*, not in ₹ *i*. They generally represent Sanskrit words ending in ऋ *ṛ* (or ऋक *ṛka*) इक *ika*, ईय *īya*, or ऋन् *in*. Such are नाति *nāti*, a grandson; दूबि *dūbi* (masculine, not feminine), *dūb* grass; पानि *pāni*, water; केहरि *kehᵃri*, a lion; डाँड़ि *ḍā̃ṛi*, a rower; सूरि *sū̃ri*, a distiller; तेलि *tēli*, an oil-man; तमोलि *tamōli*, a betel-seller; कोढ़ि *kōṛhi*, a leper; मानि *māni*, proud.

Many of these words are also pronounced with a long ई *ī*, or, in other words, have strong forms in use as well as the weak ones. Thus, we have also नाती *nātī*, केहरी *kehᵃrī*, तमोली *tamōlī*, and so on, but the forms with short ₹ *i* are the more usual. So, for feminine nouns, we have माटि *māṭi* or माटी *māṭī*, earth; कांकरि *kākarⁱ* or कंकरी *kākᵃrī*, a cucumber; कूँजि *kū̃jⁱ* or कूँजी *kū̃jī*, a key; दहि *dahⁱ* or दही *dahī*, curdled milk (this word is feminine, not masculine).

The strong form in ई *ī* also sometimes occurs as the only form for feminine nouns as in माँछी *mā̃chī*, a fly; खरी *kharī*, chalk; लगारी *lagārī*, inquisitiveness (and other similar abstract nouns, instead of with the more usual termination आई *āi*). We sometimes meet this feminine long ई *ī* in diminutives, as दाढ़ *dāṛh*, a long beard, दाढ़ी *dāṛhī*, a beard. पुजेरी *pujērī*, a priest, and मोती *motī*, a pearl, are examples of masculine words in ई *ī*, which do not also optionally end in ₹ *i*.

The long form is used, *quâ* long form, in the case of any of the foregoing nouns, and then usually has a meaning either familiar, contemptuous, or diminutive, as in माली *mālī*, a gardener, long form मालिया *māliyā* or मलिया *maliyā*, the gardener (familiarly), or (contemptuously) the wretched gardener; पोथी *pōthī*, a book, पोथिया *pothiyā*, a small book. कोढ़ी *kōṛhī*, leprous, कोढ़िया *koṛhiyā*, a poor unfortunate leper.

The same long termination is employed to indicate (*a*) a man, country, and (*b*) his profession.

Thus :—

(*a*) संन्हिया *senhiyā*, a man of Sindh ; मगहिया *mugahiyā*, a man of Magah or Magadha ; तिरहुतिया *tir^ahutiyā*, a man of Tirhut or Tirabhukti ; मथुरिया *mathuriyā*, a man of Mathurā ; नेपालिया *nepāliyā*, a man of Nēpāl ; पहाड़िया *pahăriyā*, a man of the *pahār* or mountain, a mountaineer.

(*b*) अढ़तिया *arhatiyā*, a broker ; कमरिया *kamariyā*, a blanket-wearer, a labourer ; घटिया *ghaṭiyā*, a brāhmaṇ who attends ghāṭs.

Exhibiting character more generally are फुसिया *phusiyā*, a flatterer ; चिकनिया *cikaniyā*, one who is always shining and clean (from चिक्कन *cikkan*, smooth) ; and दुखिया *dukhiyā*, one who is miserable, poverty-stricken.

58. Connected with these इ *i*-suffixes is आइ *āi* or आइ *āi*, long form अइया *aiyā*. As in Hindī, this forms abstract nouns. Thus :—भलाइ *bhalāi*, goodness ; खटाइ *khaṭāi*, acidity ; छोटाइ *choṭāi*, smallness, and hundreds of others.

It is also employed to signify the wages or price of any operation, as in चराइ *carāi*, the wages of a herdsman ; पिसाइ *pisāi*, wages of grinding ; खेवाइ *khēwāi*, ferry hire ; ढोलाइ *ḍholāi*, the cost of carriage. Connected with this are words like धोआइ *dhōāi*, the art of washing (as well as the cost of it) ; बटनाइ *baṭ^anāi*, the art of twisting ropes ; पटकनाइ *paṭ^okanāi*, a task of winnowing.

The long form in अइया *aiyā* is employed to form masculine adjectives, such as घरइया *gharaiyā*, domesticated (Hindī घरेलू *gharēlā*) ; बनइया *banaiyā*, wild ; गमइया *gamaiyā*, rustic. It also forms feminine diminutives, such as मढ़इया *marhaiyā*, a small hut. Compare (the short form) तलाइ *talāi*, a small pond (from ताल *tāl*, a pond). In Hindī, the long form तलइया *talaiyā* is preferred.

59. इम *im* (weak form), इमा *imā* (strong form).—This suffix also occurs in Bengali and Marāṭhī. In Maithilī it is found in the word ललिम *lalim* or ललिमा *lalimā*, redness.

60. ঽ *ᵘ*, weak short [form ; ঝ *ū*, strong short form ; ঝআ *uā*, long form.—Where we have weak forms in Maithili, Hindī has strong forms. Thus :—

भाऋ *bhālᵘ*, a bear ; but Hindī भालू *bhālū*.

नाऋ *nāu* § 10, iii), a barber ; ,,   नाऋ *nāū*.

बऋ *bahᵘ*, a son's wife ;   ,,   बहू *bahū*.

In some cases the imperfect ঽ *ᵘ* has altogether disappeared, so that we have—

बाऋ *bālᵘ* or बाऋ *bāl* (fem.) sand, but Hindī बालू *bālū*.

माम *mām* or even मामा *māmā*, a maternal uncle, H. मामू *māmū*.

In all these cases, the existence of the ঽ *ᵘ* as a termination is due to an accident of origin, and the termination does not necessarily indicate any special shade of meaning. Most ঝ *u*-suffixes can be referred to the Sanskrit termination ঝক *uka*, which has also survived without change, and will be found under the क *k*-suffixes.

The suffix ঝ *ū* of the strong form often has the force of the agent. Thus, ঝজাঽ *ujāṛū*, a destroyer ; ঝাক or (long form) खोआ *khauā*, an eater ; डाकू *ḍākū*, a shouter, hence, a robber ; बिगाऽ *bigāṛū*, a spoiler ; झाऽ *jhāṛū*, a sweeper, a broom. Less distinctively nouns of agency are सहरू *sahᵃrū*, a citizen (from شَهْر *shahr*, a city), and पहरू *pahᵃrū*, a watchman (from पहर *pahar*, a watch, a guard). In गमारू *gamārū*, rustic ; दुलारू *dulārū* or (long form) दुलरुआ *dularuā*, a darling ; मेहरारू *mehᵃrārū*, a woman ; and भगेऽ *bhagēṛū*, a runaway, the ঝ *ū*-suffix is simply pleonastic, as explained below, under the head of ऋ *l*- र *r*- ড় *ṛ*-suffixes. The suffix implies quality in भक्कू *bhakkū*, a fool (Hindī भकुआ *bhakuā*) ; नक्कू *nakkū*, long-nosed (Hindī, the same).

As usual, the long form ঝআ *uā* is commonly employed contemptuously as in भरुआ *bharuā*, a pimp, but not so always. In दुलरुआ *dularuā*, quoted above, it is an affectionate diminutive, while the meaning is unchanged in खौआ *khauā* and in गेड़ुआ *geruā*, a large kind of pillow.

Parallel to the आइ *āi*-suffix we have also an आऊ *āū*-suffix, with a long form अउआ or औआ *auā*. It forms adjectives, as in भगड़ाऊ *jhagᵃṛāū* or भगड़ुआ *jhagᵃrauā*, quarrelsome; रहाऊ *rahāū*, abiding, a dweller, an old inhabitant. The long form of विगाड़ू *bigāṛū*, quoted above, is not the regular विगड़ुआ *bigaṛuā*, as we might expect, but is विगड़ोआ *bigᵃṛauā*, as if formed from * विगड़ाऊ *bigᵃṛāū*.

Most causal verbs have their roots ending in आव *āw*, and from these a number of similar words are framed, such as जड़ाऊ *jaṛāū*, studded (with gems), jewelled. The termination आव *āw* is often written आओ *āo*, and this gives verbal-nouns, such as अटकाओ *aṭᵃkāo*, the act of stopping, which should be distinguished from the आऊ *āū*-suffix.

61. औन्ह *aunh* or औन *aun* (fem. औन्हि *aunh^i* or औनि *aun^i*). This termination forms adjectives generally implying a moderate degree of the quality referred to. The final consonant in every -case may be either न्ह *nh* or न *n*. It agrees in sense with the Hindī termination एला *ēlā*. Just as in Hindī we have गोरा *gōrā*, fair, light-coloured, and गोरेला *gorēlā*, fairish, rather light-coloured, so we have Maithilī गोर *gōr*, fair, गोरौन्ह *goraunh* or गोरौन *goraun*, fairish. Other examples are :—

अन्हरौन्ह *anhᵃraunh*, darkish.

अमिलौन्ह *amilaunh*, acidish.

उजरौन्ह *ujᵃraunh*, whitish (उज्जर *ujjar*, white).

उसरौन्ह *usᵃraunh*, saline (ऊसर *ūsar*, salt land).

कचौन्ह *kacaunh*, rawish.

करिऔन्ह *kariaunh*, blackish (कारि *kāri*, black).

कसौन्ह *kasaunh*, rather astringent.

गोबरौन्ह *gob°raunh*, brown land (the colour of गोबर *gōbar* or cow-dung).

गोलौन्ह *golaunh*, globular (गोल *gōl*, round).

तितौन्ह *titaunh*, bitterish.

दुधौन्ह *dudhaunh*, milky.

धुरौन्ह *dhuraunh*, dusty (धूरि *dhūri*, dust).

नेनौन्ह *nenaunh*, youthful (नेना *nēnā*, a lad).

पिरौन्ह *piraunh*, yellowish (पीअर *pīar*, yellow).

फटौन्ह *phaṭaunh*, cracked (of milk).

बुढौन्ह *buṛhaunh*, oldish (बूढ *būṛh*, old).

मठौन्ह *maṭhaunh*, sour (मट्ठा *maṭṭhā*, buttermilk).

मेघौन्ह *meghaunh*, cloudy.

ललौन्ह *lalaunh*, reddish (लाल *lāl*, red).

In all the above न *n* may be substituted for न्ह *nh*.

62.   क *k*.—A number of nouns are formed by the addition of the letter क *k* preceded by a vowel.

With अक *ak*, we have common words like सरक *sarak* or सड़क *sarak*, a road; फाटक *phāṭak*, a gate; बैठक *baiṭhak*, a seat.

Many are primary nouns,—formed from verbs whose roots end in क *k*. They are the same in form as the roots. Such are [1] अटक *aṭak*, stoppage; कड़क *karak*, a crash; कचक *kacak*, a sprain; खड़क *kharak*, a clang; खटक *khaṭak*, 'pit-a-pat'; गहक *gahak*, reeling in drink; चउंक *caŭk*, starting; चिलक *cilak*, चमक *camak*, झलक *jhalak*, झमक *jhamak*, दलक *dalak*, दमक *damak*, glitter; चटक *caṭak*, a crack, snap; and many others.

With आक *āk* or आंक *āk*, are उड़ांक *uṛāk*, one who flies (not

---

[1] See Mr. Beames' Comparative Grammar, Vol. II, p. 31. My list has been prepared by going through Mr. Beames' list with a native of Mithilá.

causal, one who causes to fly); पिषाक *piāk*, a drinker; चढ़ाक *carhāk*, a rider. Adverbs are also made with this suffix, as भटाक *jhaṭāk*, suddenly; फटाक *phaṭāk*, unawares; तड़ाक *taṛāk*, immediately; पटाक *paṭāk*, immediately; खटाक *khaṭāk*, immediately.

With उक *uk*, we have मारुक *māruk*, quarrelsome, one disposed to fight.

With बइक *aik*, we have सेबइक *sebaik* (Hindi सेवाइत *sēwāit*), a worshipper.

63. गर *gar*. This suffix implies agency. Thus कँटगर *kāṭᵃgar* thorny; हथगर *hathᵃgar*, able to use the hands; गोड़गर *goṛᵃgar*, able to use the feet. The last two examples occur in a poem describing the babyhood of *Kṛṣṇa*. As he grew big he began to be able to use his hands and his feet. I have not met the suffix elsewhere in literature, but it is very common in the colloquial language, and can be employed with almost any word in the above sense. In ordinary conversation हथगर *hathᵃgar* means 'dexterous.'

64. त *t* is mostly employed as the suffix of the present participle, usually with अइ *ai* prefixed, as in देखइत *dekhait*, seeing. When verbal roots end in vowels, the termination is lightened, as in जाइत *jāit*, going; सिउत *siut*, sewing; होअइत *hōait* or होइत *hōit*, becoming. The suffix अइत *ait*, also occurs in words like चढ़इत *carhait*, a mounted man; डकइत *ḍakait*, a robber (these two are really present participles); and नतइत *natait*, a relation (from नाता *nātā*, relationship). There are several words similarly formed from nouns in Hindi, but नतइत *natait* is the only one which I have noted in Maithilī.

65. Of a quite different origin is a group of words ending in आहटि *āhaṭⁱ*, औटी *auṭī*, or औती *autī*. These generally form abstract nouns. Thus: गड़बड़ाहटि *gaṛᵃbaṛāhaṭⁱ*, confusion; गजब-जाहटि *gajᵃbajāhaṭⁱ*, confusion; गुलगुलाहटि *gulᵃgulāhaṭⁱ*, whispering

घनघनाइटि *ghan°ghanāhaṭ^i*, a great noise; चनचनाइटि *can°-canāhaṭ^i*, speaking loudly; फरफराइटि *phar°pharāhaṭ^i*, throbbing; मनसनाइटि *san°sanāhaṭ^i*, humming in the ear, and many other similar forms. It will be observed that all these words contain reduplications, and are more or less onomatopœic. Maithili re-serves the termination आइटि *āhaṭ^i*, for this class of words, and has no words corresponding to (*e.g.*) the Hindi खिसियाहट *khisiyāhaṭ*, fretfulness: खुजलाहट *khuj°lāhaṭ*, itching. In Maithili these ideas are represented by खिसियाएब *khisiyāeb* and कुड़ियाएब *kuṛiy°eb*, re-spectively, the termination आएब *āeb* (of the infinitive or verbal noun) being usually employed in the place of the Hindi आहट *āhaṭ*. Cf. § 67.

The termination अउटी *auṭī* or अउतो *autī* which is connected with the above, is not so common as in Hindi. It forms an abstract noun in सिधउटी *sidhauṭī*, uprightness (from सिद्ध *siddh*, upright). It expresses property in words like जेठउतो *jeṭhautī*, the share of an eldest son, and बपउटो *bapautī*, the share of a father. Connected with this idea is बोड़उतो *choṛautī*, ransom ; while mere relationship is indicated in words like हरउतो *harautī*, a particular kind of bamboo with a narrow pipe (cf. Hindi हरौटी *harauṭī*, a staff, derivation doubtful); सिकउतो *sikautī*, a reed basket, from सीक *sik*, a reed ; चुनउतो *cunautī*, a box for holding lime ; कजरउटो *kajarautī*, a box for holding collyrium.

66. न *n* (fem. िन *n^i*,) weak form; ना *nā* (fem. नी *nī*) strong form.

Suffixes of which न *n* is the characteristic letter, are common in Maithili (even if we exclude the numerous *tatsama* words in *ana* borrowed from Sanskrit). Such suffixes are not employed to make infinitives as they are in Hindi.

Both weak and strong forms are frequently employed to make nouns of the instrument. Such are:—

5

(*a*) Masc. weak forms—

चपकन *cap°kan*, a close-fitting coat (√ चपक *capak*. compress).

जइन *chaṭṭan*, a gold-washer's pan.

डांसन *ḍā͂san*, a washerman's mallet.

दतुअन *datuan*, a tooth-brush (दाँत *dā͂t*. a tooth).

पडकन *paṭ°kan*, an instrument for teasing cotton.

बाढन *bāṛhan*, a broom.

मडन *mahan*, an oil-mill pestle.

लोपन *lūpan*, a poker.

From causal roots we have—

घेरान *gherān*, a fence.

अतरावन *at°rāwan*, the reeds of a loom for keeping the threads apart (cf. Skr. अन्तर *antara*).

चपरावन *cap°rāwan*, a perforated block of iron for shaping nailheads.

लगावन *lagāwan*, a stuffed calf-skin shown to a cow to make its milk flow. literally, ' an appliance.' hence ' an imposture.'

(*b*) Fem. weak forms—

चालनि *cālan^i*, a sieve.

छाओनि *chāon^i*, an encampment (छाव *chāw*. thatch).

पीअनि *pīan^i*, tobacco for smoking (as distinct from snuff).

लाडनि *lāṛan^i*, a grain-parcher's broom.

(*c*) Masc. strong forms—

अखेना *akhainā*, a threshing rake.

अँचना *ā͂c°nā*, a poker.

खिखोरना *khikhor°nā*, a weaver's scraper.

करना *kar°nā*, a curd-vessel.

झापना *jhap°nā*. ढकना *ḍhak°nā*. or ढपना *ḍhap°nā*, a cover.

झरना *jhar°nā*, a broom.

पिटना *piṭⁱnā*, a cobbler's mallet.

भरना *bhurⁱnā*, the stuffing of a quilt.

मोचना *mocⁱnā*, a barber's tweezers (मोंछ *mŏch*. a moustache).

From causal roots, we have—

खेलाओन *khelāon* or खेलौना *khelaunā*. a toy.

कोरौना *choraunā*, a door-key.

बिछाओन *bichāon* or बिछऔना *bichaonā* or बिछौना *bichaunā*. bedding.

मिलौना *milaunā*, a potter's smoother.

हथौना *hathaunā*, a toddy-vessel.

(d) Fem. strong forms. These are the most common of all—

खुरचनी *khuracⁱnī*, a pot-scraper.

उबहनी *ubahⁱnī*, a well-rope.

कटरनी *kaṭarⁱnī*, a cobbler's awl.

घिरनी *ghirⁱnī*. a pulley.

चिटकना *chiṭⁱkanī*, a door-bolt.

छेवनी *chēwⁱnī*. a potter's cutting string.

छेनी *chēnī*. a chisel.

ठेकनी *ṭhekⁱnī*. a prop.

नथुनी *nathunī*, a nose-ring.

नहरनी *naharⁱnī*, a nail parer. a gouge.

बटनी *baṭⁱnī*, a silk-reel.

बैसनी *baisⁱnī*. a seat.

मथनी *mathⁱnī*. a kind of hammer.

मधनी *mahⁱnī*, a churn-dasher.

From causal bases—

चलौनी *calaunī*. a windlass handle.

चलौनी *chalaunī*, the cover of an ass's pad.

तरौनी *taraunī*, a sweetmeat-stand.

The same suffixes are also employed to indicate an occupation, trade, or profession. Thus :—

कोड़न *kōṛan*, hoeing.

पिसान *pisān*, the trade of corn-grinding.

लेन देन *lēn dēn*, taking (and) giving, trade, traffic.

पटावन *paṭāwan*, irrigation.

उछटनी *uchᵃṭanī*, weeding.

कटनी *kaṭᵃnī*, reaping.

कमैनी *kamainī*, weeding.

करौनी *keraunī*, weeding.

टिपनी *ṭipᵃnī*, superficial weeding.

टूगनी *ṭūgᵃnī*, a special method of reaping.

फरनी *pharᵃnī*, the application of the ploughshare (फर *phar*), the first ploughing of the season.

डगौनी *ḍegaunī*, separating grain from the ears by beating on the ground.

I have not noted any strong masculine forms in ना *nā* in this sense.

The same suffixes are further extended to imply the *result* of any occupation, or even a more indefinite connection with the root. Thus :—

छारन *chāran*, a grass thatch.

धोअन *dhōan*, opium-washings.

बहारन *bahāran*, sweepings.

चटनी *caṭᵃnī* (√ चाट *cāṭ*, lick), a relish with food, ' chutnee.'

छितनी *chiṭᵃnī*, a broken basket.

Causal bases sometimes take the suffixes to indicate a ceremonial observance. Thus we have :—

चुमावन *cumāwan*, the kissing ceremony in a marriage.

ठेकौनी *ṭhekaunī*, the stopping at the door, part of a marriage ceremony.

मुदेखौनी *mudekhaunī*, presents given to a bride on showing her face.

Compare मंगनी *māg^nī*, a betrothal.

A few nouns of agency are formed with the strong form of this suffix. Those which I have noted are all vulgar and indecent abusive terms, such as हगना *hag^nā*, मुतना *mut^nā*, or पदना *pad^nā*. They all imply that the action indicated is done to excess.

67. ब *b*, अब *ab*. एब *eb*.—This forms infinitives and verbal nouns, as in देखब *dēkhab*, to see, the act of seeing. When a verbal root ends in आ *ā* or ओ *ō*, the suffix is एब *eb*, not अब *ab*. Thus पाएब *pāeb*, to obtain; जाएब *jāeb*, to go; होएब *hōeb*, to become. In देब *dēb*, to give, and लेब *lēb*, to take, the junction vowel is dropped.

When this suffix is added to intransitive roots in आ *ā*, it also forms abstract nouns, as in खिसियाएब *khisiyāeb*, fretfulness (from √ खिसिया *khisiyā*, to be fretful), कुढ़ियाएब *kuṛiyāeb*, to be angry. Cf. § 65.

68. ल *l*- र *r*- ड़ *r*-**suffixes.**—The letter ल *l* is characteristic of many noun forms.

The simplest is अल *al*, (fem. अलि *ali*), or (strong form) आला *alā* (fem. आली *ali*).

अल *al* forms past participles, such as देखल *dēkhal* (fem. देखलि *dēkhali*), seen. In the case of verbs ending in vowels, it is sometimes उल *ul*, इल *il*, एल *el* or ओल *ol*. Thus सिअल *sial* or सिउल *siul*, sewn; मुइल *muil*, dead; आएल *āel*, come : पाओल *pāol*, obtained.

It also forms adjectives on the same lines, such as दुखाएल *dukhāel*, grieved (also a past participle); निनाएल *nināel*, drowsy; डेराएल *ḍerāel*, fearful; घमाएल *ghamāel*, perspiring; अँघाएल *aṅghāel*, sleepy; सरमाएल *sar^māel* (from شرم *sharm*, shame) bashful; and many others. All these may be looked upon as participles of neuter verbs, whose roots end in आ *ā*.

The same termination is employed to make verbal nouns or

infinitives, with an oblique form in **था** *ā*, as **देखल** *dekhal*, the act of seeing; **देखला में** *dekhᵃlā sã*, from seeing.

The strong form **थला** *ᵃlā* is generally employed to make diminutives, and its feminine **थली** *ᵃlī* is used for things of a still smaller size. Thus **चकला** *cakᵃlā*, a paste-board (from **चाक** *cāk*, a wheel); **टिकुली** *ṭikulī*, a wafer: **कोठली** *koṭhᵃlī*, a small room: **तमला** *tasᵃlā*, a brass vessel, **तसली** *tasᵃlī*, a small one.

Another connected suffix is **इल** *il*, strong form **इला** *ilā*, which is not so common in Maithili as elsewhere. It forms possessive adjectives from substantives. The only true Maithili examples which I have noted with certainty are **मांझिला** *mājhilā*, the middle of three brothers, or the second of four brothers : and **सांझिल** *sājhil*, the third son of a family of four or more.

Of much more frequent occurrence is the closely related **अइल** *ail*, with the same meaning. It is often found where literary Hindi has other suffixes. Thus :—

Maithili.	Hindi
तोनरइल *tonail*, pot-bellied	**तोंदरल** *todail*.
धोधइल *dhodhail*, pot-bellied	**धोंधाला** *dhõdhālā*.
दंगइल *dāgail*, a brawler	**दंगैत** *dāgait*.
बोझइल *bojhail*, load-bearing	**बुझइल** *bujhail*.

In **बंसइला** *bāsailā*, a young bamboo, the strong form, like **थला** *ᵃlā* forms a diminutive.

Another form of **अइला** *ailā* is **एला** *ēlā*, which we have in **मउतेला** *sautēlā*, of or belonging to a co-wife, and (feminine diminutive) **खम्हेली** *khamhēlī*, a small pillar.

Parallel to **इल** *il*, we have **उल** *ul* in **काजुल** *kājul*, a worker, bread-winner. Its strong form **उला** *ulā*, fem. **उली** *ulī*, is more common, and, like the other strong forms, the feminine usually is a diminutive. Thus :—

टिकुली *ṭikulī*, a wafer.

गछुली *gachulī*, a young tree.

कठुली *kaṭhulī*, a small wooden bowl.

खटुली *khaṭulī*, a small bamboo litter.

गेड़ुली *geṛuli*, a small pillow (गेड़ुआ *geṛuā*, a large pillow).

आँठुली *āṭhulī*, a small आँठी *āṭhī* or fruit-stone.

बातुल *bātul*, a stammerer; बतुली *batulī*, a pitiful, stammering woman.

And many others. Occasionally the ड़ *u* is strengthened to ओ *ō* (cf. एला *ēlā* above), as in टिकोला *ṭikōlā*, a young mango.

69. Cognate to the ल *l*-suffixes are those whose characteristic letter is इ *y* or र *r*.

The suffix अड़ा *ªṛā* (fem. अड़ी *ªṛī*) is as pleonastic as the long form in अवा *ªwā*, which every noun can take. Perhaps in the masculine it adds a shade of contempt. In the feminine it gives a diminutive meaning. This suffix is not so common in Maithili in the west, अरा *ªṛā* (fem. अरी *ªṛī*) being more usual. An example is झाँपड़ा *jhõpªṛā* or खाँपड़ा *khõpªṛā*, a hut; feminine झाँपड़ी *jhõpªṛī* or खाँपड़ी *khõpªṛī*, a small hut. So, from मटका *maṭukā*, a large vessel, we have मटकुड़ी *maṭªkurī*, a milk-pail; टुकड़ा *ṭukªṛā* or टुकरा *ṭukªrā*, a piece; टुकड़ी *ṭukªṛī* or टुकरी *ṭukªrī*, a small piece.

The suffix is sometimes strengthened to एड़ू *ēṛū*, as in भगेड़ू *bhagēṛū*, a runaway, fugitive.

The connected अरा *ªrā*, (fem. अरी *ªrī*) is used with similar meaning, and is more often met with in Maithili. Examples are चक्की *cakkī* or चकरी *cakªrī*, a mill-stone; गेठरी *geṭhªrī*, a bundle; मूँगरी *mūgªrī*, a small grain-mallet; टुकरा *ṭukªrā*, -री *-rī*, as above.

Parallel to the suffix ओला *ōlā*, we have औरी *aurī* in घमौरी *ghamaurī*, small heat-spots, prickly-heat, from घाम *ghām*, heat.

70. There is another pair of ल *l*- and र *r*-suffixes preceded the letter आ *ā*.—Some of the examples are merely deformed

tatsamas like किरपाल् *kirᵃpāl*, Sanskrit कृपालुः *kṛpāluḥ*. But others
are *tadbhavas.* The termination is आल् *āl* (fem. आलि *ālⁱ*) or
आर *ār* (fem. आरि *ārⁱ*). Strong forms are आला *ālā* (fem. आली
ālī) or आरा *ārā* (fem. आरी *ārī*). This has several derivations,
according to the particular words with which it is used.[1] In putting them here together, no attempt is made to consider derivation. All words formed with these suffixes are of a very similar
nature, and for practical purposes they can all be considered at
the same time. The ल *l*-suffix is the less common of the pair.
We have दढ़ियाल् *daṛhiyāl*, bearded, from दाढ़ी *daṛhī*, a beard.
With the र *r*-suffix we have दुधारि *dudhārⁱ* or दुधारी *dudhārī* (feminine), milch (of a cow); पियार *piyār* (fem. पियारि *piyārⁱ*), a beloved
one, as against the Hindi प्यारा *pyārā* (fem. -री *-rī*). पेटारा *peṭārā*, a
basket-box, fem. पेटारी *peṭārī*, used in a diminutive sense; गमार
gamār, rustic; दुलार *dullār*, a darling (Skr. दुर्लभः *durlabhaḥ*). The
last two words often take an additional final *ū*-suffix. Thus गमारू
gamārū, दुलारू *dulārū* (or long form employed affectionately,
दुलरुआ *dularuā*), without change of meaning. So also the Sans-
krit-Prakrit महिला *mahilā* becomes मेहरारू *mehᵃrārū*, a woman.

71. The suffix पन *pan* प्पन *ppan*, आपन *āpan*, is as common in
Maithili as in other Indo-Aryan vernaculars. It forms abstract
nouns from adjectives or substantives. Thus :—.

चुगलपन *cugalᵃpan*, backbiting.

चुधरपन *chudharᵃpan*, meanness (चूधर *chūdhar* = शूद्र *sūdra*).

छोटपन *chotᵃpan*, smallness.

ठगपन *ṭhagᵃpan*, cheating.

दृढपन *dṛṛhᵃpan*, firmness.

धूर्तपन *dhūrtᵃpan*, knavery.

---

[1] Cf. Dr. Hoernle's Gaudian Grammar, pp. 118, 129, 135, 150.

नेनपन *nen^apan*, childhood.

बलेलपन *balel^apan*, foolishness.

बहेड़पन *baher^apan*, ne'erdoweelness.

बुड़िपन *buripan*, foolishness (बूड़ि *būri*, a fool).

बुढ़पन *burh^apan* or बुट्ठपन *burhappan*, old age.

भलापन *bhal^apan* or भलपन *bhal^apan*, honesty.

भाँड़पन *bhã̃r^apan* or भाँड़प्पन *bhã̃rappan*, roguery.

रँड़पन *rã̃^apan*, widowhood (राँड़ *rã̃r*, a widow).

लँगटपन *lãgat^apan* or नँगटपन *nãgat^apan*, blackguardliness (लंगट *lãgat*, नंगट *nãgat* or नँगटा *nãg^aṭā*, naked).

लगरपन *lagar^apan*, inquisitiveness (लगार *lagār* = ' Paul Pry ').

लड़िकपन *larik^apan*, boyhood.

सेआनपन *seãn^apan*, full-ageness (when a young lady has, as we should say in England, ' her hair up,' she is सेआनि *seãnⁱ*).

It will be observed that the suffix is added even to *tatsama* words.

72. वाह *wāh* (fem. वाहि *wāhⁱ*).—This is the regular termination of nouns of agency and is the equivalent in meaning of the Hindi वाला *wālā*. Thus :—

अनवाह *an^awāh*, the man in charge of the other (अन्य *anya*) or spare pair of bullocks, when ploughing is going on.

कतरवाह *kutar^awāh*, one who cuts sugarcane for feeding a sugarcane press.

करिनवाह *karin^awāh*, a man who works a करीन *karin* or irrigation lever.

कोदरिवाह *kodariwāh*, a worker with a कोदारि *kodārⁱ* or mattock.

गछवाह *gach^awāh*, one who climbs trees (गाछ *gāch*, a tree).

गँजवाह *gãj^awāh*, one who uses a गाँज *gã̃j*, or fish trap.

गड़िवाह *gariwāh*, a cart-driver.

गुनवाह *gun^awāh*, the man who tows a boat (गुन *gun*, a rope).

6

गैवाइ *gaiwāh*, a tender of cows.

घोड़वाइ *ghoᵃwāh*, a groom.

चरवाइ *carᵃwāh*, one who grazes cattle.

भालिवाइ *jhaliwāh*, a cymbal-player (भालो *jhālī*. cymbals).

टोकवाइ *ṭokᵃwāh*, an asker (टोक *ṭōk*, ask).

पेनवाइ *penᵃwāh*, a cattle-driver (पेना *painā*, a cattle-whip).

बधवाइ *badhᵃwāh*, a field watchman (बाध *bādh*, village lands).

मोरवाइ *mōrᵃwāh*, one who drives cattle round and round in a
mill (मोर *mōr*, a turn).

लठिवाइ *laṭhiwāh*, a wielder of cudgels.

सुनवाइ *sunᵃwāh*, one who hears complaints.

हथिवाइ *hathiwāh*, an elephant-keeper.

हरवाइ *harᵃwāh*, a ploughman.

The suffix is optionally spelt and pronounced बाइ *bāh*, so that
we may have अनबाइ *anᵃbāh*, कतरबाइ *katarᵃbāh*, and so on.
Further, an abstract noun can be formed from these nouns of
agency by adding the fem. suffix इ i. Thus गड़िवाइि *gaṛiwāhⁱ*,
the profession of a cart-driver. So from the √ चार *cār*, graze
(active), we have चरवाइ *carᵃbāh*, a cattle-grazer, and thence
चरवाइि *carᵃbāhⁱ*, cattle-grazing.

73. सार *sār*.—This is not a proper suffix, being simply a
derivative form of साला *śālā*, a house. In Maithili it is used as
a suffix, and not as a member of a compound word. The whole
compound is treated as if it were one word, with the usual shortening of the antepenultimate vowel. Thus, from—

हाथी *hāthī*, an elephant, we have हथिसार *hathisār*, an
elephant-stable.

घोड़ *ghōr*, a horse, we have घोड़सार *ghoᵃsār*, a horse-stable.

चाटि *chāṭi*, a pupil (Skr. चात्र *chātra*), चटिसार *chaṭisār*, a school.

Similarly, कनिसार *kanisār*, a furnace for parching grain, and
बनिसार *banisār*, a prison.

CHAPTER II.

GENDER, NUMBER AND CASE.

74. The noun has two Genders.—Masculine and Feminine.
Words derived direct from the Sanskrit, which were originally
neuter, generally become masculine in Maithili.

The most important exceptions to this last rule are आँखि
ākh^i, an eye; दहि *dah^i* or दही *dahī*, curdled milk; दूरि *dūr^i*, distance; and पुस्तक *pustak*, a book; which are feminine. आगि *āg^i*,
fire, though derived from a masculine Sanskrit word, is feminine
in Maithili.

75. There are two numbers, the singular and plural.

The plural number of nouns in Maithili is simply formed
by the addition of a noun signifying multitude. Those most
commonly used are सभ *sabh* and सबहि *sabah^i* [1] meaning 'all,' and
लोकनि *lok^ani* meaning 'people.' The last is only used with animate
objects. सभ *sabh* and सबहि *sabah^i* can be used indifferently either
before or after the qualified noun. Thus नेना सभक *nēnā sabhak*
नेना सबहिक *nēnā sab^ahik*, सभ नेनाक *sabh nēnāk*. सबहि नेनाक *sabah
nēnāk* and नेना लोकनिक *nēnā lok^anik* are all possible forms of the
genitive plural of नेना *nēnā*, a boy. लोकनि *lok^ani*, be it observed,
can only be used *after* the qualified noun. In all circumstances,
whatever be the order of the words, the postposition deciding
the case comes last.

76. The same rules partially apply to pronouns: but, in addition to the word signifying plurality, many of them have entirely new bases for their plural forms.

77. Throughout the following Paradigms, I shall generally
use only the word सभ *sabh* to designate the plural; but it must
always be understood that, unless specially forbidden, सबहि
sabah^i and लोकनि *lok^ani* can also be used.

---

1 The old Maithili poet Vidyápati sometimes has सबइ *sabah*, instead of
सबहि *sabah^i*. Compare song l. 6.

78. *Organic cases.*—There was a case-termination फि *hi* or फ़ि *hī* and another ड़ु *hu* or ड़ू *hū* in Apabhraṁśa Māgadhī Prakrit. These have survived in Maithili in the forms फि *hⁱ*, फ़ि *hī*, ड़ु *hᵘ* and ड़ू *hū*, which can be used for practically any oblique case. They are not often heard nowadays, except in poetry and proverbial sayings, but they are common in these. They are also frequently met in the old poetry of Vidyāpati.

Examples of the use of फि *hⁱ* and फ़ि *hī* in the various cases are as follows :—

Accusative—सत्रुफि आन *satruhⁱ ān*, he brings an enemy.

पड़रफ़ि मार *parᵃruhī mār*, beat the buffalo calves.

Instrumental—बलफि *balahⁱ*, by force, violently.

अचरफ़ि भाुरि भुरि दितहँ *acarahī jhārⁱ jhurⁱ ditahⁿ*. I would have swept it with my body-cloth.

Ablative—नेंदफि मिख चरबाफि अहीर *nẽdahⁱ sikh carabāhⁱ ahīr*. from boyhood cowherds learn cattle-tending.

Locative—जमुना हरदफ़ि *jamunā haradahⁱ*, in the Jamunā-pool.

षदंकफि मिंदुर मेट गेल *adākahⁱ sindur mēṭ gēl*, in her astonishment, the vermilion was rubbed off.

गदरौ खेतफि सुखाएल *gadᵃrī khētahⁱ sukhāel*. the unripe crop has dried up in the fields.

The following are examples of ड़ु *hᵘ* and ड़ू *hū* :—

Dative—सबड़ु जथोचित कैल परनाम *sabahᵘ jathōrit kail parᵃnām*, to all he made meet reverence.

Ablative—ओतड़ु *otahᵘ*, from there.

किछु नफ़ि ततड़ू भेल *kichᵘ nahī tatahū bhēl*. nothing came to pass from there.

Genitive.—अकरूड़ु चलएक डौल *akᵃrūṛahᵘ calaek ḍaul*. an opportunity for the coming of Akrūr.

Locative.—पछड़ु परम निपुन *pachaṛahᵘ param nipun*. exceedingly skilled in wrestling.

कोपइ॒ कठ नइिँ भाखुधि कबइ॒ *kōpah̐ kaṭ* *nah̐ bhākhathi kabah̐*,
even at any time he speaketh not harshly in anger.

Most of the above examples come from poetry, in which a final ‍इ *i* or ‍उ *u* is fully pronounced. but I have written them as if they were prose, so as to illustrate the grammatical forms.

In modern prose Maithilī the form हिँ *h̐* is contracted to ‍एँ *ē̐* and is reserved for the termination of the Instrumental while हि *hi* is contracted to ‍ए *ē*, and is reserved for the termination of the Locative. Examples will be found below, in dealing with the separate cases.

79. *Inorganic cases.*—In Maithilī (except in the organic Instrumental formed by adding ‍एँ *ē̐*, and the organic Locative formed by adding ‍ए *ē*) cases are formed by suffixing postpositions. In Hindōstānī these postpositions are added directly to the noun without any change of the latter. Thus, फल का *phal kā*, of fruit, नारी को *nārī kō*. to the woman. But. when a *tadbhava* noun (which is not a noun of relationship) ends in आ *ā*, that आ *ā* is changed to ‍ए *ē* before a postposition. Thus. from घोड़ा *ghōṛā*, a horse. we have घोड़े का *ghōṛē kā*, of a horse. In Maithilī the position is almost exactly reversed. *Tadbhava* nouns in आ *ā* are never changed, while certain other nouns do change before postpositions. In other words. the oblique form in Maithilī is always the same as the direct form except in the case of certain nouns in र *r*, ड़ *ṛ*, न *n*, ब *b*, ल *l* and र *r*. For instance घोड़ा *ghōṛā*, a horse. has its genitive घोड़ा केर *ghōṛā kēr*, not घोड़े केर *ghōṛē kēr*.

80. The following are the rules for ascertaining the oblique form *in the singular* of those nouns which take it :—

(*i*) All verbs form a feminine verbal noun by adding इ *i* to the root (see § 57). Thus देखब *dekhab*, to see ; root देख *dēkh* ; verbal noun देखि *dēkhi*, seeing, in the sense of 'the act of seeing.' All these verbal nouns in इ *i* have an oblique form in ‍औ *ai*, as in देखै कँ

dēkhai kē̃, for seeing. The oblique form itself is often used as a dative of purpose, as in ओकरा देखे गेल चलहूँ *okᵃrā dēkhai gēl chalahū̃*, I had gone for seeing him, *i.e.*, to see him. Other examples of the use of this oblique form are:—

- हम चरैक (*i.e.,* चरै+क) लेल ओकरा छाड़लें रहैत छी, *ham caraik* (*i.e., carai+k*) *lēl okᵃrā chăᵃlē rahait chī*, I have let it (a goat) loose for the sake of grazing (*i.e.*, to graze).

- दौड़ल सलहेस कें पकड़े *dauᵃral salᵃhēs kē̃ pakᵃrai*, they ran to catch Salhēs.

- चललीह हरवा बेचै *calᵃlīh harᵃwā bēcai*, she went to sell strings of beads.

- अपना चढ़ैक घोड़ी देलक *apᵃnā caṛhaik ghōṛī dēlak*, he gave the mare of his own riding (*i.e.*, his own riding mare).

In the case of the roots दे *dē*, give, and ले *lē*, an म *m* (or sometimes ब *b*) is inserted in the oblique form. Thus, देइ *dēi*, the act of giving, oblique देमै *dēmai*. Verbs whose roots end in इ *i* insert a ल *a* व *b* throughout. Thus √ पि *pi*, drink, verbal noun, पिबि *pibⁱ*, oblique पिबै *pibai*. Examples of these forms are:—

- हमरा एक बकरी लेमैक अछि *hamᵃrā ek bakᵃrī lēmaik achⁱ*, to me of taking one she-goat there is (necessity), *i.e.*, I must get a she-goat.

In the following we have also the direct verbal noun भरि *bharⁱ*, the filling :—

- नेना सभ कें पिबैक भरि भे जाइत छैक *nēnā sabh kē̃ pibaik bharⁱ bhai jāit chaik*, there becomes the filling of the drinking for the children, *i.e.*, we get enough for the children's drinking.

Note that some people write and pronounce the final ऐ *ai* of this oblique form as if it were कॅ *ā̊*. thus चरॅक *carᵃ̊k*, बेचॅ *bēcᵃ̊*, etc.

This oblique form of verbal nouns is very frequently employed in the construction of compound verbs. under the head of which several more examples will be found.

81. (*ii*) There are two other verbal nouns ending in ब *b* (§ 67) and ल *l* (§ 68), which have the same meaning. Thus देखब *dĕkhab*, the act of seeing, to see; देखल *dĕkhal*, the act of seeing. The former is commonly employed as an infinitive, but both are true nouns, and are thus declined :—

Nominative Singular	देखब *dĕkhab*	देखल *dĕkhal*
Oblique Singular	देखबा *dekh*ᵃ*bā*	देखला *dekh*ᵃ*lā*
Organic Instrumental Singular.	देखबें *dekh*ᵃ*bẽ*	देखलें *dekh*ᵃ*lẽ*
Organic Locative Singular.	देखबे *dekh*ᵃ*bẽ*, sometimes written देखबैं *dekh*ᵃ*bai*.	देखले *dekh*ᵃ*lẽ*, sometimes written देखलैं *dekh*ᵃ*lai*.

In the second noun न *n* is sometimes written for ल. We thus have the compound लेलें जाएब *lĕlẽ jāeb* or लेनें जाएब *lēnẽ jāeb*, to go by means of taking, to take away.

Examples of the employment of these two verbal nouns are :—

(*a*) 1. Direct forms—

उनक कानब सुनि *hunak kānab suni*, having heard his weeping.

छाड़ब को रहौ *chāṛab kī rahau*, what letting go was there to you, why did you let go ?

पछताएब *pach*ᵃ*tāeb*, the act of regretting. The oblique form is पछतैबा *pach*ᵃ*taibā*, see below.

2. Oblique cases—

ऊकरा मारबा में *ek*ᵃ*ra mǎr*ᵃ*bā mẽ*, in killing it.

ओकरा तकबा में in searching for it (√ ताक *tāk*, direct verbal noun ताकब *tākab*).

पछतैबाक *pach*ᵃ*taibāk*, of regretting.

रातुक चलब दिन में पहुँचल *rātuk cal*ᵃ*bẽ din mẽ pahũcal*, by travelling by night, he arrived in the daytime.

(b) 1. Direct forms—

ओ कहल करैयछि *ō kahal karaiach¹*, he does speaking, *i.e.*,
he speaks frequently.

पछतऔल *pachᵃtāol* (obl. पछतौला *pachᵃtaulā*), the act of regretting.

कैल *kail* or करल *karal*, the act of doing.

2. Oblique cases—

पानि बरिसला बिना *pāni barisᵃlā binā*, without water raining,
i.e., (owing to) the want of rain.

घरी नहि‍ भेटला सँ *carī nah¹ bheṭᵃlā sā̃*, from not getting
fodder.

घुमला सँ की लाभ यहि *ghumᵃlā sā̃ kī lābh yh¹*, what profit is
there from wandering about.

दौर धूप कैला सँ किच्छु नहि हैत *daur dhūp kailā sā̃ kicch ʷ nah¹
hait*, nothing will result (*lit.* be) from running and fussing.

पछतौला सँ की भै सकैयछि *pachᵃtaulā sā̃ kī bhai sakaiach¹*
what (good) can result from lamenting ?

लगले *lagᵃlē*, on the attaching, *i.e.*, immediately.

82.   Besides the above, several other nouns (including adjectives) ending in इ *r*, ड़ *ṛh*, न *n*, र *r*, ल *l*, and occasionally other
letters also, have oblique forms in आ *ā*. I have noted the following as certain instances :—

	Oblique form	
बड़ *baṛ*, great		बड़ा *baṛā*.
अखाड़ *akhāṛh*, an arena	..	अखाड़ा *akhāṛhā*.
आँगन *ā̃jan*, a courtyard	..	आँगना *ā̃jᵃnā*.
नैन *nain*, an eye	.,	नैना *nainā*.
दोसर *dōsar*, second	.,	दोसरा *dosᵃrā*.
तेसर *tēsar*, third	,.	तेसरा *tesᵃrā*.
पहर *pahar*, a watch	.,	पहरा *pahᵃrā*.

आंचर *ācar* or आाचर *ācar*. a body cloth.	Oblique form	अंचरा *āc⁰rā* or अचरा *ac⁰rā*.
आन्हर *ānhar*, blind	,,	अन्हरा *anh⁰rā*.
ईंगुर *īgur*, red lead	,,,	ईंगुरा *īgurā*.
कोर *kōr*, a lap	,.	कोरा *kōrā*.
दिवार *dibār*, a wall	..	दिवरा *dib⁰rā*.
दुआर *duār*, a doorway	,,	दुअरा *duarā*.
पल्लर *pallar*, a plank	,.	पल्लरा *pal⁰rā*.
बहीर *bahīr*, deaf	,,	बहिरा *bahirā*.
लिल्लार *lilār*, the forehead	,,	लिल्लरा *lil⁰rā*.
पहिल *pahil*, first	,.	पहिल्ला *pahilā*.
बदल *badal*, exchange	.,	बदला *bad⁰lā*.

To these may be added :—

अगूँ *agū̃* or आगूँ *āgū̃*, front	,,	अगाँ *agā̃*, आगाँ *āgā̃*.
पछूँ *pachū̃* or पाछूँ *pāchū̃*, rear	,,	पछाँ *pachā̃*, पाछाँ *pāchā̃*.
ठँई *ṭhã̄ī*, place	..	ठँयाँ *ṭhaĩyā̃*.
डीह *ḍīh*, a village-site	,.	डीहा *ḍīhā*.
दिस *dis*, a direction	.,	दिसा *disā*.
धनुख *dhanukh*, a bow	,,	धनुखा *dhanukhā*.

It is necessary to remark that these oblique forms are not invariably employed. We often find the direct form employed instead of the oblique one.

83. Examples are :—

(1) Direct forms—

बड़ अनुरोध बड़ा पय राख *bar* (direct) *anurōdh barā pay rākh*, lay (the burden of) a great favour upon the great.

आंगन सुन देखि *āgan sun dēkh^i*, seeing the courtyard empty.

नयन (*i.e.*, नैन) नोराएल *naen* (*i.e. nain*) *norāel*, (her) eye filled with tears.

7

दोसर रोये चन्ना *dōsar rōyē cannā*, the second one who weeps is Cannā.

तीनिक तेसर *tīnik tēsar*, the third after three.

जे परि पहर सूति गेल *jē pari pahar sūt^i gēl*, how the watch went to sleep.

चारु कन्हैया मोर आँचर *chār^u kanhaiā mōr ā̃car*, let go, O Kṛṣṇa, my body-cloth.

आन्हर कुक्कर बसातें भूखे *ānhar kukur basātē bhūkhē*, a blind dog barks at the wind.

पहिल खंड हम लेब *pahil khaṇḍ ham lēb*, I shall take the first portion.

आगू थलथल *āgū̃ thal^{a}thal*, a pendulous front.

पाछू भारी *pāchū̃ bhārī*, a heavy behind.

(2) Oblique forms—

एक सै एकैस डण्ड खेलाइत अछि अखाड़ा पर *ek sai ekais ḍaṇḍ khelāit ach^i akhāṛhā par*, he performs one hundred and twenty-one exercises upon the arena.

बड़ा पय राख *baṛā pay rākh*, as above.

कटगर तरु आँगना केओ राख *kaṭagar taru āg^{a}nā keo rākh*, does anyone keep a thorn-tree in his courtyard ?

नैना काजर पेन्हि लेलि (for लेलन्हि *lēlanh^i*) *nainā kājar pēnh^i lēl^i*, on her eyes she applied collyrium.

तेसराक अंत *tes^{a}rāk ant*, the end of the third.

सलहेसक पहरा सँ *sal^{a}hēsak pah^{a}rā sā̃*, from Salhēs's watch.

आँचरा डगरिया बहारितहुँ *āc^{a}rā ḍagariyā bahāritah^u*, I would have swept the road with my body-cloth.

बहिराक सुतलहिँ की अन्हराक जगलहिँ की *bahirāk sut^{a}lah^i kī, anh^{a}rāk jag^{a}lah^i kī*, what of a deaf man by sleeping, what of a blind man by waking (*i.e.*, what do they respectively lose by sleeping or waking ?).

लिलरा सोभैअछि ँगुराक रोरिया *lil^{a}rā sobhaiach^i ī̃gurāk roriyā*, on the forehead the fragments of red lead are beautiful.

हम सूतब तोहरा कोरा दृदा सूतब बबाक कोरा *ham sūtab toh^arā kōrā, dadā sūtab babāk kōrā*, I will sleep in your bosom, (my) brother will sleep in (my) father's bosom.

भद्रिक उड़नी-केड़नी दिबरा सटि गेल *bhadrik ehunī-kehunī dib^a-rā saṭⁱ gēl*, Bhadri's elbow, etc., (*i.e.*, elbows and knees) stuck against the wall.

दुबरा में *duarā mē*, in the doorway.

बगहा धिया पुता पलरा बेठल *bag^ahā dhiyā putā pal^arā baiṭhal*, the girls and boys of Bag^ahā were seated on a plank.

पहिला पानि भरि गेल ताड़ *pahilā pāni bharⁱ gēl tār*, the tank is filled by the first (fall of) rain.

ओकरा बदला में *ok^arā bad^alā mē*, in exchange for that.

अगां पछां बिदा भेल *agā pachā bidā bhēl*, they departed one behind the other.

बिचे ठैयां बरहो बियोगवा *bicē ṭhaiyā bur^aho biyoy^awā*, in the middle place (write) the separation of the twelve (months).

फोटरा बरा डीहा में गाइ भड़कबैत अछि *phoṭ^arā barā ḍīhā mē gāi bhar^akabait achⁱ*, Phoṭ^arā is scaring the cattle in Barā village (or Barā Ḍih).

कोन दिसा के अबैत होइ कहहु बुझाय *kōn disā kē abait hōai kahah^u bujhāy*, tell clearly towards what direction he is coming.

मारब धनुखा देब खंसाय *mārab dhanukhā dēb khā̆sāy*, I will strike him with my bow (*i.e.*, with an arrow from my bow) and fell him.

It will be seen subsequently that these oblique forms in *ā* are much more frequently employed in the case of pronouns than in the case of nouns substantive.

84. As there is no organic plural in Maithili, the question of a plural oblique form does not arise. The nouns of multitude, सभ *sabh*, सबहि *sabahi*, and लोकनि *lok^ani*, are treated exactly like singular

nouns. Thus, the organic instrumental plural of नेना *nēnā*, a boy.
may (amongst other forms) be नेना सभें *nēnā sabhē̃* or सभ नेनें *sabh
nēnē̃*.

85.   There are (counting the vocative) eight cases,—*viz.*,
Nominative. Accusative, Instrumental. Dative, Ablative, Genitive,
Locative and Vocative.

86.   The NOMINATIVE is used before all kinds and before al
tenses of verbs. There is no case of the Agent as in Hindōstānī.

87.   The ACCUSATIVE is the same in form as the nominative.
When a noun has an oblique form this is sometimes employed instead of the accusative by the vulgar.   Thus, in the Song of Salᵃhēs,
Mālin says बालपन चचरा बान्हलि *bāl*pan ac*rā* (not चाचर *ācar*)
*bānhal*ⁱ, (from my) girlhood I have kept my body-cloth tied (over
my body), *i.e.*, have kept my bosom covered.

In cases in which Hindōstānī would employ the postposition
को *kō*. Maithilī employs the dative postposition के *kē*, कें *kē̃*, कँ
kaῖ, or कँ *kā̃*. as in बनौधिआ दौड़ल मलदेस कें पकड़ै *banaudhiā
daural Salᵃhēs kē̃ pak*rai*, the Banaudhiās ran to seize Salᵃhēs.

Note that in old Maithili, the nominative and accusative often
ends in ए *ē*. which is also an old Māgadhī Prakrit termination
of the nominative case. Thus, Vidyāpatī (i, 1) says. कामिनि करए
बिमाने *kāmin*ⁱ *karae sinānē*, the fair one does bathing.

88.   The INSTRUMENTAL denotes the instrument, means, cause,
or agent, by which a thing is done. It in no way corresponds to
the 'agent case' of Hindōstānī of which the suffix is ने *nē*. It is
usually formed by the suffix सँ *sā̃* or सँ *saῖ* of which सउँ *saū̃* and
सौं *sō̃* are occasional varieties, which are more common in the older
language.

The Organic Instrumental referred to above is formed by adding एँ *ē̃*. which is sometimes (especially in old poetry) written अएँ
aῖ. It is added as follows :—

(*a*) When the noun ends in आ *ā*. the एँ *ē̃* is substituted for
the final vowel. If the noun has an oblique form ending in आ *ā*,
t is added to the oblique form in the same way. Thus कथा *kathā*

a story, instrumental कथें *kathē̃*, by a story; नेना *nēnā*, a boy, नेनें *nēnē̃*, by a boy; आंचर *ācar*, a body-cloth. oblique form अंचरा *ācᵃrā*, instrumental अंचरें *ācᵃrē̃*.

(*b*) In the case of all other nouns, the एं *ē* is added without elision of the final vowel, but if the latter is long, it is shortened, and if it is one of the imperfect vowels इ *i* and उ *u*, it is fully pronounced. Thus फल *phal*. a fruit, फलें *phalē̃*, by a fruit; पानि *pāni*, water, instrumental पानिएं *pāniē̃*; बेटी *bētī*, a daughter, instrumental बेटिएं *beṭiē̃* (not बेटीएं *beṭīē̃*); सबहि *sabahⁱ*, all, instrumental सबहिएं *sabᵃhiē̃*; भालु *bhālᵘ*. a bear, instrumental भालुएं *bhăluē̃*. The following are examples of the use of this organic instrumental :—

> कमर बांधे छुरिएं कटारें *kamar bā̃dhē churiē̃ kaṭārē̃*, he binds his waist with knife and dagger.
>
> गोरि मागु गौरबें आन्हरि *gōrⁱ māgᵘ gᵃūrᵃbē̃ ānharⁱ*. a fair woman is blinded by pride.
>
> एं कथें इ भेल *ē̃ kathē̃ i bhēl*. owing to this, it happened by conversation (*i.e.*. owing to the conversation). एं कथें *ē̃ kathē̃* is not 'by this conversation. which would be एहि कथें *ehⁱ kathē̃*.
>
> जें कानें श्रीमद्भागवत सूनल कोरान नहि सुनि सकैछी *jē̃ kānē̃ śrīmadbhāgavat sūnal korān nahⁱ sūnⁱ sakaichī*. I cannot hear the Qur'ān by the ear with which I have heard the S'rīmad Bhāgavata.

89. The DATIVE is formed by suffixing the postposition कें *kē̃*, कें *kē̃*. कैं *kaĩ*, or कां *kā̃*.

90. The ABLATIVE is formed by suffixing the postposition सैं *sã* or सैं *saĩ*, of which सऊं *saū̃* and सों *sō̃* (more common in the older language) are varieties. Verbs of speaking and asking govern the ablative of the person addressed as in Hindōstānī.

91. The sign of the GENITIVE is क *k*, which, at the present day, is no longer a postposition, but is a suffix attached to. and forming

One word with the base. Thus नेनाक *nēnāk*, of a boy ; पानिक *pānik*, of water ; नेना लोकनिक *nēnā lokᵃnik* of boys. When the base ends in an imperfect र *i* or उ *u*, this vowel is pronounced fully in the genitive. Thus सबदिक *sab*ᵃ*hik*, of all ; भालुक *bhāluk*, of a bear. When the base ends in a consonant, the vowel अ *a* is inserted before the क *k*. Thus, फलक *phalak*, of a fruit. When a noun has a separate oblique form, the क *k* is added to this. Thus बड़ *bar*, great, oblique form बड़ा *barā*, genitive बड़ाक *barāk*, of a great man; अपना चढ़क घोड़ा *apᵃnā carhaik ghōrā*, the horse of his own riding, his own riding horse.

In Southern Maithili, a long vowel is shortened before this क *k*. Thus नेनक *nĕnak*, not नेनाक *nĕnāk*, of a boy.

The postposition केर *kēr* is also employed to form the genitive. This is more common in poetry and in the older language. Examples are नेना केर *nēnā kēr*, of a boy ; फल केर *phal kēr*, of fruit. In the case of personal pronouns, the के *kē* of केर *kēr* is dropped, and the remaining र *r* becomes a suffix, as in हमर *hamar*, my.

The suffixes क *k* and केर *kēr* of the genitive are by origin adjectival, like the Hindōstānī का *kā*, के *kē*, की *kī*, but when added to nouns substantives they are in modern Maithili immutable, just as in the case of Bengali. They do not change either for gender or for case. Thus we have नेनाक बाप *nēnāk bāp*, the boy's father ; नेनाक बाप केर *nēnāk bāp kēr*, of the boy's father : नेनाक माई *nēnāk māī*, the boy's mother : नेनाक भाइ सभ *nēnāk bhāi sabh*, the boy's brothers. *This rule does not hold good in the case of pronouns, the genitives of which have an oblique form.*

92. The LOCATIVE indicates the place in, or the time at, which a thing is done. It is usually formed by the postposition में *mē̃*, of which मँ *mã* and माँ *mõ* are optional forms. Of these three माँ *mõ* is the oldest, and is generally found in poetry. The organic form of the Locative ends in ए *ē*, as explained above. It is not much used in modern prose Maithili, though it is frequent in

poetry, where it is sometimes written छ or चर *ai*. In the modern colloquial dialect it is, however, often heard in phrases such as बरे बरे *gharē ghare*, in every house; गामे गामे *gāmē gāmē*, in every village, and so on. As an example from classical poetry we may quote Vidyāpati (v. 3) जाएब घोघट घाटे *jāeb anghaṭ ghāṭē*, I shall go on the rugged river bank.

The following examples are all taken from one folk-song,— that of *Dīnā Bhadrī*.

घड़ि उक चलबे पहर बिति गेल *ghari ek cal°bē pahar biti gēl*, in (*i.e.*, after) going for one (or two) half-hours, a watch of the day passed.

चलह जौरे मिलि *calah jaurē mili*, having joined in company (with us), come along.

एहि ठामे *ehi ṭhāmē*, in this place.

बेना बरा डीहे रहथि अनेर *bēnā barā ḍīhē rahathi anēr*, Bēnā is wandering loose in Barā Dih.

मुसाहक दोकाने मना परि गेल *musāhuk dokānē manā pari gēl*, there was a prohibition (*i.e.*, they were stopped) at the shop o Musāhu. .

एक जुम तमाकू मोरा नामे नहिं चढ़ाबे *ek jum tamākū mōrā nāmē nahī carhābai*, they do not offer a single chew of tobacco in my name.

सात नींदे सुतलि चलैक फेकुनी *sāt nīdē sutali chalaik phekunī*. Phekunī was sleeping in seven sleeps (*i.e.*, was sound asleep).

बोझे बोझे बोरे बोरे नोन तमाकू तौले *bōjhē bōjhē bōrē bōrē nōn tamākū taulai*, bundle after bundle and sack after sack (*lit.* in bundle in bundle, in sack in sack) does he weigh salt and tobacco.

बड़ भोरे चेंकल दुआर *bar bhōrē chĕkal duār*, in the early morning you have obstructed my door.

93. The VOCATIVE usually takes the same form as the nominative. In speaking to a person of lower rank or age, the long form of the noun is preferred. Thus, नेना *nēnā*, a boy, becomes रौ

नेनवा *rau nen^awā.*　नेनी *nēnī,* a girl, becomes मे नेनिया *gai neniyā.* रघू *Raghŭ,* a proper name, becomes रौ रघुवा *rau Raghuā.*

The following interjections are used with the vocative :—

(*a*)　With masculine inferiors,—or familiarly, रौ *rau,* रे *rē.*

(*b*)　With masculine equals or superiors, औ *au,* हौ *hau,* हे *hē.*

(*c*)　With feminine inferiors,—or familiarly, गै *gai.*

(*d*)　With feminine equals or superiors, है *hai.*

—————o—————

CHAPTER III.

DECLENSION OF NOUNS.

94.　　There is in Maithili really only one declension, but as the forms of some classes of nouns vary slightly from each other before some of the postpositions, it will be convenient to consider nouns in three classes.

95.　　I. The first class will consist of all nouns ending in आ *ā* or आँ *ā̃.*

II. The second class will consist of all nouns ending in a consonant.

III. The third class will consist of all other nouns.

The difference between these three classes will be noticed on comparison of the Instrumental and Vocative singular.

96.　　It will be remembered that every noun has three forms, a short, a long, and a redundant (see §§ 41 ff.). In the following pages I shall only deal with the short form. As every long and redundant form ends in आ *ā* or आँ *ā̃,* they all belong to the first class. Thus, फल *phal,* a fruit, belongs to the second class. Its long form is फलवा *phal^awā,* which belongs to the first class, its instrumental singular being फलवें *phal^awē̃.*

CLASS I.

All nouns ending in चा *ā* or बिं *ã̃*.

97.　(1) Example of a Masculine noun ending in चा *ā*.

नेना *nēnā*, a boy.

Singular.

Nom.　　नेना *nēnā*, a boy.

Acc.　$\left\{ \begin{array}{l} \text{नेना } n\bar{e}n\bar{a}, \\ \text{नेना कँ } n\bar{e}n\bar{a}\ k\bar{e}, \end{array} \right\}$ a boy.

Inst.　$\left\{ \begin{array}{l} \text{नेनँ } n\bar{e}n\bar{e}, \\ \text{नेना सँ } n\bar{e}n\bar{a}\ s\bar{a}, \end{array} \right\}$ by a boy.

Dat.　　नेना कँ　*nēnā kē̃*, to a boy.

Abl.　　नेना सँ　*nēnā sā̃*, from a boy.

Gen.　$\left\{ \begin{array}{l} \text{नेनाक } n\bar{e}n\bar{a}k, \\ \text{नेना केर } n\bar{e}n\bar{a}\ k\bar{e}r, \end{array} \right\}$ of a boy.

Loc.　　नेना मँ　*nēnā mē̃*, in a boy.

Voc.　　रौ नेनवा *rau nenᵃwā*, O boy, (*or respectfully*) औ नेना *au nēnā*.

Plural.

Nom.	नेना सभ[1] *nēnā sabh*, boys.	

Acc.	नेना सभ[1] *nēnā sabh*, नेना सभ कँ[2] *nēnā sabh kĕ̃,*	} boys.

Inst.	नेना सभेँ[3] *nēnā sabhĕ̃,* नेना सभ सँ *nēnā sabh sã,*	} by boys.

Dat.	नेना सभ कँ[4] *nēnā sabh kĕ̃,* to boys.	

Abl.	नेना सभ सँ[5] *nēnā sabh sã,* from boys.	

Gen.	नेना सभक[6] *nēnā sabhak,* नेना सभ केर *nēnā sabh kēr,*	} of boys.

Loc.	नेना सभ मेँ[7] *nēnā sabh mẽ,* in boys.	

Voc.	रौ नेनवा सभ[8] *rau nenᵃwā sabh,* औ नेना सभ *au nēnā sabh,*	} O boys.

---

[1] Other forms are सभ नेना *sabh nēnā*, नेना सबहि *nēnā sabahⁱ*, सबहि नेना *sabahⁱ nēnā* and नेना लोकनि *nēnā lokᵃni*.

[2] Other forms are नेना सबहि कँ *nēnā sabahⁱ kĕ̃*, and नेना लोकनि कँ *nēnā lokᵃni kĕ̃*.

[3] Other forms are नेना सबहिएँ *nēnā sabᵒhiẽ*, नेना सबहि सँ *nēnā sabahⁱ sã*, नेना लोकनिएँ *nēnā lokᵃniẽ* and नेना लोकनि सँ *nēnā lokᵃni sã*.

[4] Other forms are नेना सबहि कँ *nēnā sabahⁱ kĕ̃* and नेना लोकनि कँ *nēnā lokᵃni kĕ̃*.

[5] Other forms are नेना सबहि सँ *nēnā sabahⁱ sã* and नेना लोकनि सँ *nēnā lokᵃni sã*.

[6] Other forms are नेना सबहिक *nēnā sabahik*, नेना लोकनिक *nēnā lokᵃnik*.

[7] Other forms are नेना सबहि मेँ *nēnā sabahⁱ mẽ* and नेना लोकनि मेँ *nēnā lokᵃni mẽ*.

[8] Other forms are रौ नेना सबहि *rau nēnā sabahⁱ*, औ नेना लोकनि *au nēnā lokᵃni*.

98. (2) Example of a feminine noun, ending in **आ** *ā.*

कथा *kathā.* a story.

Singular.

Nom.   कथा *kathā,* a story.

Acc.   { कथा *kathā.*
       { कथा कें *kathā kē̃.* } a story.

Inst. { कथें *kathē̃,*
       { कथा सॅं *kathā sā̃,* } by a story.

Dat.   कथा कें *kathā kē̃,* to a story.

Abl.   कथा सॅं *kathā sā̃,* from a story.

Gen.   { कथाक *kathāk,*
       { कथा केर *kathā kēr.* } of a story.

Loc.   कथा में *kathā mē̃,* in a story.

Voc.   हे कथा *hē kathā.* O story.

Plural.

Nom.   कथा सभ *kathā sabh,* stories.

Acc.   { कथा सभ *kathā sabh.*
       { कथा सभ कें *kathā sabh kē̃,* } stories.

Inst. { कथा सभें *kathā sabhē̃,*
       { कथा सभ सॅं *kathā sabh sā̃,* } by stories.

Dat.   कथा सभ कें *kathā sabh kē̃,* to stories.

Abl.   कथा सभ सॅं *kathā sabh sā̃,* from stories.

Gen.   { कथा सभक *kathā sabhak,*
       { कथा सभ केर *kathā sabh kēr.* } of stories.

Loc.   कथा सभ म *kathā sabh mē̃,* in stories.

Voc.   हे कथा सभ *hē kathā sabh.* O stories.

CLASS II.

99.   All nouns ending in a silent consonant.

फल *phal*, a fruit.

Singular.

Nom.   फल *phal*. a fruit.

Acc.   { फल *phal*,
        { फल कँ *phal kẽ*. } a fruit.

Inst.   { फलॅ *phalẽ*.
        { फल सँ *phal sã*. } by a fruit.

Dat.   फल कँ *phal kẽ*, to a fruit.

Abl.   फल सँ *phal sã*, from a fruit.

Gen.   { फलक *phalak*,
        { फल केर *phal kēr*, } of a fruit.

Loc.   फल में *phal mẽ*, in a fruit.

Voc.   हे फल *hē phal*, O fruit.

Plural.

Nom.   फल सभ *phal sabh*, fruit.

Acc.   { फल सभ *phal sabh*,
        { फल सभ कँ *phal sabh kẽ*. } fruit.

Inst.   { फल सभॅ *phal sabhẽ*,
        { फल सभ सँ *phal sabh sã*, } by fruit.

Dat.   फल सभ कँ *phal sabh kẽ*, to fruit.

Abl.   फल सभ सँ *phal sabh sã*, from fruit.

Gen.   { फल सभक *phal sabhak*,
        { फल सभ केर *phal sabh kēr*, } of fruit.

Loc.   फल सभ में *phal sabh mẽ*, in fruit.

Voc.   हे फल सभ *hē phal sabh*, O fruit.

As an example of a noun with an oblique form, we may take पहर *pahar*, a watch : Acc पहर *pahar* or पहरा कँ *pahᵃrā kẽ*; Inst.

पहरें *pah°rẽ* or पहरा सँ *pah°rā sã*, and so on. The plural is पहर सभ *pahar sabh*, etc., like फल सभ *phal sabh*.

CLASS III.

All nouns not ending in आ *ā* or in a consonant.

100. (1) Example of a masculine noun, ending in इ *i*.

पानि *pāni*, water.

Singular.

Nom.	पानि *pāni*. water.	
Acc.	पानि *pūni*. पानि कें *pāni kẽ*.	} water.
Inst.	पानिएं *păniẽ*. पानि सँ *pāni sã,*	} by water.
Dat.	पानि कें *pāni kẽ*, to water.	
Abl.	पानि सँ *pāni sã*. from water.	
Gen.	पानिक *pānik*. पानि केर *pāni kēr*.	} of ¡water.
Loc.	पानि में *pāni mẽ*. in water.]	
Voc.	हे पानि *hē pāni*. O water.	

Plural.

Nom.	पानि सभ *pāni sabh*. waters.	
Acc.	पानि सभ *pāni sabh*. पानि सभ कें *pāni sabh kẽ*.	} waters.
Inst.	पानि सभें *pāni sabhẽ*. पानि सभ सँ *pāni sabh sã*.	} by waters
Dat.	पानि सभ कें *pāni sabh kẽ*, to waters.	
Abl.	पानि सभ सँ *pāni sabh sã*. from waters.	
Gen.	पानि सभक *pāni sabhak*. पानि सभ केर *pāni sabh kēr*.	} of waters..
Loc.	पानि सभ में *pāni sabh mẽ*. in waters.	
Voc.	हे पानि सभ *hē pāni sabh*, O waters.	

101. (2) Example of a feminine noun ending in इ *i.*

नेनी *nēnī,* a girl.

Singular.

Nom.　नेनी *nēnī,* a girl.

Acc.　$\begin{cases} \text{नेनी } n\bar{e}n\bar{i}, \\ \text{नेनी कें } n\bar{e}n\bar{i}\ k\bar{e}, \end{cases}$ a girl.

Inst.　$\begin{cases} \text{नेनिएं } neni\bar{e}, \\ \text{नेनी सं } n\bar{e}n\bar{i}\ s\tilde{a}, \end{cases}$ by a girl.

Dat.　नेनी कें *nēnī kē̃,* to a girl.

Abl.　नेनी सं *nēnī sã,* from a girl.

Gen.　$\begin{cases} \text{नेनीक } n\bar{e}n\bar{i}k, \\ \text{नेनी केर } n\bar{e}n\bar{i}\ k\bar{e}r, \end{cases}$ of a girl.

Loc.　नेनी में *nēnī mē̃,* in a girl.

Voc.　गे नेनिया *gai neniyā,* O girl.

Plural.

Nom.　नेनी सभ *nēnī sabh,* girls.

Acc.　$\begin{cases} \text{नेनी सभ } n\bar{e}n\bar{i}\ sabh, \\ \text{नेनी सभ कें } n\bar{e}n\bar{i}\ sabh\ k\bar{e}, \end{cases}$ girls.

Inst.　$\begin{cases} \text{नेनी सभें } n\bar{e}n\bar{i}\ sabh\bar{e}, \\ \text{नेनी सभ सं } n\bar{e}n\bar{i}\ sabh\ s\tilde{a}, \end{cases}$ by girls.

Dat.　नेनी सभ कें *nēnī sabh kē̃.* to girls.

Abl.　नेनी सभ सं *nēnī sabh sã.* from girls.

Gen.　$\begin{cases} \text{नेनी सभक } n\bar{e}n\bar{i}\ sabhak. \\ \text{नेनी सभ केर } n\bar{e}n\bar{i}\ sabh\ k\bar{e}r. \end{cases}$ of girls.

Loc.　नेनी सभ में *nēnī sabh mē̃.* in girls.

Voc.　गे नेनिया सभ *gai neniyā sabh.* O girls.

102. (3) Example of a masculine proper noun ending रघू *ū.*

रघू* *Raghū,* a proper noun.

Nom.	रघू *Raghū,* Raghū.	
Acc.	रघू कें *Raghū kē,* Raghū.	
Inst.	रघुएं *Raghuē,* रघू सॅं *Raghū sā,*	} by Raghū.
Dat.	रघू कें *Raghū kē,* to Raghū.	
Abl.	रघू सॅं *Raghū sā,* from Raghū.	
Gen.	रघूक *Raghūk.* of Raghū.	
Loc.	रघू में *Raghū mē,* in Raghū.	
Voc.	रौ रघुआ *rau Raghuā,* O Raghū, (*or respectfully*) हौ रघू *hau Raghū.*	

103. As an example of a verbal noun in र *i,* with an oblique form in ढ़ै *ai,* we may take चढ़ि *carhⁱ,* mounting; acc. चढ़ि *carhⁱ* or चढ़ै कें *carhai kē*; Instr. चढ़ै सॅं *carhai sā* (चढ़ैएं *carhaiē* is not used); and so on. Instead of चढ़ै *carhai,* we may have चढ़ॅं *carhā* throughout.

———o———

CHAPTER IV.

ADJECTIVES AND GENDER GENERALLY.

104. As the rules for the formation of the feminine of adjectives are the same as those for the formation of the feminine of substantives, it will be convenient to treat the whole subject of gender at the present opportunity.

105. Adjectives are liable to change for gender. That is to say, when agreeing with a feminine noun they are put in the feminine. Thus, the word ऐसन *aisan* means 'such,' and its feminine is ऐसनि *aisanⁱ*. The word झपट *jhapaṭ,* a pounce. is feminine, and

---

* Usually spelt thus in Maithili.

.hence we have in the story of Sal^ahēs the phrase प्रेमनि झपट मारै
aisanⁱ jhapaṭ mārai, (the parrot) makes such a pounce (that—).
I have said that adjectives are *liable* to change for gender, but in
practice the change very rarely takes place. In ordinary conversation the masculine gender is quite commonly used instead of the
feminine, and, indeed, except to paṇḍits grammatical gender is
almost unknown; that is to say, adjectives only become feminine
when applied to female living creatures. The following rules as to
gender apply to substantives, as well as adjectives.

106. It is a well-known fact that in Hindōstānī the adjectives which are *tadbhavas*, and which end in आ *ā* are in reality the
only ones in that language which are affected by gender. *Tatsama*
adjectives imported direct from the Sanskrit, and forming their
feminines after the model of that language, do not form part of the
living spoken stock of the Hindī dialect, but belong rather to the
dead language of the books. The same is only partly true in
Maithilī. In this language we find not only *tadbhava* but even
some *tatsama* adjectives forming feminines distinctly the property
of the language in which they have been adopted.

107. RULE I.—The first rule to be observed is that in
Maithilī, *tadbhava words ending in a consonant form their feminine
in short* इ *i*.

Examples :—

Masculine.	Feminine.
गोर *gōr*, fair	गोरि *gōrⁱ*.
बड़ *baṛ*, great	·बड़ि *baṛⁱ*.
बुधियार *budhiyār*. wise	बुधियारि *budhiyārⁱ*.
अधलाह *adh^alāh*, bad	अधलाहि *adh^alāhⁱ*.
गमार *gamār*, rustic	गमारि *gamārⁱ*.
टेढ़ *ṭēṛh*, crooked	टेढ़ि *ṭēṛhⁱ*.

108. RULE II.—The second rule is peculiar to Maithilī, and is
as follows : *Many Tatsama words ending in a consonant form their
feminines in* इ *i*; *and that, whether in Sanskrit these words form their
feminines in long* ई *ī or not.*

Examples : —

Masculine.	Feminine.
सुन्दर *sundar*, beautiful	Sanskrit, सुन्दरी *sundarī*.
	Maithilī, सुन्दरि *sundari*.
भूसर *dhūsar*	S. भूसरा *dhūsarā* or भूसरी *dhūsarī*.
dusty	M. भूसरि *dhūsar*ⁱ.
अत्यंत *atyant*, excessive	S. अत्यन्ता *atyantā*.
	M. अत्यंति *atyant*ⁱ.

The following may here be noted as irregular :—

Masculine.	Feminine.
सुबोध *subōdh*, wise	S. सुबोधा *subōdhā*.
	M. सुबुधि *subudh*ⁱ.

109. Rule III.—*Tadbhava words ending in* आ *ā, form their feminines in* ई *ī.*

Examples :—

Masculine.	Feminine.
बेटा *bēṭā*, a son	बेटी *bēṭī*, a daughter.
नेना *nēnā*, a boy	नेनी *nēnī*, a girl.

110. Rule IV.—Long forms of nouns substantive and redundant forms of adjectives in अवा *ᵃwā* form their feminines in इया *iyā* or इआ *iā*. Redundant forms of nouns substantive in अउवा *auwā* or औआ *auā*, form their feminines in इयवा *iyᵃwā*, इअवा *iawā*, or ईवा *īwā*. Thus :—

Masculine.	Feminine.
घोड़वा *ghoṟᵃwā*, a horse	घोड़िया *ghoṟiyā* or घोड़िआ *ghoṟiā*, a mare.
छोटकवा *choṭᵃkawā* or छोटकवा *choṭakᵃwā* } small	छोटकिया *choṭᵃkiyā* or *choṭakiyā*, or छोटकिआ *choṭᵃkiā* or *choṭakiā*.

9

Masculine.		*Feminine.*
घोरौबा *ghoṛauā* or	} a horse	घोड़ियबा *ghoṛiyʰwā*, घोड़िषबा *ghori-*
घोरौबा *ghoṛauwā*		*awā* or घोड़ौबा *ghoṛiwā.*

It is necessary to give further examples, as the subject has been already discussed in §§ 41 ff.

111. RULE V.—*Tadbhava words signifying colour form their feminines as follows :*—

Masculine.		*Feminine.*
उजर *ujar*		
or उजरा *uj°rā*	}white	उजरौ *uj°rī.*
or उजरका *ujar°kā*		or उजरकौ *ujar°kī.*
कारौ *kārī*		
or करिषा *kariā*	}black	करिक्कौ *karikkī.*
or करिक्का *karikkā*		
पीरा *pīrā*		
or पीषर *pīar*	}yellow	पिषरकौ *piar°kī.*
or पिषरका *piar°kā*		
हरिषर *hariar*		
or हरिषरका *hariar°kā*	}green	हरिषरकौ *hariar°kī.*
लाल *lāl*		
or ललका *lal°kā*	}red	ललकौ *lal°kī.*

EXCEPTION.—गोर *gor* fair, which makes गोरि *gor^i*, or गोरिया *goriyā*. It will be observed that, in the feminine, all these adjectives prefer the long form.

Note also that नील *nīl*, dark blue, which also occurs in Sanskrit and which in that language forms its feminine नीला *nīlā*, or नीली *nīlī*, in Maithilī adopts नीली *nīlī* as its feminine form.

112. RULE VI.—The following classes of *Tatsama* words form their feminines generally as in Sanskrit :—

(*a*) Verbal adjectives in र *i*, and ई *ī*, corresponding to Sanskrit adjectives in रन् *in*, nominative, ई *ī*.

Examples :—

Masculine.			Feminine in Maithili.
Sanskrit मानी *mānī*	} proud	{	मानिनी *māninī*
Maithilī मानि *māni*		{ or	मानिनि *mānin*ⁱ.
S. भावी *bhāvī*	} future	{	भाविनी *bhāvinī*
M. भावी *bhāvi*		{ or	भाविनि *bhāvin*ⁱ.
S. हारी *hārī*	} seizing	{	हारिणी *hāriṇi*
M. हारी *hārī*		{ or	हारिनि *hārin*ⁱ.
S. धारी *dhārī*	} bearing	{	धारिणी *dhāriṇī*.
M. धारी *dhārī*		{ or	धारिनि *dhārin*ⁱ.
S. कारी *kārī*	} doing	{	कारिणी *kāriṇi*
M. कारी *kārī*		{ or	कारिनि *kārin*ⁱ.
S. चिरंजीवी *chirañjīvī*	} long-lived	{	चिरंजीविनी *chirañjībinī*
M. चिरंजीबी *chirañjībi*		{ or	चिरंजीबिनि *chirañjībin*ⁱ
or चिरंजिब *chirañjib*		{ or	चिरंजीबि *chirañjīb*ⁱ.

As an irregular under this head falls—

Masculine.		Feminine in Maithili.
S. सुधर्मा *sudharmā*	} virtuous	सुधर्मिणी *sudharmiṇī*.
M. सुधर्मा *sudharmā*		

113. (*b*) Participles of the reduplicated perfect in वस् *vas*, and comparatives in ईयस् *īyas*.

Examples :—

Masculine.		Feminine.
S. विद्वान् *vidvān*	} wise	{ विदुषी *biduṣī* (pronounced
M. बिद्वान *bidbān*		{ —*khī*, see § 25.)
S. गरीयान् *garīyān*	} heavier	गरीयसी *garīyasī*.
M. गरीषान *garīān*		
S. लघीयान् *laghīyān*	} lighter	लघीयसी *laghīyasī*.
M. लघीषान *laghīān*		

114.   (*c*) *Nomina agentis* terminating in क्क *ak.*

Examples :—

Masculine.		Feminine.
कारक *kārak*	a doer	कारिका *kārikā.*
पाल्लक *pālak*	a protector	पाल्लिका *pālikā.*
रच्चक *rakṣak*	a guardian	रच्चिका *rakṣikā.*
पाच्चक *pācak*	a cook	पाच्चिका *pācikā.*
सद्दायक *sahāyak*	a helper	सद्दायका *sahāyᵃkā.*

115.   (*d*) Gerundials and past participles passive.

Examples :—

Masculine.		Feminine.
मंतव्य *mantabyᵃ*	to be remarked	मंतव्या *mantabyā.*
बंद्नीय *bandanīyᵃ*	praiseworthy	बंद्नीया *bandanīyā*
जोग्य *jōgyᵃ*	worthy	जोग्या *jōgyā.*
मान्य *mānyᵃ*	reverend	मान्या *mānyā.*
साध्य *sādhyᵃ*	easy	साध्या *sādhyā.*
जुक्त *jukt*	joined	जुक्ता *juktā.*
सुद्द *suddh*	pure	सुद्दा *suddhā.*
चात्तॅ *ārt*	pained	चात्तॉ *ārtā.*
खिन्न *khinn*	broken	खिन्ना *khinnā.*

116.   (*e*) Other nouns and adjectives as :—

Masculine.		Feminine.
धूर्तॅ *dhūrt*	a knave	धूर्तॉ *dhūrtā.*
स्याम *syām*	dark	स्यामा *syāmā.*
गरिष्ठ *gariṣṭh*	heaviest (venerable)	गरिष्ठा *gariṣṭhā.*
श्रेष्ठ *srēṣṭh*	excellent	श्रेष्ठा *srēṣṭhā.*
ब्रिंद् *brind*	numerous	ब्रिंदा *brindā.*
चाज्यॅ• *ārjyᵃ*	respectable	चाज्यॉ *ārjyā.*

117. RULE VII.—The following anomalous forms should be noticed :—

(*a*) राजा *rājā*, a king, makes रानी *rānī*, a queen.

(*b*) Forms borrowed from Sanskrit *nomina agentis* in ऋ *tṛ*, have the following feminines :—

Examples :—

Masculine.		Feminine.
S. धाता *dhātā*	} creator	{ धात्री *dhātrī*.
M. धाता *dhātā*		{ धात्रि *dhātrⁱ*.
S. ज्ञाता *jñātā*	} knower	{ ज्ञात्री *jñātrī*.
M. ग्याता *gyā̃tā*		{ ग्यात्रि *gyātrⁱ*.
S. पाता *pātā*	} protector	{ पात्री *pātrī*.
M. पाता *pātā*		{ पात्रि *pātrⁱ*.

118. Adjectives do not generally change for case. In other words, like substantives, they do not usually possess oblique forms.

119. Certain adjectives ending in ऋ *ṛ*, न *n*, र *r* and ल *l* have, however, an oblique form in आ *ā*, which is employed when the noun with which they are in agreement is in an oblique case. In other words such adjectives follow the example of substantives. Examples of such adjectives are :—

बड़ *baṛ*, great.

ऐसन *aisan* or एहन *ehan*, such, and other pronominal adjectives ending in न *n*.

दोसर *dōsar*, second.

तेसर *tēsar*, third.

बहीर *bahīr*, deaf.

पहिल *pahil*, first.

Examples of these oblique forms will be found in §§ 82 and ff. The oblique forms are not often employed attributively except in the cases of ordinal numbers as in तेसरा पहरा में *tesᵉrā pahᵉrā mē̃*, in the third watch, and of pronominal adjectives. The latter will be discussed under the head of pronouns.

COMPARISON OF ADJECTIVES.

120. (*a*) *Comparative.* As in Hindōstāni, the comparative is formed, not by any change in the adjective, but by putting the word for the thing with which the comparison is made in the ablative case. Example, र गाछी ओहि गाछी सँ सुंदरि छैक *i gāchī oh*[i] *gāchī sā̃ sundar*[i] *chaik*, this grove is more beautiful than that.

121. (*b*) *Superlative.* This is formed either by prefixing सभ सँ *sabh sā̃*, the ablative case of सभ *sabh*, all, or the adjective बड़ *baṛ* (which is liable to inflection according to gender) to the principal adjective. Examples : र गाछी सभ सँ सुंदरि छैक *i gāchī sabh sā̃ sundar*[i] *chaik*, this is the most beautiful grove ; or र गाछी बड़ि सुंदरि छैक *i gāchī baṛ*[i] *sundar*[i] *chaik*, this grove is very beautiful. Usually, in such sentences, gender is neglected when the adjective is employed predicatively, so that we generally meet these expressions in the following forms : र गाछी ओहि गाछी सँ सुन्दर छैक *i gāchī oh*[i] *gāchī sā̃ sundar chaik ;* र गाछी सभ सँ सुन्दर छैक *i gāchī sabh sā̃ sundar chaik ;* र गाछी बड़ सुन्दर छैक *i gāchī baṛ sundar chaik.*

122. Certain comparatives and superlatives are also borrowed direct from the Sanskrit, which need not be noted here.

NUMERALS.

Cardinals.

123. The following are the Cardinals up to 100. It will be observed that they differ from those in use in Hindi :—

१ प्रक *ek.*	८ चाठ *āṭh.*
२ दुर *dui.*	९ नौं *nau.*
३ तीनि *tīn*[i].	१० दश *daś.*
४ चारि *cār*[i].	११ प्रगारह *egārah.*
५ पंच *pā̃c.*	१२ बारह *bārah.*
६ ब्रौ *chau.*	१३ तेरह *tērah.*
७ सात *sāt.*	१४ चोदह *caudah.*

১৫ পন্দ্রহ *pandrah.*

১৬ সোলহ *sõlah* or সোড়হ *sõṛah.*

১৭ সত্রহ *satrah.*

১৮ অঠারহ *aṭhārah.*

১৯ উনৈস *unais.*

২০ বীস *bis.*

২১ একৈস *ekais.*

২২ বাইস *bāis.*

২৩ তৈস *tais.*

২৪ চৌবীস *caubīs.*

২৫ পচীস *pacīs.*

২৬ ছব্বীস *chabbīs.*

২৭ সত্তাইস *sattāis.*

২৮ অঠাইস *aṭhāis.*

২৯ উনতীস *un^{a}tīs.*

৩০ তীস *tīs.*

৩১ একতীস *ek^{a}tīs.*

৩২ বত্তীস *battīs.*

৩৩ তেঁতীস *tẽtīs.*

৩৪ চৌঁতীস *caũtīs.*

৩৫ পৈঁতীস *paĩtīs.*

৩৬ ছত্তীস *chattīs.*

৩৭ সৈঁতীস *saĩtīs.*

৩৮ অঠতীস *aṭh^{a}tīs.*

৩৯ উনচালীস *un^{a}cālīs* or উননচালীস *unan^{a}cālis.*

৪০ চালীস *cālīs.*

৪১ একতালীস *ek^{a}tālīs.*

৪২ বেআলীস *beālīs.*

৪৩ তেঁতালীস *taĩtālīs.*

৪৪ চৌআলীস *cauālīs.*

৪৫ পৈঁতালীস *paĩtālīs.*

৪৬ ছেআলীস *cheālīs.*

৪৭ সৈঁতালীস *saĩtālīs.*

৪৮ অঠতালীস *aṭh^{a}tālīs.*

৪৯ উনচাস *un^{a}cās* or উননচাস *unan^{a}cās.*

৫০ পচাস *pacās.*

৫১ একাবন *ekāwan.*

৫২ বাবন *bāwan.*

৫৩ তিরপন *tir^{a}pan.*

৫৪ চৌবন *cauwan.*

৫৫ পচপন *pac^{a}pan.*

৫৬ ছপ্পন *chappan.*

৫৭ সতাবন *satāwan.*

৫৮ অঠাবন *aṭhāwan.*

৫৯ উনসঠি *un^{a}saṭh^i.*

৬০ সাঠি *sāṭh^i.*

৬১ একসঠি *ek^{a}saṭh^i* or একসট্ঠি *ek^{a}saṭṭh^i.*

৬২ বাসঠি *bāsaṭh^i* or বাসট্ঠি *bāsaṭṭh^i.*

৬৩ তিরসঠি *tir^{a}saṭh^i* or তিরসট্ঠি *tir^{a}saṭṭh^i.*

৬৪ চৌঁসঠি *caũsaṭh^i* or চৌঁসট্ঠি *caũsaṭṭh^i.*

৬৫ পৈঁসঠি *paĩsaṭh^i* or পৈঁসট্ঠি *paĩsaṭṭh^i.*

৬৬ ছেআসঠি *cheāsaṭh^i* or ছেআসট্ঠি *cheāsaṭṭh^i.*

৬৭ সতসঠি *sat^{a}saṭh^i* or সতসট্ঠি *sat^{a}saṭṭh^i.*

६८ अठसठि *aṭh^{a}saṭh^{i}* or अड़सठि *aṛ^{a}saṭh^{i}* or अठसट्ठि *aṭh^{a}saṭṭh^{i}*.

६९ उनहत्तरि *un^{a}hattar^{i}*.

७० सत्तरि *sattar^{i}*.

७१ अकहत्तरि *ak^{a}hattar^{i}*.

७२ बहत्तरि *bahattar^{i}*.

७३ तेंहत्तरि *tehattar^{i}*.

७४ चौहत्तरि *cauhattar^{i}*.

७५ पचहत्तरि *pac^{a}hattar^{i}*.

७६ छेहत्तरि *chehattar^{i}*.

७७ सतहत्तरि *sat^{a}hattar^{i}*.

७८ अठहत्तरि *aṭh^{a}hattar^{i}*.

७९ उनासी *unāsī*.

८० अस्सी *assī*.

८१ एकासी *ekāsī*.

८२ बेरासी *berāsī* or बेआसी *beāsī*.

८३ तेरासी *terāsī*.

८४ चौरासी *caurāsī*.

८५ पचासी *pacāsī*.

८६ छेआसी *cheāsī*.

८७ सतासी *satāsī*.

८८ अठासी *aṭhāsī*.

८९ नवासी *nawāsī*.

९० नब्बै *nabbai*.

९१ एकानबे *ekān^{a}bē*.

९२ बरानबे *barān^{a}bē* or बेआनबे *beān^{a}bē*.

९३ तेरानबे *terān^{a}bē*.

९४ चौरानबे *caurān^{a}bē*.

९५ पंचानबे *pā̃cān^{a}bē*.

९६ छेआनबे *cheān^{a}bē*.

९७ सनतानबे *san^{a}tān^{a}bē*.

९८ अंठानबे *ā̃ṭhān^{a}bē*.

९९ निनानबे *ninān^{a}bē*.

१०० सै *sai*.

Ordinals.

124. Ordinals are simple in their formation and run as follows :—

पहिल *pahil*, first.

दोसर *dōsar*, second.

तेसर *tēsar*, third.

चौठ *cauṭh*, or चारिम *cārim*, fourth.

पाँचम *pā̃cam*, fifth.

छठम *chaṭham*, sixth.

सातम *sātam*, seventh.

आठम *āṭham*, eighth.

नौम *naum*, ninth.

दशम *daśam*, tenth.

एगारहम *egār^{a}ham*, eleventh.

Etcetera ; the ordinals of the remaining numbers being formed by adding म *m* as a termination.

FRACTIONAL NUMBERS.

125.   The following are useful :—

पावो *pāo*, a quarter.

आध *ādh*, a half.

पौन *paun*, three-quarters ; or, less by a quarter.

सवैयां *sawaiyā̃*, one and-a-quarter ; or, plus a quarter.

डेवोढ़ा *deōṛhā*, one-and-a-half ; or, plus a half.

FRACTIONAL NUMBERS.

AGGREGATE NUMBERS.

126.   Note the form दुनु *dunⁿ*, both.

———o———

CHAPTER V.

PRONOUNS.

127.   The declension of Pronouns presents some important
points of difference from that of nouns, which should be carefully noted.

128.   While most nouns remain unchanged before postpositions, almost all pronouns have an oblique form.   This oblique
form falls under two heads.

129.   (1) The old oblique form.   This, in the case of the
personal pronouns, is only found in poetry.   In the case of other
pronouns it is, at the present day, rarely used except when it refers
to inanimate objects, or when the pronoun is employed as an
adjective.   Thus, the old oblique form of ई *i*, this, is एहि *ehⁱ*, and

10

 प्रि कें *ehⁱ kē̃*, to this, is only found when 'this' is something inanimate. प्रि कें *ehⁱ kē̃* could not be used if 'this' was a boy. But we can say प्रि नेना कें *ehⁱ nēnā kē̃*, to this boy, because here प्रि *ehⁱ* is used as an adjective.

The following is a list of these old oblique forms :—

Direct Form.	*Old Oblique Form.*
में *mē̃*, (old poetic form), I	मोरि *mohⁱ*.
तू *tū*, thou	तोरि *tohⁱ*.
इ *ī*, this (non-honorific)	प्रि *ehⁱ*, प्र *eh.* or प्र *aih*.
इ *ī*, this (honorific)	हिनि *hinⁱ* or हिन *hin*.
ओ *ō*, that (non-honorific)	ओरि *ohⁱ*, ओर *oh*, or ओर *auh*.
ओ *ō*, that (honorific)	हुनि *hunⁱ* or हुन *hun*.
जे *jē*, who (non-honorific)	जारि *jāhⁱ*.
जे *jē*, who (honorific)	जनि *janⁱ*.
से *sē*, he (non-honorific)	तारि *tāhⁱ*.
से *sē*, he (honorific)	तनि *tanⁱ*.
के *kē*, who ? (non-honorific)	कारि *kāhⁱ* (not used as an adjective).
के *kē*, who ? (honorific)	कनि *kanⁱ*.
की *kī*, what ? (substantive)	कथी *kathī*.
केओ *keo*, anyone	कारु *kāh^u*.

130. (2) The modern oblique form.—This is never used as an adjective. It is almost always the only form employed when the pronoun is used as a substantive and refers to an animate object. It is hence the only form used at the present day for personal pronouns. It is identical with the oblique form of the genitive, which is obtained by adding का *ā* to the direct form of that case. Thus :—

Pronoun.	GENITIVE.	
	Direct.	Oblique.
में *mē̃*, I	मोर *mōr*	मोरा *mōrā*.
हम *ham*, I	हमर *hamar* or	हमरा *hamᵃrā*.
	हमार *hamār*	
तू *tū*, thou	तोर *tōr*	तोरा *tōrā*.
तोंह *tŏh* or तों *tŏ̃*, thou	तोहर *tŏhar* or	तोहरा *tohᵃrā*.
	तोहार *tohār*	
अपनहिं *apᵃnahⁱ*, self	अप्पन *appan* or	अपना *apᵃnā*
	अपन *apan*	
इ *i*, this (non-honorific)	एकर *ēkar*	एकरा *ekᵃrā*.
इ *i*, this (honorific)	हिनक *hinak*	हिनका *hinᵃkā*.
ओ *ō*, that (non-honorific)	ओकर *ōkar*	ओकरा *okᵃrā*.
ओ *ō*, that (honorific)	हुनक *hunak*	हुनका *hunᵃkā*.
जे *jē*, who (non-honorific)	जकर *jakar*	जकरा *jakᵃrā*.
जे *jē*, who (honorific)	जनिक *janik*	जनिका *janikā*.
से *sē*, he (non-honorific)	तकर *takar*	तकरा *takᵃrā*.
से *sē*, he (honorific)	तनिक *tanik*	तनिका *tanikā*.
के *kē*, who ? (non-honorific)	ककर *kakar*	ककरा *kakᵃrā*.
के *kē*, who ? (honorific)	कनिक *kanik*	कनिका *kanikā*.

To the remaining pronouns these observations do not apply. It will be observed that in the honorific forms the genitive ends in क *k*, while all the other genitives end in र *r*.

131. We have observed (see §§ 75, 76) that nouns substantive have no proper organic plural. When the idea of plurality has to be expressed it is done by adding new words indicating plurality, such as सभ *sabh* or सबहि *sabahⁱ*, all; लोकनि *lokᵃni*, people. The same is the case with pronouns. Their plurals are formed in

the same way. In the ancient Māgadhī Prakrit from which Mai--
thilī is descended there were distinct organic plural forms, and
(except in the case of the pronouns of the first and second persons)
these old plural forms have survived in the shape of the honorific
singulars, the old singulars being relegated to a non-honorific meaning. With regard to the pronouns of the first and second persons
the case is somewhat different. In ordinary Maithilī, the old
singulars (मैं *mẽ*, I and तू *tū*, thou) have fallen into disuse and
are now only found in poetry. The old plural forms are now employed in the sense of the singular, and the plurals are now formed
by the addition of सभ *sabh*, etc. (as is also the case with the
honorific pronouns mentioned above) and are really by origin
double plurals.

132. It may be mentioned here that the pronoun of the
second person has also an honorific form अहाँ *ahā̃*, अहैं *ahaĩ* or
अपने *ap⁰ne* which will be described later on.

133. The employment of the old oblique form varies, and the
different methods of employment will be described under each
pronoun.

134. The genitives of the pronouns are freely used as possessive pronouns, and, when agreeing with a noun in an oblique case
they are put into the modern oblique form described above. It
will be convenient to give examples of this once for all here.

(*a*) DIRECT POSSESSIVE PRONOUNS AGREEING WITH NOUNS IN
THE NOMINATIVE FORM :—

> हमर रोज हरज होइत *hamar rōj haraj hōit*, my means of
> livelihood will be spoiled.

> त्रिया कारन मुदै तोर जुमल *triyā kāran mudai tōr jumal*, for
> the sake of a woman your enemy has come.

> अप्पन सभ धन उड़ाय भिखारि भै गेल *appan sabh dhan uṛāy
> bhikhār^i bhai gēl*, having wasted all his substance he
> became a beggar.

> हुनक कानब सुनि *hunak kānab sun^i*, having heard her
> lamentations.

जकर बेदुली लाइल, तकर केहन सुरखी *jakar beduli lāel, takar kehan sur^akhī*, how wonderful must be the beauty of her whose *bedulī* you have brought.

जकर खेत तकर धान *jakar khēt, takar dhān*, whose is the field, his is the paddy-crop.

तकर अकरार लिखि दाखिल करह *takar akrār likhⁱ dākhil karáh*, write and file a bond to that effect (*lit.* of that).

ककर घोड़ चैक *kakar ghōṛ chaik*, whose is the horse ?

(*b*) OBLIQUE POSSESSIVE PRONOUNS AGREEING WITH NOUNS IN THE OBLIQUE CASES :—

हमरा सिरकी में *ham^arā sir^akī mē̃*, in my hut.

तोहरा घर में *toh^arā ghar mē̃*, in your house.

गिरहस्थ अपना मन में करहलक *girhasth ap^anā man mē̃ kah^olok*, the farmer said in his own heart.

अपना चढ़क घोड़ी देल *ap^anā carhaik ghōṛī dēl*, he gave the mare of his own riding (*i.e.*, his own riding mare).

संग समाज सखी आएलि इनका फुलवाड़ी *saṅg samāj sakhī āilⁱ hun^akā phul^awāṛī*, (her) companions and friends came (into) her garden.

इनका कारन *hun^akā kāran*, for his sake.

These oblique forms are not always employed. The direct form is often used instead of the oblique form, but not *vice-versa*. The oblique form is never used instead of the direct form.

The following pairs are therefore both correct; though the second is the more usual :—

⎧ हमर सिरकी में *hamar sir^akī mē̃*, and
⎩ हमरा सिरकी में *ham^arā sir^akī mē̃*.

⎧ अपन चढ़क घोड़ी *appan carhaik ghōṛī*, and
⎩ अपना चढ़क घोड़ी *ap^anā carhaik ghōṛī*.

And so for the other examples. But the following examples, in

which an oblique form is used instead of a direct form, are
wrong :—

ञनका कानब सुनि *hun^akā kānab sunⁱ.*

अकरा खेत तकरा धान *jak^arā khēt- tak^arā dhān,* this would
mean 'to whom there is a field, to him there is a paddy-
crop,' conveying an altogether different meaning.

तकरा अकरार लिखि *tak^arā ak^arār likhⁱ.*

In phrases like हमरा सक नहिं *ham^arā sak nahⁱ,* I have no
power (to do so and so), हमरा *ham^arā* is not a genitive. It is a
dative, and the sentence literally translated is 'to me power is
not.'

The above possessive pronouns do not change for gender in the
modern language. 'My mother' is हमर माई *hamar māi,* not हमरि माई
hamarⁱ māi. In the old language, however, we now and then
come across instances of the feminine.

135. Given the oblique form, the declension of pronouns
closely follows that of nouns substantive. The principal points of
difference are :—

(1) The Accusative singular is rarely the same as the nominative, but is in the oblique form either by itself or with the postposition कें *kē,* added. Thus हम *ham,* I ; हमरा *ham^arā* or हमरा कें
ham^arā kē, me. The honorific pronoun of the second person, अपने
ap^ane or अहाँ *ahā̃,* and the interrogative pronoun की *ki,* what? are
the only exceptions to this general statement.

(2) The Genitives are formed according to a different series
of rules, as above explained.

(3) The Dative often drops the postposition कें *kē,* an idiom
which is not allowable in the case of nouns substantive. Thus
हमरा कें *ham^arā kē* or हमरा *ham^arā,* to me.

(4) Pronouns have the same form whether referring to masculine or feminine nouns.

(5) With the exception of the pronouns of the second person,
they all want the vocative case.

PERSONAL PRONOUNS.

136. There are three sets of personal pronouns, the first set referring to the first person, the second to the second person, and the third to the third. Each of the two last sets consists of two divisions—an honorific, and a non-honorific division. In other words, the pronouns of the second and third persons have each two forms, an honorific and a non-honorific. To people accustomed to deal with eastern languages, I need do no more than point out the fact, except to notice *en passant*, that in no Eastern Indo-Aryan language is this distinction carried to a greater length* than in Maithilī. The pronouns of the third person are identical with the Remote Demonstrative Pronouns, and will be dealt with under that head.

137. In order to clear the way, I commence with the two old singular forms of the pronouns of the first and second persons which at the present day are only used in poetry. These are मैं *mẽ*, I, and तू *tū*, thou, and are declined as follows :—

Nom.	मैं *mẽ*, I.	तू *tū*, thou.
Acc.	मोहि *mohi*, me.	तोहि *tohi*, thee.
Instr.	मोहि सँ *mohi sõ*, by me.	तोहि सँ *tohi sõ*, by thee.
Dat.	मोहि *mohi*, to me.	तोहि *tohi*, to thee.
Abl.	मोहि सँ *mohi sõ*, from me.	तोहि सँ *tohi sõ*, from thee.
Gen.	मोर *mõr*, my, of me.	तुअ *tua*, or तोर *tõr*, thy, of thee.
Loc.	मोहि मँ *mohi mõ*, in me.	तोहि मँ *tohi mõ*, in thee.

The oblique forms of the genitive are मोरा *mõrā* and तोरा *tõrā*. In Vidyāpati, lxxix. 13, मोरा *mõrā* is employed as a dative of possession. नहिं मोरा टका अछि *nahi mõrā* (scanned as if it were मोर *mora*) *ṭakā achi*, there is not a rupee to me, I have no money.

---

* It will be seen further on, that some verbs have not only a honorific and a non-honorific form depending on the subject, but have also another pair of honorific and non-honorific forms depending on the object.

The plural forms are not used. When necessary, the modern plurals are said to be employed instead, but I have never met an example of this.

138. It will be observed how closely the declensions of the pronouns of the first and second persons agree in the above paradigm. The same is the case in the modern pronouns, which are as follows :—

Singular.

Nom. हम *ham*, I. तोंइ *tŏh*, or तों *tŏ̃*, thou.

Acc.
{ हमरा *hamᵃrā*.
  हमरा कें *hamᵃrā kĕ̃*. } me.
{ तोहरा *tohᵃrā*.
  तोहरा कें *tohᵃrā kĕ̃*. } thee.

Instr.
{ हमरें *hamᵃrĕ̃*,
  हमरा सं *hamᵃrā sã̃*. } by me.
{ तोहरें *tohᵃrĕ̃*,
  तोहरा सं *tohᵃrā sã̃*. } by thee.

Dat.
{ हमरा *hamᵃrā*.
  हमरा कें *hamᵃrā kĕ̃*. } to me.
{ तोहरा *tohᵃrā*.
  तोहरा कें *tohᵃrā kĕ̃*, } to thee.

Abl. हमरा सं *hamᵃrā sã̃*. from me. तोहरा सं *tohᵃrā sã̃*, from thee.

Gen. हमर *hamar*, or हमार *hamār*. my, of me. तोहर *tōhar*, or तोहार *tohār*. thy, of thee.

Loc. हमरा में *hamᵃrā mĕ̃*, in me. तोहरा में *tohᵃrā mĕ̃*, in thee.

Voc. ... ... हौ तोंइ *hau tŏh*, O thou.

Plural.

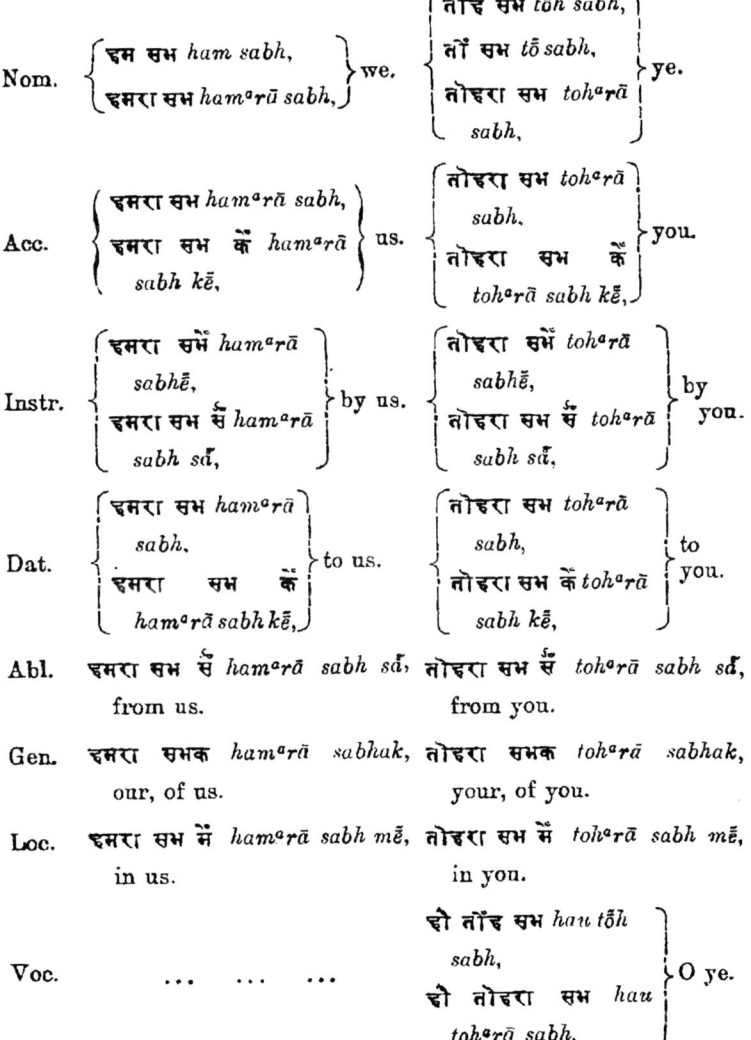

Nom.	इम सभ *ham sabh,* इमरा सभ *ham^arā sabh,* } we.	तोंइ सभ *tōh sabh,* तों सभ *tō sabh,* तोइरा सभ *toh^arā sabh,* } ye.
Acc.	इमरा सभ *ham^arā sabh,* इमरा सभ कँ *ham^arā sabh kē,* } us.	तोइरा सभ *toh^arā sabh,* तोइरा सभ कँ *toh^arā sabh kē,* } you.
Instr.	इमरा सभें *ham^arā sabhē,* इमरा सभ सँ *ham^arā sabh sā,* } by us.	तोइरा सभें *toh^arā sabhē,* तोइरा सभ सँ *toh^arā sabh sā,* } by you.
Dat.	इमरा सभ *ham^arā sabh,* इमरा सभ कँ *ham^arā sabh kē,* } to us.	तोइरा सभ *toh^arā sabh,* तोइरा सभ कँ *toh^arā sabh kē,* } to you.

Abl. इमरा सभ सँ *ham^arā sabh sā,* from us. तोइरा सभ सँ *toh^arā sabh sā,* from you.

Gen. इमरा सभक *ham^arā sabhak,* our, of us. तोइरा सभक *toh^arā sabhak,* your, of you.

Loc. इमरा सभ में *ham^arā sabh mē,* in us. तोइरा सभ में *toh^arā sabh mē,* in you.

Voc. ... ... वो तोंइ सभ *hau tōh sabh,*
वो तोइरा सभ *hau toh^arā sabh,* } O ye.

11

Instead of सभ *sabh* we may as usual employ सबहि *sabah*[i] or
लोकनि *lok*[a]*ni* throughout, except that it is not customary to use them
with the direct forms हम *ham*, and तोंह *tŏh* or तों *tŏ̃*. Thus we
do not hear हम सबहि *ham sabah*[i], or तोंह लोकनि *tŏh lok*[a]*ni*. In the
genitive plural we can, as usual, have सभ केर *sabh kēr*, instead of
सभक *sabhak*.

The terminations हि *h*[i] and हूँ *h*[u] are often added to these pronouns. The former gives emphasis, and the second means 'also.'

Thus हमहि *hamah*[i], I (emphatic), I alone, as distinguished
from other people; हमहूँ *hamah*[u], I also; तोंहूँ *tŏh*[u], thou also ;
हमरहूँ *ham*[a]*rah*[u] (with shortening of the final vowel of हमरा
ham[a]*rā*), to me also.

139. तोंह *tŏh* and तों *tŏ̃* are non-honorific pronouns of the
second person. There are two honorific pronouns of this person.
अहाँ *ahã* or अहैं *ahaĭ*, and अपने *up*[a]*ne*.

These are declined exactly like substantives, and have no
oblique form. Thus, genitive अहाँक *ahãk*, or अहैंक *ahaĭk*, and
अपनेक *ap*[a]*nek*, your. The only irregularity is the instrumental
singular, the various forms of which are:—

अहैं *ahaĭ*, अहाँ सँ *ahã sã*, or अहैं सँ *ahaĭ sã*,   ⎫
    and अपने सँ *op*[a]*ne sã*,   ⎬ by you.
                                     ⎭

The plural is, as usual :—

अहाँ (or अहैं) सभ *ahã* (or *ahaĭ*) *sabh*, सबहि *sabah*[i], or लोकनि
lok[a]*ni*,

अपने सभ *ap*[a]*ne sabh*, etc.

अपने *ap*[a]*ne* is more honorific than अहाँ *ahã*. The latter is
sometimes even used when talking to inferiors. अहाँ *ahã*, in fact,
is *polite* ; while तोंह *tŏh* is *rude* or *vulgar*.

In Hindōstānī आप *āp*, your honour, is construed with the verb
in the third person plural, as in आप कहाँ जावे ऍ *āp kahã jātē*

haĩ, where is your honour going ? In Maithilī, on the contrary, हर्तं *ahã̄* and अपनें *ap^ane*, are construed with the second person honorific of the verb, as in अपने बड़त नीक कथा कहल *ap^ane bahut nik kathā kahal*, your honour made a very excellent remark.

THE REFLEXIVE PRONOUN.

140. Closely connected with the foregoing is the Reflexive Pronoun अपनहिं *ap^anah^i* or अपनें *ap^ane*, self, which is employed exactly like the Hindōstānī आप *āp*, genitive अपना *ap^anā*, always referring to the person of the subject of the sentence.

The genitive of अपनहिं *ap^anah^i* is अपन *upan*, or अप्पन *appan*, own, with an oblique form अपना *ap^anā*, which is also used as an oblique base. Thus, Acc. Dat. अपना *ap^anā*, or अपना कें *ap^anā kẽ*, to oneself.

The nominative plural is अपनहिं (or अपनें) सभ *ap^anah^i* (or *ap^ane*) *sabh*, सबहिं *sab^ah^i*, or लोकनि *lok^ani*. The oblique cases of the plural are formed from the base अपना सभ *ap^anā sabh*, etc. Thus Gen. plural अपना सभक *ap^anā sabhak*, अपना सबहिक *ap^anā sab^ahik*, अपना लोकनिक *ap^anā lok^anik*, of selves.

The Locative plural, अपना सभ में *ap^anā sabh mẽ*, or (as frequently happens) with the plural suffix dropped, अपना में *ap^anā mẽ* means 'amongst themselves,' like the Hindōstānī आपस में *āpas mẽ*.

The following are examples of the use of this pronoun :—

अपनहिं बिलास सँ गेल सर्लोगवा *ap^anah^i bilās sã̄ gēl sar^alog^awā*, he himself, after enjoyment (of this life), went to heaven.

अपने ब्राह्मनीक रूप धैं कँगनिया चढ़लि *ap^ane brah^amanĩk rūp dhai kũganiã carhal^i*, she herself, taking the form of a Brāhman woman, ascended the bank.

अपन मरौटी अपने गाय गबैत चलू जोगिया गाम, *apan marauṭi apane up⁴ne gāy yabait calū jogiyā gām,* having sung our own death-song let us go singing to the village of Jogiyā.

अपन बड़ बेटी रखलन्हि घर सुताय *apun bah⁴ bēṭī rakh⁴lanh⁴ ghar sutāy,* he has put his own daughter-in-law and daughter to sleep at home.

बैरी अपना बस में आबि जाय *bäirī up⁴nā bas mē̃ ābⁱ jāy,* (if) an enemy come into one's own power.

अपना में मेलि कें कँ रहबँह *up⁴nā mē̃ mēlⁱ kai kã̄ rah⁴bãh,* you will remain at peace amongst yourselves. *i.e.,* with each other.

THE DEMONSTRATIVE PRONOUNS, AND PRONOUN OF THE THIRD PERSON.

141. There are two Demonstrative Pronouns,—a Proximate, ए *i* or ई *ī,* this, and a Remote, ओ *ō.* that. The Remote Demonstrative Pronoun is also used as a Pronoun of the third person, with the meaning of 'he,' 'she,' or 'it.'

142. Each of these pronouns has two forms, a non-honorific and an honorific. Each of these latter, again, has two oblique forms, the old, and the modern.

143. These pronouns may be either substantives or adjectives. When used as substantives they are declined throughout. When used as adjectives they are unchanged when the substantive with which they are in agreement is in the form of the nominative, and are put in the old oblique form when the substantive is not in that form. Thus, ई नेना *i nēnā,* this boy ; ओ नेना *ō nēnā,* that boy ; ई सभ नेना *i sabh nēnā,* or ई नेना सभ *i nēnā sabh,* these boys ; ओ सभ नेना *ō sabh nēnā.* or ओ नेना सभ *ō nēnā sabh,* those boys ; but एहि नेनाक *ehⁱ nēnāk,* of this boy ; ओहि नेनाक *ohⁱ nēnāk,* of that boy ; एहि सभ नेनाक *ehⁱ sabh nēnāk,* or एहि नेना सभक *ehⁱ nēnā subhak,* of these boys ; ओहि सभ नेनाक *ohⁱ subh nēnāk,* or ओहि

नेना सभक *oh* *nēnā sabhak*, of those boys. The modern oblique forms
are never used in this way.

Other examples of the adjectival use of these pronouns are:—

एहि बेकूफ कें कहाँ तक नीक अकिल हैतैक, *eh* *bēkūph kē̃ kahā̃ tak nīk akil haitaik*, how far will wisdom come to this fool.

एहि फसिलक की रंग अछि *eh* *phasilak kī rañg uch*. what is the prospect of this harvest.

ओहि राति कें कतहूँ चलैत गेल *oh* *rāt* *kē̃ katah* *calait gēl*, that night he went away somewhere.

ओहि रसायनीक ठेकान नहिं लागल *oh* *rasāy* *nīk ṭhēkān nah* *lāgal*, no trace was found of that alchemist.

144. When used as substantives, the non-honorific pronouns
have two forms.—one referring to inanimate objects and using the
old oblique form. while the other refers only to animate objects
and uses the modern oblique form. Thus एहि में *eh* *mē̃*. in this
(thing); एकरा में *ek* *rā mē̃*. in this (living creature); ओहि में *oh*
mē̃, in that (thing). in it : ओकरा में *ok* *rā mē̃*. in that (living
creature). in him. in her.

There are thus three declensions of Demonstrative Pronouns
when used as substantives. *viz*:—

    (a) Non-honorific inanimate.

    (b) Non-honorific animate.

    (b) Honorific animate.

It stands to reason that an honorific inanimate declension is not
likely to occur. The following is the declension of Demonstrative
Pronouns.

145. (*a*) Non-Honorific Inanimate.

Singular.

 इ *i* or ई *î*, this.   ओ *ô*. that.

Nom.	इ *i* or ई *î*, this	ओ *ô*. that.
Acc.	इ *i*, ई *î*, एहि *ehi*. एहि कें *ehi kē̃*, this.	ओ *ô*, ओहि *ohi*. ओहि कें *ohi kē̃*, that.
Instr.	एं *ē̃*, एहि सँ *ehi sā̃*, by this.	ओहि सँ *ohi sā̃*, by that.
Dat.	एहि *ehi*. एहि कें *ehi kē̃*, to this.	ओहि *ohi*. ओहि कें *ohi kē̃*, to that.
Abl.	एहि सँ *ehi sā̃*, from this.	ओहि सँ *ohi sā̃*, from that.
Gen.	एकर *ēkar*, of this.	ओकर *ōkar*, of that.
Loc.	एहि में *ehi mē̃*, in this.	ओहि में *ohi mē̃*, in that.

Plural.

Nom.	इ सभ *i sabh*, or ई सभ *î sabh*. these.	ओ सभ *ô sabh*, those.
Acc.	एहि सभ (कें) *ehi sabh* (*kē̃*). these.	ओहि सभ (कें) *ohi sabh* (*kē̃*), those.
Instr.	{ एं सभ *ē̃ sabh*, एहि सभ सँ *ehi sabh sā̃*, } by these.	ओहि सभ सँ *ohi sabh sā̃*, by those.
Dat.	एहि सभ (कें) *ehi sabh* (*kē̃*), to these.	ओहि सभ (कें) *ohi sabh* (*kē̃*). to those.
Abl.	एहि सभ सँ *ehi sabh sā̃*. from these.	ओहि सभ सँ *ohi sabh sā̃*, from those.
Gen.	एहि सभक *ehi sabhak*, of these.	ओहि सभक *ohi sabhak*. of those.
Loc.	एहि सभ में *ehi sabh mē̃*. in these.	ओहि सभ में *ohi sabh mē̃*. in those.

Instead of प्रहि *eh*[i], we may have, throughout, प्रह *eh* or प्रेह *aih*, and similarly for ओहि *oh*[i]. we may have ओह *oh* or ओेह *auh*. I have not noted any instrumental form of ओ *ō*, corresponding to the ॅ *ē* of इ *ī*. The genitives singular एकर *ēkar* and ओकर *ōkar* are contractions of प्रहि कर *eh*[i] *kar* and ओहि कर *oh*[i] *kar* respectively. I have not met with forms like प्रहिक *ehik* or ओहिक *ohik*, as we might expect. The plural suffix may be सबहि *sabah*[i] instead of सभ *sabh*. लोकनि *lok*[a]*ni* cannot be used. as the pronouns refer only to inanimate objects.

As examples of these inanimate non-honorific pronouns, we may quote :—

इं एकर छाठम बिश्रान थिकै *i ēkar āṭham biān thikai*. this is the eighth calving of this one (referring to a cow).

इं ले जाह *i lē jāh*, take away this.

प्रहि नहिं जनल्ली अहाँ भद्री छी *eh*[i] *nah*[i] *jan*[a]*lī uhā̃ bhadrī chī*, I did not know this. that your honour is Bhadri.

प्रहि सँ इं फल बहरारअहि *eh*[i] *sā̃ i phal bah*[a]*rāi-ach*[i], from this this fruit comes out, *i.e.*, the moral of this is the following :—

ओहि में किच्छु लाभ नहिं *oh*[i] *mē̃ kicch*[u] *lābh nah*[i]. in that there is no profit.

कौआ ओकर गुद्दा खाप्र गेल *kauā ōkar guddā khāe gēl*, the crow ate up its kernel.

As an emphatic form of these pronouns we have इहे *ihe*, this indeed, and उहे *uhe* or वैह *waih*, that indeed, as in दीना भद्री जिबैत चल उहे गबैत रहै *dinā bhadrī jibait chal, uhe gabait rahai*, (when) Dinā and Bhadrī were alive, that is the very song they used to sing ; वैह चोराप्र कै ले गेल अहि *waih corāe kai lai gēl ach*[i], it is he who has stolen (the property) and carried it off.

146.　　(*b*) Non-Honorific Animate.

This is declined like the inanimate pronoun, except that प्रकरा
ekᵃrā is substituted for प्रहि *ehⁱ* and ओकरा *okᵃrā* for ओहि *ohⁱ*.
Thus :—

Singular.

Nom.　ए *i* or ई *ī*, this.　　　　　　ओ *ō*, that.

Instr.　$\left\{ \begin{array}{l} \text{प्रकरें } ekᵃr\~ē, \\ \text{प्रकरा सँ } ekᵃrā\ s\~a, \end{array} \right\}$ by this.　ओकरा सँ *okᵃrā sā̃*, by that.

Dat.　$\left\{ \begin{array}{l} \text{प्रकरा } ekᵃrā, \\ \text{प्रकरा कें } ekᵃrā\ k\~ē. \end{array} \right\}$ to this.　$\left\{ \begin{array}{l} \text{ओकरा } okᵃrā, \\ \text{ओकरा कें } okᵃrā\ k\~ē, \end{array} \right\}$ to that.

Gen.　एकर *ēkar*, of this.　　　　　ओकर *ōkar*, of that.

Plural.

Nom.　ए सभ *i sabh*. ई सभ *i sabh*, etc.,　ओ सभ *ō sabh*, etc., those.
　　　these.

Dat.　प्रकरा सभ (कें)*ekᵃrā sabh (k\~ē)*.　ओकरा सभ (कें) *okᵃrā sabh*
　　　to these.　　　　　　　　　　　　　(*k\~ē*), to those.

Similarly for the other cases. I have not noted any instrumental form of ओ *ō*, corresponding to the प्रकरें *ekᵃr\~ē* of ए *ī*. In
the plural, instead of सभ *sabh*, we can, as usual, have सबहि *sabahⁱ*
or लोकनि *lokᵃni*. As examples of these animate non-honorific pronouns, we may quote :—

　ओ आइकाल्हि गाभिनि अछि *ō āikālhⁱ gābhinⁱ achⁱ*, nowadays she
　is in calf (referring to a cow).

　ओकरा प्रहि तरहें घबड़ाएल देखि कँ *okᵃrā ehⁱ tarᵃh\~ē ghabᵃrāᵊl
　dēkhⁱ k\~a*, having seen him distracted in this manner.

In the following ओकरा *okᵃrā* is irregularly used to refer to an
inanimate object.　तखन ओ सभ ओकरा भट पट तोड़ि देलक *takhan ō
sabh okᵃrā jhaṭ-paṭ tūṛⁱ dēlak*, then they at once broke it (*sc.* a
stick).

एकर आठम बिआन *ēkar āṭham biān*, her eighth calving.

जेहि सौं ओकर परबरस सोदक से अबस्य॰ कर्तब्य॰ थीक *jehi saũ ūkar parᵃbaraś hūik sē abasya kartabya thīk*, we must certainly do what is necessary for its (the child's) support.

प्रकरा सभ कें किछु के देखाबी *ekᵃrā sabh kē kichᵘ kai dekhābī*, having done something, let me show it to all these (*viz.* to his sons).

प्रकरा सबहि कें हमरा लग पठाए देह *ekᵃrā sabahi kē hamᵃrā lag paṭhāe daih*, send all these (*viz.*, dogs) to me.

हि *hⁱ* added to these oblique forms gives emphasis, while हूँ *hū* when suffixed, means 'also.' Thus प्रकरहि कें *ekᵃrahⁱ kē*, it is to *this* one; ओकरहूँ पठाए दिऔक *okᵃrahᵘ paṭhāe diauk*, send him also. Observe that the final आ *ā* of प्रकरा *ekᵃrā* and ओकरा *okᵃrā* is shortened before these suffixes.

147. (c) HONORIFIC.

The old honorific oblique forms of ई *ī* and ओ *ō* are हिनि *hinⁱ* and हुनि *hunⁱ* respectively. We meet them variously spelt. Sometimes we have हिन *hin* and हुन *hun*; sometimes हिनहि *hinhⁱ* and हुनहि *hunhⁱ*, and sometimes हिनह *hinh* and हुनह *hunh*. For the sake of convenience I shall only employ हिनि *hinⁱ* and हुनि *hunⁱ* in the paradigms, but it should be remembered that the other forms are often met with. Indeed, the most usual form of the genitive is हिनक *hinak* and हुनक *hunak*, and not हिनिक *hinik* and हुनिक *hunik*. These old oblique forms are only employed as adjectives, and, being honorific, rarely occur in the literary style, though one hears them in conversation. We have an example in हुनि स्वामिक कारन *hunⁱ swāmik kāran*, for the sake of that (respected) husband (the prospective wife is speaking), in the song of Salhēs.

12

148. The modern oblique form is the oblique genitive of the old oblique form. Thus, हिनका *hin^{a}kā* and इनका *hun^{a}kā*, of which हिनिका *hinikā*, हिन्हका *hinh^{a}kā*, हिन्हिका *hinhikā*, and इनिका *hunikā*, इन्हका *hunh^{a}kā*, इन्हिका *hunhikā*, are optional varieties.

149. The declension of the honorific pronoun is the same as that of the non-honorific, substituting हिनका *hin^{a}kā* and इनका *hun^{a}kā*, or any of the optional spellings, for एकरा *ek^{a}rā* and ओकरा *ok^{a}rā*, respectively. Thus :—

Singular.

Nom.	इ *i* or ई *ī*, this.	ओ *ō*, that.	
Instr.	हिनका सँ *hin^{a}kā sã̄*, by this.	इनका सँ *hun^{a}kā sã̄*, by that.	
Dat.	{ हिनका *hin^{a}kā*, हिनका कँ *hin^{a}kā kẽ*, } to this.	{ इनका *hun^{a}kā*, इनका क *hun^{a}kā kẽ*, } to that.	
Gen.	{ हिनक *hinak*, हिनकर *hin^{a}kar*. } of this.	{ इनक *hunak*, इनकर *hun^{a}kar*. } of that.	

Plural.

Nom. इ सभ *i sabh*, ई सभ *ī sabh*, etc., these.   ओ सभ *ō sabh*, etc., those.

Dat. हिनका सभ (कँ) *hin^{a}kā sabh* (*kẽ*), to these.   इनका सभ (कँ) *hun^{a}kā sabh* (*kẽ*), to those.

Similarly for the other cases. As usual, in the plural we can use सबहि *sabah^i* or लोकनि *lok^{a}ni* instead of सभ *sabh*. Examples of the use of this form of the demonstrative pronoun are :—

हिनका फुरसति देब *hin^{a}kā phursat^i dēb*. I will give him leave to depart.

इनका माए बाप गारी देलक *hun^{a}kā māe bāp gārī dēlak*, have the father and mother given abuse to her (*i.e.*, have they abused her).

इनिका माता नहिं *hunikā mātā nahⁱ*, to him there is no mother, he has no mother.

इनक कानब सुनि *hunak kānab sunⁱ*, hearing her weeping.

150. The above genitives एकर *ēkar*, ओकर *ōkar*, हिनक *hinak*, or हिनकर *hin^akar* and इनक *hunak* or इनकर *hun^akar*, are usually all put into the oblique form when agreeing with a noun in an oblique case. Examples of this will be found in § 134 *ante*.

THE RELATIVE AND CORRELATIVE PRONOUNS.

151. The Relative Pronoun is जे *jē*. who, which, and its Correlative is से *sē*, he, she, it. that.

152. As in the case of the Demonstrative Pronouns, each has two forms, a non-honorific and an honorific ; and the non-honorific form, again, may be animate or inanimate. There is, however this difference. that in the Instrumental, Ablative, and Genitive singular, and throughout the plural, the form usually employed for inanimate nouns may also be employed for animate ones.

153. When used as adjectives, the oblique forms (जाहि *jāhⁱ* and ताहि *tāhⁱ*) of the non-honorific inanimate declension are used when in agreement with a noun in an oblique case. Examples of the adjectival use of these pronouns are as follows :—

जे चीज बस्तु सभ अहाँक नोकसान भेल अछि, से सभ पहुँचत *jē cīj bast^u sabh ahāk nok^asān bhel achⁱ, sē sabh pahūcat*, all your property which has been spoilt. will arrive (*i.e.,* be restored).

जे लोक आएल चल से लोक गेल *jē lōk āel chal. sē lōk gēl.* the man who came, went.

जाहि लोकक खेत ताहि लोकक धान *jāhⁱ lōkak khēt, tāhⁱ lōkak dhān*, the person who owns the field. owns the paddy.

आधि बन सिकिबो नं डांलै ताधि बन हन्सा के लड़ै *jāhⁱ ban siki-ō ne ḍōlai, tāhⁱ ban hansā chai laṛai,* (in) the forest where even the reeds are motionless, his soul is fighting.

154.   When used as a substantive, the inanimate non-honorific form is declined as follows.   The Instrumental, Ablative, and Genitive singular, and the whole of the plural can be also used to refer to animate nouns.

155.   (a) NON-HONORIFIC INANIMATE.

Singular.

जे *jē,* which, who.   से *sē,* he, she, it, that.

Nom.	जे *jē,* which.	से *sē,* that.
Acc.	जाधि (कें) *jāhⁱ (kē),* to which.	ताधि (कें) *tāhⁱ (kē),* to that.
Instr.	{ जें *jē̃* / जाधि सें *jāhⁱ sā̃,* } by which, by whom.	{ तें *tē̃* / ताधि सें *tāhⁱ sā̃.* } by that, by him.
Dat.	जाधि (कें) *jāhⁱ (kē),* to which.	ताधि (कें) *tāhⁱ (kē),* to that.
Abl.	जाधि सें *jāhⁱ sā̃.* from which, from whom.	ताधि सें *tāhⁱ sā̃,* from that, from him.
Gen.	जसु *jasᵘ,* of which, of whom.	तसु *tasᵘ,* of that, of him.
Loc.	जाधि में *jāhⁱ mē̃,* in which.	ताधि में *tāhⁱ mē̃,* in that.

Plural.

Nom.	जे सभ *jē sabh,* which, who.	से सभ *sē sabh,* those, they.
Acc.	जाधि सभ (कें) *jāhⁱ subh kē.* which, who.	ताधि सभ (कें) *tāhⁱ sabh (kē),* those, they.
Instr.	जाधि सभ सें *jāhⁱ sabh sā̃,* by which, by whom.	ताधि सभ सें *tāhⁱ sabh sā̃,* by those, by them.
Dat.	जाधि सभ (कें) *jāhⁱ sabh (kē),* to which, to whom.	ताधि सभ (कें) *tāhⁱ sabh (kē),* to those, to them.

Abl. जाहि सभ सँ *jāhⁱ sabh sã*, from ताहि सभ सँ *tāhⁱ sabh sã*, from
which, from whom.   those, from them.

Gen. जाहि सभक *jāhⁱ sabhak*. of ताहि सभक *tāhⁱ sabhak*. of
which, of whom.   those, of them.

Loc. जाहि सभ में *jāhⁱ sabh mē̃*, in ताहि सभ में *tāhⁱ sabh mē̃*, in
which. in whom.   those, in them.

Instead of जाहि *jāhⁱ* and ताहि *tāhⁱ*, we sometimes find in poetry
जा *jā* and ता *tā*. We also sometimes have जेहि *jehⁱ* and तेहि *tehⁱ*,
which are properly Bhojpuri. From this last we have an instrumental जेहिं *jehⁱ̃* and तेहिं *tehⁱ̃*, which are used adverbially, to mean
'as,' 'so.' The Genitives जसु *jasᵘ*, and तसु *tasᵘ*, are only used in
proverbs and poetry. In one place Vidyāpati has तासि *tāsⁱ* (xviii,
7). I have not met forms like जाहिक *jāhik* and ताहिक *tāhik*, which
we might expect. The plural suffix may, as usual, be सबहि *sabahⁱ*
or लोकनि *lokᵃni* instead of सभ *sabh*. As examples of this form of
the honorific pronoun we may quote :—

जे आएल से गेल *jē āel sē gēl*, he who came, went.

जाहि सँ नाम चलैन्हि से हमर किरिया करह *jāhⁱ sã nãm calainhⁱ,
sē hamar kiriyā karᵃh*, in order that (*lit.* from which) our
name may continue, so perform our funeral rites.

In the following the final ि *i* of जाहि *jāhⁱ* has been lengthened
for the sake of metre.

आहो सँ किछु पाबिअँ सहिअँ कड़ुर बेन *jāhī sã kichᵘ pābiã, sahiã
karui bēn*, from whomsoever you would receive benefits, you
must bear abusive words.

कैएक कथा सभ सिखाए दिअह कि जाहि सँ तोहरा लाभ हैतह *kaiek
kathā sabh sikhāe diahᵘ, ki jāhⁱ sã tōhᵒrā lābh haitahᵘ*, I will
teach you several sayings from which there will be gain to
you.

जकरा जा सँ रीती दुरडक दुरि गेलॆ दोगुन पिरीती *jakarā jā sẽ rītī durahuka duri gēlẽ doguna pirītī*, to whom, with whom there is affection (*i.e.*, when there is mutual affection), the love is twice as strong the more distant they are from each other (Vidyāpati, xlvi. 1).

ता सम *tā sama*, like that (Vidyapati, xvi. 2).

जेहि सौ ओकर परबरस होइक *jeh^i saü ōkar par^abaras hōik*, so that (*lit.* from which) its support may be. (we must take precautions for the child's support).

तेहि अबसर *teh^i abasara*, at that time (Vid. xxviii. 4).

जेहिं ऐलाच तेहिं गेला, *jeh^i ailắh teh^i gēlā*, as he came, so he went.

जसु मन परम तरासे *jasu mana parama tarāsē*. in whose heart there is exceeding fear (Vid. vii. 5).

तसु साहस नहिं सीमा *tasu sāhasa nahĩ sīmā*, there is no limit to her courage (Vid. vii. 4).

तासि रिपु *tāsi ripu*, his foe (Vid. xviii. 7).

156. Several emphatic forms of these pronouns have been noted. Such are जॆइ *jaih*, who, सॆइ *seh*, सइ *saih*, सोए *sōe*, even he : सेओ *sēō*, सेहो *sēhō*, सेहओ *seh-o*, he also. Thus,—

सॆइ चतुर जन जॆइ बुझत अबधारी *saiha catura jana jaiha bujhata abadhārī*, they alone are wise who can understand it correctly (Vid. xvii. 7).

तनिका सॆइ पै नाइ *tanikā seh pai nāh*, he alone (will be) a husband to her.

चानन लाग बिखम सर सोए *cānana lāga bikhama sara sōe*, the application of sandalwood,—even that is an intolerable arrow (Vid. xvii. 3).

सेहओ दुरि गेला *seha-o duri gelā*, that also went far away (Vid. lxxiii. 4).

सेहो थिक ओहि ठामा *sēhō thika ohi ṭhāmā*, that also is in that place (Vid. xvii. 3).

157. It will have been noticed from the above that while से *sē* is generally employed as a correlative, it is sometimes used as an independent demonstrative pronoun. Its Instrumental singular appears under various forms, such as तैं *taĩ*, तौं *taũ*, तौ *tau*, तो *tō*, or with emphatic ई *i*, तेई *tēĩ*, or with emphatic ओ *o*, तेओ *tēo*, तैओ *taio*, or तैअओ *taiao*, all of which are commonly used adverbially. Thus :—

तें नहिं करथि गरासे *tē̃ nahĩ karathi gurāsē*, *therefore* he does not devour it (Vid. xiv. 8).

तैं नहिं कमल सुखाइं *taĩ nahĩ kamala sukhāĩ*, *therefore* the lotus does not wither (Vid. xiv. 6).

तौं पय जीबे अधर सुधा रस जौं पय पीबे *taũ paya jībē, adhara sudhā-rasa jaũ paya pībē*, *so long* will it live, as long as it sips the nectar of the lower lip (Vid. ii. 5).

तो पय जीबथि जीबे *tō paya jībathi jībē*, *so long* will he remain living (Vid. x. 10).

तेई बहि गेल हावा *tēĩ bahi gēl hāwā*, *exactly so* did the wind blow.

तेओ धसल केस पासे *tēo dhasala kēsa pāsē*, *therefore also* my hair was disordered (Vid. xl. 7).

तैओ तुलित नहिं भेला *taio tulita nahĩ bhēlā*, *still* it did not equal (the beauty of thy face) (Vid. vi. 4).

तैअओ कुमुदिनि करय अनंदा *taiao kumudini karaya anandā*, *nevertheless* the water-lily rejoices (Vid. xlvi. 6).

158. (*b*) NON-HONORIFIC ANIMATE.

This is declined like the inanimate pronoun, except that जकरा *jak^arā* is substituted for जाहि *jāhⁱ*. and तकरा *tak^arā* for ताहि *tāhⁱ*. Thus :—

Singular.

Nom. जे *jē*, who. से *sē*, he, she, that.

Instr. $\begin{cases} \text{जकरें } jak^aṛ\bar{e}, \\ \text{जकरा सँ } jak^arā \ sằ, \end{cases}$ $\begin{matrix} \text{by} \\ \text{whom.} \end{matrix}$ $\begin{cases} \text{तकरें } tak^aṛ\bar{e}, \\ \text{तकरा सँ } tak^arā \ sằ, \end{cases}$ $\begin{matrix} \text{by} \\ \text{him,} \\ \&\text{c.} \end{matrix}$

Dat. जकरा (कें) *jak^arā* (*kḗ*), to whom. तकरा (कें) *tak^arā* (*kḗ*), to him, &c.

Gen. जकर *jakar*, whose. तकर *takar*, his, her, its.

Plural.

Nom. जे सभ *jē sabh*, who. से सभ *sē sabh*, they.

Dat. जकरा सभ (कें) *jak^arā sabh* (*kḗ*), to whom. तकरा सभ (कें) *tak^arā sabh* (*kḗ*), to them.

Similarly for the other cases. In the plural, as usual, सबहि *subahⁱ* or लोकनि *lok^ani* may be substituted for सभ *sabh*. Occasionally we come across जेकर *jēkar* instead of जकर *jakar*, जेकरा *jek^arā* instead of जकरा *jak^arā*, तेकर *tēkar* instead of तकर *takar*, and तेकरा *tek^arā* instead of तकरा *tak^arā*. These are properly Bhojpurī forms.

As examples of these non-honorific animate pronouns we may quote :—

जकर खेत तकर धान *jakar khēt. takar dhān*, whose is the field, his is the paddy-crop.

जकर लाठी तकर मङैस *jakar lāṭhī takar mahīs*. he who owns the cudgel owns the buffalo.

जकरा सँ रस चूबि रहल अछि *jakₐrā sā̆ ras cūb' rahal ach'*, (grapes) from which the juice is exuding (here the pronoun is, exceptionally, inanimate).

जेकर बनल अखड़वा तेकर बारहो मास *jēkar banal akharₐwā tēkar bă̆rₐho mās*, he whose (fields) are ready in *Āṣāḍh*, is ready also all the year round.

हिं *h'* (even), and हूँ *h̆ū* (also), are added as in the case of demonstratives. Thus (Vid. l. 4).

एहि अबसर पहु मिलन जेहन सुख ।

जकरहिं होए से जान ॥

ehi abasara pahu milana jehana sukha ।
jakarahī hoe sē jāna ॥

Only she that hath experienced them, knows the bliss of the tryst with the beloved at such a time.

159. (c) HONORIFIC ANIMATE.

The honorific oblique forms of जे *jē* and से *sē* are जनि *jan'* and तनि *tan'*, respectively. We thus get the following declension which is exactly parallel to that of ई *ī* and ओ *ō* :—

Singular.

Nom.	जे *jē*, who.	से *sē*, he, she, that.
Instr.	जनिका सँ *janikā sā̆*, by whom.	तनिका सँ *tanikā sā̆*, by him, her.
Dat.	जनिका (कें) *janikā* (*kē̆*), to whom.	तनिका (कें) *tanikā* (*kē̆*), to him, her.
Gen.	जनिक *janik*, जनिकर *janikar*, whose.	तनिक *tanik*, तनिकर *tanikar*, his, hers.

13

Plural.

Nom.   जे सभ *jē sabh*, who.   से सभ *sē sabh*, they.

Dat.   जनिका सभ (कँ) *janikā sabh*   तनिका सभ (कँ) *tanikā sabh*
      (*kē̃*), to whom.   (*kē̃*), to them.

And so on for the other cases. As usual, in the plural we can use सबहि *sabahⁱ*, or लोकनि *lokᵃni* instead of सभ *sabh*. Examples of these honorific forms are :—

    जेहन जनिकर चाकरी तेहने एन भरि देथि *jehᵃn janikar cākᵃrī, tehᵃnē̃-san bharⁱ dēthⁱ*, as is each one's (*lit.* whose) service, exactly so he pays in full.

    केयो जमानत दे कें बचलाह जनिका अमला नेही *keō jamᵃnat dui kē̃ bacᵃlāh, janikā amᵃlā nēhī*, some, to whom there was affection on the part of the court officials, got off by giving bail.

    जनिक एहन धनि *janika ehana dhani*, (a man) whose wife is so (beautiful), (Vid. li. 2).

    कि कहब तनिक ज्ञाने *ki kahᵃba tanika· geᵃnē*, what shall I say (about) his wisdom ? (Vid. xxii. 2).

160. I have not noted any occurrence of the employment of the oblique genitive of जे *je*, though, of course, it is commonly heard colloquially. For से *sē*, we have the following pair of examples :—

     Direct Genitive—

       लाख गारि देलैं, तकर उतर हम नहि किछु कहलौक *lᵃkh gārⁱ dēlē̃, tᵃkar utᵃr hᵃm nᵃhⁱ kichᵘ kahᵃlᵃuk*, a thousand abuses didst thou give me, but I said to thee no answer to (*lit.* of) it.

     Oblique Genitive—

       तकरा बल सँ गुलामी जट चरबैत अछि *takᵃrā bal sē̃ gulᵃmī jaṭ ca·ᵃbᵃit achⁱ*, through her might Gulāmī Jaṭ is grazing (cattle).

161. INTERROGATIVE PRONOUNS.

There are two interrogative pronouns, *viz.*, के *kē*, who ? and
की *kī*, what ? The former only refers to animate objects, and the
latter only to inanimate.

162. When employed as adjectives के *kē* and की *kī* become
कोन *kōn* or कौन *kaun*, but when agreeing with a noun in the nominative singular की *kī* may remain unchanged. Examples of the
adjectival use of these pronouns are :—

के *kē*,—ओ कोन लोक थीक *ō kōn lōk thīk*, what caste is he ?

कोन लोकक घोड़ ैक *kōn lōkak ghōṛ chaik*, of what person is
(this) the horse, *i.e.*, what person owns the horse ?

कोन गरू परलौ *kaun garū par^alau*, what misfortune has befallen
you ?

पुछैत छन्हि जे कोन लोगक हबेली छीक *puchait chainh^i jē kaun
lōgak habēlī chīk*, you are asking, '(of a man) of what caste is
this the house ? '

कोन उपाय जाएब जोगिया नगर *kaun upāy jāeb jogiyā nagar*, by
what device shall we go to Jogiyā town ?

की *kī*,—ई कोन बिआन थिकैक *i kōn biān thikaik*, what calving is
this ? (*i.e.*, how many times has she calved before ?)

थोकरा में क.न गुन छैक *ck^arā mē kōn gun chaik*, what virtue is
there in it ?

कोन लोटा में पानि लाएल छैह *kōn lōṭā mē pāni lāel chĉh*, in
what vessel have you brought the water ?

कोन दिसा के अबैत होए कहह बुझैय *kaun disā kē abait hōai kahah^u
bujh^u^y*, tell (me) in what direction he may be coming.

फेरि की भगड़ा छिक *phēr^i kī jhag^o^rā ach^i*, then what (cause of)
quarrel can there be ?

की नाम छिक *kī nām chhik*, what name is it ?

163. The declension of के *kē* (the animate pronoun) closely follows that of the animate forms of जे *jē*.

There are, as usual non-honorific and honorific declensions. They are as follows :—

Singular.

	Non-honorific.	*Honorific.*
Nom.	के *kē*, who ? which ?	के *kē*, who ? which ?
Instr.	ककरें *kak^arē̃*, ककरा सँ *kak^arā sā̃,* } by whom ?	कनिका सँ *kanikā sā̃*, by whom ?
Dat.	ककरा (कें) *kak^arā* (*kē̃*), to whom ?	कनिका (कें) *kanikā* (*kē̃*), to whom ?
Gen.	ककर *kakar*, whose ?	कनिक *kanik*. कनिकर *kanikar*, whose ?

Plural.

Nom.	के सभ *kē sabh*, who ?	के सभ *kē sabh*, who ?
Dat.	ककरा सभ (कें) *kak^arā sabh* (*kē̃*), to whom ?	कनिका सभ कें *kanikā sabh kē̃*, to whom ?

and so on for the other cases. In the plural, as usual, सबहि *sabhi* or लोकनि *lak^ani*, may be substituted for सभ *sabh*. Occasionally we come across केकर *kēkar* instead of ककर *kakar*, and केकरा *kek^arā* instead of ककरा *kak^arā*, but these are properly Bhojpuri forms. I have not come across कासि *kāhi* corresponding to जासि *jāhi* in the modern language, but Vidyāpati employs it in passages such as कासि कहब दुख *kāhi kahaba dukha*, to whom shall I tell my distress ? (lxi. 2.)

As examples of these animate interrogative pronouns, we may quote :—

ककर घोड़ कंक *kakar ghōṛ chaik,* whose horse is it ?

केकर ऍहन जमाऍ *kēkara ehana jamāe,* who has such a son-in-law (Vid. lxxxi. 4) ?

ककरा दे कं जोगिया जाँजरि भेजब समाद *kak^arā dĕ ke jogiyā jā̃jarⁱ bhējab samād,* having given whom (*i.e.,* by means of whom) shall we send word to Jogiyā Jā̃jari.

लुबुधल नयन हटय के पार *lubudhala nayana haṭaya kē pāra,* who can turn aside a greedy eye ? (Vid. iv. 3).

I have not come across any instances of the honorific forms in literature, but they are occasionally heard colloquially.

164. The inanimate interrogative pronoun is कि *ki* or की *kī,* what ? It is often written किञ *kia* or किए *kiē,* especially in poetry. Its declension is quite irregular, and is as follows :—

Singular.

Nom. कि *ki,* की *kī,* or किञ *kia,* what ?

Acc. कथी कें, *kathī kĕ,* or की *kī.* what ?

Instr. कथीं *kathī̃.* कथी में *kathī sĕ.* by what ?

Dat. कथी लें *kathī lai.* किऍ *kiai.* किए *kiē,* or किऍ *kie.* to or for what ? why ?

Abl. कथी सें *kathī sĕ.* from what ?

Gen. कथीक *kathīk,* of what ?

Loc. कथी में *kathī mĕ,* in what ?

Plural wanting. Note the form of the Dative. This case has many variations. I have noted कि ला *ki lā,* कि लें *ki lai,* की ला *kī lā,* की लें *kī lai,* कथी ला *kathī lā,* कथी लें *kathī lai.* लें *lai* is often written लय *lay* or लाऍ *lae,* and instead of कथी *kathī,* we often have कथि *kathi.* Like the dative, the instrumental कथीं *kathī̃* is used to mean 'why ? '

Examples of this pronoun are :—

कि कहब तनिक ३.ब्याने *ki kahaba tanika geānē*, what shall I say (about) his wisdom ? (Vid. xxii. 2).

अपनेक बकरी की भेल *apᵃnek bakᵃrī kī bhēl*, what has happened to your goat ?

की ंक *kī chaik*, what is it ?

किय भेल *kia bhēl*, what has happened ?

किय कहौ ंं मुसाङ्र *kia kahau, hē musāhᵘ*, O Musāhu, what have you to say ?

किर विभाता लिखि मोहि देल *kiē bidhātā likhi mohi dēl*, why hath God written (it) for me (in my fate) ? (Vid. lvii. 1).

कथी में पानि लाप्रल ंं *kathī mē pāni lāel chāh*, in what have you brought the water ?

कथीं हमरा चोर बनबैछी *kathī hamᵃrā cōr banᵃbaichī*, why do you make me out a thief ?

कथि लए कंश पटकलंं मोहि *kathi lae kaṁśu patakalāha mōhi*, why, O Kaṁśa, didst thou dash me down (Manbōdh's *Harivaṁśa*. i. 37).

फोटरा गीदर कथि ला मरद औतार लेलें *phoṭᵃrā gīdar kathi lā marad autār lēlē*, O Phoṭᵃrā, the jackal, why has a man taken your form ?

क्यो कह नन्द महर किए मान *kyō kaha nanda mahara kie māna*, others (*lit.* some) said. 'Why does King Nanda agree ?' (Manbōdh. vii. 45).

INDEFINITE PRONOUNS.

165. These are केओ *keo*, anyone, someone ; किछ *kichᵃ*, anything, something ; and केएक *kaiek*, several.

166. कंञो *keo*, anyóne, someone, appears under various forms. I have noted कंञो *keŏ*, क्यो *kyŏ*, and कंञञो *keao*. In old poetry we sometimes meet केदुङ *kĕduhu*.

167. When used as an adjective, it usually takes the form कोनो *kŏno* or कौनो *kauno*, but we sometimes find कंञो *keo* used instead.

The following are examples of its use as an adjective :—

कोनो नेना नहिं आग्ल *kŏno nenā nahĭ āel*, no boy came.

कोनो गटहस्थक फुलवाड़ी में *kŏno grhasthak phulᵃwārī mẽ*, in the garden of a certain householder.

कोनो बातक मन में अंदेशा मति राखो *kŏno bātak man mẽ andĕśā matĭ rākhī*, do not have anxiety in your mind about anything.

कौनो मुसहर ने घर से होइत अछि बाहिर *kauno musahar nĕ ghar se hŏit achĭ bāhir*, no Musahar comes out of the house.

कौनो बात के हरकति नहिं *kauno bāt kĕ harᵃkatĭ nahĭ*, there is no inconvenience for (want of) anything.

कंञो अपूर्ब ढंगक लोक *keo apūrb ḍhaṅgak lōk*, a man of some extraordinary kind, or some man of an extraordinary kind.

It will be seen that when used as an adjective, it can refer to inanimate objects as well as animate ones.

168. When used as a substantive, it has an oblique form ककरङ *kakᵃrahū*, often written ककरो *kakᵃrō*. Its genitive is ककर *kakᵃrō*. In poetry we sometimes find a form काङ *kāhu* instead of ककरङ *kakᵃrahū*, with a genitive काङक *kāhuka*. It is therefore thus declined :—

Singular.

Nom.	केओ *keo,* केऔ *keū,* क्यो *kyū,* or केअओ *keaō,*	anyone, someone.
Acc.	ककरऊ *kak^arah^ū,* or ककरऊ कें *kak^arah^ū kē*	someone, or anyone.
Inst.	ककरऊ सें *kak^arah^ū sā,* by anyone, etc.	
Dat.	ककरऊ *kak^arah^ū,* or ककरऊ कें *kak^arah^ū kē*	to anyone. etc.
Abl.	ककरऊ सें *kak^arah^ū sā,* from anyone. etc.	
Gen.	ककरो *kak^arō,* of anyone, etc.	
Loc.	ककरऊ में *kak^arah^ū mē.* in anyone, etc.	

The plural is the same as the singular. ' ककरो *kak^arō* may be used for ककरऊ *kak^arah^ū* throughout.

Examples of the use of this pronoun are :—

केओ नहिं आएल *keo nahi̇̄ āel.* no one came.

क्यो घर थंगना केअओ दुआरि *kyū ghara āganā keao duāri,* some (danced) in the courtyard of the house and some in the doorway (Manbōdh's *Harivaṁsā.* ii. 45).

निज भुज बल ककरऊ नहिं गनए *nija bhuja bala kakarahū nahi̇̄ ganae,* (on account of) the strength of their own arms they esteem no one (Manbōdh. vi. 33).

किछु नहिं ततऊ कांङ सों भेल *kichu nahi̇̄ tatahū kāhu sō bhela* from that quarter nothing (*i.e..* no help) came from anyone (Manbōdh, i. 7).

क्यो नहिं मानए कांङ्क ऽटल *kyū nahi̇̄ mānae kāhuku haṭalu,* no one heeds the remonstrances of anyone (Manbōdh, iv. 17).

169. The indefinite pronoun inanimate is किछु *kich^u* or किच्छु *kicch^u*. It means 'anything' and 'something.' When it means 'anything,' the oblique form is the same as the nominative, but

when it means 'something' its oblique form is कथू *kathū*. We therefore have the following declensions :—

170. किछु *kich^u*. or किच्छु *kicch^u* anything.

Nom.   किछु *kich^u*. anything.

Acc.   किछु कें *kich^u kē̃*, anything.

Inst.   किछु सें *kich^u sā̃*, by anything.

Dat.   किछु कें *kich^u kē̃*, to anything.

Abl.   किछु सें *kich^u sā̃*, from anything.

Gen.   किछुक *kichuk*, of anything.

Loc.   किछु में *kich^u mē̃*, in anything.

171. किछु *kich^u*. or किच्छु *kicch^u* something.

Nom.   किछु *kich^u*, something.

Acc.   कथू कें *kathū kē̃*, something.

Inst.   कथू सें *kathū sā̃*, by something.

Dat.   कथू कें *kathū kē̃*, to something.

Abl.   कथू सें *kathū sā̃*, from something.

Gen.   कथूक *kathūk*, of something.

Loc.   कथू में *kathū mē̃*, in something.

Examples of the use of this pronoun are :—

ओहि ग्राम में ककरो किछु नहि छैक *oh^i grām mē̃ kak^{a}rō kich^u nah^i chaik*, in that village no one has anything.

किछु अमोट पठबिहँ *kich^u amōṭ paṭhabihă*, send (me) some mango conserve.

ओ औखध कथू में धेल होतैक *ō aukhadh kathū mē̃ dhail hotaik*, that medicine must be put into something.

172. The Indefinite pronoun केप्क *kaʾek*, some, several, is an adjective, and is not declined. An example of its use is :—

तोचरा केप्क कथा सभ सिखाप दिञ्ङ *tohᵃra kaiek kathā sabh sikhāe diuhᵘ*. I will teach you several matters.

DERIVATIVE PRONOMINAL FORMS.

173. The following table gives in a succinct shape the various derivative pronominal forms. It explains itself, and further comment is unnecessary :—

	Near Demonstrative.	Remote Demonstrative.	Interrogative.	Relative.	Correlative.
	ई *i*, this.	ओ *ō*, that.	के *kē*, who?	जे *jē*, who, which.	से *sē*, that.
Time.	एखन *ekhun*, now.	तखन *takhun*, then.	कखन *kukhun*, when?	जखन *jakhun*, when.	तखन *takhun*, then.
Place.	एतय *etuy*, here.	ओतय *otuy*, there.	कतय *katay*, where?	जतय *jatay*, where.	ततय *tutuy*, there.
	एम्हर *ēmhur*, hither.	ओम्हर *ōmhur*, thither.	केम्हर *kēmhur*, whither?	जेम्हर *jēmhur*, whither.	तेम्हर *tēmhur*, thither.
Manner.	एना *ēnā*, thus.	ओना *ōnā*, in that way.	केना *kēnā*, how?	जेना *jēnā*, as.	तेना *tēnā*, so.
Likeness.	एहन *ehun*, or ऐसन *aisun*, like this.	ओहन *ohun*, like that.	केहन *kehun*, like what?	जेहन *jehun*, like as.	तेहन *tehun*, like the same.
Quantity or Number.	एतक *utek*, this much.	ओतेक *otek*, that much.	कतक *kutek*, how much?	जतेक *jatek*, as much.	ततेक *tatek*, so much.

PART III.

CONJUGATION.

—●●—

CHAPTER I.

PRELIMINARY.

A. General Remarks.

174. The conjugation of the verb forms the most complicated part of Maithilī Grammar. Like the verbs of many partially cultivated languages, it has few parts for which there are not two or three optional forms. These are not local peculiarities. but may often be used by the same speaker as his fancy or as the rhythm of the sentence dictates. In many cases I cannot find that they represent different shades of meaning.

175. Maithilī verbs may conveniently be divided into the two classes of *Transitive* and *Intransitive*. These differ in the conjugation of the tenses formed from the past participle. In the paradigms of the regular verb, the verb देखब *dēkhab*, to see, will be used as the example of a transitive verb, and the verb सुतब *sūtab*, to sleep, as the example of an intransitive verb. It will be observed that in both these verbs the root-vowel is long, and it must be carefully remembered that in the conjugation of all such verbs, the root-vowel is liable to be shortened, under the rules given in § 32 and ff. *ante*. It is most important to bear this in mind, as the whole system of conjugation is full of it.

176. There is one exception to this rule of the shortened antepenultimate. and this is that when ऐ *ai*, or औ *au*, is *final*. it counts as only one syllable (even when written अइ *ai*, अए *ae*, or अउ *au*, अओ *ao*, respectively) and not as two (see §§ 13, 33 *ii*). Thus under the general rule. we should expect the *ē* in the form देखै *dēkhai*, to be shortened ; but it is not. The reason for this apparent irregularity is that in verbal forms a final ऐ *ai* always

represents an older अहि *ah*ⁱ, and a final औ *au* always represents
an older अहु *ah*ᵘ, each of which. under the rule, counts only as
one syllable. देखे *dēkhai* is for देखहि *dēkhah*ⁱ, and देखौ *dekhau* is
for देखहु *dekhah*ᵘ, and in both of these older forms the long *ē* is
quite regular. The apparent exception disappears when ऐ *ai* or
औ   ceases to be final. Thus in देखैक *dekhaik* (for देखहिक
dekhahik) and देखौक *dekhauk* for देखहुक *dekhahuk*), the shortening
of the *ē* to *e* is quite regular.

B. Root. Verbal Nouns and Participles.

177. It will be more convenient to deal with the finite tenses
after we have described the root and the various verbal nouns
and participles. The **Root** of every verb is the same as the
shortest form of the second person non-honorific of the Old Present.
Thus the 2nd pers. non-hon. Old Present of देखब *dēkhab*, to see,
is देख *dēkh*, which is also the root.

178. The **Verbal nouns** are three in number.

(*a*) The first verbal noun is formed by adding इ ⁱ to the
root. Thus देखि *dēkh*ⁱ the act of seeing (see § 57). The final इ ⁱ
is often omitted in writing and pronunciation, so that we have
देख *dēkh* instead of देखि *dēkh*ⁱ. Its oblique form is देखे *dēkhai* or
देखँ *dēkha*, and the rules for its declension together with examples
are given in § 80 *ante*. Some roots ending in vowels are irregular
in the formation of the first verbal noun.

179. (*b*) The second verbal noun is usually formed by adding
अब *ab* to the root (see § 67) and is generally employed as the infinitive: thus देखब *dēkhab*. the act of seeing, to see. Its oblique form is देखबा *dekh°bā*, and the rules for its declension
together with examples are given in § 81 *ante*.

Verbs whose roots end in आ *ā* form their infinitives in एब
eb. Thus from जा *jā*, we have जाएब *jāeb*, to go.

Those whose roots end in आब *āb*, also form their infinitives
in एब *eb*, but with the elision of the ब *b* of the root. Thus

from the root पाब *pāb*, obtain, we have the infinitive पाएब *pāeb*, to obtain. In poetry we often find ओब *ob* instead of एब *eb* in this case. Thus पाओब *pāob*.

Those verbs whose roots end in ि *i* or ी *ī*, form the infinitive in अब *ab* or उब *ub*. Thus, सि *si*, sew, makes सिअब *siab* or सिउब *siub*.

Those verbs whose roots end in ू *ū*, form the infinitive in अब *ab* or ीब *ib*. Thus चू *cū*, drip, makes चूअब *cūab*, or चूीब *cūib*, to drip.

Those verbs whose roots end in ो *ō*, form the infinitive in अब *ab* or एब *eb*. Thus the root धो *dhō*, wash, makes धोअब *dhōab* or धोएब *dhōeb*, to wash.

Irregular are :—

✓ हो *hō*, become, Infinitive होएब *hōeb* or हैब *haib*.

✓ दे *dē* give, Infinitive देब *dēb*.

✓ ले *lē* take, Infinitive लेब *lēb*.

This verbal noun is derived from the Sanskrit future passive participle in तव्य *tavya*, and is hence employed in the formation of the future tense.

189. (c) The third verbal noun is formed by adding अल *al* to the root (see § 63). thus देखल *dēkhal*, the act of seeing. The oblique form is देखला *dēkhᵃlī*, and the rules for its declension together with examples are given in § 81, *ante*. This verbal noun is generally the same as the past participle, but when the latter is irregular the verbal noun sometimes takes the regular form. Thus the ✓ जा *jā*, go, has its past participle (irregular) गेल *gēl*, but its third verbal noun is जाएल *jāel*. From this example it will be seen that (compare the second verbal noun), it ends sometimes in एल *el* instead of अल *al*. The rule is the same as in the case of उब *ub*.

The instrumental or locative of this verbal noun (or perhaps of the past participle) in अल *al*, is often used absolutely to indicate continued action. Thus :—प्रक गमारि गोश्वारिनि माथ पर मटकुरी घेलें चलि जाइबलि *ek gamᾱrⁱ goᾱrinⁱ māth par maṭᵃkurī dhailē calⁱ jᾱichalⁱ*, a foolish milkmaid, *by placing a curd-pot on her head*, was going along. That is to say, she was going along with a curd-pot on her head.

Similarly we have from the √ ले *lē*, take, लेलें जाइप्रब *lēlē jᾱeb*, to take away with one, लेलें श्राप्रब *lēlē ᾱeb*, to bring with one. In such common phrases न *n* is often substituted for ल *l*, so that we have लेनें जाप्रब *lēnē jᾱeb* or even नेनें श्राप्रब *nēnē ᾱeb*. These forms are different in meaning from forms such as लै जाप्रब *lai jᾱeb* (Hindi ले जाना *lē jᾱnᾱ*) to take away or लै श्राप्रब *lai ᾱeb* (Hindi ले आना *lē ᾱnᾱ*) or लाप्रब *lᾱeb* (Hindi लाना *lᾱnᾱ*) to bring. They correspond rather to the Hindi लिये जाना *liye jᾱnᾱ*, to take away *with one*.

Examples of such forms are :—

हमरा समाद नेहर लेनें जाह्ड *humarō samᾱda naihara lēnē jᾱhū*, take away with you a message for my father's house also (*Vid.* lxxix. 10).

अहिरा गोश्वार समाद नेनें अबैत छैक *ahⁱrᾱ goᾱr samᾱd nēnē abait chaik*, Ahirā Goār is bringing the news with him.

लै जाह मलहेस कें ... कचे बांस के फठा सौं पीठि छोदारि देब *lai jᾱh sulᵃhēs kē ... kacē bᾱs ke phaṭhᾱ saū p ṭhi adᵃrⁱ deb*, take away Salhēs ... with a split piece of green bamboo flay his back. (बांस के *bᾱs ke* is not a Maithili form. It is borrowed, as often happens in folktales, from another dialect, *viz.*, Bhojpuri. The correct Maithili would be बांसक *bᾱsak* or बांस केर *bᾱs kēr*.)

जकर बंटुलो लाप्रल तकर तिरिश्रा केहन सुरखी *jakar beduli lᾱel takar tⁱrⁱᾱ kᵉhan sᵘrᵃkhī*, how fair must the woman who owns the spangle which you brought !

181. The **Noun of Agency**, corresponding to the Hindi noun in वाला *wālā*, is formed by adding बाह *bāh* or वाह *wāh* to the root. Thus देखबाह *dekh*ᵃ*bāh* or देखवाह *dekh*ᵃ*wāh*, a seer, one who sees. See § 72.

182. The **Present Participle** is formed by adding ऐत *ait*, often written अइत *ait* or अयित *ayit*, to the root (see § 64). Thus देखैत *dekhait*, देखइत *dekhait*, or देखयित *dekhayit*, seeing. The ऐ *ai* of this termination is very unstable. Thus with verbs whose roots end in a long vowel, the termination becomes इत *it*, as in जाइत *jāit*, going ; होइत *hōait*, or होइत *hōit*, becoming. The √ सि *si*, sew, has सिऐत *siait*, सिअत *siut*, and सिइत *siit*, but √ पी *pī*, drink, makes पिबैत *pibait*, just as √ पाब *pāb*, obtain, has पबैत *pabait*. The √ दे *dē*, give, and the √ ले *lē*, take, have, respectively, दैत *dait* and लैत *lait* for their present participles. In the Past Conditional tense, which is formed from this participle, the ऐत *ait* is, as a rule, similarly weakened. Thus देखितहुँ *dekhitah*ᵘ, (if) I had seen.

183. By adding the oblique termination हिं *h*ⁱ to the weakened present participle we get a form called the "**Adverbial Participle.**" Thus देखितहिं *dekhitah*ⁱ, on seeing, in the act of seeing, immediately on seeing, equivalent to the Hindī देखते-ही *dēkh*ᵃ*tē-hī*. The following are examples of the employment of these participles :—

कनैत खिजैत धामी आएल *kanait* (√ कान *kān*) *khijait* (√ खीज *khīj*) *dhāmī āel*, Dhāmī came weeping and feeling angry (note the shortening of the antepenultimate vowel).

हमरा सबहिक देखैत स्वामि-धन वृथा नष्ट होइछ *ham*ᵃ*rā sub*ᵃ*hik dekhait swāmi-dhan vṛthā naṣṭ hōich*, in our presence [*lit.* (in the) seeing of us] our master's property is being destroyed.

दीना राम के धरितहिं भद्रीक एहुनी केहुनी छुटि गेल *dinā rām kē dharitah*ⁱ *bhadrīk ehunī kehunī chuṭ*ⁱ *gēl*, immediately on (Phoṭ*ᵃ*rā's) seizing Dīnā Rām, Bhadri's knees and elbows were freed.

184. The Past Participle is usually formed by adding ਅਲ *al* to the root (see § 68). When the root ends in a vowel, or in ਆਬ *āb*, the vowel of the suffix is liable to change, much as the termination ਅਬ *ab* of the second verbal noun is changed. Thus :—

Verbs whose roots end in ਆ *ā*, add ਏਲ *el*. Thus √ ਘਬੜਾ *ghab^arā*, to be agitated, past participle ਘਬੜਾਏਲ *ghab^arāel*.

Verbs whose roots end in ਆਬ *āb*, add ਔਲ *ol*. Thus, from √ ਪਾਬ *pāb*, obtain, ਪਾਔਲ *pāol*.

Verbs whose roots end in ਿ *i* or ੀ *ī*, add ਅਲ *al* or ਉਲ *ul*. Thus from √ ਸਿ *si*, sew, ਸਿਅਲ *sial* or ਸਿਉਲ *siul*, from √ ਪੀ *pī*, drink, ਪੀਉਲ *pīul*.

Verbs whose roots end in ਉ *ū* take ਅਲ *al* or ਇਲ *il*. Thus, from √ ਚੂ *cū*, drip, ਚੂਅਲ *cūal* or ਚੂਇਲ *cūil*.

Verbs whose roots end in ਓ *ō* take ਅਲ *al* or ਏਲ *el*. Thus, from √ ਧੋ *dhō*, wash, ਧੋਅਲ *dhōal* or ਧੋਏਲ *dhōel*.

Six verbs have irregular past participles as follows :—

√ ਕਰ *kar*, do	Past Participle	ਕੈਲ *kail*.
√ ਧਰ *dhar*, seize, place	..	ਧੈਲ *dhail*.
√ ਮਰ *mar*, die	.,	ਮਰਲ *maral* or ਮੁਇਲ *muil*.
√ ਦੇ *dē*, give	..	ਦੈਲ *dēl*.
√ ਲੇ *lē*, take	.,	ਲੈਲ *lēl*.
√ ਹੋ *hō*, become	..	ਭੈਲ *bhēl*.

The past participle ਭੈਲ *bhēl*, added to another past participle, imparts to it more of the character of an adjective, and, at the same time, adds completeness to the idea. Thus, ਸੂਤਲ ਭੈਲ *sūtal bhēl*, asleep ; ਦੇਖਲ ਭੈਲ *dēkhal bhēl*, seen.

The instrumental of the past participle is employed in conjugation to form the perfect and pluperfect tenses.

I have not come across many good instances in literature of the use of the past participle as an adjective. It is, of course,

15

extremely commonly employed in the formation of the tenses. The
following may be taken as examples of the adjectival use :—

एक गरीब परोसिया जाड़क मारल घर सँ निकसि आएल, *ek garib
parosiyā jāṛak māral ghar sā̃ nikas*[i] *āel*, a poor neighbour.
struck of (*i.e.* by) cold. came forth from (his) house.

एक कंगाल कोनो पहुँचल अतीथि सँ पुछलक, *ek kaṅgāl kōno pahū̃-
ral atīth*[i] *sā̃ puchalak*, a beggar once asked from a certain
arrived pilgrim (*i.e.* a pilgrim who had arrived).

185. **The Conjunctive Participle** corresponds to the Hindi
देख कर *dēkh kar*, having seen, and is properly the same in form
as the first verbal noun. Thus, देखि *dēkh*[i] (or देख *dēkh*), having
seen. This is the form we generally find in poetry or proverbs.
but in the modern language it is usual to add the suffixes कें *ke*.
कै *kai*, कँ *kā̃*, or कैकँ *kaikā̃*. Thus देखि कें *dēkh*[i] *ke*. देखि कै *dēkh*[i]
kai, देखि कँ *dēkh*[i] *kā̃*, or देखि कैकँ *dēkh*[i] *kaikā̃*. having seen. A
poetical form of कँ *kā̃* is कहुँ *kah*[u]. thus डूबि कहुँ *dūb*[i] *kah*[u], having
dived. The following verbs have irregular conjunctive participles.
Only the short form is given in each case. The suffixes can be
added as usual :—

✓ कर *kar*, do Conj. Part. करि *kar*[i], कें *ke*. कै *kai*, or कय *kay*.
                            कए *kae*, कँ *kā̃*.

✓ धर *dhar*, seize.   ..   धरि *dhar*[i], धै *dhai*, or धय *dhay*. धए
   place.   *dhae*, धँ *dhā̃*.

✓ आ *ā*, come   ..   आबि *āb*[i], आइ *āi*, or आय *āy*.

✓ दे *dē*, give   ..   दे *dē*, दै *dai*, दय *day*, दए *dae*. देइ *dei*.
                            दँ *dā̃*.

✓ ले *lē*, take   ..   ले *lē*, लै *lai*, लय *lay*, लए *lae*, लेइ *lei*.
                            लँ *lā̃*.

✓ हो *hō*, become   ..   होइ *hoi*, भै *bhai*. भय *bhay*, भए *bhae*.

C. Finite Tenses.

186. **Gender.**—As in the case of nouns, the Maithilī verb
has two genders, Masculine and Feminine. Feminine forms are,

as a rule. only used when the subject is a feminine animate being.
The first person never shows any distinction of gender, nor do
those forms (see § 188, below) in which respect is shown to the
object. It follows that only those forms of the 2nd and the 3rd
persons, whose objects are non-honorific (Groups 1 and II below),
ever change for the feminine gender. Even in these persons there
are many forms which are of common gender.

187. **Long and Redundant Forms.**—Verbs have short,
long, and redundant forms just like nouns. I have not discovered
any difference in their meaning. The long form is most often
made by adding ऐ *ai* to the short form, and the redundant form
by adding क *k* to the long form. Thus we have (short form) देखेची
dekhaichī, I see, of which the long form is देखेिचऐ *dekhaichiai*, and
the redundant form is देखेिचऐक *dekhaichiaik*. Similarly, we have
(short form) देखलक *dekhᵃlak*, he saw, long form देखलकै *dekhalᵃkai*,
redundant form देखलकैक *dekhalᵃkaik*. In some forms of the second
person the long form is made by adding अँह *āh* or अझ *ahᵘ* and the
redundant form by adding अहँक *ᵃhāk* or अझक *ᵃhuk* with variations of spelling, which will appear in the paradigms. Thus,
देख *dēkh*, thou seest, long form देखँह *dēkhāh* or देखझ *dēkhahᵘ*, redundant form देखँहक *dᵣkhᵃhāk* or देखझक *dᵣkhᵃhuk*.

These long and redundant forms are confined to those groups
of inflexions in which the object is non-honorific (*vide* § 188).
Even then, there is no long or redundant form for the third person
when the subject is honorific. They are thus confined to the
following cases.

First and second persons—Subject non-honorific, object non-
honorific (Group I), or subject honorific, object non-honorific (Group II).

Third person—Subject non-honorific, object non-honorific
(Group I).

These groups are described below in § 188.

Examples of the employment of these long and redundant
forms are as follows :—

1st Person. Short Form :—मारब धनुखा देब खँसाब, *mārab*

dhannkhā, dēb khāsāy. I will strike him (with an arrow) from the bow, I will fell him.

Long Form:—प्रि बेरिया मांरबे धरती देबे लोटाय, *eh¹ beriyā mǎr⁰buī, dhar⁰tī dēbuī lot⁰y,* at this time I will strike him, I will cause him to roll upon the ground.

Redundant Form :—तिहि ठ.म दे्वेक धुनी ह्ँसाय, *tⁱhⁱ ʈhǎm debaⁱk dhunī khāsⁿy,* at that place we shall set (*lit.* cause to fall) our fire (on the ground).

3rd Person.   Short Form :—घड़ि प्रक चलबे. पहर बिति ग्ल *ghaṭⁱ ek cal⁰bē puhar bit̃ⁱ gēl,* after travelling a few (*lit.* one) half-hours, a watch (of the day) passed.

Long Form :—तखन गेलै गंगुआ हजमुआ, *takh⁰n gēlaⁱ Gāgnā hⁱja-muā,* then Gangū the barber went.

Redundant Form.—सात नींदे सुतलि छलैक फेकुनी कांचे नींद में उठलैक चिहाय, *sāt nī̃dē sūtalⁱ chalⁿⁱk phekunī, kǎcē nī̃d mē̃ uṭh⁰laⁱk cihⁿy,* Phekuni was sleeping in seven sleeps (at once), and in drowsiness she started up.

188.   **Number.   Non-honorific and Honorific forms.**— Before going further it must be explained once for all that the Maithilī verb does not change for number.   There is no distinction between singular and plural.   On the other hand, there is a distinction between the non-honorific and honorific forms (which, indeed, by derivation, are respectively singular and plural).   In the finite tenses there are thus four groups of forms for each person, according as the subject or as the object is treated honorifically.

These four groups are :—

(I)   Subject non-honorific ; object non-honorific. *E.g.,* he (a slave) or it sees him (a slave) or it.

(II)   Subject honorific ; object non-honorific. *E.g.,* he (a king) sees him (a slave) or it.

(III)   Subject non-honorific ; object honorific. *E.g.,* he (a slave) or it sees him (a king).

(IV)   Subject honorific ; object honorific. *E.g.,* he (a king) sees him (a king).

Except in the case of the 3rd person of group IV, all the

forms of groups III and IV (in which the object is honorific)
are made from the long forms of groups I and II (in which it is
non-honorific) respectively, by lengthening the final vowels when
necessary, and adding फ़ि *nh*[i].

In the case of the 3rd person of group IV, there is no long
form of the 3rd person of group II from which to make it. It is
therefore made from the short form of the 3rd person of group II,
in a manner similar to that of the formation of the other persons
of group IV.

Examples of these third and fourth groups are :—

1st person :   long form, groups I and II, देखिछिअइ *dekhaichiai*,
I see ; groups III and IV, देखिछिअइन्हि *dekhaichiainh*[i].

2nd person :   long form, group I, देखछहु *dekhaichhah*[u]. you
see ; group III, देखछहुन्हि *dekhaichahunh*[i].

2nd person :   long form, group II, देखिछिअइ *dekhaichiai*, you
(honorific) see ; group IV, देखिछिअइन्हि *dekhaichiainh*[i].

3rd person :   long form, group I, देखछइ *dekhaichai*, he sees ;
group III, देखछइन्हि *dekhaichainh*[i].

3rd person :   short form, group II, देखछथि *dekhaichath*[i], he
(honorific) sees ; group IV, देखछथीन्हि *dekhaichathinh*[i].

In the above explanations I have employed the words "slave"
and "king" to illustrate the non-honorific and honorific forms
respectively, but, in common use, the distinction is not nearly
so marked as this. As a practical guide, we may say that human
beings are generally referred to by honorific forms, unless they are
distinctly inferior, such as low-caste people, slaves, etc. On the
other hand, inanimate things and irrational animals are almost
always referred to as non-honorific.

In regard to Groups III and IV, I have said that the *object*
must be honorific. The object may be the direct object or may be
the indirect object. Either has the same effect on the verbal form.
Thus, in the second, fourth and sixth of the following examples,
of the use of these forms, the honorific object is indirect :—

**First person (Groups I and II) and second person (Group
II) (long forms)** (as will be seen from § 190, these three

are always the same in form). एहि बेरिया मारबै धरती देबै
लोटाय, *ehᶦ bᵉriyā mărᵃbai, dharᵃtī dēbai loṭāy,* this time
I will strike him and cause him to roll over (on) the
ground.

First person (Groups III and IV) and second person
(Group IV). सभ मशाला लक्ष्मी दाइ कें अपने चुप्पे देबैन्हि, *sᵤbh
maśālā Lachᵃmī Dᵃi kē ᵘpᵃne cuppē dᵉbainhᶦ,* your Honour
will give all the spices privately to (the respected)
Lakṣmī Dāi.

Second person (Group I) (long form). कोन दिसा के अबैत
होइ कहुहु बुझाय, *kōn disā kē abait hŏai kahᵤhᵘ bujhāy,* explain and tell in what direction he is coming.

Second person (Group III). कालू सदा अम्मा निरसो के कहहुन्हि
जोगिया जाई, *Kālū Sᵃdā Ammā Nirᵃsō kē kahᵃhūnhᶦ Jogiyā
jᵃī,* say to (the respected) Kālū Sadā and mother Nirsō,
'go to Jogiyā.'

Third person (Group I) (long form). ओकरा एहि तरहें
घबड़ाएल देखि कें एक मनुष्य० कहलकै, *okᵃrā ehᶦ tarᵃhē ghubᵃ-
rāel dēkhᶦ kᵃ ek mannṣya kᵃhalᵃkai,* seeing him (the fool)
thus agitated a certain man said to him —.

Third person (Group III). मोनशी कहलथीन्हि नहिं हौ, अर्जी
लिखैछी । ओ कहलकैन्हि तँ हमारो सही कै दिअ, *monᵃśī
kᵃhalᵃthīnhᶦ* (Group IV), '*nahᶦ hau, arjī likhaichī.*'
Ō kᵃhulᵃkainhᶦ, 'tā hamᵃrō sahī kai diᵃ, the (respected)
scribe I said (politely) to (the unknown and respected
stranger), 'it is not (what you think it is, —*hau* not *hai.*
see § 1J1), I am writing a petition.' He (*i.e.* the stranger
who was an impudent fool) said (to the respected scribe),
' then please to put my signature also.'

Third person (Group II) (short form). देहि दुनू भाइ छोड़ि
देलथि, *dēhᶦ dᵤnū bhᵃi chōrᶦ dēlathᶦ,* the two (famous)
brothers (the heroes of the story) left their bodies.

Third person (Group IV). कालू सदा दीना भद्री के बैसे देलथीन्हि,
Kālū Sᵃdā Dīnā Bhᵃdrī kē baisai delᵃthīnhᶦ, (the respect-

·ed) Kālū Sadā made (the two famous brothers) Dīnā and Bhadri sit down.

Another example occurs above under 'Third person (Group III).'

189. So far we have been dealing only with transitive verbs. Intransitive verbs have only an indirect object, and, in their case, the use of Groups III and IV is rather lax. They are, of course, employed when the indirect object is honorific, but they are also found when the verb has no object at all and when the *subject*, not the object is honorific. Thus : –

तखन गंगा-जी कहे लगलथीन्हि, *takhan Gaṅgā-jī kahai lagal*ᵘ*-thīnh*ⁱ, then they began to say to (the holy) Ganges.

बड़त दिन भेलेन्हि अहाँ लोकनि तकाजा नहि करैछिऐन्हि, *bahut din bhelainh*ⁱ *ahā̃ lok*ᵃ*ni tukājā nah*ⁱ *karaichiainh*ⁱ, many days (have) passed (since) you (*honorific*) have pressed (the respected Bhōlā Sāhu) (for the money he owes).

In the former of these two examples it will be seen that the honorific object is indirect. In the second example the close connection with a sentence having an honorific subject and an honorific direct object as well, is responsible for the form of भेलेन्हि *bhelainh*ⁱ.

Instances of intransitive verbs with an honorific subject are much more common, especially when the subject is plural. In fact we have here a survival of the old plural signification of these forms (see the first paragraph of § 188).

Thus :—

दीना भद्री मरि गेलेन्हि, *Dīnā Bhadrī mar*ⁱ *gelainh*ⁱ (Group III), Dīnā and Bhadrī are dead. Here, if the verb were transitive, the subject would be non-honorific, as the form belongs to Group III. In an intransitive verb it is honorific plural.

जाहि सँ नाम चलेन्हि से हमर किरिया करह, *jāh*ⁱ *sã̃ nām calainh*ⁱ *sē hamar kiriyā karah*, perform our funeral rites that our (famous) names may be current (*i.e.* endure).

कीनो धनिक कें दुद बेटा रहैन्हि । जखन उनक बाप मरि गेलथीन्हि

kōno dhanik kē dui bēṭā ,ahainh^i (Group III). *Jakh'n hunak b^ip mar^i gel^athinh^i*, to a certain (respected) rich man there were two (respected) sons. When the (respected) father of (the respected) them died ....

190. **Pers'n.**—It is in denoting the persons that the complex character of the Maithili verb is most manifest. There are many forms for each person. The following is a brief sketch of personal terminations.

In the first case we must note that the first person is the same whether the subject is honorific or not ; also that the second person honorific is always the same as the first person. Thus देखैची *dekhaichī* means I or we (non-honorific), or I or we (honorific) see, or thou (honorific) seest, or you (honorific) see.

191. **The rule of attraction.**—In the case of some of the personal terminations, there is an important rule to be applied. It is called *the rule of attraction*, and is peculiar to Bihārī. We have seen that when the object of a verb is honorific certain special forms are used. Similarly, there are special forms when the object is in the second person. These forms only occur in the case of forms with a non-honorific object whose terminations contain the letter ऐ *ai*, and are made by changing ऐ *ai* to औ *au*. Thus देखलक *dekh^alak*, देखलकै *dekhal^akai*, or देखलकैक *dekhal^akaik*, he saw, but देखलक *dekh^alak*, देखलकौ *dekhal^akau*, or देखलकौक *dekhal^akauk*, he saw *you*. The relationship of the second person with the object need not be very direct, as will be seen from the fourth of the following examples :—

सुरता नैना कें मारलकै, *Mur^atā nēnā kē măral^akai*, Murtā struck the boy.

सुरता तोहरा कें मारलकौ, *Mur^atā toh^arā kē măral^akau*, Murtā struck you.

ओकरा गाड़ी में कोन माल छै, *ok^arā gāṛī mē kōn māl chai*, what goods are there in his cart ?

तोहरा गाड़ी में कोन माल छौ *toh^arā gāṛī mē kōn māl chau*, what goods are there in your cart ?

Note further, as to spelling, that the ऐ *ai* is quite frequently ·written अइ *ai*, अए *ae* or even अय *ay*, so that instead of कै *chai* in the penultimate example we may have कइ *chai*, कए *chae* or कय *chay*. Similarly instead of औ *au*, we may have अउ *au* or अओ *ao*. Thus instead of कौ *chau* we sometimes see written कउ *chau* or कओ *chao*. Historically, these औ *au* terminations are contractions of अहु *ahᵘ*, and we sometimes come across this spelling, especially in poetry. Thus for दिऔ *diaᵘ*, let me give you, I have met दिअहु *diahᵘ*, which has the same meaning.

192. It will be remembered that the 2nd person honorific is always the same as the first person. With regard to this there is one reservation, viz., *that the rule of attraction does not apply to the second person.* Thus देखबिऔ *dekhᵃichiau*, means only ' I, or we. see you '; it does not mean ' you (honorific) see you. ' In the second person the termination औ *au* is only used to refer to the subject. Thus in the *Gīt Dīnā-bhadrī* (149), we have जेबौ जोगिया *jaibau Jogiyā jahā̃ yā*ᵐ, you will go to where is the village of Jogiyā. In the first person जेबौ *jaibau* would mean ' I will go to your (house, or some such word).' Moreover ' you see you ' would be an impossible idea in Maithilī. We should have to say ' you see (your) self, ' which is a different thing altogether and does not bring in the rule of attraction. It thus follows that the rule of attraction only applies to the first and third persons. Examples are :—

First person, देखलिऐ *dekhᵃliai*, देखलिऐक *dekhᵃliaik*, I or we saw ; देखलिऔ *dekhᵃliau* or देखलिऔक *dekhᵃliauk*, I or we saw you.

Third person, non-honorific subject, non-honorific object देखलकै *dekhalᵃkai* or देखलकैक *dekhalᵃkaik*, he or they saw ; देखलकौ *dekhalᵃkau* or देखलकौक *dekhalᵃkauk*, he or they saw you.

I have very rarely come across forms like देखलकौन्हि *dekhalᵃkaunhⁱ* (from देखलकैन्हि *dekhalᵃkainhⁱ*), he (non-honorific) saw you (honorific) (Group III), but I doubt if they were correct. I have never met such in conversation. At the same time it may be noted that in the present conjunctive there is a form in ओन्हि *aunhⁱ*, which is peculiar to this tense, and which has no special reference to the 2nd person. It has nothing to do with the rule of attraction.

On the other hand, just as a redundant form is obtained by changing ऐ *ai* to ऐक *aik*, so a redundant form is quite commonly made by changing औ *au* to औक *auk*. Thus the redundant form of देखलिऔ *dekh^aliau* is देखलिऔक *dekh^aliauk*. as in the above examples.

193. **Other Personal Terminations.**—Before taking up the general aspect of this question, we may notice the frequently occurring terminations अथि *athⁱ* and अन्हि *anhⁱ*. These are peculiar in the third person in the second group, in which the subject only is honorific. *In the tenses formed from the past participle,* अथि *athⁱ* is used only with transitive verbs, but अन्हि *anhⁱ* is not subject to this restriction.

In the case of intransitive verbs, we have आह *äh*, instead of अथि *athⁱ*, in the tenses formed from the past participle. But आह *äh* is not confined to the 3rd person. In the 3rd person it is honorific like अथि *athⁱ*, but it can also be employed for the second person *non-honorific*. Thus सुतलाह *sut^aläh* means either 'he or they (honorific) slept.' or else 'thou or you (non-honorific) slept.'

आह *äh*, is also used honorifically in the third person of the future of both transitive and intransitive verbs.

आह *äh* has a feminine form ईह *īh* or ईहि *īhⁱ*. Thus सुतलीह *sut^alih* or सुतलीहि *sut^alihⁱ*, she or they (fem.) (honorific) slept or thou or you (fem. non-hon.) slept. अथि *athⁱ* and अन्हि *anhⁱ* have no special feminine forms. They are of common gender.

We may give the following examples of the use of these terminations :—

अन्हि *anh*[i].

Past Conditional (formed from present participle)—ओतन्हि दुरागमन करैतन्हि जमैया जाँजरि, *autanh*[i] (intransitive), *durāgaman karaitanh*[i] (transitive) *jamaiyā Jā̃jar*[i] (if) (the two famous) sons-in-law had come, they would have performed (the ceremony of) *durāgaman* at Jānjari.

Past Indicative (formed from past participle)—बड़ फजैत दीना भद्री कैलन्हि दुनू भाइ, *bar phajhait Dinā Bhadrī kailanh*[i] (transitive) *dunū bhāi*. great indignity did the two (famous) brothers, Dinā and Bhadrī (to me).

Perfect (formed from past participle)—फेर ऐलन्हि अछि से देखलक लोग सभ, *pher ailanh*[i] *ach*[i] *sē dekhᵃlak lōg sabh*, the people saw (that) (the respected Dinā and Bhadrī) have come back.

In old poetry, this termination is often written as a suffix, without the disappearance of the initial अ *a*. Thus, we have in Manbōdh's *Haribans :—*

कनक मुकुट झलकल-अन्हि द्वार, *kanaka mukuṭa jhalakala-anhi dwāra*, the golden diadem gleamed in the doorway.

जनि झपटल-अन्हि बाज बटेरि, *jani jhᵃpaṭala-anhi bāju baṭēri*, as a falcon swooped upon a quail

In the old poetry we even find this termination suffixed to the termination आइ *āh* as in the following passage from the same poem :—

कहु खन नाचथि गावथि गीत ।

खैताइ-अन्हि से परलए बीत ॥

Kahu khana nācathi gābathi gīta.

Khaităha-anhi sē paralae bīta.

(The child Kṛṣṇa) sometimes danceth and sometimes singeth songs. (if) he will eat (transitive future), a whole age passeth away (*i.e.,* an age used to pass even in getting him away from his play to eat).

So we have it added to the termination ष्षथि *athⁱ*, in the following from the same :—

पूष्षथि-ष्न्हि तो भद्वा कह्ब, *pūchathi-anhi taũ bhadⁿbā kahaba,* if he, (Kṛṣṇa) ask you, then you will say that it is an unlucky day.

ष्षथि *athⁱ*.

Old Present (formed from the root) :—

कनक धामी के कहिहौन्हि बुभाय । दुनू बेटीक कहिहौन्हि जे कोह्बर कर्ष्थ तैयार । दुनू जमाय मारल गेलैन्हि ।

Kanak Dhāmī kē kahihaunhⁱ bujhⁿy, dunū bēṭīk kahihaunhⁱ jē koh*bar karathⁱ (transitive) *taiyār, dunū jamāy mārul gelainhⁱ,*

Tell and explain to (the respected) Kanak Dhāmī. Tell him that the two (respected) sons-in-law for whom he (the respected one) is preparing the marriage bowers of his two daughters, have been slain.

कालू सदा बैठल रहथि दरबाजा, *Kālū Sadā baiṭhul rahathⁱ* (intransitive) *darⁿbⁿjā* (the respected) Kālū Sadā was (*lit.* remains) seated at his doorway.

Past indicative (formed from past participle) :—

देहि दुनू भाइ छोड़ि देलथि, *dēhⁱ dunū bhāⁱ chōⁱ dēlathⁱ,* the two (famous) brothers left their bodies

ष्षाह *āh. Third person honorific.*

Future Indicative (transitive or intransitive) :—राजा भीम सेन कह्ताह हाल हम नहिं जानी, *rājā Bhīm Sain kah*tāh hāl, ham nahⁱ jānī,* Rājā Bhīm Sēn will tell (transitive) the affair, we do not know.

जाहि तरह जाति में रह्ताह से उपाय के देबहीन्हि, *jⁿhⁱ tarah jātⁱ mē rah*tāh sē upⁿy ke deb*hinhⁱ,* you will arrange so that they may remain (intransitive) in caste.

Past Indicative (only intransitive) :—भद्रीक ब्रागू सच्हेस मै गेलाँच ठाढ़ि, *Bhadrik āgū Salhēs bhai ge'āh ṭhārhⁱ*, before Bhadrī (the famous) Salhēs took his stand.

Feminine examples are :—डेगे डेगे चल्लीच जोजन भरि जाद जुमलीच ब्रपना फुन्नवाड़ी, *ḍēge ḍēge calᵃlih, jōjun bharⁱ jāi jumᵃlih apᵃnā phulᵃwārī*, step by step she went, having gone a full league she arrived at her garden.

धामीक सबद् सुनि उठलीहि दीना भद्रीक माद चिहाय, *Dhāmik sabad sunⁱ uṭhᵃlih̄ⁱ Dīnā Bhadrik māi cihāy*, hearing Dhāmi's voice, the mother of Dīnā and Bhadrī started up.

Second person non honorific: कोन गरू परल जे सुतलाच खटबारि, *kaun garū paral jē sutᵃlāh khaṭᵃbārⁱ*, what calamity has befallen (you) that you are sleeping on your bed ?

194. **Tenses.** The tenses of the Maithilī verb are the same as in Bengali, and are conjugated very similarly in their main principles.

We may divide them into—

(a)—Tenses formed from the root.

(b)—The Future.

(c)—Tenses formed from the Present Participle.

(d)—Tenses formed from the Past Participle.

The first three classes are conjugated in the same way whether a verb is transitive or intransitive ; but the tenses formed from the past participle are conjugated differently according to whether the verb is transitive or intransitive. In this respect, we may note that the verb substantive is treated as intransitive.

The following is a list of the more usual tenses :—

(a) (1) Old Present Indicative

(2) Present Conditional

(3) Imperative

formed from the root.

(b) (4) Future Indicative

of mixed formation.

  (*c*) (5)   Past Conditional
       (6)   Present Indicative
       (7)   Imperfect Indicative
              formed from the present participle.
  (*d*) (8)   Past Indicative
       (9)   Perfect Indicative
      (10)   Pluperfect Indicative
              formed from the past participle.

195. I now proceed to give the personal terminations of these tenses in the case of regular verbs whose roots end in consonants. When a root ends in a vowel, the addition of the termination causes some anomalies which will be discussed under the head of Vocalic Roots in Chapter IV. Similarly, there are a few irregular verbs which will be specially dealt with in Chapter V.

Some of the examples which I give of the various terminations, are instances of these anomalous formations. I had to do this when no other examples were available. In such cases I have invariably drawn attention to the fact, or have given a reference to the section where the anomaly is dealt with.

When there are two or more forms in use for one person of one group or section of a group, I put the one most commonly employed first. The order of forms in the following paradigms has nothing to do with derivation. In fact, the oldest forms. being seldom employed, usually come last. For instance, the termination *iah*ᵘ of the long form of the first person, Groups I and II with the object in the second person, of the Old Present. is certainly the original of the termination *iau*. But I put *iau* first because it is the one commonly met with. *Iah*ᵘ is seldom heard. and the third termination given in the paradigms, *iŏ*, only occurs in poetry. Unless feminine forms are specially given, all forms are of common gender.

196. The three tenses formed from the root,—the Old Present, the Present Conditional. and the Imperative,—are all really variants of one tense. Custom has, however, ordained slight variations in the conjugation according to the use to which the tense is put. It will be seen (§ 201) that this tense is also employed as a future.

(*a*) (1) The **Old Present** is not much used now-a-days, except in poetry and proverbs and in idiomatic phrases, such as कौ कहौ *ki kahī*, what am I to say? It is conjugated by adding the personal terminations to the root direct. These are as follows :—

PERSON	SHORT FORM — GROUP I. (Subject: non-honorific. Object: non-honorific.)	SHORT FORM — GROUP II. (Subject: honorific. Object: non-honorific.)	LONG FORM — GROUP I. (Subject: non-honorific. Object: non-honorific.)	LONG FORM — GROUP II. (Subject: honorific. Object: non-honorific.)	REDUNDANT FORM — GROUP I. (Subject: non-honorific. Object: non-honorific.)	REDUNDANT FORM — GROUP II. (Subject: honorific. Object: non-honorific.)	REDUNDANT FORM — GROUP III. (Subject: non-honorific. Object: honorific.)	REDUNDANT FORM — GROUP IV. (Subject: honorific. Object: honorific.)
1	ĭ,		iai Or (with object in 2nd person). iau, iahu, or *iā		iaik. Or (with object in 2nd person). iauk.		iainhi	iainhi
2	(The bare root).	Same as 1st person.	āh, ahu, au ; fem. ahī, āhī.	Same as 1st person, but no forms for object in 2nd person.	ahāk, ahuk, ahīk,	Same as 1st person, but no forms for object in 2nd person.	ahānhi.	Same as 1st person.
3	ĭ. *u, *ū *ahī.	athī.	ai (ae). Or (with object in 2nd person.) au (or ahu).	......	aik. Or (with object in 2nd person.) auk.	......	ainhi.	athĭnhĭ. athānhĭ.

In the above, forms which are chiefly employed in poetry are marked with an asterisk Besides these we may mention a non-honorific first person singular in *ō* occasionally used by the vulgar, and an old form of the second person in *asi*, found in Vidyāpati. Thus:—

पुरबहि बन्दौं सुरुज *purubahi̐ bandō suruj*, in the East I worship the sun.

म्रगमद पंक करसि अंग राजा *mr̥ga-mada paṅka karasi aṅga rājā*, with paste of musk dost thou anoint (thy) limbs Vid. xii. 2)

As examples of the use of this tense, we may quote the following:—

First Person: मरौं पिञास पिञाबङ पानि, *marī piṅsa piñbahu pāni*, I die of thirst, give me water to drink (Vid. xii, 2).

      आज देखिहे सखि बड़ि अनुमनि सनि, *ājạ* (for *āja*) *dekhini sakhi bari anumani sani*, to-day, O friend, I see her very melancholy (Vid. xxxiv, 1).

      कहियो न जनिश्रो पँचा उधार, *kahiyō na janiaṅ* (√ *jān*) *paṅca udhār*, never do we know (of) borrowing or taking (things) on credit from you.

      देखिअ तुय अपरुब सभ साज, *d khiā tua aparuba sabha sāja*, I see thee arrayed in wondrous raiment (Vid. xii, 1).

      दौरी गाम सुनिश्रैक, *Dauri g-m suniaik*, I hear (the name of) the village Daurī.

Second Person:—(I have not come across any instance of the second person of this tense used in literature There are examples of this person in the Present Conditional, and in the Imperative.)

Third Person: नहिं नहिं करै नयन ढर लोरे, *nahi̐ nahi̐ karē nayana ḍhara lōrē*, she says 'no, no,' and tears flow from her eyes (Vid. xxviii 5).

साजनि ताक जिबन थिक सार । जे मन दइ करु पर उपकार *sājani tāka jibana thika sāra, jē mana dai karu para upakāra*, O friend, behold, his life is precious, who willingly rendereth assistance to others (Vid. iii, 3).

राङु दुरि बसु निश्रारो न आबथि तें नहिं करथि गरासे, *Rāhu dūri basu niaro na ābathi, tē nahi̐ karathi garāsē*, Rāhu (the demon of eclipse) (*i.e.*, her hair) dwelleth afar off, and doth not approach (the sun and moon, *i.e.*, her eyes), and therefore he doth not eclipse them (Vid. xiv, 8).

कटला तरु जक खसु अररॉय, *kaṭalā taru jaka khasu araṟāya*, she falls screaming like a severed tree (Man. ii, 52).

भनहिं बिद्यापति, *bhanahĩ Bidyāpati*, saith Vidyāpati (Vid. passim).

आगु आगु डोली चलॅ पाछू पाछू दुनू भाइ, *āgū āgū ḍolī calai*, *pāchū pāchū dunū bhāi*, in front go the litters (and) behind the two brothers.

हाथ माँथ मीड़ॅ पीटॅ, *hāth mãth miṟai piṭai*, she wrings her hands and beats her head (in sorrow).

दौरी गाम सुनिऐक बसैक हिरिया तमोलिनि जिरिया लोहाइनि, *Daurī gām suniaik basaik Hiriyā Tamōlin*[i] *Jiriyā Lohāin*[i], I hear (the name of) a village called Daurī, (where) dwell Hirā Tamōlini and Jīrā Lohāini.

इतनी लिखैक मिनतिया, *it*[a]*nī likhaik minatiyā*, so much (in the way of) respectful salutations he writes.

दीना भद्रीक कनैन्हि जोगिया दोस्त महीम, *Dīnā Bhadrīk kanainh*[ⁱ] (√ *kān*) *Jogiyā dōst mahīm*, the friends and lovers of (the respected) Dīnā and Bhadrī all weep in Jogiyā.

198. (*a*) (2). The **Present Conditional** is only a variant of the Old Present, from which it is derived. It prefers to substitute औ *au* for ऐ *ai*, in the third person. In this case the औ *au* (also written बऽ *ahu* or ओ *o*) does not indicate that the object is in the second person. The forms in ऐ *ai* of the Old Present are also occasionally met in this tense. The following are the terminations. Those marked with an asterisk are chiefly used in poetry :—

PERSON.	SHORT FORM.		LONG FORM.		REDUNDANT FORM.			
	GROUP I. (Subject: non-honorific. Object: non-honorific.)	GROUP II. (Subject: honorific. Object: non-honorific.)	GROUP I. (Subject: non-honorific. Object: non-honorific.)	GROUP II. (Subject: honorific. Object: non-honorific.)	GROUP I. (Subject: non-honorific. Object: non-honorific.)	GROUP II. (Subject: honorific. Object: non-honorific.)	GROUP III. (Subject: non-honorific. Object: honorific.)	GROUP IV. (Subject: honorific. Object: honorific.)
1	?	Same as 1st person.	Or (with object in 2nd person.) *iau, iahu,* *iä	Same as 1st person, but no forms for object in 2nd person.	Or (with object in 2nd person). *iauk* 〔*iaik*; *iauk*〕	Same as 1st person, but no forms for object in 2nd person.	*iainhí*	*iainhí.*
2	(The bare root).	Same as 1st person.	*ái, ahu, au;* fem. *ahé, áhé.*	Same as 1st person, but no forms for object in 2nd person.	*ahák, ahuk, ahik.*	Same as 1st person, but no forms for object in 2nd person.	*ahánhí.*	Same as 1st person.
3	*é,* **a,* **u,*	*athé, athu.*	*au, ahu, ô,* (sometimes *ai*).	...	*auk* (sometimes *aik*)	...	*ainhí auuhí.*	*athínhí, athänhí.*

The following are examples of the use of this tense :—

First person :—आठम दीन चोर, माल हाजिर करी नहिं हाजिर करी तो नौम दीन तोहरा सौ विबाह करी, *āṭham dīn cōr māl hājir karī* (future) ; *nahⁱ hājir karī* (pres. conditional), *tau naum dīn tohᵃrā saũ bibāh karī* (future), on the eighth day I will produce the thief (and) the stolen), property ; (if) I do not produce (them), then on the ninth day I will marry you.

की कहिऔक *kī kahiauk,* what am I to say (on your behalf).

Second person :—जखन अपने चाही तखन तोड़वा लेल जाई, *jakhan apᵃne cāhī, takhan torᵃwā lēl jāī,* when you, sir, may desire, then have (the fruit) plucked and take it away.

सत्य॰ पूबी *satya pūchī,* (if) your honour ask the truth.

Third person :—आगि लागल भोंपड़ी जे निकसे से लाभ, *agⁱ lāgal jhõpᵃṛī, jē nikᵃsē sē lābh,* when a cottage is on fire whatever may come out (may be rescued), that is (clear) profit.

कौन दिसा के अबैत होइ कहहु बुझाय, *kaun disā kē abait hŏai kahahᵘ bujhāy,* tell clearly in what direction he is (*lit.* may be) coming.

नहिं पतियाहु तो आबिहैं, *nahⁱ patiyāhᵘ* (√ *patiyā + ahᵘ*) *to ăbihẽ,* if she do not believe you, then come.

जाहि सँ नाम चलैन्हि से हमर किरिया करह, *jāhⁱ sằ nām calainhⁱ sē hamar kiriyā karăh,* perform our funeral rites that our name may endure.

199. (*a*) (3). The **Imperative** is again a variant of the Present Conditional. The first person usually ends in अ *ă*, instead of ई *ĭ*, although the latter is also used. There are a number of alternative forms of the second person. To these the termination न् *yă*, also employed for the future, is often added without affecting the sense. Terminations marked with an asterisk are chiefly used in poetry.

PERSON.	SHORT FORM.		LONG FORM.		REDUNDANT FORM.			
	GROUP I. (Subject: non-honorific. Object: non-honorific.)	GROUP II. (Subject: honorific. Object: non-honorific.)	GROUP I. (Subject: non-honorific. Object: non-honorific.)	GROUP II. (Subject: honorific. Object: non-honorific.)	GROUP I. (Subject: non-honorific. Object: non-honorific.)	GROUP II. (Subject: honorific. Object: non-honorific.)	GROUP III. (Subject: non-honorific. Object: honorific.)	GROUP IV. (Subject: honorific. Object: honorific.)
1	*ū* (sometimes *i*)		Or (with object in 2nd person.) *iau, iahᵘ, *iū* — *iui*		Or (with object in 2nd person.) *iaik* — *iauk* — *iaiuhⁱ*			
2	(The bare root.) also *ē*.	Same as 1st person.	*ăh, ahᵘ, au, aū;* fem. *ahĭ, ahⁱ*	Same as 1st person, but no forms for object in 2nd person.	*ahăk (ahŏk), ahuk, ahik, auk.*	Same as 1st person, but no forms for object in 2nd person.		
3	*ē, *ᵤ, *ᵤ.*	*athĭ, athᵘ.*	*au, ahᵘ, ŏ,* (sometimes *ai.*)	...	*auk,* (sometimes *aik.*)	...	*aunhⁱ* — *ahĭnhⁱ*	*athinhⁱ othĭnhⁱ*

The following are examples of the use of this tense:—

First Person :—चलू तौनू मामा भगिना कटैया सिकार, *calū tinū māmā bhaginā Kaṭaiyā sikār,* let us three, uncle and nephews, go to hunt in the Kaṭaiyā forest.

बाप माइ के कह्-गँ ठेकान, *bāp māi ke kahū-gā ṭhekān,* let us tell our father (and) mother our whereabouts.

तौर खँचि मुसाऊ बनियाँ के मारी, *tīr khaïc¹ Musāhu Baniyā ke mārī,* drawing an arrow let me kill Musāhu Baniyā.

किच्छु सीखि लेइ तँ पठाय दिऐक, *kicch⁴ sīkh¹ lēē, tā paṭhāy diaik,* let him learn something (first), and then let me send him.

Second Person :- जेहि मुँचे धैलें कटैया औहि मुँचे धर अपना बाप के, *jeh¹* (for *jāh¹*) *mūhē dhailē Kaṭaiyā, oh¹ mūhē dhar apᵃnā bāp ke,* with the mouth with which you (non-honorific) seized (me) (in) Kaṭaiyā, with the same mouth seize your own father (an abusive phrase).

अपना अपना घर में सुन्दर खाऐक करे-गँ, *apᵃnā apᵃnā ghar mē sunnar khāek karē-gā,* each in your own house prepare beautiful food. (A mother-in-law is addressing her daughters-in-law. Hence non-honorific terms are used).

आबि कै अप्पन मुदे बान्हू, *āb¹ kai appan mudai bānhū,* having come, bind your foe. (A wife is addressing her husband respectfully).

चलू सामी भोजन करू, *calū sāmī bhōjan karū,* come, my husband, make your meal.

एहन बात मति कहाह् बहुत तामस मति करह, *chan bāt·mat¹ kahāh, bahut tāmas mat¹ karāh,* say not such words, make not much anger. (One brother addresses another familiarly).

ताकह् ममा हरिन सुगरक ठाठ, *tākah⁴, mamā, harin sugarak ṭhāṭh,* look, uncle, for herds of deer and boar.

एक बेरि हुकुम दिह्, *ek bēr¹ hukum dih⁴,* give (me) the order but once (cf. the example of दिहँ *diā,* in § 200).

भनहिं विद्यापति सुनिऐ मनाइनि, *bhanahī Bidyāpati suniai Manāini,* saith Vidyāpati, 'hear, O Manāini.' (Vid. lxxxii., 8).

कहहक जे जातिक योगी छी, *kahᵃhăk jē jātik Jōyī chī,* say 'we are Jōgīs by caste.'

पुछहुक जे कोन लोग छी, *puchᵃhuk jē kōn lōg chī,* ask (them), 'what is your Honours' caste ? '

बहोरन ममा के लाबहोक बोलाय, *Bahōran mamā kē lăbᵃhŏk bolāy,* call and bring Bahōran (our) uncle.

हमरा बालकक संग ओकरहुँ पठाय दिओक, *hamᵃrā bālakak sang okarahᵘ pathāy diauk,* send him also with my boy.

कालू सदा अम्मा निरसो के कहहुन्हि जोगिया जाई, *Kālū Sadā ammā Nirᵃsō kē kahᵃhūnhⁱ Jogiyā jāi,* say to the respect-ed Kālū Sadā and mother Nirsō 'go to Jogiyā.'

Third Person :—किच्छु सीखि लेए तँ पठाय दिऐक, *kicchᵘ sīkhⁱ lēē tă̐ pathāy diaik,* let him learn something, then let me send him.

जाहि मुँहें धैलक फोटरा गीदर जेठ भाइ के ताहि मुँहें धरौ हमरा के, *jāhⁱ mū̃hē̃ dhailak Photᵃrā gidar jēṭh bhāi kē, tāhⁱ mū̃hē̃ dharau hamᵃrā kē,* with the mouth with which Photrā the jackal has seized my elder brother, with the same mouth let him seize me.

200. There are various forms of a respectful imperative in the second person, made by adding इहें *ihē̃,* इआ *iă* (or इयाँ *iyă̐*), इअह *iăh,* इहाँ *ihă̐,* इओक *iauk,* इहौक *ihauk,* इहौन्हि *ihaunhⁱ,* इहथि *ihathⁱ,* or बहीन्हि *bahīnhⁱ* to the root. These I call **Mild Imperatives.** There are also some periphrastic respectful forms made by com-bining the 2nd verbal noun in ल *l,* with the Imperative or Future of the √ जा *jā,* go, which I call the **Respectful Imperative** and the **Respectful Future** respectively. Examples of these are as follows :—

नहिं पतियाङ तो आबिहें, *nahⁱ patiyāh°, to ăbihē̃,* if she do not believe you, then please to come.

दौष निगम दुर आनि मिलाबिय ।
तांहि दिञ्च बिधि मुख आध ॥

Dīsa nigama dui āni milābiyu (m.c. for *milābiyá*).
Tǎhi dia (m.c. for *diá*) *Bidhi-mukha ādha* (Vid. xvii., 4).
Join the (ten) directions to the (four) vēdas, and to that add
half the (four) faces of Brahmā.

प्रक बेरि ङक्कुम दिञ्च, *ek bēr[i] hukum diá*, please give (me) the
order but once.   (cf. the example of दिङ्घ *dih[u]*, in § 199).

हम तोंहरा प्रक कहिनी सुनबंछिञङ्ङ् जकरा सभ दीन मन रखिञंङ्,
ham toh[a]rā ek kahinī sun[a]baichiah[u] jak[a]rā sabh dīn man rakhiáh,
I tell you a story, which please remember all your days.

तञ्चां तों बैसिहं हम जाइत छी दौरी गाम, *tahā̃ tõ baisihá, ham jāit*
chī Dauri gām, please sit there, I am going to Dauri village.

चढ़िञौक ममा परसाक गाछ, *carhiauk mamā par[a]sāk gāch*, O uncle
please climb up the *parsā* tree.

दादा हो अहिरा गोञार के कहिहौक जाई बथान, *Dādā hō, Ahirā*
Goār kē kahihauk jāī bathān, O brother, say to Ahirā Goār, 'go to
(your) cow-shed.'

दुनू बेटीक कहिहौन्हि जे कोञ्चबर करथि तैयार दुनू जमाय मारल
गेलैन्हि, *dunū bēṭīk kahihaunh[i] jē koh[a]bar karath[i] taiyār, dunū jamāy*
māral geluinh[i], please tell (him) that the two sons-in-law for whom
he is preparing the marriage bowers of his two daughters have
been killed.

से हो सारा मानिनिहथि हमर दिनमा, *sē hō sārā mǎnihath[i] hamar*
din[a]mā (for *din[a]wā*), therefore, O brother-in-law, accept (or, ' let
my brother-in-law accept ') my day (*i.e.*, the date fixed by me).

प्रक सेर अन्न घटि नहिं देबञ्चौन्हि, *ek sēr ann ghat[i] nah[i] deb[a]hinh[i]*,
please do not give one seer of grain less (than the right
amount).

Respectful Imperative :—अखन अपने चाही तखन तोड़बा लेल जाय,
jakhan ap[a]ne cāhī, takhan tor[a]bā lēl jāy, when you, sir, may desire,
then be good enough to have the fruit plucked and take it.

Respectful Future :—देखल जाएत, *dēkhal jáet*, you will be
pleased to see, *i.e.*, be good enough to look and see.

NOTE.—The Respectful Imperative and Respectful Future are really impersonal passives. लेल जाय *lēl jāy*, is, literally, 'let it be taken.' So देखल जाएत *dēkhal jāet*, is, 'it will be seen (by you).' This use of the impersonal passive as a form of respect, is carried to great lengths in the Naipāli language spoken immediately to the north of Mitbilā.

201 (b). The **Future** tense in Maithilī is formed in three ways. In the first place it may be the same as the present conditional. We often find the forms of the present conditional or imperative employed in the sense of the future. It may be noted that, in the cognate Kāśmīrī language, the only form of the future is made in the same way.

In the second place, a number of the forms of the future are based on the second verbal noun, which ends in ब *b* (देखब *dēkhab*, to see).

In the third place, a number of the forms of the future are based on the present participle, ending in प्रत *ait* (देखैत *dēkhait*, seeing). In this case the termination of the participle is lightened by changing प्रत *ait* to अत *at* (देखत *dēkhat*) or रत *it* (देखित *dēkhit*).

202. The idea of future time can be emphasized by adding गॉं *gå* (in old Maithili गै *gai* or गए *gae*) to any of these forms. The addition of this termination is quite optional, and is most common in conversation. Examples of the use of this termination taken from literature are as follows. Those of गै *gai* and गए *gae* are in poetry and are taken from Manbōdh's Haribans :—

प्रचि दरी कें बेचब-गॉं आथोर कंचा सबचि सँ आम कौनि लेब, *chi dahī kē̃ bēcab-gå, āor kañcā sabah¹ så ām kin¹ lēb*, I'll sell these curds, and with the pice (I get for them) I will buy mangoes. (This example shows how purely optional the use of गॉं *gå* is. It is employed with one future and not with the other).

बाप मार कें कह्-गॉं ठंकान, *bāp māi-kē kahū-gå ṭhekān*, we shall (*i.e.*, let us) inform (our) parents as to (our) whereabouts.

अपना अपना घर में सुन्नर खाएक करें-गॉं, *ap°nā ap°nā ghar mē̃ sunnar khāek karē̃-gå*, you will prepare beautiful food each in her own room.

मारब-गे हम कालिह बथान, *māraba-gai hama kālhi buthāna,* to-morrow will I destroy the cowsheds.

तखनुक हरख कहब-गए कहि, *takhanuka harakha kahaba-gae kāhi,* to whom shall I tell the joy of that moment?

The second and third of the above examples have also been given as examples of imperatives. Grammatically, the termination गे *gā* shows that they are futures, used in the sense of polite imperatives. They are the first form of the future, which is identical with the present conditional and imperative.

It is hardly necessary to point out the correspondence of this termination with the Hindī गा *gā* in forms such as देखूँ-गा *dēkhū̃-gā,* I shall see.

It is unnecessary to give a table of the terminations of the first form of the future. They are identical with those of the present conditional and imperative. One example may be given in which the same word is used once as a future conditional, and once as a future indicative :—

नहिं हाजिर करी तौ नौम दीन तोहरा साँ बिबाह करी, *nahⁱ hājir karī, tau naum dīn tohⁱrā saũ bibāh karī,* If I shall not produce (the thief) then I will marry you on the ninth day.

Other examples are :—

एहि उपकारक बदला तोहरा केएक कथा सिखाय दिअ‍ङ, *ehⁱ upᵃkārak badᵃlā tohⁱrā kaiek kathā sikhāy diahᵘ,* in return for this favour I will teach you (object in second person) certain things.

किच्छु सीखि लेअ तँ पठाय दिएक, *kicchᵘ sīkhⁱ lēē, tã pathāy diaik,* let him learn something, and then I will send him (to school).

203. (*b*, 4). **Future Indicative, second form,** based on the second verbal noun in ब *b*. The terminations are added directly to the root. Vulgarly, we often hear म *m* instead of ब *b*. Thus देखबौक *dekhᵃmauk* instead of देखबौक *dekhᵃbauk*, I shall see you. This second form only occurs in the first and second persons. After roots ending in vowels, the junction vowel is often some other vowel instead of ᵃ, following in this the second verbal noun.

PERSON	SHORT FORM		LONG FORM		REDUNDANT FORM			
	GROUP I. (Subject: non-honorific. Object: non-honorific.)	GROUP II. (Subject: honorific. Object: non-honorific.)	GROUP I. (Subject: non-honorific. Object: non-honorific.)	GROUP II. (Subject: honorific. Object: non-honorific.)	GROUP I. (Subject: non-honorific. Object: non-honorific.)	GROUP II. (Subject: honorific. Object: non-honorific.)	GROUP III. (Subject: non-honorific. Object: honorific.)	GROUP IV. (Subject: honorific. Object: honorific.)
1	*ab, abalū̃, abō̃,*		*abui* Or (with object in 2nd person.) *abau, abalᵘ*		*abaik* Or (with object in 2nd person.) *abauk*		*abainlᵗ*	
2	*abē*	Same as 1st person.	*abᵃh, abau, abahō;* fem. *abᵃlᵗ.*	Same as 1st person, but no forms for object in 2nd person.	*abalᵃk, abalaik.*	Same as 1st person, but no forms for object in 2nd person.	*abahīnlᵗ.*	Same as 1st person.
3	Wanting.	Wanting.	Wanting.	Wanting.	Wanting.	Wanting.	Wanting.	Wanting.

The following are examples of this form of the future:—

First Person: नहिं पतियाहु तो आबिहें देबहूँ गोआही गुजराय,
nahᶦ patiyāhᵘ to ăbihẽ, dēbahᵘ (dē + ᵃbahᵘ) goāhī gujarāy,
if she do not believe you, please come, (and) I will bear
testimony.

सभ के देबौं हम चारि सेर बोनि, *sabh kē dēbẽ (dē + ᵃbẽ)
ham cārᶦ sēr bonᶦ,* to all will I give four seers (of grain)
as daily wages.

मारब धनुखा देब खसाय, *mārab dhanukhā, dēb khasāy,*
I will smite him with (an arrow from my) bow and fell
him.

कजरा नदी कैसन उतरब पार, *Kajᵃrā nadī kaisan utᵃrab
pār,* how shall we cross the river Kajᵃrā ?

[*N.B.*—This form in अब *ab* is the one in general use].

नहिं हो मामा घुरबै चलह कठैया मिकार, *nahᶦ, hō māmā,
ghurᵃbai; calăh Kaṭaiyā sikār,* we will not return, O
uncle ; come to hunt in Kaṭaiyā.

दुरमति लागल रे कौंड़ा पूत तोरा एक थापड़ मारबौ,
durᵃmatᶦ lāgal rē chaũṛā pūt, tōrā ek thāpaṛ mārᵃbau, are
you mad, you son of a boy ? I will give you a slap.

घर में चोरी भेल चोर माल पकड़ि कै हाजिर कै दह तखन
तोहरा फुरसति देबह बीच में नहिं देबह, *ghar mẽ cōrī bhēl ;
cōr māl pakaṛᶦ kai hājir kai dăh, takhan tohᵃrā phurᵃsatᶦ
dēbahᵘ ; bîc mẽ nahᶦ dēbahᵘ,* a theft has taken place in
(my) house ; arrest the thief and his booty, then will I
release you ; till then I will not set you free.

उनटि के हम नहिं किच्छु कहबैक, *unaṭᶦ ke ham nahᶦ
kicchᵘ kahᵃbaik,* I will make no reply (to her).

Second Person: हमरा गाइक दूध पीबैं, *hamᵃrā gāik dūdh pîbẽ,*
will you drink the milk of *my* cow ? (a rude question.)

निरसो अम्मा के कहबौ बुझाय, *Nirᵃsō ammā kē kahᵃbau
bujhāy,* you will explain to mother Nirsō.

धाबाक धारि तोरि मांछी हाँक हो मामा । मांछी बैठत

चमरा देह पर । कहब हबाल । परसाक गाछ पर से हेठ होबहो,
dhābāk dhār^i tōr^i mãchi hauk, hō māmā. Mãchi baithat
(3rd person) *ham^{a}rā dēh par. Kahab* (1st person) *habāl.*
Par^{a}sāk gāch par sē hẽth hob^{a}hō (2nd person), tear off a
branch of the *dhābā* tree, and drive off the flies. The
flies will settle on our corpses. I will tell you a circum-
stance (that concerns us). Will you come down from
the *parsā* tree ?

तखन जाय पुछबहुन्हि सखी कँ, *takhan jāy puch^{a}bahūnh^i*
sakhī kẽ, (one girl addresses another) then you will go
and ask our (respected) friend.

आधा आधा सभ मशाला लछमी दाइ कँ अपने चुप्पे देबैन्हि,
ādhā ādhā sabh masālā Lach^{a}mī Dāi kẽ ap^{a}ne cuppē
debainh^i, your Honour will give half of each of the deli-
cacies privately to the respected Lachmī Dāi.

The following is an example of the suffix अन्हि *anh^i* as used
by Maubōdh (see § 193).

    कहलन्हि कुबलए पिड़ लै आनि ।
    द्वार धरब-अन्हि भिनसर जानि ॥

    kah^{a}lanhi kubalae piṛa lai āni,
    dwāra dharaba-anhi (for *dhar^{a}bainh^i*) *bhinasara jāni.*

He said, "having brought (the Elephant) Kuvalaya Piḍa at
dawn, warily you will place him at the door."

204. (b) (4). **Future**, third form, based on the present participle ending in ইত *ait*, of which the ঐ *ai* is usually weakened to অ *a*, but sometimes to ই *i*. The terminations are to be added to the root direct. This form is mainly used in the third person. In the first person it is only found in groups I and II, and in the 2nd person only in group II, and even here it is not common.

PERSON	SHORT FORM		LONG FORM		REDUNDANT FORM			
	GROUP I	GROUP II	GROUP I	GROUP II	GROUP I	GROUP II	GROUP III	GROUP IV
	(Subject: non-honorific.) Object: non-honorific.)	(Subject: honorific.) Object: non-honorific.)	(Subject: non-honorific.) Object: non-honorific.)	(Subject: honorific.) Object: non-honorific.)	(Subject: non-honorific.) Object: non-honorific.)	(Subject: honorific.) Object: non-honorific.)	(Subject: non-honorific.) Object: honorific.)	(Subject: honorific.) Object: honorific.)
1	*itahĕ.*		Or (with object in 2nd person.) *atai, atahu.*	Same as 1st person, but no forms for object in 2nd person.	Or (with object in 2nd person.) *ataik, atauk.*	Same as 1st person, but no forms for object in 2nd person.	Wanting.	
2	Same as 1st person.		Wanting.	......	Wanting.	......	Wanting.	Wanting.
3	*at*; fem. *at.*	*atahĭ, atahu, atĭh;* fem. *aĭh* or *atĭhĭ*	*atai* Or (with object in 2nd person). *atau, atahu.*	......	*ataik* Or (with object in 2nd person). *atauk.*	......	*atanhĭ*	*atinhĭ atinhĭ*

Examples of this form of the future as follows. Only one example has been noted in literature of the 1st person, and none of the 2nd person. The example of the first person will be found in the third sentence below :—

Third Person : जिब जाएत परान बचत तैखो ने परसा गाछ पर से हेंठ होबो, *jib jāet, parān bacat, taio nē parᵃsā gāch par sē hēṭh hōbō,* (whether) my life will go (*i.e.*, will be lost), (or whether) my life will be saved, still I will not descend from the Parsā tree.

मधुपुर रमनि जखन हरि देखति ।
हरखित जनम कृतारथ लेखति ॥

madhupura ramani jakhana hari dekhati,
harakhita janama kṛtāratha lekhati. (Manbōdh.)

When a damsel of Madhupur will see Hari,
She will rejoice and will consider her life's desire
fulfilled.

सामी सलहेस जौं मिलतथि सामी सलहेस लै राज भोगितहुं । नहिं मिलतांह हिआ हारि घुरब । सोग सन्ताप सौं पानि धसि खसब, *sāmī salᵃhēs jaŭ milᵃtathⁱ, sāmī salᵃhēs lai rāj bhogitahū* (1st person). *Nahⁱ milᵃtāh, hiā hārⁱ ghurab. Sōg santāp saŭ pāni dhasⁱ khasab,* (if) my lord Salhēs will be met (by me), with my lord Salhēs will I enjoy the kingdom. If he will not be met (by me). losing my heart (heart-broken) will I return. In sorrow and affliction will I plunge into water (and drown myself).

[Note in this example two different forms of the first person and two different forms of the third person honorific. In each case the two forms of each pair are quite identical in meaning.]

निरसो देलन्हि बजर केवाड़ ठोकि जे बाबू सुतले रहतांह नहिं जेतांह *Nirᵃsō dēlanhⁱ bajar kewāṛ ṭhōkⁱ, jē bābū sutᵃlē rahᵃtāh nahⁱ jaitāh,* Nirsō shut adamantine doors (*i.e.*, shut the door tightly) saying, 'my sons will remain asleep, and will not depart.'

मोरंग चैक पनियां कुपनियां बहिरे धरतै साहुक कलबुज, *Mōrang chaik paniyā ku-paniyā, bahirē dharᵃtai sāhuk kalᵃbuj,* in the

Mōrang the water is bad water, and will seize from without the body of the Sāhu (and fill him with disease).

नादिर मीर्याँक बेटी छे बड़ जोगतान । एक थापड़ मारतौ पानि नहिं पीबैं, *tāhir mīyā̃k bēṭi chai baṛ jōgatān. Ek thāpaṛ mărᵃtau pāni nahⁱ pībē̃*, Tāhir Miyā̃'s daughter is a great sorceress. She will give you one slap and you will never drink water (again) (*i.e.*, you will be killed).

पांचो मिलि के करतझ् सम्स्कार, *pā̃cō milⁱ ke karᵃtahᵘ sanskār*, the five will unite and perform your funeral ceremonies.

तोहरा सभक केसो टेढ़ नहिं चैतझ़, *tohᵃrā sabhak kēs-ō ṭeṛh nahⁱ haitahᵘ* (indirect obj. in 2nd pers.), not even a hair of one of you will be bent.

बरख बारह लगतैक खेपवा, *barakh bārah lagᵃtaik khepᵃwā*, the expedition will last twelve years.

As an example of Manbōdh's suffix अन्हि *anhⁱ*, we have खैताह-अन्हि, *khaităh-anhi*, already quoted in § 193.

205. (*c*) (5). The **Past Conditional** is formed from the present participle, to which the personal terminations are added directly. In the short form of group I, no termination is added in the third person, the bare present participle being here employed alone.

The present participle ends in ऐत *ait*, as in देखैत *dekhait*, seeing. When personal terminations are added, this termination is usually lightened to इत *it*, thus देखित *dēkhit*. This lightening is not however obligatory, and we sometimes hear the ऐ *ai* retained. This is not a peculiarity of any particular form, but depends entirely on the personal equation of the writer or the speaker. Sometimes the ऐत *ait* is lightened to अत *at* (देखत *dēkhat*), instead of इत *it*. This also is a case of personal equation.

The following are the terminations of this tense. I have included the lightened participial termination in each instance, so that the terminations as given, are to be added to the root direct. In every instance *ai* or ᵃ may (as has been explained) be substituted for the initial *i* of the termination. The terminations commencing with *i* are, however, much the most usual.

206. (c) (5) **Past Conditional.** The terminations are added to the root direct.

PERSON	SHORT FORM — GROUP I. (Subject: non-honorific. Object: non-honorific.)	SHORT FORM — GROUP II. (Subject: honorific. Object: non-honorific.)	LONG FORM — GROUP I. (Subject: non-honorific. Object: non-honorific.)	LONG FORM — GROUP II. (Subject: honorific. Object: non-honorific.)	REDUNDANT FORM — GROUP I. (Subject: non-honorific. Object: non-honorific.)	REDUNDANT FORM — GROUP II. (Subject: honorific. Object: non-honorific.)	GROUP III. (Subject: non-honorific. Object: honorific.)	GROUP IV. (Subject: honorific. Object: honorific.)
1	*itahũ**, -ti (seldom used).	Same as 1st person.	*itai* — Or (with object in 2nd person.) *itiau, itiahũ.*	*itiai* — Same as 1st person.	*itaik* — Or (with object in 2nd person). *itiauk.*	*itaik itiauk.* — Same as 1st person, but no forms for object in 2nd person.	*itiainĩ.*	*itiainĩ.*
2	*itē̃.*	(Same as 1st person.)	*itāi*; fem. *itahĩ* or *itāhĩ.*	Same as 1st person, but no forms for object in 2nd person.	*itahik, itiahik.*		*itiainhĩ.*	Same as 1st person.
3	*ait*; fem. *aiti.*	*itahĩ, itanhĩ.*	*itai* — Or (with object in 2nd person.) *itiau, itiahu.*	......	*itaik* — Or (with object in 2nd person.) *itiauk.*	......	*itiainĩ.*	*itiathinhĩ* / *itiathũnhĩ.*

* or *aitahₐ* or *ₑtahₐ* and so throughout except in the short form of the 3rd person of group I.

The following are examples of the use of this tense :—

First Person :—जौं हमहूँ तोहरा जकाँ बनीज-ब्यापार करितहूँ आऔर अन्न तौलितहूँ तखन आद पाऔ भरि अन्न एम्हर ओम्हर सँ माँगि नहिं खैतहूँ, *jaŭ hamah^ū toh^arā jakā̃ banīj-byāpār karitah^ū, āor ann taulitah^ū, takhan āi pāo bharⁱ ann ēmhar ōmhar sā̃ māgⁱ nahⁱ khaitah^ū* (for *khā + itah^ū*), if I also, like you, had done trading and had weighed out food, I should not have eaten to-day a quarter of a seer of food begged from here and there.

जनितहूँ तो बगहा में बरदी तमाकू लद॰बैतिऐ, *janitah^ū to bag^ahā mē̃ bar^adī tamōkū lad^abaitiai,* if I had known, I would have loaded a bullock in Baghā with tobacco.

Second Person (also *Third Person*) :—जौं तौं हमरा नहिं छाड़ितँछ आऔर मारि दितँछ तखन ओ मोती तोहरा हाथ लगैत, *jō̃ tō̃ ham^arā nahⁱ chāritāh āor mārⁱ ditāh, takhan ō mōtī toh^arā hāth lagait,* if you had not let me go and had killed me, then that pearl would have come into your hand.

Third Person :—जिबैत रहैत तो जोगिया अबैत पलटि, *jibait rahait to jogiyā abait palaṭⁱ,* if they had been alive they would have come back to Jogiyā.

आन केओ रहितऐ मारितहूँ मुक्का दितहूँ खँसाय, *ān keo rahitathⁱ māritah^ū mukkā ditah^ū khāsāy,* if it had been any other person (than you, our respected mother), we should have struck him with a blow of the fist, and knocked him down.

ओतन्हि दुरागमन करैतन्हि जमैया जाँजरि, *autanhⁱ durāgaman karai-tanhⁱ jamaiyā jā̃jarⁱ,* if they had come to Jā̃jari his sons-in-law would have performed the ceremony of *durāgaman.*

Sometimes the imperfect tense indicative is employed in the sense of the past conditional. An example is जो जिबैत रहाँछ दीना भद्री जोगिया नगर कौनो मुसहरनी नहिं कैलक सिंगार, *jo jibait chalāh dīnā bhadrī jogiyā nagar, kauno musahar^anī nahⁱ kailak sīgār,* if Dīnā and Bhadrī had been alive in Jogiyā town, no Musahar's wife would have dared to adorn herself. In this example the past tense indicative is also employed in the apodosis in the sense of the past conditional.

207. (c) (6)   **Present Indicative.**
      (c) (7)   **Imperfect Indicative.**

These two tenses are formed by combining the present participle with Auxiliary Verbs. They will be dealt with under the head of periphrastic tenses (Chapter III).

208.   (d) (8)   **Past Indicative.**—This tense is formed from the past participle in चल *al* (देखल *dēkhal)*, which in the case of transitive verbs is a passive. Thus देखल, *dēkhal,* means ' seen,' and when we want to say 'I saw' we must say 'seen by me.' We have observed that nouns and pronouns have nothing corresponding to the agent case in Hindi. The ' by me,' ' by you,' or ' by him,' etc., which forms the subject of the verb, is therefore indicated by the terminations suffixed in conjugating the tense. देखलहुँ, *dekh^alah^ũ*, means 'seen by me,' 'I saw'; देखलैं, *dekh^alăh,* means ' seen by you', ' you saw '; देखलक *dekh^alak,* means ' seen by him,' ' he saw '; and so on.

On the other hand the past participle of an intransitive verb is not necessarily passive. सुतल, *sūtal* means ' slept,' and in conjugation ' I slept ' may be represented by either ' it was slept by me ' or by ' slept I.' In Maithilī both principles are followed in conjugating intransitive verbs. This is most manifest in the periphrastic tenses formed from the past participle, the perfect and the pluperfect, but we also see clear traces of it in the conjugation of the past indicative. Here there is a mixture of forms. For ' I slept ' we usually say 'it was slept by me '; but for ' you slept ' we do not say ' it was slept by you ' (सुतलैं *sut^alăh*) but we say सुतलाह *sut^alăh,* i.e., slept you. It thus follows that the conjugation of the past tense of an intransitive verb sometimes agrees with that of the past tense of a transitive verb, and sometimes differs.

At the present day all sense of the *reason* for this difference has disappeared from the language. No native of Mithilā, when employing the past tense of a transitive verb, is aware that he is using a passive idiom. To him the pasts of both kinds of verbs are conjugated in as straightforward a manner as the English, I loved, thou lovedst, he loved. All that he is conscious of is that in the tenses formed from the past participle, the conjugation of transitive verbs differs from that of intransitive ones, and, for practical purposes this is all that need be known. It is unnecessary to consider देखलहुँ *dekhᵃlah*ᵁ as meaning ' it was seen-by-me,' and it is quite sufficient to consider it as meaning ' I saw,' just as सुतलहुँ *sutᵃlah*ᵁ means ' I slept '; but it is useful to know the origin of the difference, and for that reason the above explanation has been given.

We commence with giving the terminations of the past tense of the **transitive** verb.

209. (*d*) (8) **Past Indicative of a Transitive verb.** The terminations to be added to the root direct.

PERSON.	SHORT FORM.		LONG FORM.		REDUNDANT FORM.			
	GROUP I. (Subject: non-honorific. Object: non-honorific.)	GROUP II. (Subject: honorific. Object: non-honorific.)	GROUP I. (Subject: non-honorific. Object: non-honorific.)	GROUP II. (Subject: honorific. Object: non-honorific.)	GROUP I. (Subject: non-honorific. Object: non-honorific.)	GROUP II. (Subject: honorific. Object: non-honorific.)	GROUP III. (Subject: non-honorific. Object: honorific.)	GROUP IV. (Subject: honorific. Object: honorific.)
1	alahĭ, al, alĭ; fem. alĭ.	Same as 1st person.	alai, aliai. Or (with object in 2nd person.) alau, alahu, aliau, alialu		aliaik, aliaik. Or (with object in 2nd person.) alauk, aliauk		aliainki, aliainhĭ	
2	alē, alai	Same as 1st person.	alāh; fem. aĭļhĭ, alĭhĭ.	Same as 1st person, but no forms for object in 2nd person.	alahik, alahĭk	Same as 1st person, but no forms for object in 2nd person.	alahānhĭ.	Same as 1st person.
3	alak (al; fem. alĭ.)	alanhĭ (alathĭ.)	aləkai Or (with object in 2nd person) aləkau.	...	aləkaik Or (with object in 2nd person.) aləkauk.	aləkaik Or (with object in 2nd person.) aləkauk.	aləkainhĭ.	aləthinhĭ. aləthănhĭ.

In the above paradigm the termination *al* (fem. *al*[i]) properly belongs to the first person in the short form of Group I. In the case of intransitive verbs, it is not used in the first person, but is used in the third person of the same group. In old (*e.g.*, in Manbōdh's *Haribans*) poetry, and in the speech of the illiterate (*e.g.*, in the song of Salhēs), this termination is, however, also used in the third person of the transitive verbs. I have, therefore, inserted it also under the third person, placing it within marks of parenthesis to show that its use in this person is not regular.

In the third person of Group II, the termination *alanh*[i] is the one in common use. I have only noted one occurrence in literature of the form *alath*[i].

The following are examples of the use of this tense :—

*First Person :—*भन मनबोध पछाँ किछु रहल ।

कथा प्रसंग आगु हम कहल ॥

Bhana Manabōdha pachā kichu rahala.[1]
Kathā prasanga āgu hama kahala.[1]

Saith Manbōdh, 'this occurred (intransitive, 3rd person) somewhat subsequently. In the order of (my) tale I said (transitive, 1st person) it too soon.'

कहियो न देखल गेहुमनक फेंच पर खंजन फहराइत *kahiyō na dēkhal gehumanak phēc par khañjan phah*[a]*rāit,* never (before) did I see a khañjan-bird hovering over the hood of a cobra.

गोड़ लगैत छी, पैयाँ परैत छी, एहि नहिं जनली अहाँ भद्री छी *gōr lagait chī, paiyā parait chī, eh*[i] *nah*[i] *janalī ahā bhadrī chī,* I clasp (your) legs, I fall at (your) feet, I did not know this, that Your Honour was Bhadrī.

जनम सँ पुजलहुँ मोकामा गढ़ में, *janam sā puj*[a]*lah*[u] *mokāmā garh mē,* from (my) birth, did I worshipped (thee) in Mokāmā fort.

बालपन अचरा बान्हलि पर एरख सुँद नहिं देखलि जनम पाछु सिन्दुर नहिं माँग परिरलि । इनका कारन कांचे बाँसक कोहबर बान्हलि लाल पलंग सभ रंग सेज ओढ़ाओलि सिकिया चौंरि कें बनिया बनाओलि,

---

*bāl*ᵃ*pan acᵃrā bānhal*ⁱ, *par purukh mūh nah*ⁱ *dēkhal*ⁱ, *janam pāe sindur nah*ⁱ *mãg pahiral*ⁱ ; *hun*ᵃ*kā kāran kãcē bãsak koh*ᵃ*bar bānhal*ⁱ, *lāl palang sabh rang sēj ochāol*ⁱ (for *ochāb + al*ⁱ), *sikiyā cīr*ⁱ *kai beniyā banāol*ⁱ (*banāb + al*ⁱ), (a woman speaks) I tied up my girlhood with my body-cloth, the face of another man I did not see, from my birth I did not wear vermilion on the parting of my hair. For him did I build a bridal arbour of fresh bamboos, on a crimson bed did I overspread a mattress of varied colours, and with a split reed did I apply silver spots to my brow.

लाख अपराध कैलौक । लाख गारि देलें । तकर जतर हम नहिं किछु कहलौक, *lākh ap*ᵃ*rādh kailauk, lākh gār*ⁱ *dēlē̃, takar ūtar ham nah*ⁱ *kich*ᵘ *kah*ᵃ*lauk,* I committed a hundred thousand faults against you ; a hundred thousand abusive words did you give me ; (and yet) no answer of that (abuse) did I say to you.

Second Person : जाहि मरद लै जोबन संबलें से मरद बैसल चौक देबहा नदीक धार, *jāh*ⁱ *marad lai jōban seb*ᵃ*lē̃, sē marad baisal chauk deb*ᵃ*hā nadīk dhār,* the man for whom you have kept your virginity, is seated for you by the stream of the river Debhā.

कौन गरू परलौ बड़ भोरे चैंकल दुआर, *kaun garū par*ᵃ*lau bar bhōrē chē̃kal duār,* what misfortune has befallen you that your Honour has obstructed my door very early in the morning ?

बिनु अपराधें गरदनियाँ देलाह, *bin*ᵘ *ap*ᵃ*rādhē̃ gar*ᵃ*daniyā̃ dēlāh,* without fault (*i.e.,* for no fault) you gave them neck-thrusting (*i.e.,* you thrust them away by the neck).

Third Person : केओ नहिं चिन्हलक जोगियाक लोग, *keo nah*ⁱ *cinh*ᵃ*lak, jogiyāk lōg,* none of the people of Jogiyā recognised them.

देखलक सल्हेस जे बड़ अजगुत भेल, *dekh*ᵃ*lak salhēs jē bar aj*ᵃ*gut bhēl,* Salhēs saw that (something) very extraordinary (had) happened.

चटि दे धैलक पटि दे मारलक बान्हलक पछुआरि धै के, *cat*ⁱ *dē dhailak, pat*ⁱ *dē mār*ᵃ*lak, bānh*ᵃ*lak pachuār*ⁱ *dhai ke,* giving abruptness (*i.e.,* suddenly) he seized (him), giving instantaneousness (*i.e.,* instantly) he struck (him), seizing him from behind he bound him.

This termination ᵃ*lak* is very common.

The following are examples of the irregular omission of the final *ak*.

हँसि हँसि कुसल पुछल ब्रजनाथ, *hāsi hāsi kusala puchala braja-nātha,* smilingly Vrajanāth asked his welfare. (Manbōdh, vii, 28)

के देव सबए सबहुँ एह कहल ।

निज अनुचर सभ कहल हकार ।

' *kai deba sabai*' *sabahũ eha kahala,*......

nija anucara sabha kahala hakāra. (Manbōdh, ii, 34, 35).

All of them said this ' we will do everything '............His attendants all uttered a howl.

बाजे लागल भद्री दीना सौं साजल जबाब, *bājai lāgal* (intransitive) *bhadrī, dinā saū sājal* (for *sॉj^alak*) *jabāb,* Bhadrī began to speak, to Dīnā he arranged his answer.

तखन दौना मालिनि दछिनक चीर पहिरि लेलि पाटी सम्हारि लेलि नैना काजर पेन्हि लेलि ...... असले कसबीनि भेलि, *takhan daunā mālinⁱ dachinak cīr pahirⁱ lēlⁱ* (transitive), *pātī samhārⁱ lēlⁱ, nainā kājar pēnhⁱ lēlⁱ*.......... *ās^alē kas^abīnⁱ bhēlⁱ* (intransitive), then Daunā Mālin apparelled herself in garments of the south, arranged her flat temple-locks, (and) applied collyrium to her eyes...........(in appearance) she became a real harlot.

[It will be seen that in the last two examples, taken from modern prose, the irregular form of the transitive verbs seems to be suggested by the neighbourhood of an intransitive verb with the same subject.]

फेर मारलन्हि दौना राम फोटरा के देलन्हि खसाय, *pher mār^alanhⁱ dīnā rām phoṭ^arā kē dēlanhⁱ khasāy,* again (the respected) Dīnā Rām smote Phoṭrā and dashed him down (*dēlanhⁱ* for *dē +* ^a*lanhⁱ*).

अपन बड़ बेटी रखलन्हि घर सुताय । हमर बेटी पुतुह् देखलन्हि नांगट उघारि, *apan bah^u bēṭī rakh^alanhⁱ ghar sutāy, hamar bēṭī putuh^u dekh^alanhⁱ nāगaṭ ughārⁱ,* he (the respected one) put his own daughter-in-law and daughter to sleep in his house, and (came here and) having uncovered them saw my daughter and daughter-in-law naked.

[As an example of Manbōdh's method of employing the suffix स्न्हि *anhi* (§ 193), we may quote:—

सबहु देखल-स्न्हि जे चल जागल, *sabahu dekhala-anhi jē chala jāgala*, every one who was awake saw (what happened).]

[The solitary example of the form in *ᵃlathi* which I have noted occurs in the song of Dīnā Bhadrī. It is as follows:—

देहि दुनू भाद कोड़ि देलथि, *dēhi dunū bhāi chōri dēlathi* (for *dē + ᵃlathi*), the two brothers left their bodies (and disappeared).]

कथा सभ सौ बहुत बुभौलकि परंतु केओ किच्छु नहिं मानलकै, *kathā sabh saū bahut bujhaulᵃkui* (for *bujhāb + alᵃkai*), *parantᵘ keo kicchᵘ nahi mānalᵃkai*, he remonstrated much with them by words, but no one heeded (him) at all.

ददा हो नहिं बुभालको, दुनू पुतुङ् के फजिहति कैलक, *dadā hō, nahi bujhalᵃkau; dunū putuhᵘ kē phajihati kailak*, brother, she did not understand you; she has done indignity to her daughters-in-law.

तखन ओकरा सभक बाप कहलकैक, *takhan okᵃrā sabhak bāp kahalᵃkaik*, then their father said to them.

ओ कहलकैन्हि हमरो नमस्कार लिखि दिऔन्हि । मोनसी कहलथीन्हि नहिं हौ *ō kahalᵃkainhi 'hamᵃrō namaskār likhi diaunhi'; monᵃsī kahalᵃthīnhi 'nahi hau*,' he (the ignorant fool, not respected) said (politely to the respected scribe) 'please write my compliments also.' The (respected) scribe said (politely, to the fool, whom he treated with respect) 'it is not (what you think).'

210. (d) (8) **Past Indicative** of an **Intransitive** verb. The terminations to be added to the root direct.

PERSON	SHORT FORM. Group I. (Subject: non-honorific. Object: non-honorific.)	SHORT FORM. Group II. (Subject: honorific. Object: non-honorific.)	LONG FORM. Group I. (Subject: non-honorific. Object: non-honorific.)	LONG FORM. Group II. (Subject: honorific. Object: non-honorific.)	REDUNDANT FORM. Group I. (Subject: non-honorific. Object: non-honorific.)	REDUNDANT FORM. Group II. (Subject: honorific. Object: non-honorific.)	REDUNDANT FORM. Group III. (Subject: non-honorific. Object (indirect): honorific.)	REDUNDANT FORM. Group IV. (Subject: honorific. Object (indirect): honorific.)
1	alah² aĭi.		aĭai / Or (with indirect object in 2nd person.) aĭau, aĭahu.		aĭaik / Or (with indirect object in 2nd person.) aĭauk.		aĭainhi	
2	alā, aĭai.	Same as 1st person.	alăh; fem. alih, alihĭ.	Same as 1st person, but no forms for object in 2nd person.	alahăk, alahik.	Same as 1st person, but no forms for object in 2nd person.	alahĭnhĭ.	Same as 1st person.
3	al; fem. al.	alăh (fem. alih, alihĭ); aĭanhĭ.	alai / Or (with indirect object in 2nd person.) alau, alahu.	...	alaik / Or (with indirect object in 2nd person.) alauk.	...	aĭainhĭ	aĭathĭnhĭ aĭathĭnhĭ.

20

Regarding the employment of those forms of Groups I and
II which refer to the object in the second person, and the forms
(Group III and IV) in which the object is honorific, reference
should be made to §§ 191, 192 and § 189.

The following are examples of the use of this tense :—

First Person:—आन दिन भरि क्वा उतरलहुँ पार, *ān din bhar^i
chawā utaralah^ū pār*, on other days I crossed (the river) (with the
water only) up to the calves of my legs.

बारह बरख जोगिया जाँजरि बसलहुँ, *bārah barakh jogiyā jā̃jar^i
bas^{a}lah^ū*, for twelve years lived we in Jogiyā Jānjari.

बारह बरिस नेहर सासुर बसली, *bārah baris naihar sāsur bas^{a}lī*,
for twelve years did we live in our fathers' houses and in those
of our fathers-in-law.

Second Person :—रे गमार तों हमर तीनू कथा प्रखनहि बिसरि गेलें,
rē gamār, tõ hamar tīnū kathā ekhanah^i bisar^i gēlē (for *gē+^{a}lē*)
O fool, you already forgot my three statements.

कौन गरू परल जे सुतलांह खटबारि, *kaun garū paral jē sut^{a}lăh
khat^{a}bār^i*, what calamity befell (you) that you (the respected one)
slept (*i.e.*, art lying prone) upon (your) bed.

Third Person :—अम्माक सबद सुनि दीना भद्री उठल चिहाय, *ammāk
sabad sun^i dīnā bhadrī uṭhal cihāy*, when they heard their mother's
words, Dīnā and Bhadrī started up.

गोसाँउनीक घर पैसलि दीना भद्रीक सिरमा बैसलि, *gosā̃unīk ghar
paisal^i ; dīnā bhadrīk sir^{a}mā baisal^i*, she entered the shrine of the
family Goddess ; she sat by the head of Dīnā and Bhadrī's bed.

चललांह भद्री गुलामी के उदेस, बाँड़ाक रूप धेलक। भद्री चलल बरा
डीह बथान, *cal^{a}lăh bhadrī gulāmī kē udēs : chaŭrāk rūp dhailak
bhadrī calal barā ḍih bathān*, (the respected) Bhadrī went to
search for Gulāmī : he took the shape of a little boy : (now no
longer respected, being but a village lad) Bhadrī went to the
cowshed in Barā Ḍih.

दिया चारि कें चललीच मालिनि । कनेति चललीच मालिनि खामीक
उदेस । डेगे डेगे चललीच । जोजम भरि आय जुमलीच अपना फुलबाड़ी ।
फूल देखि धरती खसलीच सुरक्षाय । तखन लोटि लोटि कानें लगलीचि
फुलबाड़ी में । इनक कानब सुनि मंग समाज सखी बड़ीन भोर दोरत आछत्रि,

*hiyā hār^i kai cal^alīh mālin^i : kanait^i cal^alīh mālin^i swāmīk udēs :
ḍēgē ḍēgē cal^alīh : jōjan bhar^i jāy jum^alīh ap^anā phul^abāṛī : phūl
dēkh^i dhar^atī khus^alīh mur^achāy : takhan lōṭ^i lōṭ^i kānai lag^alīh
phul^abāṛī mē : hunak kānab sun^i saṅg samāj sakhī buhīn bhōr
hōit āel^i*, broken-hearted went (the respected) Mālin : weeping
went Mālin to search for her husband : step by step she went :
she travelled for a whole league and arrived at her garden : seeing the flowers she fell fainting : then, rolling on the ground, she
began to weep : hearing the sound of her weeping her (not respected) companions, female friends, (and) sisters came at dawn.

As a specimen of Manbōdh's use of the suffix *anh^i* (§ 193),
we may quote :—

पैर परल-ञ्हि प्रेम जनाए । *paira parala-anhi prēma janāe*
(The respected) Akrūra expressing (his) affection fell at (Kṛṣṇa's)
feet (Man. vii, 27).

Similarly भापटल-ञ्हि *jhapaṭala-anhi*, he swooped (Man. x,
17), and भलकल-ञ्हि *jhalakala-anhi*, he glittered (Man. ix, 11).

कानै लगलै बरुआ चारु गुनबें, *kānai lag^alai baruā* (long form of
bār, a boy) *cārū gun^abē*, the boy began to weep in a pretty way.

कौन गरू परलौ, *kaun garū par^alau*, what misfortune has befallen you ?

किछु बाकी रहलैक कार्ल्हि सोम दिन के ले जैहें, *kich^u bākī rah^alaik,
kālh^i sōm din kē lē jaihē*, something remained wanting (to complete the full weight), let her take that away on Monday.

फोटरा के देखि अजगुत भेलौक, *phoṭ^rā kē dēkh^i aj^agut bhelauk*,
having seen Phoṭrā, it was wonderful to you.

दीना भद्री मरि गेलैन्हि, *dinā bhadrī mar^i gelainh^i*, (the respected) Dinā and Bhadrī (have) died.

तखन गंगा-जी कहै लगलथीन्हि जे नाओ गेल भसिया, *takhan gaṅgā-
jī kahai lagal^a thīnh^i jē 'nāo gēl bhasiyā,'* then the holy Ganges
began to say that 'the boats were washed away.'

211. In order to make the Transitive and Intransitive conju-
gations of this tense quite clear, the student may be reminded
that some terminations are common to transitive and intransitive
verbs, while others are peculiar to transitive, and others again to
transitive verbs. This is made plain in the two following tables :—

(*d*) (8). **Past Indicative.** Terminations common to Transitive and to Intransitive verbs.

PERSON.	SHORT FORM.		LONG FORM.		REDUNDANT FORM.			
	GROUP I. (Subject: non-honorific. Object: non-honorific.)	GROUP II. (Subject: honorific. Object: non-honorific.)	GROUP I. (Subject: non-honorific. Object: non-honorific.)	GROUP II. (Subject: honorific. Object: non-honorific.)	GROUP I. (Subject: non-honorific. Object: non-honorific.)	GROUP II. (Subject: honorific. Object: non-honorific.)	GROUP III. (Subject: non-honorific. Object: honorific.)	GROUP IV. (Subject: honorific. Object: honorific.)
1	*alī, alahū̃.*		*aliai.* Or (with object in 2nd person.) *aliau, aliahu.*		*aliaik.* Or (with object in 2nd person.) *aliauk.*		*aliainhi.*	
2	*alẽ, alai.*	Same as 1st person.	...	Same as 1st person, but no forms for object in 2nd person.	*alahầk* *alahik.*	Same as 1st person, but no forms for object in 2nd person.	*alahūnhi.*	Same as 1st person.
3	...	*alanhī.*	...	...	...	...	...	*alathinhi,* *alathūnhi.*

(d) (8). **Past Indicative.** Terminations used only by Transitive or by Intransitive verbs, respectively.

PERSON.	SHORT FORM. GROUP I. (Subject: non-honorific.) (Object: non-honorific.)	SHORT FORM. GROUP II. (Subject: honorific.) (Object: non-honorific.)	LONG FORM. GROUP I. (Subject: non-honorific.) (Object: non-honorific.)	LONG FORM. GROUP II. (Subject: honorific.) (Object: non-honorific.)	REDUNDANT FORM. GROUP I. (Subject: non-honorific.) (Object: non-honorific.)	REDUNDANT FORM. GROUP II. (Subject: honorific.) (Object: non-honorific.)	REDUNDANT FORM. GROUP III. (Subject: non-honorific.) (Object: honorific.)	REDUNDANT FORM. GROUP IV. (Subject: honorific.) (Object: honorific.)
1	Transitive: *al*: fem. *ati* (spans Groups I–II)		Transitive: *alái*; fem. *alíhí, alíhí*; Intransitive: *aláh*; fem. *alih, alíhí*. — Transitive: *alai* Or (with object in 2nd person.) Transitive: *alau, alahu*.		Transitive: *alaik* Or (with object in 2nd person.) Transitive: *alauk*. (spans Groups I–II)		Transitive: *alainhi*. (spans Groups III–IV)	
2	Same as 1st person. (spans Groups I–II)		Same as 1st person, but no forms for object in 2nd person. (spans Groups I–II)		Same as 1st person, but no forms for object in 2nd person. (spans Groups I–II)		Same as 1st person. (spans Groups III–IV)	
3	Transitive: *alak*; Intransitive: *al*; fem. *ali*.	*alathi*; *aláh*; fem. *alih, alihi*.	Trans. *alokai*. Intrans.: *alai* Or (with object in 2nd person.) Trans.: *alokau*. Intrans.: *alau*.	...	Trans.: *alokaik*. Intrans.: *alaik*. Or (with object in 2nd person.) Trans.: *alokauk*. Intrans.: *alauk*.	...	Transitive: *alokainhi*. Intransitive: *alainhi*.	...

212. (*d*) (9). **Perfect Indicative.**

(*d*)(10). **Pluperfect Indicative.**

These two tenses are formed by combining the past participle with auxiliary verbs. They will be dealt with under the head of periphrastic tenses (Chapter III).

———o———

CHAPTER II.

Verbs Substantive and Auxiliary Verbs.

213. The Verb Substantive is freely employed in the formation of periphrastic tenses;—*viz.* of the Present Indicative, the Imperfect Indicative, the Perfect Indicative, and the Pluperfect Indicative. There are several forms of the verb substantive, all of which are in common use.

214. The verb substantive most frequently met with is that formed from the root अछ *ach*, be. It is defective in its conjugation, the only parts used being the present and past tenses and the present participle. Moreover, in the modern language, except in one form of the 3rd person of the present, and in the present participle, the initial अ *a* is always dropped, so that the word for ' I am ' is छी *chī*, not अछी *achī*. In the older language, however, of poetry and occasionally in folktales, the initial अ *a* is commonly preserved. In poetry, moreover, the final ऐ *ai* of the long form of the first person (including the 2nd person honorific), is often weakened to अ *a*, so that we have छिअ *chia* for छिऐ *chiai* for ' I am,' ' you are.' In the following paradigm such poetical forms are given within marks of parenthesis.

The conjugation of the present tense of this verb is based on the conjugation of the old Present (see § 197) of the regular verb, but presents a few abnormal forms. The conjugation of the past tense follows that of the past tense of the regular intransitive verb. This verb is conjugated as follows :—

√ अछ *ach*. be.

Present Participle :—अछैत *achait ;* fem. अछैति *achaiti*, being.

215. Present, *I am*, &c.

PERSON	SHORT FORM — GROUP I. (Subject: non-honorific. Object: non-honorific.)	SHORT FORM — GROUP II. (Subject: honorific. Object: non-honorific.)	LONG FORM — GROUP I. (Subject: non-honorific. Object: non-honorific.)	LONG FORM — GROUP II. (Subject: honorific. Object: non-honorific.)	REDUNDANT FORM — GROUP I. (Subject: non-honorific. Object: non-honorific.)	REDUNDANT FORM — GROUP II. (Subject: honorific. Object: non-honorific.)	REDUNDANT FORM — GROUP III. (Subject: non-honorific. Object: honorific.)	REDUNDANT FORM — GROUP IV. (Subject: honorific. Object: honorific.)
1	छी *chī*, (अछी *achī*.)	Same as 1st person.	छिऐ *chiai*, (छिऔ *chiau*) Or (with object in 2nd person.) छियौ *chiau*, छियह *chiahu*.	Same as 1st person, but no forms for object in 2nd person.	छिऐक *chaik* Or (with object in 2nd person.) छियौक *chiauk*.	Same as 1st person, but no forms for object in 2nd person.	छिऐन्हि *chitinhi*	बयान्हि *chatlinhi*.
2	छे *chĕ*, छ *chai*.	बचि *chathi*	छ *chah*; fem. छिहि *chahĭ*.	Same as 1st person.	छैक *chahaik*, छौक *chahaik*.	…	बहून्हि *chahunhi*.	बयान्हि *chatlinhi*.
3	अचि *achī*; or छिक *chik*, छक *chik*; fem. छीकि *chiki*.		छ *chai*, छिक *chikai* (अछ *achai*) Or (with object in 2nd person.) छिकौ *chikau*, छिकह *chikahu*.	…	छैक *chaik*, छिकैक *chikaik* Or (with object in 2nd person.) छौक *chauk*, छिकौक *chikauk*.		छैन्हि *chainhi*	

216. Past. I was, &c.

PERSON	SHORT FORM		LONG FORM		REDUNDANT FORM		GROUP III. (Subject: non-honorific. Object: honorific.)	GROUP IV. (Subject: honorific. Object: honorific.)
	GROUP I. (Subject: non-honorific. Object: non-honorific.)	GROUP II. (Subject: honorific. Object: non-honorific.)	GROUP I. (Subject: non-honorific. Object: non-honorific.)	GROUP II. (Subject: honorific. Object: non-honorific.)	GROUP I. (Subject: non-honorific. Object: non-honorific.)	GROUP II. (Subject: honorific. Object: non-honorific.)		
1	चलहुँ *chalahũ*, चली *chalī.*	Same as 1st person.	चलिऔ *chaliai* Or (with object in 2nd person.) चलिऔ *chaliau,* चलिऔ *chaliahu.*		चलिऐक *chaliaik* Or (with object in 2nd person.) चलिऔक *chaliauk.*		चलिऔन्हि *chaliainhi*	Same as 1st person.
2	चलह *chalah*, चलि *chalai.*	चलाह *chalāh*; (चलाहि *achalāhi*) fem. चलिहि *chalihi.*	चलाह *chalāh*; fem. चलिह *chalih,* चलिहि *chaliht.*	Same as 1st person, but no forms for object in 2nd person.	चलहिक *chalahaik,* चलहीक *chalahik.*	Same as 1st person, but no forms for object in 2nd person.	चलहिन्हि *chalahinhi.*	…
3	चल *chal*; fem. चलि *chali.*		चल *chalai* Or (with object in 2nd person.) चलौ *chalau,* चलहु *chalah.*	…	चलक *chalaik* Or (with object in 2nd person.) चलौक *chalauk.*	…	चलिन्हि *chalainhi.*	चलथीन्हि *chalathinhi,* चलथुन्हि *chalathunhi.*

The following are examples of the use of this verb, as a verb substantive. Many other examples will be found under the head of the periphrastic tenses.

217. **Present.** *First Person :*—জাতিক জোগী ছী, *jātik jōgī chī,* by (lit. of) caste we are Jōgīs.

হম ধরমক বেটা ছী, *ham dhar^amak bēṭā chī,* I am the son of Virtue (*i.e.,* I am telling the truth).

হম হলধর অনুচর ছিয় জকরু ।
চউদহ ভুবন হুকুম চল তকর ॥

hama haladhara anucara chia jakaru ।
caudaha bhuban hukuma cala takara ॥ (Man. ix, 66.)

The fourteen worlds move at His commands, whose servants I and Haladhara are.

Second Person :—কোন লোগ ছী, *kōn lōg chī,* what caste are Your Honours ?

এহি নহি জনলী অহাঁ ভদ্রী ছী, *ehⁱ nahⁱ jan^alī ahā̃ bhadrī chī,* this I did not know (that) Your Honour is Bhadrī.

Third Person :—কখন জাএত দিন কত অছি বেরি, *kakhana jăeta* (m.c. for *jāet*) *dina kata achi bēri,* when will the day go how much time is (left) ? (Vid. xii, 3).

এহি অছি কালী ফনি দুরবার, *ehi achi kālī phani durabāra,* (in) this (place) is the invincible snake Kālī (Man. iv, 19).

চারিম এক কথা আঙোর অছি, *cārim ek kathā āor achⁱ,* there is one more, a fourth, statement (which I am going to tell you).

হমরা বেটা জেহন কথি সে খুব জনৈছী, *ham^arā bēṭā jehan chathⁱ sē khūb junai-chī,* you know well what sort (of temper) there is to my (respected) son.

কমল ভমর জগ অছএ অনেক, *kamala-bhramara jaga achae* (for *achai*) *anē^ka,* lotus(-loving) bees there are many in (this) world (Vid. xlv, 1).

সন্ততি আঁকর আজ ধরি অছএ, *santati ā̃kara ăja* (m. c. for *āja*) *dhari achae* (for *achai*), his descendants exist to this day (Man. xiii, 18).

21

तान्हिर मौयाँक बेटी छै बड़ ओगतान, *tāhir miyãk bēṭī chai bar joyᵃtān*, Tāhir Mīyã's daughter is a great sorceress.

जे काल घेल्लक अछि तोहरा से छौ लगे में, *jē kāl dhailak ahⁱ tohᵃrā sē chau lagē mē̃*, the death (*i.e.*, the murderer) which has seized you is still close to you.

तोहरा घर में एक चन्द्रहार छहु, *tohᵃrā ghar mē̃ ek candrahār chahᵘ*, in your house there is to you a necklace.

बकस में छौ-टा रुपैआ चैक ओ मसाला सभ चैक, *bakas mē̃ chau-ṭā rupaiā chaik ō masālā sabh chaik*, in the box are six rupees, and there are dainties.

की नाम छिक । कालू सदा नाम छीक, *kī nām chik ? kālū sadā nām chīk*, what is (your) name ? (my) name is Kālū Sadā.

श्री लछमी देबि कें नेना छोट छैन्हि, *śrī lachᵃmī dēbⁱ kē̃ nēnā chōṭ chainhⁱ*, to the respected Lakṣmī Dēvī there is a little baby (not respected), *i.e.*, she has had a baby.

सामीक अरजल चथीन्हि कुटुम भल, *sāmik arᵃjal chathīnhⁱ kuṭum bhal*, the welfare of (a respected wife's) relations is the gain of (the respected) husband.

218. Past. *First Person :*—नान्हि-टा छली हम बाप माइक नाम नहिं जनली, *nānhi-ṭā chalī ham bāp māik nām nahⁱ janᵃlī*, (a man is speaking) I was a baby, and did not know the name of my father and mother.

हम तोहर बैरी छलिअहु, *ham tōhar bãirī chaliahᵘ*, I was to you your enemy.

Second Person :—I have not come across any example of this person in literature.

Third Person :—हमरा पेट में मुर्गीक अंडहु सँ पैघ एक मोती छल, *hamᵃrā pēṭ mē̃ murgīk aṇḍa-hᵘ sã̃ paigh ek mōtī chal*, in my belly there was a pearl bigger than even a hen's egg.

> गोबिंद गमन सुनल ब्रज-नारि ।
> जे छलि जतए बैसलि हिय हारि ॥

> *gōbīda gamana sunala braj-nāri ।*
> *jē chali jatae baisali hia hāri ॥*

When the women of Braj heard of the departure of Kṛṣṇa, they all sat down broken-hearted (Man. vii, 33).

अचलाच मोट चोट जे भेल ।

कोट गेलाच नहिं लाजक लेल ॥

achalăha mŏṭa chŏṭa jē bhēla |
kŏṭa gelăha nahĩ lājaka lēla ॥

Those who had been (lit. were) (so) stout (and valiant, and) had (now) become (so) small, out of shame did not return to the fortress (Man. x, 50).

प्रक चिलहोरिक लोल में प्रक घोंघा चलै, *ek cilªhŏrik lŏl mẽ ek ghŏghā chalai*, there was a shell-fish in the beak of a kite.

भाइ जेठ चलङ्ग से मारल गेल कटैया, *bhāi jēṭh chalahᵘ sē māral gēl kaṭaiyā*, he who was to-you your eldest brother has been killed in Kaṭaiyā.

Present Participle. तोहरा अचैत घर में चोरी भेल, *tohªrā achait* (a sort of ' ablative absolute ') *ghar mẽ cŏrī bhēl*, while you were present (*i.e.*, while you were in charge) a theft took place in the house.

निज धनि अचैति नइ उपभोगब ।

केबल परहिक आसे ॥

nija dhani achaiti nai upabhŏgaba |
kēbala parahi-ka āsē ॥

You, while having your own wife, will not be content with her but your hope is only for another's wife (Vid. li, 6).

अचैत बस्तु न करिय निरासे *achaita bastu na karia* (m. c. for *kariă*) *nirāsē*, do not disappoint him as long as any thing remaineth (to thee) (Vid. iii, 4).

This verb is very frequently used with a genitive or dative of possession to mean 'to have.' Thus from Manbŏdh (vi, 34, 35).

चानुर मुष्टि हमर अछि माल ।......

करि बर अछि मोहि कुबलय पीड़ ।

cānura muṣṭi hamara achi māla |......
kari bara achi mohi kubalaᵉ pῑraʳ

Of me are (*i.e.*, I have) (two) wrestlers, Cānura and Muṣṭi…
to me is (*i.e.*, I have) an excellent elephant (named) Kuvalaya
Piḍa. Similarly Vidyāpati (lxxix, 7).

नहिं मोरा टका अछि नहिं धेनु गाई *nahī morā ṭakā achi nahī
dhēnu gāī,* I have no money and no milch cow.

√ अह *ah*, be.

219. Another form of the verb substantive which we frequently hear in conversation is connected with the Hindi है *hai,* is, and
may be said to be based on the root अह *ah,* be. It is still more
defective than the root अछ *ach* ; indeed. I have only met two
forms of it, *viz.* :

अहि *ahⁱ,* he is.

हौ *hau,* he is (object in 2nd person).

The latter form would postulate the existence of है *hai,* but I have
not come across it. Examples of the use of these two forms are :—

थोरेक आम हमरा संग अहि *thōrek ām humᵃrā saṅg ahⁱ,* a few
mangoes are in my possession.

देस देस आओर गाम गाम घुमला सँ की लाभ अहि *dēs dēs āor gām
gām ghumᵃlā sā̃ kī lābh ahⁱ,* what profit is there from wandering
about from country to country and from village to village ?

मोनसी कहलथीन्हि नहिं हौ *monᵃsī kahalᵃthīnhⁱ 'nahⁱ hau,'* the
(respected) scribe said (politely) 'it is not (what you think).'

The use of this root is regular in the Magᵃhī and Bhojᵃpuri
dialects of Bihārī. In them the verb is much more fully conjugated.

√ थिक *thik*, be.

220. Instead of the verb √ अछ *ach,* the verb √ थिक *thik*
may be substituted, but only in the present tense.

221. The √ थिक *thik* is by origin the strong form of the
√ थि *thi,* which is derived from the Sanskrit स्थित *sthita,* stood.
स्थित *sthita* is the past participle of the Sanskrit intransitive
√ स्था *sthō,* stand. It should therefore be remembered that √ थिक
thik is by origin a past participle of an intransitive verb.

Although, therefore, it is now only used in the sense of the present tense, it takes the terminations of the past tense of an intransitive verb, the letter ल *l* being omitted. It will be remembered that this ल *l* is the sign of the past tense, and in this case it is not required, as the ✓ थिक *thik* is already in the past.

The following is therefore the conjugation of the ✓ थिक *thik* in the present tense. It is not used in any other tense.

222. Present, 1 am, &c.

PERSON	SHORT FORM — GROUP I. (Subject: non-honorific. Object: non-honorific.)	SHORT FORM — GROUP II. (Subject: honorific. Object: non-honorific.)	LONG FORM — GROUP I. (Subject: non-honorific. Object: non-honorific.)	LONG FORM — GROUP II. (Subject: honorific. Object: non-honorific.)	REDUNDANT FORM — GROUP I. (Subject: non-honorific. Object: non-honorific.)	REDUNDANT FORM — GROUP II. (Subject: honorific. Object: non-honorific.)	GROUP III. (Subj.: non-honorific. Object: honorific.)	GROUP IV. (Subject: honorific. Object: honorific.)
1	छिकहुँ *thikahũ*	Same as 1st person.	छिकिऐ *thikaiẽ* — Or (with object in 2nd person.) छिकिऔ *thikiau*, छिकिचङ्क *thikaũ*	छिकिऐ *thikiai* — Or (with object in 2nd person.)	छिकिऐक *thikaiaik* — Or (with object in 2nd person.) छिकिकौक *thikiauk*	छिकिऐक *thikiaik*	छिकिऐन्हि *thikainhĩ*	छिकिऐन्हि *thikaiẽnhĩ*
2	छिकैं *thikẽ*, छिकैा *thikaũ*	Same as 1st person.	छिकाच *thikaĩ*; fem. छिकौच *thikih*, छिकौचि *thikihĩ*	Same as 1st person, but no forms for object in 2nd person.	छिकाचक *thikahak*; fem. छिकौकि *thikaik*	Same as 1st person, but no forms for object in 2nd person.	छिकहिन्हि *thikahĩnhĩ*	Same as 1st person.
3	छिक *thik*, छौिक *thik*; fem. छिकि *thikih*, छौिक *thikihĩ*	Same as 1st person.	छिक *thikai*; Or (with object in 2nd person.) छिकौ *thikau*, छिकचङ्क *thikahũ*	...	छिकक *thikaik*; Or (with object in 2nd person.) छिकौक *thikauk*	...	छिकन्हि *thikainhĩ*	छिकथिन्हि *thikathinhĩ*, छिकथुन्हि *thikathũnhĩ*

The following are examples of the use of this form of the present of the Verb Substantive.

First Person :—पहिल खंड हम लेब किप्रेक-तँ हम जंगलक राजा थिकहुँ *pahil khaṇḍ ham lēb, kiaik-tå ham jangalak rōjā thikah*, the first portion I shall take because I am king of the forest.

जाति के हम नटिन थिकहुँ *jāt¹ kē ham naṭin thikah*, by caste I (fem.) am a *naṭin.*

Second Person :—के तौं थिकांच ककर कुल जानि ।
बिनु परिचय नहिं देब पिढ़ि पानि ॥
थिकहुँ पथुकजन राज कुमार ।
धनिक बिञोग भरमि संसार ॥

kē tō thikāha kakara kula jāni ।
binu paricaya nahī debu piṛhi pāni ॥
thikahū pathukajana rāja-kumāra ।
dhani-ka biōya bharami (m.c. for *bharami*) *sansāra* ॥

' Who are you (respected) and of what family ?   Without previous acquaintance I give no man a seat or water.'

' I am a traveller and a Rājpūt ; and, separated from my love, I roam over the world ' (Vid. lxxx, 2, 3).

Third Person :—दीना भद्रीक गीत सपनोंतौ थिक *dīnā bhadrīk gīt sap*ᵃ*nautī thik*, the song of Dīnā (and) Bhadrī is (like) a dream (to us).

बिद्यापति एह गाओल सजनी गे
इं थिक नब रस रीती ।
बयस जुगल सम चित थिक सजनी गे
दुङ मन परम हुलासे ॥

bidyāpati eha gāola, sajanī gē,
i thika naba rasa ritī ।
bayasa juga¹a, sama cita thika, sajanī gē,
duhu mana parama hulāsē ॥

(Saith) Vidyāpati, ' this I sang, O friend. This is the way of new delights. Their ages are equal, their souls are in unison,

O friend. In the hearts of both is supremest rapture.' (Vid. xxiii, 11, 12).

तखन सलहेस कहैत ऱ्थीन्हि जे कोन चोर थीक *takhan salᵃhēs kahait chathīnhⁱ jē 'kŏn cōr thīk,'?* then Salhēs says, 'who is the thief'?

भैलक तरह जेहन गोट थीक *dhailaka taraha jehana goṭa thīka,* he took every form which was (possible for him to take). (Man. vii, 3).

तो-हूँ थीकि मोर माइ *tŏ-hⁿ thīkⁱ mŏr māi,* my mother is you also (*i.e.,* you also are my mother).

हमर सक नहिं थीकि *hamar sak nahⁱ thīkⁱ,* my power is not (*i.e.,* I am not able). Here, quite exceptionally, an inanimate word is treated as a feminine, and has a feminine verb after it.

ई कोन बिआन थिकैक । ई एकर आठम बिआन थिकै *i kŏn biᾱn thikaik ? ī ēkar ᾱṭham biᾱn thikai,* what calving (of the cow) is this? It is her eighth calving.

चानन सौं अनुरागल थिकइन्हि
भसम चढ़ाबथि अंग ।
भनहिं बिद्यापति सुनिऐ मनाइनि
थिकाह दिगंबर भंग ॥

> *cānana sŏ anurᾱgᵃla thikainhi,*
> *bhasama curḥābuthi aṅga* |
> *bhanahī bidyᾱpati suniai manᾱini*
> *thikᾱha digumbara bhaṅga* ‖

He is painted with sandal-wood,
He smears ashes on his body.
Saith Vidyᾱpati, 'hear, O Mēnᾱ,
It is the god Digambar Bhang.'

(Vid. lxxxii, 6, 8).

√ रह *rah,* remain.

223. Instead of the verb √ अछ *ach,* the verb √ रह *rah* may be substituted, but only in the past tense. That is to say, instead of चली *chalī,* I was, we may say रही *rahī.*

The verb √ रह *rah* means literally 'remain,' and when used as a verb substantive this meaning is retained. The verb is taken to signify 'I was such and such, and I remain so.' Hence 'I remain' is considered as equivalent to 'I was.' When used in the sense of 'I was' although the signification is one of past time, the verb is therefore conjugated in the old present and not in the form of the past tense.

The following is therefore the conjugation of the verb √ रह *rah* in the sense of the past tense of the verb substantive. It is not used for any other tense of the verb substantive. In the sense of 'remain' this verb is conjugated throughout, and is quite regular.

224. Old Present for Past. 'I was,' &c.

PERSON.	SHORT FORM. GROUP I. (Subject: non-honorific. Object: non-honorific.)	SHORT FORM. GROUP II. (Subject: honorific. Object: non-honorific.)	LONG FORM. GROUP I. (Subject: non-honorific. Object: non-honorific.)	LONG FORM. GROUP II. (Subject: honorific. Object: non-honorific.)	REDUNDANT FORM. GROUP I. (Subject: non-honorific. Object: non-honorific.)	REDUNDANT FORM. GROUP II. (Subject: honorific. Object: non-honorific.)	REDUNDANT FORM. GROUP III. (Subj.: non-honorific. Object: honorific.)	REDUNDANT FORM. GROUP IV. (Subject: honorific. Object: honorific.)
1	रही *rahi.*	Same as 1st person.	रहिऐ *rahiai.* Or (with object in 2nd person.) रहिऔं *rahiau,* रहिञ्जु *rahiahu*	रहिऐक *rahiaik*	रहिऐक *rahiaik* Or (with object in 2nd person.) रहिऔक *rahiauk*	Same as 1st person, but no forms for object in 2nd person.	रहिऐन्हि *rahiainhi*	Same as 1st person.
2	रहें *rahē,* *रह *raha.*	रहथि *rahathi*	रहें *rahē;* रहाहि, रहाहिं *rahāhi* Or (with object in 2nd person.) रहो *rahau,* रहह *rahah.*		रहँक *rahak* Or (with object in 2nd person.) रहोक *rahauk*		रहैन्हि *rahainhi*	रहथिन्हि *rahathinhi,* रहथुन्हि *rahathunhi.*
3	रह *rah.*	Same as 1st person.	रहइ *rahai;* रहे *raha* Or (with object in 2nd person.) रहँह *rahah*	Same as 1st person, but no forms for object in 2nd person.	रहँक *rahak* Or (with object in 2nd person.) रहोक *rahauk*	Same as 1st person, but no forms for object in 2nd person.	रहैन्हि *rahainhi*	Same as 1st person.

The following are examples of the use of the √ रह *rah* as a Verb Substantive.

First Person :—I have not noted any instances of the use of this person as a verb substantive. It occurs as an auxiliary verb.

Second Person :—The same remarks apply.

Third Person : प्रलए काल तहँ रह नहिं घाटि, *pralae kāla tahā raha nahī ghāṭi*, (the crash) was not less than (that at) the time of the general destruction of the universe (Man. v, 39).

रहथि मिथिला में बीरेश्वर नामक मन्त्री, *rahathi mithilā mē bīrēśwar nāmak mantrī*, in Mithilā there was a prime-minister named Virēśwara.

गुड़कल गुड़कल भिड़कल जाए ।
जतए रहए दुर ब्रिच्छ अकाए ॥

guṛakala guṛakala bhiṛukala jāe ।
jatae rahae (for *rahai*) *dui briccha akāe ॥*

Rolling, rolling, bouncing, it goes to where were two huge trees (Man. iii, 10).

जखन धै लेलें कलें तखन छाड़ब की रहौ, *jakhan dhai lēlē chalē takhan chāṛab kī rahau*, (lit.) when you had seized me, then what letting go was there (to you) (*i e.* why did you let me go)?

छाड़ जे मुँह में रहैक से-हो गमौलक, *hāṛ je mūh mē rahaik, sē-ho gamaulak*, the bone which was in his mouth, he lost that also.

कोनो धनिक कें दुइ बेटा रहैन्हि, *konō dhanik kē dui bēṭā rahainhi*, to a certain rich man there were two (respected) sons.

225.   It is thus seen that there are several forms of the verb substantive. All these can also be used as auxiliary verbs in the formation of periphrastic tenses. The √ अछ *ach* is the one generally employed, but we frequently meet the others used instead of it. This should be borne in mind, as, in the paradigms, I shall in the main confine myself to the forms with √ अछ *ach*.

The following summary of the short forms of the 3rd person will serve as a reminder.

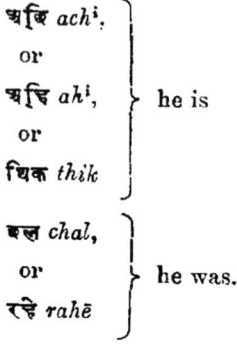

अछि *ach^i*,
or
अहि *ah^i*, } he is
or
थिक *thik*

चल *chal*,
or
रहे *rahē* } he was.

---

226. The √ हो *hō*, become, as a Verb Substantive, and as an Auxiliary Verb.

It will have been observed that the Verbs Substantive just described are all defective, possessing amongst them all only two finite tenses,—the present indicative, and the past indicative. The remaining tenses, when required, are furnished by the corresponding forms of the √ हो *hō*, become. This verb is also employed in the formation of some of the rarer periphrastic tenses (see § 241).

The verb √ हो *hō* is anomalous in several of its forms, and will be fully described under the head of irregular verbs (§ 322).

For our present purposes it is sufficient to note here the following tenses, which are employed as auxiliaries :—

    (2)   *Present Conditional* :—होइ *hōi*, (if) I become,
                                             (if) I be.
    (4)   *Future Indicative* :—हैब *haib* or होएब *hoeb*, I
                                      shall become, I shall be.
    (5)   *Past Conditional* :—होइतहुँ *hōitah^u*, (if) I had
                                  become, (if) I had been.

The past is भेलहुँ *bhĕlah^u*, I became. It is not employed either as a Verb Substantive or as an Auxiliary Verb.

CHAPTER III.

PERIPHRASTIC TENSES.

227. In the list of tenses given in § 194, the following are periphrastic :—

    (c) (6)   Present Indicative
        (7)   Imperfect Indicative
               Formed from the Present Participle.
    (d) (9)   Perfect Indicative
       (10)   Pluperfect Indicative
               Formed from the Past Participle.

Besides these there are six rare tenses, which can theoretically be made with the aid of the √ हो *hō*, become, as an auxiliary verb. They run parallel to the corresponding tenses in Hindi, but I have met only one instance of them in my reading. They are dealt with in § 241.

228. (c) (6) The **Present Indicative** is formed by conjugating the present tense of the auxiliary verb with the present participle. Thus देखत *dekhait.* seeing; की *chī*, I am ; देखत की *dekhait chī,* I see. Or we may have देखत अछि *dekhait ah²*, he sees (there is no first person for this form of the auxiliary) ; or देखत थिकहुँ *dekhait thikah*ᵃ, I see. Of course, instead of की *chī*, we can have छिऐ *chiai*, छिऔ *chiau*, छिऐक *chiaik*, and so on. In all cases that goes without saying.

In this tense (and also in the imperfect) it is very common to drop the final त *t* of the present participle, and to write it as one word with the auxiliary. Thus देखकी *dekhai-chī,* I see. and so throughout. Here, although *written* in the Nāgari character as one word, the two do not form a real compound This is seen in cases in which the present participle does not end in ऐत *ait*, but, as is the case with some vocalic roots, in इत *it* preceded by a long vowel (see Chapter IV). In such cases the suffixed auxiliary does not bring in the rule of the short antepenultimate, as it would if it was really compounded with the participle. Thus, the present participle of the √ खा *khā*, eat, is खाइत *khāit*, and the present indicative is खाइछी *khāi-chī*, not खइछी *khaichī*, I am eating. In transliteration, I, therefore, insert a hyphen between the participle and the auxiliary as shown above.

In the short form of Group I in the 3rd person there is a further slight optional irregularity. For " he sees," the usual (but not, by any means, the only) form is देखइछि *dekhaïch*[i] or even देखइछ *dekhaïch*, as well as देखैत अछि *dekhait achh*[i] or देखैअछि *dekhai-uchh*[i]. It should be noted carefully that this is always pronounced *dekha-ichh*[i] or *dekha-ichh*, and that the *a* and the *i* never coalesce into ऐ *ai* as is usually the case (see § 13). Here the two letters always form two distinct syllables.

In the feminine, the feminine of the present participle (देखैति *dekhait*[i]) should be used. The final ति *t*[i] is elided exactly like the masculine त *t*.

It will be remembered that there are various ways of spelling the present participle. We may have देखैत *dekhait*, or देखइत *dekhaït* or देखएत *dekhaet*, or देखयित *dekhayit*. As explained in § 13, this is only a matter of spelling, not of pronunciation.

The following are therefore the terminations of this tense :—

229 (c) (6). **Present Indicative.** Uncontracted form. The terminations to be added to the root direct.

PERSON	SHORT FORM. GROUP I. (Subject: non-honorific. Object: non-honorific.)	SHORT FORM. GROUP II. (Subject: honorific. Object: non-honorific.)	LONG FORM. GROUP I. (Subject: non-honorific. Object: non-honorific.)	LONG FORM. GROUP II. (Subject: honorific. Object: non-honorific.)	REDUNDANT FORM. GROUP I. (Subject: non-honorific. Object: non-honorific.)	REDUNDANT FORM. GROUP II. (Subject: honorific. Object: non-honorific.)	REDUNDANT FORM. GROUP III. (Subject: non-honorific. Object: honorific.)	REDUNDANT FORM. GROUP IV. (Subject: honorific. Object: honorific.)
1	*ait chiai*; fem. *ait chī.*	Same as 1st person.	*ait chiai*; fem. *ait chiai* Or (with object in 2nd person.) *ait chiau*; fem. *ait chiau.*		*ait chuik*; fem. *ait chaik* Or (with object in 2nd person.) *ait chiauk*; fem. *ait chiauk.*		*ait chainh*; fem. *ait chainh.*	
2	*ait chē*; fem. *ait chē.*		*ait chah*; fem. *ait chauk.*	Same as 1st person, but no forms for object in 2nd person.	*ait chahâk*; fem. *ait chahâk.*	Same as 1st person, but no forms for object in 2nd person.	*ait chahinh*; fem. *ait chahinh.*	Same as 1st person.
3	*ait achī*; fem. *ait achī.*	*ait chathī*; fem. *ait chathī.*	*ait chai*; fem. *ait chai.* Or (with object in 2nd person.) *ait chau*; fem. *ait chau*		*ait chaik*; fem. *ait chahâk.* Or (with object in 2nd person.) *ait chauk*; fem. *ait chauk*		*ait chainh*; fem. *ait chainh.*	*ait chathinh*; fem. *ait chathinh.*

230. (c) (6) **Present Indicative.** Contracted forms. The terminations to be added to the root direct. All forms are common gender, unless special feminine forms are given.

PERSON	SHORT FORM — GROUP I. (Subject: non-honorific. Object: non-honorific.)	SHORT FORM — GROUP II. (Subject: honorific. Object: non-honorific.)	LONG FORM — GROUP I. (Subject: non-honorific. Object: non-honorific.)	LONG FORM — GROUP II. (Subject: honorific. Object: non-honorific.)	REDUNDANT FORM — GROUP I. (Subject: non-honorific. Object: non-honorific.)	REDUNDANT FORM — GROUP II. (Subject: honorific. Object: non-honorific.)	GROUP III. (Subject: non-honorific. Object: honorific.)	GROUP IV. (Subject: honorific. Object: honorific.)
1	*ai-chī.*	*ai-chī.*	*ai-chiai* Or (with object in 2nd person.) *ai-chiau.*	*ai-chiai* Or (with object in 2nd person.) *ai-chiau.*	*ai-chaik* Or (with object in 2nd person.) *ai-chauk.*	*ai-chaik* Or (with object in 2nd person.) *ai-chauk.*	*ai-chiainh¹.*	*ai-chiainh¹.*
2	*ai-chĕ.*	Same as 1st person.	*ai-chăh;* fem. *ai-chăh¹.*	Same as 1st person, but no forms for object in 2nd person.	*ai-chǎk.*	Same as 1st person, but no forms for object in 2nd person.	*ai-chahǎnh¹.*	Same as 1st person.
3	*ai-achí* or (more usually) *aíchí* or *aích.*	*ai-chathí.*	*ai-chai* Or (with object in 2nd person.) *ai-chau.*	…	*ai-chaik* Or (with object in 2nd person.) *ai-chauk.*	…	*ai-chainh¹.*	*ai-chathinh¹.*

23

In the above paradigms I have omitted duplicate forms of the Verb Substantive. They can easily be supplied.

It is unnecessary to do more than remind the student that any other form of the verb substantive (अछि *ahⁱ*, छौ *hau*, थिकहुँ *thikahⁱ*, &c.), can be used instead of those given above.

The following are examples of the use of this tense :—

First Person :—गोड़ लगैत छी पैंयाँ परैत छी एहि नहि जनली अहाँ भद्री छी, *gōṛ lagait chī, paĩyā̃ parait chī, ehⁱ nahⁱ janⁱlī ahā̃ bhadrī chī,* I clasp (your) legs, I fall at (your) feet, this I did not know that your Honour is Bhadrī.

भार चिट्ठी लिखैछी, *bhāi ciṭṭhī likhai-chī,* brother, I am writing a letter.

देखैत अछी सूखल डारि पर बादिल कागा बोलैत अछि मरन मरन, *dekhait achī* (old form of *chī*) *sūkhal ḍārⁱ par bādil kāgā bolait achⁱ maran maran,* I see on a branch the fearful crow is saying 'Death, Death.'

भेद बताए दैति छी, *bhēd batāe daitⁱ chī,* I (fem.) tell an artifice.

एहि कथा पर हम तोहरा एक कहिनी सुनबैछिअड्, *ehⁱ kathā par ham tohªrā ek kahinī sunªbai-chiahᵘ,* on this account I (fem.) cause you to hear (*i.e.*, tell you) a story.

हम रे अहिरा पुछैत छिऔक बड़ साधु भाब, *ham, rē ahirā, puchait chiauk baṛ sādhᵘ bhāb,* I am asking you, O cowherd, in a very gentle manner.

आन दिन देखिऔक कटैया बड़ सोहाबन आजू कटैया देखैछिऔक बड़ भयाबन, *ān din dekhiauk* (old present) *kaṭaiyā baṛ sohāban, ājū kaṭaiyā dekhai-chiauk baṛ bhayāban,* on other days I see (*i.e.*, used to see) the Kaṭaiyā (forest) (about which you speak) very pleasant. To-day I see it very terrible.

Second Person :—कहलन्हि जे अहिरा कहाँ जाइछेँ, *kahªlanhⁱ jē* 'ahirā, kahā̃ jāi-chaⁱ' (the present participle of √जा *jā* is *jāit*, not *jāit*, see §§ 282, 310), (the respected Bhadrī) said, 'O cow herd, where are you (not respectful) going.'

जाहि मरद लाय प्रतेक मगरूमी देखबैति कँ ताहि मरद के हम बरा
डीहे देखब, *jāhⁱ marad lāy etek mag^arūmī dekh^abaitⁱ chaĭ, tāhⁱ
marad kē ham barā ḍihē dēkhab,* the man on whose account you
(fem.) show so much pride, I will see at Barā Ḍih.

हे बाबू स्वेलौक की पुछैत छी मुसहरक हबेली छीक, *hē bābū, habē-
līk kī puchait chī ? Musah^arak habēlī chīk,* O gentlemen, Are you
asking (the caste) of the house ? It is the house of a Musahar.

हमरा बेटा जेहन कथि से खूब जनैछी, *ham^arā bēṭā jehan chathⁱ, sē
khūb janai-chī,* you (fem.) know well what sort of (temper) there
is to my son (*i.e.*, what a temper he has).

केना के मारैत छँच हो भगिना फोटरा फेर भेल तैयार, *kenā ke mărait
chăh, hō bhaginā, phoṭ^arā pher bhēl taiyār,* how are you hitting
(him), O Nephews ? Phoṭarā is again ready (to attack you).

एक ठाम रहि कँ स्वामी में लय किऐ नहिं लगबैछँच आओर कोनो मठ
में बैसि कँ दाताक गुन किऐ नहिं गबैछँच, *ek ṭhām rahⁱ kă swāmī mē
lay kiai nahⁱ lag^abai-chăh ? Āor kōnō maṭh mē baisⁱ kă dātāk gun
kiai nahⁱ gabai-chăh,* why do you not remain in one place and
devote yourself to the contemplation of the Master ? Why do you
not sit in some temple and sing the goodness of the Giver ?

किएक सबहु होइछिय मति मूढ, *kieka sabahu hoi-chia* (the present participle of √हो *hō* often takes the form होइत *hoit,* see § 322)
mati mūṛha, why are you all of foolish mind (Manbōdh, v. 22) ?

अहाँ लोकनि तकाजा नहिं करैछिऐन्हि, *ahā lok^ani takājā nahⁱ karai-
chiainhⁱ,* you (respected people) are not pressing (the respected
person) (to pay his debts).

Third person :—ओकर नाम केओ ने बाट बटोही धरैत अछि, *ōkar
nām keo nē bāṭ baṭōhī dharait achⁱ,* no traveller on the road takes
(*i.e.*, utters) his name.

फोटरा बरा ढीहा में गाइ भड़कबैत अछि, *phoṭ^arā barā ḍīhā mē
gāi bhar^akabait achⁱ,* Phoṭarā is scaring the cattle in Barā Ḍih.

सदा भूकि भूकि कँ हमरा सभ कँ भड़कबैअछि, *sadā bhūkⁱ bhūkⁱ kaĭ
ham^arā sabh kē bhar^akabai-achⁱ,* always on the bark (the dogs)
are scaring us (*or* causing us to quarrel).

भद्री के पांच से फजिहति करैति अछि, *bhadrī kē pā̃c sai phajihat[i] karait[i] ach[i]*, to Bhadri she makes use of five hundred infamies (*i.e.*, abuses him).

तिरिया पुछैअछि जातिक ठेकान, *tiriyā puchai-ach[i] jātik ṭhekān*, a woman is asking (fem.) information as to (our) name.

> बिद्यापति भन इहो न निक थिक ।
> जग भरि करइछि निंदा ॥
>
> *Bidyāpati bhana ' ihō na nika thika ।*
> *jaya bhari karaïchi nindā ' ॥*

Saith Vidyāpati, 'this also is not right, the whole world blames it' (Vid. xxxv, 6).

> जनि जल-हीन मीन जक फिरइछि ।
> अहोनिसि रहइछि जागी ॥
>
> *jani jala-hīna mīna jaka phiraïchi ।*
> *ahonisi rahaïchi jāgī ॥*

Like a fish without water, she twists and turns, and day and night she remains awake (Vid. lxxvi, 8).

अपनेक ओतय कतेक मोट चलैअछि, *ap[a]nek otay katek mōṭ calai-ah[i]*, how many well-buckets are working in your (farm)?

स्वामि-धन बृथा नष्ट होइछ, *swāmi-dhan bṛthā naṣṭ hoïch* (the present participle of √हो *hō* is होइत *hoit*, see § 322), my master's property is being needlessly wasted.

केबल आलसी कां स्वामी बस्तु देअबयित छथि कपट सों निरालसी लोक भी खायित छथि, *kēbal ālasī kā̃ swāmī bast[u] deabayit chath[i]; kapaṭ sõ nirālasī lōk bhī khāyit chath[i]*, (my) master is causing goods (*i.e.*, food) to be given only to lazy people; (but) by means of deceit people who are not lazy are also eating. (This and the preceding are from Candā Jhā's version of the *Puruṣa Parīkṣā*, p. 51. Note the spelling of the present participle).

दीना राम कहैत छथि. *dinā rām kahait chath[i]*, Dinā Rām says (so and so).

ओ लोकनि गमार थिकाः जे बैरी कें सत्यबादी बुझैछथि, *ō lok^ani ga-mār thikäh, jē bāīrī kē satyabādī bujhai-chathⁱ*, those people are fools who consider enemies as speakers of the truth.

मालिनि कर जोरि मिनती करैछथि, *mālinⁱ kar jōrⁱ minatī karai-chathⁱ*, (the respected) Mālini (name of a woman) is making supplication with hands joined together.

अबैति को गोश्राही गुजराव, *abaitⁱ chau goñhī guj^arāb,* she is coming to make you bear testimony.

अम्मा निरसो कालू सदा ओ अहिरा गोश्रार समाद नेनें अबैत छैक, *ammā nir^asō, kālū sadā, o ahirā goār samād nēnē abait chaik,* Mother Nirsō, Kālū Sadā, and Ahirā the cowherd, are coming with the news.

एक जानवर दच्छिन सौं अबैत चौक, *ek jān^abar dacchin saū abait chauk,* an animal is coming towards you from the south.

दीना भद्री ठाढ़ भेलाः पुछैत छैन्हि जे कोन लोगक हबेली चीक, *dīnā bhadrī ṭhāṛh bhēläh, puchait chainhⁱ jē 'kōn, lōyak habēlī chīk,'* Dīnā Bhadri stood, they are asking (politely) 'of what caste is (this) the house?'

कालू सदा के कहैत छथीन्हि जे हमहूँ मुसहर छी, *kālū sadā kē ka-hait chathīnhⁱ jē hamah^ū musahar chī,* they (the respected ones) say (politely) to Kālū Sadā that, 'we also are Musahars.'

तखन पुछैछथीन्हि चंपा *takhan puchai-chathīnhⁱ campā,* then (the respected) Campā (name of a woman) asks (politely).

No example of the use of the √थिक *thik* as an auxiliary occurs in the above examples. I have failed to find such in literature, where it seems to be only used as a verb substantive. We, however, occasionally hear it employed as an auxiliary in conversation.

231. (c) (7). The **Imperfect Indicative** is formed by conjugating the past tense of the Auxiliary Verb with the present participle. Thus देखैत *dekhait,* seeing; चलहुँ *chalah^ū,* I was; देखैत चलहुँ *dekhait chalah^ū,* I was seeing. Or we may say देखैत रही *dekhait rahī.*

As in the present tense it is very common to drop the final न *t* of the present participle, and to write it as one word with the auxiliary. Thus देखैलहुँ *dekhai-chalah^u*, and so throughout.

In the feminine, the feminine of the present participle (देखैति *dekhaitⁱ*) should be used. The final ति *tⁱ* is elided exactly like the masculine न *t*.

As in the Present Indicative (see § 228) there are the usual variations of spelling of the present participle.

The following are therefore the terminations of this tense :—

232. (c) (7). **Imperfect Indicative.** Uncontracted form. The terminations to be added to the root direct.

PERSON.	SHORT FORM.		LONG FORM.		REDUNDANT FORM.			
	GROUP I. (Subject: non-honorific.) (Object: non-honorific.)	GROUP II. (Subject: honorific.) (Object: non-honorific.)	GROUP I. (Subject: non-honorific.) (Object: non-honorific.)	GROUP II. (Subject: honorific.) (Object: non-honorific.)	GROUP I. (Subject: non-honorific.) (Object: non-honorific.)	GROUP II. (Subject: honorific.) (Object: non-honorific.)	GROUP III. (Subject: non-honorific.) (Object: honorific.)	GROUP IV. (Subject: honorific.) (Object: honorific.)
1	*ait chalĕ; fem. aitŧ chalğ.*	*ait chalahñ; fem. aitŧ chalahū.*	*ait chaliai; fem. aitŧ chaliai* Or (with object in 2nd person.) *ait chaliau; fem. aitŧ chaliau.*	*ait chaliai; fem. aitŧ chaliai* Or (with object in 2nd person.) *ait chaliau; fem. aitŧ chaliau.*	*ait chaliaik; fem. aitŧ chalohãik* Or (with object in 2nd person.) *ait chaliauk; fem. aitŧ chaliauk.*	*ait chaliaik; fem. aitŧ chaliaik* Or (with object in 2nd person) *ait chaliauk; fem. aitŧ chaliauk.*	*ait chaliainhi; fem. aitŧ chaliainhi.*	*ait chaliainhi; fem. aitŧ chaliainhi.*
2	Same as 1st person.	Same as 1st person.	*ait chṛlãh; fem. aitŧ chalih.*	Same as 1st person, but no forms for object in 2nd person	*ait chalohãk; fem. aitŧ chalohãk*	Same as 1st person, but no forms for object in 2nd person.	*ait chalohãn-hĭ; fem. aitŧ chalohãnhĭ.*	Same as 1st person.
3	*ait chṛl; fem. aitŧ chalĕ.*	*ait chṛlĕh; fem. aitŧ chalih.*	*ait chalŏi; fem. aitŧ chalŏi* Or (with object in 2nd person.) *ait chŏlau; fem. aitŧ chalŏau.*	......	*ait chalŏik; fem. aitŧ chalŏik* Or with object in 2nd person.) *ait chalŏauk; fem. aitŧ chalŏauk.*	......	*ait chalŏinhĭ; fem. aitŧ chalŏinhĭ.*	*ait chalŏinhĭ; fem. aitŧ chalŏhinhĭ.*

233. (c) (7). **Imperfect Indicative.** Contracted form. Terminations to be added to the root direct. All forms are common gender, unless feminine forms are given.

PERSON	SHORT FORM		LONG FORM		REDUNDANT FORM			
	GROUP I. (Subject: non-honorific.) (Object: non-honorific.)	GROUP II. (Subject: honorific.) (Object: non-honorific.)	GROUP I. (Subject: non-honorific.) (Object: non-honorific.)	GROUP II. (Subject: honorific.) (Object: non-honorific.)	GROUP I. (Subject: non-honorific.) (Object: non-honorific.)	GROUP II. (Subject: honorific.) (Object: non-honorific.)	GROUP III. (Subject: non-honorific.) (Object: honorific.)	GROUP IV. (Subject: honorific.) (Object: honorific.)
1	ai-chelahā.		ai chelai Or (with object in 2nd person.) ai cheliau.		ai-chelaik Or (with object in 2nd person.) ai-chelauk.		ai-chelaianhi.	
2	aichalē.	Same as 1st person.	ai-chelah; fem. ai-chelih.	Same as 1st person, but no forms for object in 2nd person.	ai-chelahāk.	Same as 1st person, but no forms for object in 2nd person.	ai-chelahānhi.	Same as 1st person.
3	ai-chal; fem. ai-chalī.	ai-chelah; fem. ai-chelih.	ai chelai Or (with object in 2nd person.) ai-cheliau.	......	ai-chelaik Or (with object in 2nd person.) ai-chelauk.	... ...	ai-chelainhi	ai-chela-thinhī.

24

In the course of my reading. I have only noted this tense
in the third person. All three persons are heard in conversation.
The following are examples of the third person :—

ओ बाहर ठाढ़ भेल हाथ मिड़ैत चल, *ō bāhar ṭhāṛh bhēl hāth mi-
ṛait chal,* he stood outside (and) was wringing his hands.

दीना भद्री जिबैत चल उहे गबैत रहे, *dīnā bhadrī jibait chal uhe
gabait rahai,* (when) Dinā (and) Bhadrī were living, they were
singing (*i.e.,* used to sing) that very song.

एक मौनसी बजार में बैसल चिट्ठी लिखैछल, *ek monᵃsī, bajār mẽ
baisal, citṭhī likhai-chal,* a scribe, seated in the market, was writing a letter.

एक गमारि गोआरिनि माथ पर मटकुरी धैले चलि जाइछलि, *ek gamārⁱ
goārinⁱ māth par maṭᵃkurī dhailē cal ⁱ jāi-chalⁱ* (the present participle of the √जा *jā* is जाइत *jāit,* see §§ 282, 310), a foolish milkmaid was going along with a pot of curds on her head.

234.　(*d*) (9). **Perfect Indicative.**—This tense is conjugated
in two ways. The first form is the one most commonly met with,
and is made on the same principle both for transitive and intransitive verbs. All that is necessary is to take the corresponding
form of the past indicative and to suffix to it the third person of
the present of the auxiliary verb,—usually in the form अछि *achⁱ* or
अछि *ahⁱ*. Note that in whatever person the verb may be, the
auxiliary is always in the third person. Thus :—

Past,　　देखलहुँ *dekhᵃlahᵘ,* I saw.

Perfect,　देखलहुँ अछि *dekhᵃlahᵘ achⁱ* or　देखलहुँ अछि *dekhᵃlahᵘ
ahⁱ,* I have seen.

Past,　　देखल *dēkhal,* I saw.

Perfect,　देखल अछि *dēkhal achⁱ* or　देखल अछि *dēkhal ahⁱ,* I have
seen.

Past,　　देखलंह *dekhᵃlåh,* you saw.

Perfect,　देखलंह अछि *dekhᵃlåh achⁱ* or　देखलंह अछि *dekhᵃlåh ahⁱ*
you have seen.

Past,   देखलक *dekhªlak*, he saw.

Perfect,   देखलक अछि (or अहि) *dekhªlak achⁱ* (or *ahⁱ*), he has
             seen.

Past,   सुतलहुँ *sutªlahū*, I slept.

Perfect,   सुतलहुँ अछि (or अहि) *sutªlahū achⁱ* (or *ahⁱ*) I have
             slept.

Past,   सुतलाँच *sutªlăh*, you slept.

Perfect,   सुतलाँच अछि (or अहि) *sutªlăh achⁱ* (or *ahⁱ*) you have
             slept.

Past,   सुतलै *sutªlai*, he slept.

Perfect,   सुतलै अछि (or अहि) *sutªlai achⁱ* (or *ahⁱ*) he has
             slept.

It will be remembered that the short form of the third person of
the past tense of transitive verbs ends in *ªlak* (thus देखलक *dekhªlak*,
he saw), while in the case of intransitive verbs it ends in *al*
(सूतल *sūtal*, he slept). We never say सुतलक *sutªlak*. In the perfect tense, however, the form सुतलक *sutªlak* is regularly employed,
and is, indeed, the customary form. Thus सुतलक अछि (or अहि)
sutªlak achⁱ (or *ahⁱ*), he has slept.

The origin of this mode of forming the perfect is well
illustrated by this last form. It will be remembered that all the
terminations of the past of transitive verbs and most of those of
the past of intransitive verbs are really pronouns in the case of
the agent. अहुँ *ahū*, means 'by me,' अक *ak*, means 'by him,'
and so on. Thus देखल + अहुँ *dekhªl + ahū*, means 'seen-by-me,'
i.e., I saw, and देखल + अक *dekhªl + ak* means 'seen by him,' he
saw. Adding अछि *achⁱ* (or अहि *ahⁱ*) we get देखल + अहुँ अछि
dekhªl + ahū achⁱ, (it) is seen by me, a sort of impersonal verb
with the resultant meaning 'I have seen.' Similarly देखल + अक
अछि *dekhªl + ak achⁱ* is, 'it is seen by him,' *i.e.*, he has seen. In
the case of intransitive verbs, सूतल *sūtal*, meaning simply 'asleep,'
is a past participle, employed like the Hindi past participle सोया *sōyā*,

to mean 'he slept.' But if we want to say 'he has slept,' we must make an impersonal verb सुतल + अक अछि *sut⁰l + ak ach*ⁱ, it is slept by him, *i.e.*, 'he has slept.' सूतल अछि *sūtal ach*ⁱ (see below) would mean rather 'he is asleep.'

This one case of the use of सुतलक *sut⁰lak* instead of सूतल *sūtal* is the only instance in which the conjugation of this form of the perfect differs from that of the past (omitting, of course, consideration of the added अछि *a*ₜ*h*ⁱ or अहि *ah*ⁱ), and it is quite unnecessary to give a table of the terminations.

235. The following are examples of this form of the perfect :—

First Person :—एक बकस पठायोल अछि से अहांक हेतु, *ek bakas paṭhāol* (see § 273) *ach*ⁱ, *sē ahāk hēt*ᵘ. I have sent a box, it is for you.

सूपत बेंचि के देली अहि, *sūpat bēc*ⁱ *ke dēlī* (see § 314) *ah*ⁱ, I have given in barter (*lit.* having sold) the full weight.

रोपलहुँ अछि, *rop⁰lah*ᵘ *ach*ⁱ, I have planted (see below).

अहाँ कें खोलायोलि अछि, *ahā̃ kē kholāol*ⁱ (see § 273) *ach*ⁱ, I (fem.) have caused you to be freed.

Second Person :—कोन जिआन भेल अछि जे हमरा बांधि देल अछि से हाल कह, *kōn jiān bhēl ach*ⁱ *jē ham⁰rā bā̃dh*ⁱ *dēl* (see § 314) *ach*ⁱ, *sē hāl kah*, explain what fault has occurred that you have bound me.

एहि बेरि कुसिआर रोपलहुँ अछि बा नहिं। कुसिआर तँ रोपलहुँ अछि, *eh*ⁱ *bēr*ⁱ *kusiār rop⁰lah*ᵘ *a*ₜ*h*ⁱ (2nd person) *bā nah*ⁱ? *Kusiār tã̄ rop⁰lah*ᵘ *a*ₜ*h*ⁱ (1st person), this time have you planted any sugarcane or no? I have indeed planted sugarcane (but it has not turned out well).

Third Person :—केबार अम्मा निरसो ठोकलक अहि, *kebār ammā nir⁰sō thok⁰lak ah*ⁱ, Mother Nirsō has shut the door.

दीना भद्री मरि गेलैन्हि तखन फेर ऐलन्हि अछि, *dinā bhadrī mar*ⁱ *gelainh*ⁱ, *ta*ₖ*ha*ₙ *pher ailanh*ⁱ *a*ₜ*h*ⁱ, Dinā and Bhadrī died (*past*), then (*i.e.*, now) they have come (*perfect*) back again.

सौदा रेइ पुराय औरो बकिए रहलोक अछि, *saudā·dēhᵘ purāy, auro bakiē ruhᵃluuk aₜhⁱ*, give the goods in full weight, more also has remained in arrear (with you) (*i.e.*, you have still to give more to make full weight).

236. The second form of the perfect is not so common as the first form. It is made in exactly the reverse way to the method of making the first form. Here it is the present tense of the auxiliary verb which is conjugated with the past participle. In the case of transitive verbs the participle is put in the instrumental case,—thus देखलें की *dekhᵃlē ₜhī*, I have seen—or in the locative,—thus देखले की *dekhᵃlē chī*. In both of these forms न *n* is often substituted for ल *l*, especially by the vulgar,—thus देखनें की *dekhᵃnē ₜhī* or देखने की *dekhᵃnē chī*. The past participle, whether in the instrumental or in the locative, does not change for gender.

In the case of intransitive verbs, the past participle is in the nominative form, and is liable to inflection for gender. Thus सूतल की *sūtal chī*, fem. सूतलि की *sutalⁱ chī*, I have slept. This form of intransitive verbs has very often (in fact generally) very little of the *meaning* of the perfect tense about it. सूतल की *sūtal chī*, for instance, generally means 'I am asleep' rather than 'I have slept.' Sometimes, however, the sense of the perfect is quite plain. Examples of both uses will be found below.

It is unnecessary to give tables of the termination of this form of the perfect. In transitive verbs the past participle (in the instrumental or locative) is unchangeable (either for person or for gender). In intransitive verbs it is only changeable for gender. The only thing that changes for person is the auxiliary verb, and of this any appropriate form may be used.

237. The following are examples of this form of the perfect of transitive verbs :—

First Person :—अपनेक औतय कतेक मोट चलै अछि । तीनि मोट तँ लधलें की, *apᵃnek otay katek mōṭ calai-ahⁱ ? Tinⁱ mōṭ tā ladhᵃlē chī*, how many well-buckets (worked by cattle) are in use in your (farm) ? Well, I have yoked three well-buckets.

हम प्रकरा मारवा में बड्डत दौड़-धूप कैलें की, *ham ek*ᵃ*rā măr*ᵃ*bā mē bahut dauṛ-dhūp kailē* (see § 306) *chī*, I have made great exertions in killing it.

Second Person :—ई कहिनी नहिं सुनलें कंह, *ī kahinī nah*ⁱ *sun*ᵃ*lē chăh*, have you not heard this saying?

I have not noted in literature any instance of the occurrence of the third person of this form of the perfect of a transitive verb.

The following are examples of the use of this tense in an intransitive verb :—

First Person :—सबेरेक चलल की, *saberēk calal chī*, I have started (*i.e.,* I started) at dawn.

सुनँह गंगा चोरि कै आयल की, *sunăh gaṅgā, cōr*ⁱ *kai āel* (see § 312) *chī*, hear, O Ganges, having committed theft, I have come (*or* am come).

I have not come across any example of the second person.

Third Person :—पानि बरिसला बिना बड़ हानि भेल अछि, *pāni barisᵃlā binā baṛ hān*ⁱ *bhēl* (see § 322) *ach*ⁱ, owing to the rain not falling there has been great loss.

अंगूर सभक एहन गुच्छ सभ पाकल टट्टी में लटकि रहल अछि कि जकरा सँ रस चूबि रहल अछि, *ăgūr sabhak ehan gucch sabh pākal taṭṭī mē latak*ⁱ *rahal ach*ⁱ, *ki jak*ᵃ*rā sằ ras cūb*ⁱ *rahal ach*ⁱ, such ripe bunches of grapes having hung from the trellis have remained (*i.e.,* are there), that the juice has remained dripping (cf. § 342) (*i.e.,* keeps dripping).

से जनमल अछि (*v.l.* इथि) मारत तोहि, *sē janamala achi* (or *chathi*) *mārata tōh*ⁱ, he has taken birth (who) will kill thee (Man. i. 377).

जाहि मरद लै जोबन सेबलें से मरद बैसल चौक देबहा नदीक धार, *jāh*ⁱ *marad lai jōban seb*ᵃ*lē, sē marad baisal chauk deb*ᵃ*hā nadik dhār*, the man for whom you kept your virginity, that man is seated (for you) by the stream of the river Debhā.

238. The **Pluperfect Indicative** is formed on the same principles as the second form of the perfect, substituting the past tense of the verb substantive for the present of the verb substan-

tive.   Thus देखलें *dekhªlē̃*, (देखले *dekhªlē*, देखनें *dekhªnē̃*, देखने *de-khªnē*) कलहुँ *chalahū*, I had seen ; सूतल कलहुँ *sūtal chalahū*, I had slept.   Instead of कलहुँ *chalahū*, etc., we may as usual have रही *rahī*, etc.   There is nothing corresponding to the first form of the perfect ; we never meet forms like देखलहुँ कल *dekhªlahū chal.*

This tense not only has the sense of a pluperfect, but is also used to signify that the action happened a long time ago.   Thus, देखलें कलहुँ *dekhªlē̃ chalahū* means either 'I had seen,' or 'I saw a long time ago.'

I have given सूतल कलहुँ *sūtal chalahū* (fem. सूतलि कलहुँ *sūtalⁱ chhalahū*) as the form of the pluperfect of an intransitive verb. It is necessary to add that natives of Mithilā tell me that (in this tense only) intransitive verbs may also be treated as if they were transitive so that we can also have सूतलें कलहुँ *sutªlē̃ chalahū*. I have, however, never met such a form in literature.

It is unnecessary to give a table of the terminations of this tense.   The following are examples of its use in literature :—

239.   (*a*) Transitive verbs—

First Person :—हम तोहरा पहिले हस्सी में उड़ौने रहिबझु, *ham tohªrā pahilē hassī mē uṭaunē* (see § 273 ff.) *rahiahu*, formerly (long ago) I ridiculed you in sport.

Second Person :—जखन धैं लेलें (or लेनें or लेने) कलें तखन चाडब की रहौ, *jakhan dhai* (see § 314) *lēlē̃* (or *lēnē̃* or *lēnē*) *chalē̃ takhan chārab kī rahau*, when you had caught me, then what letting go was there to you (*i.e.*, why did you let me go) ?

Third Person :—जतवा जनि कर लेनें कलि सुन्दरि ।
से सभ सोपलक ताही ॥

jatawā jani kara lēnē chali sundari ।
sē sabhu sopalaka tāhi ॥

The fair one made over everything to those from whom she had taken them (Vid. x. 2).   Here लेनें *lēnē̃* is shortened to लेनें *lēnē* for the sake of metre.

240.   (*b*) Intransitive verbs—

First Person :—रानि हम सूतल बलहुँ अपन (for अपना) सिरकी
में, *rāt*[i] *ham sūtal chalah*[u] *oppan* (for *ap*[a]*nā*) *sir*[a]*kī mē̃*, at night
I was asleep in my own tent.

गेल बलहुँ *gēl chalah*[u], I had gone.   See next example.

Second Person :—कथी ले ओतय गेल बलहुँ । ओतय हमर खेत
अछि । ओकरा देखे गेल बलहुँ, *kathī lai otay yēl chaluh*[u] ? *otuy hamar
khēt ach*[i].   *Ok*[a]*rā dēkhai yēl chaluh*[u], why had you gone there ?
My field is there. I had gone to see it.

Third Person :—अपन सभ धन उड़ाय भिखारि में गेल बल, *apan
sabh dhan urāy bhikhāri bhai gēl chal,* having squandered all his
property, he had become a beggar.

राम राम कहि के उठल बलाह, *rām, rām, kah*[i] *ke uṭhal chalăh,*
crying 'Rām, Rām' he was arisen (*i.e.,* arose).

अहिरा गोयार गेल कटैया भद्री बैसल रहै, *ahirā goār gēl kaṭaiyā,
bhadrī baisal rahai,* Ahirā Goār went to Kaṭaiyā ; Bhadrī was
seated (there).

सात नींदे सूतलि चलि फेकुनी, *sāt nī̃dĕ sūtal*[i] *chal*[i] *phekunī,*
Phekuni (name of a woman) was asleep in seven sleeps.

It will be noted that, as in the case of the perfect, many of
the examples of the intransitive verb are not true pluperfects (so
far as sense goes) at all.

The √हो *hŏ as an Auxiliary.*

241.   In Hindi there is a set of periphrastic tenses formed
with the √हो *hō,* become, as the auxiliary. Most of them are
very rare. As given in the grammars, under various fancy names,
they are :—

चलता होऊँ, *cal*[a]*tā hŏ*ū̃, I may be going.
चलता होऊँगा, *cal*[a]*tā hŏū̃gā,* I shall be going.
चलता होता, *cal*[a]*tā hŏtā,* had I been going.
चला होऊँ, *calā hŏū̃,* I may have gone.
चला होऊँगा, *calā hŏū̃gā,* I shall have gone.
चला होता, *calā hŏtā,* had I gone.

It would be, no doubt, possible to concoct parallel tenses in Maithili, but I have never met any example of any of them except one of the first, which, also, I may add, is the one which is most common in Hindī.

The one example which I have noted is :—

कोन दिसा के अबैत होइ कहह^u बुझाय, *kŏn disā kē abait hŏui kahah^u bujhāy*, having explained tell (*i.e.*, tell clearly) in what direction he may be (*i.e.*, is probably) coming.

It will be sufficient to dismiss this and the other connected tenses with these remarks. I shall not refer to them again. If met with they will be easily recognized.

In the following chapter I give a complete paradigm of the conjugation of the regular transitive and of the regular intransitive verb, with roots ending in consonants. The roots chosen as examples are √देख *dēkh*, see, and √छुत *sūt*, sleep.

——o——

CHAPTER IV.

CONJUGATION OF THE REGULAR VERB.

242.. In the following paradigms attention must be again called to the regular shortening of the antepenultimate vowel as explained in §§ 32 and ff and § 176. When the vowel of the root is आ *ā*, the practice is to shorten it to अ *a*, not to आ *ă*, unless this would cause ambiguity. Thus one form of the third person past indicative of the √लाग *lāg*, begin, is लगलै *lag^alai*, not लागलै *lăg^alai*, because in Maithili there is no √लग *lag*, begin, with which it can be confused. But the long form of the first person of the same tense of the √मार *mār*, strike, is मारलै *măr^alai*, not मरलै *mar^alai*, because the latter might be confused with the मरलै *mar^alai*, he died, the long form of the third person of the √ *mar*, die.

25

A. TRANSITIVE VERB.

√देख *dēkh*, see.

243. (a) (1) Old Present, 'I see,' &c.

PERSON	SHORT FORM		LONG FORM		REDUNDANT FORM			
	GROUP I. (Subject: non-honorific. Object: non-honorific.)	GROUP II. (Subject: honorific. Object: non-honorific.)	GROUP I. (Subject: non-honorific. Object: non-honorific.)	GROUP II. (Subject: honorific. Object: non-honorific.)	GROUP I. (Subject: non-honorific. Object: non-honorific.)	GROUP II. (Subject: honorific. Object: non-honorific.)	GROUP III. (Subject: non-honorific. Object: honorific.)	GROUP IV. (Subject: honorific. Object: honorific.)
1	देखि *dēkhi*, *देखौँ *dēkhā*.		देखिऐ *dekhiai* — Or (with object in 2nd person.) देखिऔ *dekhiau*, देखिऔ *dekhiau*, *देखिऐ *dekhid*.		देखिऐक *dekhiaik* — Or (with object in 2nd person.) देखिऔक *dekhiauk*.		देखिऔन्हि *dekhiainhi*.	देखिऔन्हि *dekhiainhi*.
2	देख *dēkh*, *देखसि *dēkhasi* — Same as 1st person.		देख *dēkhah*, देखऽ *dēkhahu*, देखौ *dēkhau* ; *देखिँ *dēkhali*, देखिँ *dēkhahi*. — Same as 1st person, but no forms for object in 2nd person.		देखक *dekhahak*, देखकऽदेखलक *dekhkadekhalak*, देखिकदेखिक *dekhikdekhik* — Same as 1st person, but no form for object in 2nd person.		देखक *dekhahak*	Same as 1st person
3	देखे *dēkhē*, *देख *dēkha*, *देखऽ *dēkhu*, *देखिँ *dēkhali*	देखथि *dēkhathi*	देखै *dēkhai* — Or (with object in 2nd person.) देखौ *dēkhau*, देखऽ *dēkhauk*. GROUP I.		देखैक *dekhaik* — Or (with object in 2nd person.) देखौक *dekhauk*. GROUP I.	देखैक *dekhaik*	देखैन्हि *dekhainhi*	देखथिन्हि *dekhathinhi*, देखयून्हि *dekhathinhi*.

* Chiefly used in poetry, or in the old language. Regarding the long ē in देखै *dēkhai*, देखौ *dēkhau*, see § 176.

244. (a) (2) Present Conditional, '(if) I see, I may see,' &c.

PERSON	SHORT FORM GROUP I. (Subject: non-honorific. Object: non-honorific.)	SHORT FORM GROUP II. (Subject: honorific. Object: non-honorific.)	LONG FORM GROUP I. (Subject: non-honorific. Object: non-honorific.)	LONG FORM GROUP II. (Subject: honorific. Object: non-honorific.)	REDUNDANT FORM GROUP I. (Subject: non-honorific. Object: non-honorific.)	REDUNDANT FORM GROUP II. (Subject: honorific. Object: non-honorific.)	REDUNDANT FORM GROUP III. (Subject: non-honorific. Object: honorific.)	REDUNDANT FORM GROUP IV. (Subject: honorific. Object: honorific.)
1	देखूँ *dēkhū̃.*	Same as 1st person.	देखिऐ *dēkhiai* Or (with object in 2nd person.) देखिबौ *dēkhiau,* देखिबहु *dēkhiahu,* *देखिब *dēkhiă.*	Same as 1st person, but no forms for object in 2nd person.	देखिबैक *dēkhiaik* Or (with object in 2nd person.) देखिबौक *dēkhiauk.*	Same as 1st person, but no form for object in 2nd person.	देखिबन्हि *dēkhiainhi*	Same as 1st person.
2	देखु *dēkh.*	Same as 1st person.	देखह *dēkhah,* देखहु *dēkhahu,* देखौ *dēkhau;* f. देखिहि *dēkhahi,* देखहि *dēkhahĭ.*	Same as 1st person, but no forms for object in 2nd person.	देखहक *dēkhohak,* देखक *dēkhahuk,* देखहिक *dēkhohik.*	Same as 1st person, but no form for object in 2nd person.	देखहन्हि *dēkhohinhi.*	Same as 1st person.
3	देखे *dēkhē,* *देखा *dēkha,* *देखु *dēkhu.*	देखथि *dēkhathi,* देखथुं *dēkhathŭ.*	GROUP I. देखौ *dēkhau,* देखह *dēkhah,* देखो *dēkho,* (sometimes) देखुइ *dēkhai*		GROUP I. देखैक *dēkhaik,* (sometimes) देखक *dēkhaik.*		देखैन्हि *dēkhainhi,* देखौन्हि *dēkhaunhi.*	देखथिन्हि *dēkhothinhi,* देखथुन्हि *dēkhothŭnhi.*

* Chiefly used in poetry or in the old language.

245. (a) (3) Imperative, 'let me see, see thou,' &c.

PERSON	SHORT FORM — GROUP I. (Subject: non-honorific. Object: non-honorific.)	SHORT FORM — GROUP II. (Subject: honorific. Object: non-honorific.)	LONG FORM — GROUP I. (Subject: non-honorific. Object: non-honorific.)	LONG FORM — GROUP II. (Subject: honorific. Object: non-honorific.)	REDUNDANT FORM — GROUP I. (Subject: non-honorific. Object: non-honorific.)	REDUNDANT FORM — GROUP II. (Subject: honorific. Object: non-honorific.)	REDUNDANT FORM — GROUP III. (Subject: non-honorific. Object: honorific.)	REDUNDANT FORM — GROUP IV. (Subject: honorific. Object: honorific.)
1	देखूँ *dēkhũ*, (sometimes) देखी *dēkhī*	Same as 1st person.	देखिऐ *dekhiai* Or (with object in 2nd person.) देखिऔ *dekhiau*, देखिअड् *dekhiaũ*, *देखिऐ *dekhiā*.	देखिऐक *dekhiaik* Or (with object in 2nd person.) देखिऔक *dekhiauk*	देखिऐक *dekhiaik* Or (with object in 2nd person.) देखिऔक *dekhiauk*	Same as 1st person, but no form for object in 2nd person.	देखिऔन्हि *dekhiainh*	देखिऔन्हि *dekhiainh*. Same as 1st person.
2	देख *dēkh*, देखें *dēkhẽ*	Same as 1st person.	देखह *dēkhah*, देखहु *dēkhahu*, देखौ *dēkhau*, f. देखिं *dekhaũ*, देखिन्हिं *lēkhihī*, देखिन्हिं *lēkhihĩ*. Same as 1st person, but no forms for object in 2nd person.		देखहिक *dekhohâk*, देखोक *dekhohôk*, देखुक *dekhohuk*, देखिक *dekhohik*, देखौक *dekhauk*. Same as 1st person, but no form for object in 2nd person.		देखहन्हि *dekhainh*	
3	देखे *dēkhe*, *देखा *dēkha*, *देखु *dēkhu*	देखथि *dēkhathi*, देखथु *dēkhathu*	GROUP I. देखौ *dēkhau*, देखहु *dēkhahu*, देखौ *dēkhō*, (sometimes) देखै *dēkhai*		GROUP I. देखौक *dekhauk*, (sometimes) देखक *dekhaik*.		देखौन्हि *lekhathinh*	देखुन्हि *lekhathinhl*

* Chiefly used in poetry, or in the old language.

246. Mild Imperative.

Second person.—देखिहें *dekhihẽ*, देखिअं *dekhiā*, देखियं *dekhiyā̇*, देखिअंद *dekhiāh*, देखिहं *dekhihā*, देखिऔक *dekhiauk*, देखिऔक *dekhihauk*, देखिहौम्ह *dekhihaunh[i]*, देखिहथि *dekhihath[i]*, देखबहौम्ह *dekha-bahīnh[i]*, please to see.

247. Respectful Imperative.

Second person.—देखल जाई *dēkhal jāī*, देखल जाओ *dēkhal jāo*, be pleased to see.

248. Respectful Future.

Second person.—देखल जाएत *dēkhal jāet*, देखल जाएत-गं *dēkhal jāet-gā̇*, you will be pleased to see, be good enough to see.

249. Future Indicative.

First Form.—This is the same as the present conditional (a) (2), to which the termination गं *gā̇* (poetically गै *gai* or गए *gae*) may optionally be added. Thus देखी *dēkhī* or देखी-गं *dēkhī-gā̇*, I shall see.

250. (*b*) (4) **Future Indicative.** Second form. 'I shall see,' &c. The termination ं *gå* (ं *gai* or गु *gae*) may be added throughout.

PERSON	SHORT FORM		LONG FORM		REDUNDANT FORM		GROUP III	GROUP IV
	GROUP I. (Subject: non-honorific. Object: non-honorific.)	**GROUP II.** (Subject: honorific. Object: non-honorific.)	**GROUP I.** (Subject: non-honorific. Object: non-honorific.)	**GROUP II.** (Subject: honorific. Object: non-honorific.)	**GROUP I.** (Subject: non-honorific. Object: non-honorific.)	**GROUP II.** (Subject: honorific. Object: non-honorific.)	(Subject: non-honorific. Object: honorific.)	(Subject: honorific. Object: honorific.)
1	देखब *dekhab*	देखबँ *dekhabahă*, देखबॅ *dekhabŏ*.	देखबि *dekhabai* Or (with object in 2nd person.) देखबौ *dekhabau*, देखबलु *dekhabalu*.	देखबि *dekhabai* Or (with object in 2nd person.)	देखबैक *dekhabaik* Or (with object in 2nd person.) देखबौक *dekhabauk*.	देखबैक *dekhabaik* Or (with object in 2nd person.) देखबौक *dekhabauk*.	देखबैन्हि *dekhabainhĭ*	देखबैन्हि *dekhabainhĭ*
2	देखबॅ *dekhabĕ*.	Same as 1st person.	देखबह *dekhabăh*, देखबौ *dekhabau* देखबहो *dekhabahŏ*; fem. देखबिहि *dekhabahĭ*.	Same as 1st person, but no forms for object in 2nd person.	देखबहक *dekhabahăk*, देखबौक *dekhabahik*.	Same as 1st person, but no form for object in 2nd person.	देखबह्नि *dekhabahănhi*.	Same as 1st person.
3	Wanting.	Wanting.	Wanting.	Wanting.	Wanting.	Wanting.	Wanting.	Wanting.

251. (b) (4) **Future Indicative.** Third Form. 'I shall see,' &c. The termination नैं *gú* (नैं *gui* or नय *gue*) may be added throughout.

PERSON.	SHORT FORM.		LONG FORM.		REDUNDANT FORM.			
	GROUP I. (Subject: non-honorific. Object: non-honorific.)	GROUP II. (Subject: honorific. Object: non-honorific.)	GROUP I. (Subject: non-honorific. Object: non-honorific.)	GROUP II. (Subject: honorific. Object: non-honorific.)	GROUP I. (Subject: non-honorific. Object: non-honorific.)	GROUP II. (Subject: honorific. Object: non-honorific.)	GROUP III. (Subject: non-honorific. Object: honorific.)	GROUP IV. (Subject: honorific. Object: honorific.)
1	देखूँहँ *dekhúhuṅ.*	देखितहुँ *dekhitahuṅ.*	देखिनि *dekhatai* Or (with object in 2nd person.) देखिनौ *dekhatau,* देखिनइ *dekhatahu.*	देखनि *dekhatai* Or (with object in 2nd person.) देखनौ *dekhatau,* देखनइ *dekhatahu.*	देखनिक्रैक *dekhataiak,* Or (with object in 2nd person.) देखनिखौक *dekhataук.*	देखनिऐक *dekhataiaik,* Or (with object in 2nd person.) देखनिखौक *dekhatauk.*	*Wanting.*	*Wanting.*
2	*Wanting.*	Same as 1st person.	*Wanting.*	Same as 1st person, but no forms for object in 2nd person.	*Wanting.*	Same as 1st person, but no form for object in 2nd person.		
3	देखत *dekhat;* देखब *dekhatab;* देखब *dekhatah;* fem. देखति *dekhatih,* देखन्ह *dekhatih,* देखति *dekhatih.*	देखबु *dekhatathí,* देखबु *dekhatathu,* देखबि *dekhotah;* देखबहिं *dekhotaih,* देखति *dekhath.*	GROUP I. देखने *dekhatai* Or (with object in 2nd person.) देखनौ *dekhatau,* देखन्ह *dekhatahu*	Same as 1st person, but no forms for object in 2nd person.	GROUP I. देखनक *dekhataik* Or (with object in 2nd person.) देखनौक *dekhatauk.*	Same as 1st person, but no form for object in 2nd person.	देखनिक्क *dekhataiuk.*	देखयौकि *dekhataiinhí,* देखयूकि *dekhatainhí.*

252. (c) (5) Past Conditional, '(if) I had seen,' &c.; 'I should have seen,' &c.

PERSON	SHORT FORM — GROUP I. (Subject: non-honorific. Object: non-honorific.)	SHORT FORM — GROUP II. (Subject: honorific. Object: non-honorific.)	LONG FORM — GROUP I. (Subject: non-honorific. Object: non-honorific.)	LONG FORM — GROUP II. (Subject: honorific. Object: non-honorific.)	REDUNDANT FORM — GROUP I. (Subject: non-honorific. Object: non-honorific.)	REDUNDANT FORM — GROUP II. (Subject: honorific. Object: non-honorific.)	REDUNDANT FORM — GROUP III. (Subject: non-honorific. Object: honorific.)	REDUNDANT FORM — GROUP IV. (Subject: honorific. Object: honorific.)
1	देखितहुँ *dekhitahũ*,* देखिती *dekhiti* (rare).	Same as 1st person.	देखितिऐ *dekhitiai* Or (with object in 2nd person.) देखितियौ *dekhitiau*, देखितियहँ *dekhitiahũ*	देखितिऐ *dekhitiai*	देखितिऐक *dekhitiai* Or (with object in 2nd person.) देखितियौक *dekhitiauk*, देखितियैक *dekhitiahik*	देखितिऐक *dekhitiaik* Or (with object in 2nd person.) देखितियौक *dekhitiauk*	देखितियुन्हि *dekhitiaũnhĩ*	Same as 1st person.
2	देखितें *dekhitẽ.*	Same as 1st person.	देखितहिँ *dekhitahĩ*, fem. देखितहि *dekhitahi*, देखितँहिँ *dekhi-tāhĩ.*	Same as 1st person, but no forms for object in 2nd person.	देखियहाँक *dekhijahãk*, देखितहिक *dekhitahik.*	Same as 1st person, but no form for object in 2nd person.	देखितहुन्हि *dekhitahũnhĩ*	Same as 1st person.
3	देखैत *dekhait*; fem. देखैति *dekhaiti.*	देखितथि *dekhitathĩ*, देखितन्हि *dekhitanhĩ.*	GROUP I. देखित *dekhitai* Or (with object in 2nd person.) देखितिऔ *dekhitiau*, देखितिन्हु *dekhitinhũ.*		GROUP I. देखितैक *dekhitaik* Or (with object in 2nd person) देखितौक *dekhitauk.*		देखितैन्हि *dekhitainhĩ.*	देखितियैन्हि *dekhitiaĩnhĩ* देखितयुन्हि *dekhit(i)aũnhĩ* देखितयँन्हि *dekhit(i)athãnhĩ.*

* Or देखैतहुँ *dekhaitahũ* or देखलहुँ *dekhḷatahũ*, and so throughout, except in the short form of the 3rd person of Group I.

253. (c) (6) **Present Indicative.** Uncontracted form. 'I see,' &c.; 'I am seeing,' &c.
(The Auxiliary verb does not change for gender, except in the second person of the long form of Group I.)

PERSON	SHORT FORM		LONG FORM		REDUNDANT FORM			
	GROUP I. (Subject: non-honorific. Object: non-honorific.)	GROUP II. (Subject: honorific. Object: non-honorific.)	GROUP I. (Subject: non-honorific. Object: non-honorific.)	GROUP II. (Subject: honorific. Object: non-honorific.)	GROUP I. (Subject: non-honorific. Object: non-honorific.)	GROUP II. (Subject: honorific. Object: non-honorific.)	GROUP III. (Subject: non-honorific. Object: honorific.)	GROUP IV. (Subject: honorific. Object: honorific.)
1	देखल छी dekhait chī; fem. देखलि छी dekhait chī.	Same as 1st person.	देखल छिऎ dekhait chiai; fem. देखलि छिऎ dekhait chiai. Or (with object in 2nd person.) देखल छिऔ dekhait chiau; fem. देखलि छिऔ dekhait chiau.	Same as 1st person, but no forms for object in 2nd person.	देखल छिऐक dekhait chiaik; fem. देखलि छिऐक dekhait chiaik. Or (with object in 2nd person.) देखल छिऔक dekhait chiauk; fem. देखलि छिऔक dekhait chiauk.	Same as 1st person, but no forms for object in 2nd person.	देखल छिऐन्हि dekhait chiainh; fem. देखलि छिऐन्हि dekhait chiainh.	Same as 1st person.
2	देखल छह dekhait chah; fem. देखलि छह dekhait chah.	Same as 1st person.	देखल छह dekhait chah; fem. देखलि छह dekhait chah.	Same as 1st person, but no forms for object in 2nd person.	देखल छह dekhait chalak; fem. देखलि छह dekhait chalak.	Same as 1st person, but no forms for object in 2nd person.	देखल छह dekhait chahunh; fem. देखलि छह dekhait chahunh.	Same as 1st person.
3	देखल अछि dekhait achi; fem. देखलि अछि dekhait achi.	देखल बधि dekhait chathi; fem. देखलि बधि dekhait chathi.	GROUP I. देखल बे dekhait chai; fem. देखलि बे dekhait chai. Or (with object in 2nd person.) देखल बो dekhait chau; fem. देखलि बो dekhait chau.		GROUP I. देखल बेक dekhait chaik; fem. देखलि बेक dekhait chaik. Or (with object in 2nd person.) देखल बोक dekhait chauk; fem. देखलि बोक dekhait chauk.	देखल बेक dekhait chaik; fem. देखलि बेक dekhait chaik.	देखल बन्हि dekhait chainh; fem. देखलि बन्हि dekhait chainh.	देखल बथिन्हि dekhait chathinh; fem. देखलि बथिन्हि dekhait chathinh.

26   92

254. (c) (6) **Present Indicative.** Contracted form. 'I see,' &c.; 'I am seeing,' &c. (The feminine is the same as the masculine, except in the second person of the long form of (group I.)

PERSON	SHORT FORM		LONG FORM		REDUNDANT FORM			
	GROUP I. (Subject: non-honorific. Object: non-honorific.)	GROUP II. (Subject: honorific. Object: non-honorific.)	GROUP I. (Subject: non-honorific. Object: non-honorific.)	GROUP II. (Subject: honorific. Object: non-honorific.)	GROUP I. (Subject: non-honorific. Object: non-honorific.)	GROUP II. (Subject: honorific. Object: non-honorific.)	GROUP III. (Subject: non-honorific. Object: honorific.)	GROUP IV. (Subject: honorific. Object: honorific.)
1	देखबी *dekhai-chī*	Same as 1st person.	देखबिछि *dekhai-chiai* Or (with object in 2nd person) देखबिछो *dekhai-chiau*	Same as 1st person, but no forms for object in 2nd person.	देखबिछिऐक *dekhai-chiaik* Or (with object in 2nd person.) देखबिछिओक *dekhai-chiauk*	Same as 1st person, but no forms for object in 2nd person.	देखबिछिऐन्हि *dekhai-chiainh*	Same as 1st person.
2	देखबह *dekhai-chĕ*	Same as 1st person.	देखबर *dekhai-ciadh*, fem. देखबरि *dekhai-chathī.*		देखबएक *dekhai-elahăk.*		देखबछृन्हि *dekhai-chăhănhī.*	देखबचौन्हि *dekhai-chathīnhī.*
3	देखबधि *dekhai-achĕ*; more usually, देखादि *dekhaichĕ*, देखबह *dekhaïch.*	देखबधि *dekhai-chathĭ*	GROUP I. देखब *dekhai-chai* Or (with object in 2nd person.) देखबो *dekhai-chau.*		GROUP I. देखबक *dekhai-chaik* Or (with object in 2nd person.) देखबोक *dekhai-chauk.*		देखबन्हि *dekhai-chainhĭ.*	देखबचौन्हि *dekhai-chathīnhĭ.*

In both the above forms of the Present Indicative, any optional form of the present tense of the auxiliary verb may be employed, as explained in § 230.

255. (c) (7) **Imperfect Indicative.** Uncontracted form. 'I was seeing,' &c. (The auxiliary verb does not change for gender, except in the third person of the short form of Group I and of Group II, and in the long form of the second person of Group I).

PERSON.	SHORT FORM.		LONG FORM.		REDUNDANT FORM.			
	GROUP I. (Subject: non-honorific. Object: non-honorific.)	GROUP II. (Subject: honorific. Object: non-honorific.)	GROUP I. (Subject: non-honorific. Object: non-honorific.)	GROUP II. (Subject: honorific. Object: non-honorific.)	GROUP I. (Subject: non-honorific. Object: non-honorific.)	GROUP II. (Subject: honorific. Object: non-honorific.)	GROUP III. (Subject: non-honorific. Object: honorific.)	GROUP IV. (Subject: honorific. Object: honorific.)
1	देखत बलिऐ *dekhait chalaĩ*; f. देखिति बलिऐ *dekhait chalaḧ*	देखत बलिऐं *dekhait chalala*; f. देखिति बलिऐं *dekhait chalah*	देखत बलिऐ देखिति बलिऐ देखिति बलिऐ *dekhait chalai*; fem. *dekhait chalai dekhait chalian*	Same as 1st person, but no forms for object in 2nd person.	देखत बलऐक देखत बलिऐक देखिति बलिऐक *dekhait chalaik dekhait chalaik*; f. *dekhait chalauk*	Same as 1st person, but no forms for object in 2nd person.	देखत बलिऐन्हि देखिति बलिऐन्हि *dekhait chalaind*; fem. *dekhait chalainihi*	Same as 1st person. देखत बलैन्हि देखिति बलैन्हि *dekhait chalaind*; f. *dekhait chalainihi*
2	देखत बलें *dekhait chalĕ*; fem. देखिति बलें *dekhait chalĕḧ.*	Same as 1st person.	देखत बलेह *dekhait chalĕh*; f. देखिति बलेह *dekhait chalĕh.*	Same as 1st person, but no forms for object in 2nd person.	देखत बलऐक *dekhait chalalak*; f. देखिति बलऐक *dekhait chalalak.*			
3	देखत बल *dekhait chal*; fem. देखिति बलि *dekhait chalḧ.*	देखत बलाह *dekhait chalalaḧ*; f. देखिति बलिह *dekhait chalḧ.*	देखत बल *dekhait chalal*; fem. देखिति बलि *dekhait chalai* Or (with object in 2nd person.) देखत बली देखिति बली *dekhait chalau dekhait chalau.*		देखत बलक देखिति बलक *dekhait chalalak*; f. Or (with object in 2nd person.) देखत बलौक देखिति बलौक *dekhait chalauk dekhait chalau.*	देखत बलैक देखिति बलैक *dekhait chalaik*; f. Or (with object in 2nd person.) देखत बलैक देखिति बलैक *dekhait chalaik*; fem. *dekhait chalau.*	देखत बलिन्हि देखिति बलिन्हि *dekhait chalainhi*; fem. *dekhait chalainhi.*	

256. (c) (7) **Imperfect Indicative.** Contracted Form. 'I was seeing,' &c. (The feminine is the same as the masculine, except in the third person of Group I and of Group II, and in the long form of the second person of Group I.)

PERSON	SHORT FORM GROUP I. (Subject: non-honorific. Object: non-honorific.)	SHORT FORM GROUP II. (Subject: honorific. Object: non-honorific.)	LONG FORM GROUP I. (Subject: non-honorific. Object: non-honorific.)	LONG FORM GROUP II. (Subject: honorific. Object: non-honorific.)	REDUNDANT FORM GROUP I. (Subject: non-honorific. Object: non-honorific.)	REDUNDANT FORM GROUP II. (Subject: honorific. Object: non-honorific.)	REDUNDANT FORM GROUP III. (Subject: non-honorific. Object: honorific.)	REDUNDANT FORM GROUP IV. (Subject: honorific. Object: honorific.)
1	देखलिऐं *dekhai-chaḷaĩ̃*	Same as 1st person.	देखलिऐ *dekhai-chaḷiai* Or (with object in 2nd person) देखलिऔ *dekhai-chaḷiau*	Same as 1st person, but no forms for object in 2nd person.	देखलिऐक *dekhai-chaḷaik* Or (with object in 2nd person.) देखलिऔक *dekhai-chaḷauk*	Same as 1st person, but no forms for object in 2nd person.	देखलिऐन्हि *dekhai-chaḷainhi*	Same as 1st person.
2	देखलें *dekhai-chaḷẽ*	Same as 1st person.	देखलाढ़ *dekhai-chaḷãḍh,* देखली *dekhai-chaḷih.*	Same as 1st person, but no forms for object in 2nd person.	देखलैक *dekhai-chaḷaik*	Same as 1st person, but no forms for object in 2nd person.	देखलहिन्ह *dekhai-chaḷahãnh.*	Same as 1st person.
3	देखल *dekhai-chaḷ,* fem. देखलि *dekhai-chaḷih.*	देखलाढ़ *dekhai-chaḷãḍh;* fem. देखलीह *dekhai-chaḷih.*	GROUP I. देखलै *dekhai-chaḷai* Or (with object in 2nd person.) देखलौ *dekhai-chaḷau.*		GROUP I. देखलक *dekhai-chaḷaik* Or (with object in 2nd person.) देखलौक *dekhai-chaḷauk.*		देखलैन्हि *dekhai-chaḷainhi.*	देखलथिन्हि *dekhai-chaḷa-thinhi.*

In both the above forms of the Imperfect Indicative any optional form of the past tense of the auxiliary verb may be employed, as explained in § 231.

257. (d) (8) Past Indicative. 'I saw,' &c.

PERSON	SHORT FORM		LONG FORM			REDUNDANT FORM				
	GROUP I. (Subject: non-honorific. Object: non-honorific.)	GROUP II. (Subject: honorific. Object: non-honorific.)	GROUP I. (Subject: non-honorific. Object: non-honorific.)	GROUP II. (Subject: honorific. Object: non-honorific.)		GROUP I. (Subject: non-honorific. Object: non-honorific.)	GROUP II. (Subject: honorific. Object: non-honorific.)	GROUP III. (Subject: non-honorific. Object: honorific.)	GROUP IV. (Subject: honorific. Object: honorific.)
1	देखलुँ dekhaluṅ, देखल dekhal; f. देखली dekhali; instead of देखल dēkhal.	Same as 1st person.	देखल dekhlaṅi, देखलि dekhali. Or (with object in 2nd person.) देखलौ dekhalau, देखल्हुँ dekhalhuṅ deklhalauḥ	देखलिँ dekhalini Or (with object in 2nd person.) देखलौक dekhalauk, देखलिउक dekhaliuk.		देखलक dekhalahik, देखलौक dekhalalik.	देखलौक, देखलिउक dekhalaink, देखलिउक dekhalink. Or (with object in 2nd person.) देखलौक dekhalauk, देखलिउक dekhaliuk.	देखलिन्हि dekhalahiṅ deklhalāhinhi	Same as 1st person.
2	देखलें dekhalē, देखलइ dekhalaī.	Same as 1st person.	देखलेँ dekhalaiṅ; fem. देखलिहि dekhalihi देखलुँ dekhalhi.	Same as 1st person, but no forms for object in 2nd person.		देखलक dekhalahik, देखलिक dekhalaik.	Same as 1st person, but no forms for object in 2nd person.	देखलहिन्हि dekhlahinhi	Same as 1st person.
3	देखलक dekhalak, *देखल dēkhal; f *देखलि dēkhali.	देखलिन्हि dekhalainhi, *देखलथि dekhalathi	देखलक dekhalakai Or (with object in 2nd person.) देखलौ dekhalakau.	GROUP I. देखलक dekhalakai Or (with object in 2nd person.) देखलौक dekhalakau.	GROUP I. देखलकैक dekhalakaik Or (with object in 2nd person.) देखलकौक dekhalakauk.			देखलकि dekhala katink	देखलधिन्हि dekhalathinhi, देखलथिन्हि deklhalathinhi

* These forms are peculiar to poetry. In the modern language they are only used by the vulgar.

258. (*d*) (9) **Perfect Indicative. First Form. 'I have seen,' &c.**

PERSON	SHORT FORM GROUP I. (Subject: non-honorific. Object: non-honorific.)	SHORT FORM GROUP II. (Subject: honorific. Object: non-honorific.)	LONG FORM GROUP I. (Subject: non-honorific. Object: non-honorific.)	LONG FORM GROUP II. (Subject: honorific. Object: non-honorific.)	REDUNDANT FORM GROUP I. (Subject: non-honorific. Object: non-honorific.)	REDUNDANT FORM GROUP II. (Subject: honorific. Object: non-honorific.)	REDUNDANT FORM GROUP III. (Subject: non-honorific. Object: honorific.)	REDUNDANT FORM GROUP IV. (Subject: honorific. Object: honorific.)
1	देखलूँ चुकि *dekhalũ achi*	Same as 1st person.	देखल चुकि *dekhalaũh achi* / Or (with object in 2nd person.) देखलिहि चुकि *dekhalaiũh achi*	Same as 1st person, but no forms for object in 2nd person.	देखलक चुकि *dekhalahãk achi* / देखलौक चुकि *dekhalahãk achi*	Same as 1st person, but no forms for object in 2nd person.	देखलैन्हि चुकि *dekhalainhi achi*	Same as 1st person
2	Same as 1st person.	Same as 1st person.					देखलहुन्हि चुकि *hidnhi achi*	Same as 1st person
3	देखलक चुकि *dekhalak achi*	देखलन्हि चुकि *dekhalanhi achi*	देखलक चुकि *dekhalakai achi* / Or (with object in 2nd person.) देखलकौ चुकि *dekhalakau achi*		देखलकक चुकि *dekhalakaik achi* / Or देखलकौक चुकि *dekhalakauk achi*	देखलकक चुकि *dekhalakaik achi* / Or (with object in 2nd person.) देखलकौक चुकि *dekhalakauk achi*	देखलकन्हि चुकि *kainhi achi* / चुकि dekhala. *kainhi achi*	देखलथीन्हि चुकि *dekhala-thinh achi* / चुकि dekhala. *thinh achi*

Any other optional form of the preterite indicative may be substituted for those given above. Thus देखल चुकि *dekhal achi*, देखलिऐ चुकि *dekholiai achi*, etc. Also, instead of चुकि *achi* we may substitute any other optional form of the third person of the present of the auxiliary verb; but the ones in ordinary use are चुकि *achi* and चुकि *ahi*.

259. (*d*) (9) **Perfect Indicative. Second Form.** 'I have seen,' &c.

PERSON	SHORT FORM		LONG FORM		REDUNDANT FORM			
	GROUP I. (Subject: non-honorific. Object: non-honorific.)	GROUP II. (Subject: honorific. Object: non-honorific.)	GROUP I. (Subject: non-honorific. Object: non-honorific.)	GROUP II. (Subject: honorific. Object: non-honorific.)	GROUP I. (Subject: non-honorific. Object: non-honorific.)	GROUP II. (Subject: honorific. Object: non-honorific.)	GROUP III. (Subject: non-honorific. Object: honorific.)	GROUP IV. (Subject: honorific. Object: honorific.)
1	देखल छी *dekhalõ chi.*	Same as 1st person.	देखल चिऐ *dekhalõ chiai* Or (with object in 2nd person.) देखल चिऔ *dekhalõ chiau.*	देखल चिऐ *dekhalõ chiai* देखल चिऔ *dekhalõ chiau.*	देखल चिऐक *dekhalõ chaik* Or (with object in 2nd person.) देखल चिऔक *dekhalõ chiauk.*	देखल चिऐक *dekhalõ chaik* देखल चिऔक *dekhalõ chiauk.*	देखल चिऐथि *dekhalõ chaith*	Same as 1st person.
2	देखल छ *dekhalõ chë.*	Same as 1st person.	देखल छह *dekhalõ chah;* देखल बहि *dekhalõ chahi.*	Same as 1st person, but no forms for object in 2nd person.	देखल चहैक *dekhalõ chahãk.*	Same as 1st person, but no forms for object in 2nd person.	देखल चहुनि *dekhalõ chahũnĩ*	
3	देखल चि *dekhalõ achi.* देखल चिथि *dekhalõ chathí.*		GROUP I. देखल क *dekhalõ chai* Or (with object in 2nd person.) देखल को *dekhalõ chau.*		GROUP I. देखल कैक *dekhalõ chaik* Or (with object in 2nd person.) देखल कौक *dekhalõ chauk.*		देखल चैनि *dekhalõ chainĩ* देखल कैनि *dekhalõ chainĩ.*	देखल चथिनि *dekhalõ chathinĩ* देखल चथिनि *dekhalõ chathinĩ.*

Instead of देखल *dekhalõ*, we often hear देखने *dekholẽ*. The vulgar often substitute देखने *dekhané* or देखने *dekhoné*, and these forms are also occasionally used by the educated.

Any optional form of the present tense of the auxiliary verb may be employed, as explained in § 236.

260. (*d*) (10) Pluperfect Indicative. 'I had seen,' &c.; 'I saw a long time ago,' &c.

PERSON.	SHORT FORM. GROUP I. (Subject: non-honorific. Object: non-honorific.)	SHORT FORM. GROUP II. (Subject: honorific. Object: non-honorific.)	LONG FORM. GROUP I. (Subject: non-honorific. Object: non-honorific.)	LONG FORM. GROUP II. (Subject: honorific. Object: non-honorific.)	REDUNDANT FORM. GROUP I. (Subject: non-honorific. Object: non-honorific.)	REDUNDANT FORM. GROUP II. (Subject: honorific. Object: non-honorific.)	REDUNDANT FORM. GROUP III. (Subject: non-honorific. Object: honorific.)	REDUNDANT FORM. GROUP IV. (Subject: honorific. Object: honorific.)
1	देखल कहुँ *dekhalẽ chalẽ.*	Same as 1st person.	देखल चलिहुँ *dekhalẽ chalai* / Or (with object in 2nd person.) देखल चलिऔ *dekhalẽ chaliau*	देखल चलाइ *dekhalẽ chalai* — Same as 1st person, but no forms for object in 2nd person.	देखल चलिऐक *dekhalẽ chaliaik* / Or (with object in 2nd person.) देखल चलिऔक *dekhalẽ chaliauk*	Same as 1st person, but no forms for object in 2nd person.	देखल चलिऐन्हि *dekhalẽ chaliainhi.*	Same as 1st person.
2	Same as 1st person.	—	देखल चलाह *dekhalẽ chalah ;* f. देखल चलीह *dekhalẽ chalih.*	Same as 1st person, but no forms for object in 2nd person.	देखल चलऽक *dekhalẽ chalauk*	Same as 1st person, but no forms for object in 2nd person.	देखल चलऽहि *dekhalẽ chalahunhi.*	Same as 1st person.
3	देखल चल *dekhalẽ chal ;* f. देखल चलि *dekhalẽ chalih.*	देखल चलाह *dekhalẽ chalah ;* f. देखल चलीह *dekhalẽ chalih.*	देखल चल *dekhalẽ chalai* / Or (with object in 2nd person.) देखल चलौ *dekhalẽ chalau.*	देखल चलाइ *dekhalẽ chalai* / Or (with object in 2nd person.) देखल चलाउ *dekhalẽ chalau.*	देखल चलैक *dekhalẽ chalaik* / Or (with object in 2nd person.) देखल देलक *denalẽ chalauk.*	देखल चलैक *dekhalẽ chalaik* / Or (with object in 2nd person.) देखल चलऽक *dekhalẽ chalauk.*	देखल चलैन्हि *dekhalẽ cha-lainhi.*	देखल चलथिन्हि *dekhalẽ chala-thinhi.*

As in the perfect देखने *dekhlẽ,* देखनऐ *dekhlõe* or देखने *dekhlõne* are found instead of देखल *dekhalẽ.*

Any optional form of the past tense of the auxiliary verb may be employed, as explained in § 238.

261.   Verbal Nouns and Infinitives.

(1) देखि *dēkh*[i] (or देख *dēkh*) (oblique form, देखे *dēkhai* or देखँ *dēkhá̃*), the act of seeing.

(2) देखब *dēkhab* (obl. form, देखबा *dekh*ᵃ*bā*), the act of seeing, to see.

(3) देखल *dēkhal* (obl. form, देखला *dekh*ᵃ*lā*), the act of seeing.

262.   Noun of Agency.

देखबाइ *dekh*ᵃ*bāh* or देखवाइ *dekh*ᵃ*wāh*, one who sees.

263.   Participles.

Present :—देखैत *dekhait* (fem. देखैति *dekhait*[i]), seeing.

Past :—देखल *dēkhal* (fem. देखलि *dēkhal*[i]), seen.

Conjunctive :—देखि *dēkh*[i] (देख *dēkh*), देखि कँ *dēkh*[i] *kai*, देखि कँ *dēkh*[i] *kã̃*, or देखि कँकँ *dēkh*[i] *kaikã̃*, having seen.

Adverbial :—देखितहिं *dekhitah*[i], on seeing, in the act of seeing, immediately on seeing.

B.   INTRANSITIVE VERB.

√छत *sūt*, sleep.

264.   It is only necessary to give paradigms of those tenses of the intransitive verb which are formed from the past participle. In the other tenses it is conjugated exactly like the transitive verb.

As the intransitive verb has no direct object, those forms of the verb which have special reference to the object, *viz.*, Groups III and IV, and the long forms in औ *au* of Groups I and II can only refer to the indirect object.   The mode of their employment is explained in § 189.

265. (d) (8) Past Indicative. 'I slept,' &c.

PERSON	SHORT FORM		LONG FORM		REDUNDANT FORM			
	GROUP I. (Subject: non-honorific. Object: non-honorific.)	GROUP II. (Subject: honorific. Object: non-honorific.)	GROUP I. (Subject: non-honorific. Object: non-honorific.)	GROUP II. (Subject: honorific. Object: non-honorific.)	GROUP I. (Subject: non-honorific. Object: non-honorific.)	GROUP II. (Subject: honorific. Object: non-honorific.)	GROUP III. (Subject: non-honorific. Object (indirect): honorific.)	GROUP IV. (Subject: honorific. Object (indirect): honorific.)
1	सुतलहुँ *suṭalaḥũ*, सुतली *suṭalī*.	Same as 1st person.	सुतलिऐ *suṭaliai* Or (with indirect object in 2nd person.) सुतलिऔ *suṭaliau*, सुतलिअहु *suṭaliahu*.	Same as 1st person, but no forms for object in 2nd person.	सुतलिऐक *suṭaliaik* Or (with indirect object in 2nd person.) सुतलिऔक *suṭaliauk*.	Same as 1st person, but no forms for object in 2nd person.	सुतलिऐन्हि *suṭaliainhĩ*	Same as 1st person.
2	सुतलह *suṭalaḥ*, सुतलें *suṭalaẽ*.	Same as 1st person.	सुतलेँ *suṭalaẽ*; fem. सुतलिहि *suṭalili*, सुतलेँहि *suṭalililĩ*.	Same as 1st person, but no forms for object in 2nd person.	सुतलेँक *suṭalaḥik*, सुतलेँक *suṭalalik*.	Same as 1st person, but no forms for object in 2nd person.	सुतलेँहि *suṭalalainhĩ*.	सुतलेँयौहि *suṭalathãnhĩ*, सुतलेँयुहि *suṭalalyũnhĩ* *suṭalalainhĩ*.
3	सुतल *sūtal'*; fem. सुतलि *sūtali*.	सुतलाह *suṭalāh* (fem. सुतलिह *suṭalili*, सुतलेँहि *suṭalilĩ*); सुत-लिहि *suṭalainhĩ*	सुतल *suṭalai* Or (with indirect object in 2nd person.) सुतलो *suṭalau*, सुतलहु *suṭalahu*	GROUP I. सुतलैक *suṭalaik* Or (with indirect object in 2nd person.) सुतलौक *suṭalauk*.				

266. (d) (9) **Perfect Indicative.** First form. ' I have slept,' &c.

PERSON	SHORT FORM			LONG FORM			REDUNDANT FORM			
	GROUP I. (Subject: non-honorific. Object: non-honorific.)	GROUP II. (Subject: honorific. Object: non-honorific.)		GROUP I. (Subject: non-honorific. Object: non-honorific.)	GROUP II. (Subject: honorific. Object: non-honorific.)		GROUP I. (Subject: non-honorific. Object: non-honorific.)	GROUP II. (Subject: honorific. Object: non-honorific.)	GROUP III. (Subject: non-honorific. Object (indirect): honorific.)	GROUP IV. (Subject: honorific. Object (indirect): honorific.)
1	सुतलहुँ चुकि *sutalẽ achi.*	सुतलहुँ चुकि *sutalahũ achi*; fem. सुतलिहुँ चुकि *sutalih achi.*		सुतलिहुँ चुकि *sutalai achi* ; f. सुतलिहुँ चुकि *sutalih achi.* Or (with ind. obj. in 2nd person.) सुतलिहुँ चुकि *sutalai achi.* सुतलिहौ चुकि *sutaliau achi.*	सुतलिहिक चुकि *sutalaik achi* Or (with ind. obj. in 2nd person.) सुतलिचौक चुकि *sutliauk achi.*				सुतलिहौन्हि चुकि *sutalaiainhi achi*	Same as 1st person.
2	सुतलक चुकि *sutalak achi.*	Same as 1st person.		सुतलक चुकि *sutalk achi.* Or (with ind. obj. in 2nd person.) सुतलौक चुकि *sutalauk achi.*	Same as 1st person, but no forms for object in 2nd person.		सुतलहिन्हि चुकि *sutalahinhi achi.*		Same as 1st person.
3	सुतलक चुकि *sutaldh achi*; fem. सुतलीक चुकि *sutalih achi.*			सुतलैक चुकि *sutlak achi* Or (with ind. obj. in 2nd person.) सुतलौक चुकि *sutlauk achi.*			सुतलिहिन्हि चुकि *sutalainhi achi.*			सुतलहौन्हि चुकि *sutalathinhi achi.*

Any optional form of the Past Indicative may be substituted for those given above. Thus सुतल्ही चुकि *sutali achi*, I have slept, instead of सुतलहुँ चुकि अछि *sutalahũ achi.*

Also, instead of चुकि *achi* we may substitute any of the optional forms of the present of the auxiliary verb; but the ones in ordinary use are चुकि *achi* and चुकि *ah.*

267. (*d*) (9) **Perfect Indicative.** Second Form. 'I have slept,' &c.; 'I am asleep,' &c.

PERSON.	SHORT FORM.		LONG FORM.		REDUNDANT FORM.			
	GROUP I. (Subject: non-honorific. Object: non-honorific.)	GROUP II. (Subject: honorific. Object: non-honorific.)	GROUP I. (Subject: non-honorific. Object: non-honorific.)	GROUP II. (Subject: honorific. Object: non-honorific.)	GROUP I. (Subject: non-honorific. Object: non-honorific.)	GROUP II. (Subject: honorific. Object: non-honorific.)	GROUP III. (Subject: non-honorific. Object (indirect): honorific.)	GROUP IV. (Subject: honorific. Object (indirect): honorific.)
1	खतल छों *sätal chĕ*; fem. छतलि छो *sätalĭ chĕ.*	Same as 1st person.	खतल छिइ *sätal chai*; fem. छतलि छिइ *sätal chiai.* Or (with indirect object in 2nd per.) छतलि छिञौ *sätal chiau*; fem. छतलि छिञौ *sätal chiau.*	खतल छिइ *sätal chiai*; fem. छतलि छिञौ *sätal chiau.*	खतल कइक *sätal chahăk*; f. छतलि कछेक *sätalĭ chahăk.*	खतल छिइक *sätal chiaik*; छतलि छिइक *sätal chiaik.* Or (with indirect object in 2nd per.) छतलि छिञौक *sätal chiauk*; fem. छतलि छिञौक *sätal chiauk.*	छतल छिञेन्हि *sätal chiainh*; fem. छतलि छिञेन्हि *sätal chiainhĭ.*	Same as 1st person.
2	खतल छें *sätal chĕ*; fem. छतलि छें *sätalĭ chĕ.*		खतल छेंह *sätal chăih*; fem. छतलि छेंहि *sätal chahĭ.*	Same as 1st person, but no forms for object in 2nd person.	खतल कछंक *sätal chahăk*; f. छतलि कछंक *sätalĭ chahăk.*	Same as 1st person, but no forms for object in 2nd person.	खतल कछेंहि *sätal chahăihĭ*; f. छतलि कछेंहि *sätalĭ chahăihĭ.*	Same as 1st person.
3	खतल अछि *sätal achĭ*; fem. छतलि अछि *sätalĭ achĭ.*	खतल छथि *sätal chathĭ*; f. छतलि छथि *sätalĭ chathĭ.*	खतल छइ *sätal chai*; f. छतलि छइ *sätalĭ chai.* Or (with ind. obj. in 2nd person.) छतलि छौ *sätal chau*; f. छतलि छौ *sätalĭ chau.*		खतल कैक *sätal chaik*; f. छतलि कैक *sätalĭ chaik.* Or (with ind. obj. in 2nd person.) छतलि कौक *sätal chauk*; f. छतलि कौक *sätalĭ chauk.*	खतल छैक *sätal chaik*; f. छतलि छैक *sätalĭ chaik.*	खतल छैंहि *sätal chainhĭ*; fem. छतलि छैंहि *sätalĭ chainhĭ.*	खतल छथीन्हि *sätal chathĭnhĭ*; fem. छतलि छथीन्हि *sätalĭ chathĭnhĭ.*

Any optional form of the present tense of the auxiliary verb may be employed, as explained in § 236.

268. (d.) (10) **Pluperfect Indicative.** 'I had slept,' &c.; 'I slept a long time ago,' &c.; 'I was asleep,' &c.

PERSON	SHORT FORM		LONG FORM				REDUNDANT FORM		
	GROUP I. (Subject: non-honorific. Object: non-honorific.)	GROUP II. (Subject: honorific. Object: non-honorific.)	GROUP I. (Subject: non-honorific. Object: non-honorific.)	GROUP II. (Subject: honorific. Object: non-honorific.)	GROUP III. (Subject: non-honorific. Object (indirect): honorific.)	GROUP IV. (Subject: honorific. Object indirect: honorific.)	GROUP I. (Subject: non-honorific. Object: non-honorific.)	GROUP II. (Subject: honorific. Object: non-honorific.)	GROUP III. (Subject: non-honorific. Object (indirect): honorific.)
1	सूतल* कहूँ *sūtal chalaũ*; f. सूतलि* कहूँ *sūtali chalaũ*.	Same as 1st person.	सूतल कहलिहुँ *sūtal chaliũ* Or (with ind. obj. in 2nd person) सूतलि कहलियो *sūtali chaliau*; fem. सूतलि कहलियो *sūtali chaliau*.	Same as 1st person, but no forms for object in 2nd person.	सूतल कहलिहुनि *sūtal chaliainhĩ*; fem. सूतलि कहलिहुनि *sūtali chaliainhĩ*.	Same as 1st person.	सूतल कहलिहक *sūtal chaliaik*; fem. सूतलि कहलिहक *sūtali chaliaik*. Or (with ind. obj. in 2nd person.) सूतल कहलियोक *sūtal chaliauk*; f. सूतलि कहलियोक *sūtali chaliauk*.	Same as 1st person, but no forms for object in 2nd person.	सूतल कहलिहुनि *sūtal chaliainhĩ*; fem. सूतलि कहलिहुनि *sūtali chaliainhĩ*.
2	सूतल कहें *sūtal chalẽ*; fem. सूतलि कहें *sūtali chalẽ*.	Same as 1st person.	सूतल कहलह *sūtal chalah*; f. सूतलि कहली *sūtali chalih*.	Same as 1st person, but no forms for object in 2nd person.			सूतल कहलहक *sūtal chalahak*; f. सूतलि कहलहक *sūtali chalahak*.	Same as 1st person, but no forms for object in 2nd person.	सूतल कहलहुनि *sūtal chalahũ-nhĩ*; f. सूतलि कहलहुनि *sūtali chalahũnhĩ*.
3	सूतल कह *sūtal chal*; fem. सूतलि कहलि *sūtali chali*.	सूतल कहलाह *sūtal chalāh*, fem. सूतलि कहलीह *sūtali chalih*.	सूतल कहल *sūtal chalai*; fem सूतलि कहलि *sūtali chalai* Or (with ind. obj. in 2nd person.) सूतल कहलौ *sūtal chalau*; fem. सूतलि कहलौ *sūtali chalau*.	सूतल कहलैक *sūtal chalaik*; fem सूतलि कहलैक *sūtali chalaik* Or (with ind. obj. in 2nd person.) सूतल कहलौक *sūtal chaliauk*; f. सूतलि कहलौक *sūtali chaliauk*.			सूतल कहलक *sūtal chalaik*; fem. सूतलि कहलक *sūtali chalaik* Or (with ind. obj. in 2nd person.) सूतल कहलौक *sūtal chaliauk*; fem. सूतलि कहलौक *sūtali chaliauk*.		सूतल कहलैनि *sūtal chalai-nhĩ*; f. सूतलि कहलैनि *sūtali chalainhĩ*.

* Or (both masc. and fem.) सूतलैं *sutaĩ*, or (less commonly, and mostly by the uneducated) सूतलें *sutalẽ*, सूतलैं *sutalaĩ*, or सूतनें *sutanĕ*.

Any optional form of the past tense of the auxiliary verb may be employed, as explained in § 238.

CHAPTER V.

Vocalic Roots.

269. The roots of the verbs conjugated in the preceding chapter end in a consonant. If a root ends in a vowel, the same terminations are added, but when these commence with a vowel, changes, which require explanation, occur in the method of suffixing them to the root.

The same is the case with verbs whose roots end in आब *āb*, in which the ब *b* represents an older semi-vowel व *v*, which is, as a general rule, ultimately derived from a Sanskrit प *p*. The conjugation of these verbs runs parallel with that of verbs in आ *ā*, but at the same time differs from them in certain particulars. Owing to the nature of these roots in आब *āb*, I class them as vocalic roots for convenience of treatment.

Vocalic roots may end in आ *ā*, आब *āb*, इ *i*, ई *ī*, ए *ē*, ऊ *ū* or ओ *ō*. They will be dealt with in that order.

Roots in आ *ā* and आब *āb*.

270. Of all vocalic roots these are by far most common. Verbs whose roots end in आ *ā* include all potential passives (see § 333), a large number of intransitive verbs, and the transitive verb √ खा *khā*, eat.

Verbs whose roots end in आब *āb* include nearly all causals and double causals (see §§ 334 and ff), a certain number of transitive verbs, and the intransitive verbs √गाब *gāb*, sing., √पश्चताब *pachᵃtāb*, repent, and √आब *āb*, come. √आब *āb* is irregular in some of its forms and will be dealt with in § 312, although in this chapter I have freely used regular forms in the examples. √गाब *gāb* follows the other roots in आब *āb*, except that as they are transitive and it is usually intransitive, it in such cases takes the intransitive forms of the past tenses. When used as a tran-

sitive verb it is conjugated as such. Thus,—गाओल *gāol*, he sang
(intransitive) : but (Vid. xxiii, 11) प्रह गाओल *eh gāol*, I sang this
(transitive).

271. As a great many verbs have both potential passive
and causal forms, we frequently notice pairs of each conjugation
running side by side. Thus from the √देख *dēkh*, see, we have
the potential passive √देखा *dēkhā*, be visible, and the causal
√देखाब *dēkhāb*, cause to see, show. The past participle of the
former would be देखाएल *dekhāel* and of the latter देखाओल *dekhāol*.
देखैलहुँ *dekhailah^u* would mean ' I was visible.' देखौलहुँ *dekhaulah^u*
would mean ' I caused to see.'

The following are examples of these roots, with the past participle in each case :—

A. Verbs in आ *ā*.

Root.	Past Participle.
देखा *dēkhā*, be visible,	देखाएल *dekhāel*.
अघा *aghā*, be satiated.	अघाएल *aghāel*.
घबड़ा *ghab^arā*, be confused.	घबड़ाएल *ghab^arāel*.
हड़बड़ा *har^abarā*, be flurried.	हड़बड़ाएल *har^abarāel*.
खा *khā*, eat,	खाएल *khāel*.

B. Verbs in आब *āb*.

देखाब *dēkhāb*, show,	देखाओल *dekhāol*.
पाब *pāb*, obtain,	पाओल *pāol*.
गाब *gāb*, sing,	गाओल *gāol*.
पछताब *pach^atāb*, repent.	पछताओल *pach^atāol*.

272. As usual (*vide* §§ 32 ff) the termination आ *ā* or आब *āb*
is liable to be shortened in the antepenultimate. It is usually,
however, retained long before a final ऐ *ai* or औ *au*. Thus पावै
pābai. पावौ *pābau*, as explained in § 176. Before ऐत *ait* of the

present participle आब *āb* is as usual shortened, as in पबैत *pabait.*
Verbs in आ *ā*, on the other hand. make the present participle as in
खाइत *khāit* or खायित *khāyit.*

When the final vowel of a root in आ *ā* comes before a termination beginning with अ *a*, the two together become आए *āe*.
Thus खा *khā* + अल *a* becomes खाएल *khāel* (really for खायल
khāyal, with euphonic य *y* inserted), eaten or I ate ; खा *khā* + अब *ab*
becomes खाएब *khāeb*, to eat or I shall eat. Before ऐ *ai*, it
usually remains unchanged, as in देखाऐ *dekhāai*, he sees, but in the
present participle, the termination ऐत *ait* becomes इत *it*, and
before the इ *i* the आ *ā* either remains unchanged or inserts a
य *y* ; thus, as above, खाइत *khāit* or खायित *khāyit*, eating. As usual
(see §§ 11, 14) इ *i* is often employed for ए *e*, and *vice versa*, so that
we may meet forms such as खाइल *khāil*, खाइब *khāib* or खाएत *khāet*.
In all these cases, when the आ *ā* is shortened under the antepenultimate rule, the two vowels together become ऐ *ai* (often
written, as usual अइ *ai* or अए *ae*. see § 13). Thus खैलहुँ *khailahů*,
I ate, खैबै *khaibai*, I shall eat, खैतहुँ *khaitahů* (if) I had eaten.

273. With roots ending in आब *āb*, the procedure is somewhat different. As a general rule, before अ *a*, the आब *āb* plus
अ *a* becomes आओ *āo*. Thus देखाब *dekhāb* + अब *ab* becomes
देखाओब *dekhāob* (poetical form ; for the usual form see below). I
shall show ; देखाब *dekhāb* + अल *al* becomes देखाओल *dekhāol*, I
showed. In the form देखाबथि *dekhābathi* (3rd person, Short Form,
Group II, Old Present), the ब *b* is preserved unchanged.

Before terminations commencing with ऐ *ai* or औ *au* the ब *b* is
usually retained. Thus देखाबै *dekhābai*, देखाबौ *dekhābau* (3rd person, Long Form, Group I, Old Present) ; Present Participle देखबैत
dekhᵃbait, with shortening of the antepenultimate. Before इ *i*
or ई *ī*, आब *āb* remains unchanged, as in देखाबी *dekhābī*, I show.

274.   In the modern language there is a tendency to assimilate the conjugation of roots in आब *āb* to that of those in आ *ā*.   A glance at the paradigm will show that many optional forms are borrowed from the latter conjugation.   In the 2nd verbal noun and in the future the conjugation in आ *ā* has almost ousted the original one.   We have just seen that the old poetical form of the first person future was देखाओब *dekhāob*, I shall show.   In the modern language it is, however, always देखाएब *dekhāeb*.   A reference to the paradigm will show how completely the original *o*-conjugation has disappeared in the future.   It has only survived in the third form of the tense.

On the other hand, the past tense, the one most frequently employed, strongly preserves the *o*-conjugation.   The conjugation of roots in आ *ā*, has here entirely failed to gain a footing.   In this tense, and elsewhere in similar circumstances, when आओ *ā-o* becomes अओ *a-o*, under the antepenultimate rule, the two adjacent vowels coalesce, and are usually written औ *au*.   Thus, देखाओल *dekhāol* or देखौलहुँ *dekhaulah*[u], I showed.

275.   In the following paradigms, I take as the model of a root in आ *ā* the √देखा *dekhā*, be visible, and as the model of a root in आब *āb*, √देखाब *dekhāb*, show.   I only give the short and long forms of Groups I and II.   The redundant forms of these two groups, and the forms of Groups III and IV can be made from these without any difficulty.   In cases where any difficulty is likely to arise, I solve it in additional notes.   It is only necessary to give the four simple tenses, the verbal nouns, and the participles.   The periphrastic tenses can easily be made from these materials.   Even for the four simple tenses, I only give the most common forms.

One other remark should be made.   I have throughout spoken of roots ending in आब *āb*.   This termination is very often written आव *āw* or *āv*, and is even so pronounced in South Mithilā.   Thus, instead of देखाबी *dekhābī*, we hear देखावी *dekhāwī* or *dekhāvī*,

28

and so throughout. There is no doubt that in the best standard Maithili the correct forms are those with ब *b*, though व *w* forms will often be found in literature (generally due to careless writing).

276. (a) (1) **Old Present.**

'I am visible,' &c.   'I show,' &c.

PERSON	I am visible — SHORT FORM		I am visible — LONG FORM		I show — SHORT FORM		I show — LONG FORM	
	GROUP I. (Subject: non-honorific. Object: non-honorific.)	GROUP II. (Subject: honorific. Object: non-honorific.)	GROUP I. (Subject: non-honorific. Object: non-honorific.)	GROUP II. (Subject: honorific. Object: non-honorific.)	GROUP I. (Subject: non-honorific. Object: non-honorific.)	GROUP II. (Subject: honorific. Object: non-honorific.)	GROUP I. (Subject: non-honorific. Object: non-honorific.)	GROUP II. (Subject: honorific. Object: non-honorific.)
1	देखाैं *dekhaĩ*, देखाउ *dekhāũ*	Same as 1st person.	देखाइ *dekhāai*. Or (with object in 2nd person) देखाओ *dekhāaũ*, देखाज्ञ *dekhāṽ*.	Same as 1st person, but no forms for object in 2nd person.	देखाबी *dekhābī*, देखाबौं *dekhābaũ*	देखाबि *dekhābi* (देखाज *dekhāū*).	देखाबिउ *dekhābiũ* (*dekhābiaĩ*) Or (with obj. in 2nd pers) देखाबिअु *dekhābiau* (देखाबौं *dekhābiaũ*).	Same as 1st person, but no forms for object in 2nd person.
2	देखाए *dekhāe*, (often spelt देखाय *dekhāy*), देखाओ *dekhāo* (देखाव *dekhāv*)	देखाुश्चि *dekhāthi*	देखाल *dekhāl*.	Same as 1st person, but no forms for object in 2nd person.	देखाब *dekhāb*.	Same as 1st person.	देखाबह *dekhābah*, Red. form देखाबहक *dekhābahak*.	Same as 1st person, but no forms for object in 2nd person.
3	Same as 1st person.	देखाथि *dekhāthi*	GROUP I. देखाउ *dekhāũ* Or (with object in 2nd person.) देखाओ *dekhāau*, देखाज *dekhāṽ*		देखाबे *dekhābe* (देखाए *dekhāe*.)	देखाबथि *dekhābathi*.	GROUP I. देखाबइ *dekhābai*. Or (with object in 2nd person.) देखाबौ *dekhābau*.	

For ā-verbs, in Groups III and IV, we have (1) देखेंहिं *dekhaĩinhĩ* ; (2) देखाइहिं *dekhāihĩ* ; (3) देखाउंहिं *dekhāũhĩ* ; *dekhāũinhĩ* ; देखाथिंहिं *dekhāthĩnhĩ*.

277. (*b*) (4) **Future Indicative. Second Form.**

'I shall be visible, &c.'

'I shall show,' &c.

PERSON	SHORT FORM — GROUP I. (Subject: non-honorific. Object: non-honorific.)	SHORT FORM — GROUP II. (Subject: honorific. Object: non-honorific.)	LONG FORM — GROUP I. (Subject: non-honorific. Object: non-honorific.)	LONG FORM — GROUP II. (Subject: honorific. Object: non-honorific.)	SHORT FORM — GROUP I. (Subject: non-honorific. Object: non-honorific.)	SHORT FORM — GROUP II. (Subject: honorific. Object: non-honorific.)	LONG FORM — GROUP I. (Subject: non-honorific. Object: non-honorific.)	LONG FORM — GROUP II. (Subject: honorific. Object: non-honorific.)
1	देखाएब *dekhaeb* / देखैब *dekhaibĕ*	Same as 1st person.	देखैबै *dekhaibai* — Or (with object in 2nd person) देखैबौ *dekhaibau.*	Same as 1st person, but no forms for object in 2nd person.	देखाएब *dekhaeb* (poetical) देखाओब *dekháob.* / देखैब *dekhaibĕ.*	Same as 1st person.	देखैबै *dekhaibai* — Or (with object in 2nd person.) देखैबौ *dekhaibau.*	Same as 1st person, but no forms for object in 2nd person.
2	Wanting.	Wanting.	देखैबैह *dekhaibáh.*		Wanting.	Wanting.	देखबैह *dekhaibáh.*	
3	Wanting.		GROUP I. Wanting.		Wanting.		GROUP I. Wanting.	

278. (b) (+) Future Indicative. Third Form.

'I shall be visible,' &c.   'I shall show,' &c.

'I shall be visible,' &c.

PERSON.	SHORT FORM. GROUP I. (Subject: non-honorific. Object: non-honorific.)	SHORT FORM. GROUP II. (Subject: honorific. Object: non-honorific.)	LONG FORM. GROUP I. (Subject: non-honorific. Object: non-honorific.)	LONG FORM. GROUP II. (Subject: honorific. Object: non-honorific.)
1	देखबूँ *dekhaitaũ.*	देखबूँ *dekhaitaũ.*	देखबिते *dekhaitai* Or (with object in 2nd person). देखबिताँ *dekhaitaũ*	देखबिते *dekhaitai* Or (with object in 2nd person). देखबिताँ *dekhaitaũ*
2	Wanting.	Same as 1st person.	Wanting.	Same as 1st person, but no forms for object in 2nd person.
3	देखारत *dekhãit.*	देखबाद *dekhaitãh.*	GROUP I. देखब *dekhaitai* Or (with object in 2nd person). देखबताँ *dekhaitau*	

'I shall show,' &c.

PERSON.	SHORT FORM. GROUP I. (Subject: non-honorific. Object: non-honorific.)	SHORT FORM. GROUP II. (Subject: honorific. Object: non-honorific.)	LONG FORM. GROUP I. (Subject: non-honorific. Object: non-honorific.)	LONG FORM. GROUP II. (Subject: honorific. Object: non-honorific.)
1	देखबूँ *dekhautaũ.*	देखबाऊ *dekhautaũ.*	देखबिते *dekhautai* Or (with obj. in 2nd person.) देखबिताँ *dekhautiaũ.*	देखबाते *dekhautiai* देखबाऊताँ *dekhautiau.* Same as 1st person, but no forms for object in 2nd person.
2	Wanting.	Same as 1st person.	Wanting.	Same as 1st person, but no forms for object in 2nd person.
3	देखाबत *dekhãot.*	देखबाद *dekhautãh.*	GROUP I. देखबत *dekhautai* Or (with obj. in 2nd person.) देखबताँ *dekhautau.*	

279. (c) (5) Past Conditional.

'If I had been visible,' &c.; 'I should have been visible,' &c.   'If I had shown,' &c.; 'I should have shown,' &c.

PERSON	SHORT FORM — GROUP I (Subject: non-honorific. Object: non-honorific.)	SHORT FORM — GROUP II (Subject: honorific. Object: non-honorific.)	LONG FORM — GROUP I (Subject: non-honorific. Object: non-honorific.)	LONG FORM — GROUP II (Subject: honorific. Object: non-honorific.)	SHORT FORM — GROUP I (Subject: non-honorific. Object: non-honorific.)	SHORT FORM — GROUP II (Subject: honorific. Object: non-honorific.)	LONG FORM — GROUP I (Subject: non-honorific. Object: non-honorific.)	LONG FORM — GROUP II (Subject: honorific. Object: non-honorific.)
1	देखितहुँ *dekhaitahū*	Same as 1st person.	देखैतिऐ *dekhaitiai* / Or (with object in 2nd person.) देखैतिऔ *dekhaitiau*	Same as 1st person, but no forms for object in 2nd person.	देखबितहुँ *dekhabitahū°*, देखौतहुँ *dekhautahū*	देखबिलन्हुँ *dekhabitalahū*, देखौलन्हुँ *dekhautalahū*	देखबितिऐ *dekhabitiai*, देखबितिऔ *dekhabitiau*	Same as 1st person, but no forms for object in 2nd person.
2	देखैतैं *dekhaitē*	देखैतथि *dekhaitathī*	देखैतह *dekhaitāh*	Same as 1st person, but no forms for object in 2nd person.	देखबितें *dekhabitaĩ*, &c.	Same as 1st person.	देखबितलाह *dekhabitalāh*, &c.	Same as 1st person, but no forms for object in 2nd person.
3	देखात *dekhāt*	देखैतथि *dekhaitathĩ*	देखैत *dekhaitau* / Or (with object in 2nd person.) देखैतौ *dekhaitau*		देखबित *dekhabit*	देखबलथि *dekhabitalathĩ*, &c.	देखबितलाह *dekhabitalāh* / Or (with obj. in 2nd pers.) देखबितनी *dekhabaitan*, &c.	Same as 1st person, but no forms for object in 2nd person.

Optional forms for *áb*-verbs throughout as in the first person, except in the short form of the 3rd person of Group I.

280. (d) (8) Past Indicative.

'I become visible,' &c.					'I showed,' &c.				
	SHORT FORM.		LONG FORM.		SHORT FORM.		LONG FORM.		
PERSON.	GROUP I. (Subject: non-honorific. Object: non-honorific.)	GROUP II. (Subject: honorific. Object: non-honorific.)	GROUP I. (Subject: non-honorific. Object: non-honorific.)	GROUP II. (Subject: honorific. Object: non-honorific.)	GROUP I. (Subject: non-honorific. Object: non-honorific.)	GROUP II. (Subject: honorific. Object: non-honorific.)	GROUP I. (Subj.: non-honorific. Object: non-honorific.)	GROUP II. (Subject: honorific. Object: non-honorific.)	
1	देखलिहुँ dekhliuṁ	देखलिअहँ, देखी dekhliahã, dekhliu.	देखलिअह dekhliaiḥ	देखलिहु dekhliaiau Or (with object in 2nd person.) देखलिआ dekhliaiau.	देखौलिहुँ dekhauliuṁ, देखौलि dekhāol, देखौली dekhauli.	देखौलहुँ* dekhauluhiḥ देखौली dekhauli.	देखौलिहुँ dekhauliaḥ देखौलिअ dekhaulaiat, देखौलिओ dekhaulaii Or (with obj. in 2nd person.) देखौलिओ dekhaulaiau, देखी- ली dekhaulaulian	देखौलाता dekhaulata, देखौलिा dekhaulaii Or (with obj. in 2nd person.) dekhaulaiai	
2	Same as 1st person.		देखलिह dekhliaiḥ Or (with object in 2nd person.) देखलिओ dekhliaian. Same as 1st person, but no forms for object in 2nd person.		देखौलि dekhaulē	Same as 1st person.	देखौलिह dekhaulaiḥ Or (with object in 2nd person.) देखौली dekhaulaiau. Same as 1st pers., but no forms for obj. in 2nd pers.		
3	देखलि dekhliei	देखलि dekhliai	देखलि dekhliai Or (with object in 2nd person.) देखलिआ dekhliaian.		देखौलक dekhaulak.	देखौलिन्हि dekhaulanhḥ.	GROUP I. देखौलकी dekhaulakai Or (with obj. in 2nd person.) देखौलकी dekhaulakau.		

* Here and elsewhere the diphthong is often written as in देखौलिहुँ or देखउलिहुँ (see § 13).

281.　Verbal Nouns and Infinitives.

(1)

देखाय *dekhāy* (an optional and usual spelling of देखाइ *dekhāi* or देखाए *dekhāe*), the condition of being visible ; obl. देखाए *dekhāe* or देखाय *dekhāy.*

देखाबि *dekhāb*[i] or देखाय *dekhāy* (often spelt देखाइ *dekhāi* or देखाए *dekhāe*), the act of showing. The oblique form of देखाबि *dekhab*[i] is देखाबे *dekhābai* (with the usual variations of spelling), or देखाबँ *dekhābã.* That of देखाय *dekhāy* is देखाए *dekhāe* or देखाय *dekhāy.*

(2)

देखाएब *dekhāeb ;* obl. देखेबा *dekhaibā ;* the condition of being visible, to be visible.

देखाएब *dekhāeb ;* obl. देखेबा *dekhaibā :* the act of showing, to show.

(3)

देखाएल *dekhāel ;* obl. देखेला *dekhailā ;* the condition of being visible.

देखाओल *dekhāol ;* obl. देखौला *dekhaulā ;* the act of showing.

282.　Participles.

Present.

देखाइत *dekhāit,* seeing.

देखबैत *dekh*[a]*bait,* showing.

Past.

देखाएल *dekhāel,* seen.

देखाओल *dekhāol,* shown.

283.　The following are examples of the use of verbs whose roots end in आ *ā.*

(*a*) (1) **Old Present :—**

फोटरा के तीर चढ़ाय कें भड़ौ मारै । मरि जाय, *pho*ṭ[a]*rā kē tir caṛhāy kē* ke *bhadrī mārai* ; *mar*ⁱ *jāy*, Bhadrī having aimed an arrow strikes Photrā. He dies.

अम्मत अंगूर के खायो, *ammat āgūr kē khāo,* who eats sour grapes ?

से कोन ठाम जते नहिं जाथि । कै बेरि अंगनहुँ सों बहराथि ॥
कै बेरि साँप धरए ले जाथि । कै बेरि चून दही बदि खाथि ॥

*sē kona thāma jatai nah*ⁱ *jāthi* । *kai beri āganahū sō baharāthi* ॥
kai beri sāpa dharae lai jāthi । *kai beri cūna dahī badi khāthi* ॥

What place is there where he does not go! How often does he go outside the court-yard! How often does he catch hold of a snake and carry it away (thinking it a piece of rope)! How often does he eat lime thinking it is curds. (Man. iii. 2. 4).

(*a*) (2) **Present Conditional :—**

नहिं पतियाङ् तो आबिहैं, *nah*ⁱ *patiyāh*ᵘ *to ābihẽ.* (if) she do not have faith in you. then come.

(*a*) (3) **Imperative :—**

यार राखू मोर बात जाङ् जोगिया घर ... ... अहाँ घुरि जाउ *yār rākhū mōr bāt. jāh*ᵘ *jogiyā ghar ... ahā ghuri jāū,* friend, heed my word, go home to Jogiyā ... let Your Honour return (home).

कहलकैन्हि हे अम्मा जाह जाह घर, *kahal*ᵃ*kainh*ⁱ, 'hē ammā, jāh jāh ghar,' he said respectfully, ' O mother, go, go home.'

खाह पिबह चैन करह, *khāh, pibáh, cain karáh,* eat, drink, be happy.

*Precative Form :—*कालि्हक दिन ले जैहैं *kālhik din lē jaihẽ,* please take (it) away tomorrow.

(*b*) (4) **Future Indicative :—**

तीनु सम्मा भगिना जाएब कटैया सिकार, *tinū mamā bhaginā jāeb kataiyā sikār.* we three, uncle and nephews, will go to Kataiyā to hunt.

हमरो समधिया ले कं जैबौ जोगिया, *ham*ᵃ*rō samadhiyā lē ke jaibau jogiyā.* having taken our message also, you will go to Jogiyā.

हमरा पेटक आगि एहि सँ नहिं मिझाएत (for मिझाइत, § 271) *ham*ᵃ-*rā pētak āg*ⁱ *ehi sã nah*ⁱ *mijhāet* (for *mijhāit*), the fire of my belly cannot be extinguished (potential passive) by this.

29

बाबू सुतले रहतोह नहिं जैतोह, *bābū sut^alē rah^atāh ; nah^i jaitāh.*
(my) sons will remain asleep ; they will not go.

खैतोह-अन्हि से परलए बीत, *kaitāha-anhi sē parulae bīta,* (if)
he will eat, a whole age passeth away (see § 193).

(c) (5) Past Conditional :—

जौं हमहूँ तोहरा जकाँ अन्न तौलितहूँ तखन आइ पाश्रो भरि एम्हर
ओम्हर सँ माँगि नहिं खैतहूँ, *jaũ hamah^ū toh^arā jakā̃ ann taulitah^ū
takhan āi pāo bhur^i ēmhar ōmhar sā̃ mā̃g^i nah^i khaitah^ū,* if, like you,
I had (traded and) weighed out food, I should not to-day have
eaten after begging a quarter of a seer (of food) from here and
there.

(c) (6) Present Indicative :—

कह्लन्हि जे 'अहिरा कहाँ जाइछैं ।' कह्लक जे जाइछी गाइक बथान,
kah^alanh^i jē ' ahirā kahā̃ jāichai ?' kah^alak jē jāi-chī gāik bathān,
he (honorific) said, ' O Ahirā, where are you (non-honorific) going ? ' he (non-honorific) said, ' I am going to (my) cowshed.'

ठेहनी धैनें जाइत अछि उरसीक डीह, *theh^anī dhainē jāit ach^i
ur^asik dīh,* taking his crutch along with him, he is going to Ursī
village.

(d) (8) Past Indicative :—

चित्ता आओर हुँड़ार नाँगड़ि सुटकाए कँ पड़ाएल, *cittā āor hūṛār nā̃-
gaṛ^i sut^akāe kā̃ paṛāel,* the leopard and the wolf, hiding their tails,
ran away.

तखन सबहु मिलि खाएल तार, *takhana sabahu mili khāela tāra,*
then all, having united, ate (poetic for खेलक *khailak*) the *tāl*
fruits. (Man. v, 11).

अग्रि प्रज्वलित देखि धूर्त सभ पड़यलाह (for पड़ैलाह) *agn^i prajwalit
dēkh^i dhūrt sabh paray^alāh (for paṛailāh),* seeing the fire blazing.
the knaves ran away.

(*Note.*—Here we have an honorific form used in its original
signification of a non-honorific plural. This sometimes occurs in
literature).

जत पौलन्हि खेलन्हि सभ बस्तु, *jata paulanhi (√पाब pāb) khailanhi
(√खा khā) sabha bastu,* all the things that he could get he ate.
(Man. v, 30).

Verbal Nouns.

एतबाँ बचन सुनि दीना भद्री गेल खिसियाय, *etᵃbā̃ bacan sun*ⁱ *dīnā bhadrī gēl khisiyāy*, so much words having heard, Dīnā and Bhadrī became angry. (See § 342).

The genitive of खाय *khāy*, the act of eating, *viz.*, खाएक *khāek*, is used to mean "food." Thus अपना अपना घर में सुन्दर खाएक करे-गं *apᵃnā apᵃnā ghar mē sunnar khāek karē̃-gá*, you will, each in your own house, prepare beautiful food.

ओना लेने जेबे तो लोग कहतौ जे उढ़रा उढ़री छी, *onā lēnē jaibē to lōg kahᵃtau jē uṛʰᵃrā uṛʰᵃrī chī*, in taking them away with us (*i.e.*, if we take them away with us) in that way people will say to you that we are each a pair in concubinage.

नेव हेरेनें जेहन धेनु गाइ, *nēru herainē* (for *herailē*) *jehanu dhenu gāi*, like a cow on losing her calf. (Man. iii, 17).

Present Participle :—See *Present Indicative.*

Cf. also निरालसी लोक भोज्य खायित छथि, *nirālᵃsī lōk bhōjya khāyit* (for *khāit*) *chath*ⁱ, people who are not lazy are eating food. (*Purush Parīkṣā*, p. 51).

Past Participle : See Past Indicative.

Conjunctive Participle :

धामीक सबद सुनि उठलीचि दीना भद्रीक माइ चिहाय, *dhāmik sabad sun*ⁱ *uṭʰᵃlīh*ⁱ *dīnā bhadrik māi cihāy*, having heard the voice of Dhāmī, the mother of Dīnā and Bhadrī, being startled, rose up.

284. The following are examples of the use of verbs whose roots end in आब *āb*.

(1) (*a*) (*b*) Old Present, and Present Conditional :—

जँ एकरा सभ कें किछु कें देखाबी तँ चाहे जे बुझि जाय, *jā̃ ᵉkᵃrā sabh kē̃ kicch*ᵘ *kai dekhābī tā̃ cāhē jē buyh*ⁱ *jāy*, if, having done something I show it to them, then they ought to understand.

अबैति हो गोषाची गुजराब, *abait*ⁱ *chau goāhī guj*ᵃ*rāb*, she is coming to you (that) she may cause you to bear testimony.

बीछि बान कै फल सभ पाइ, *bichi bāna kai phula sabha pāe.* they all obtain as the fruit arrows (sharp as) scorpions. (Man. x, 52).

स्‍ति उठि नित दिन सुरुज कै हाँथ उठाबे, *sūt*[i] *uth*[i] *nit din suruj kē hāth uthābai.* daily, when they go to rest, and when they rise, they raise their hands to the sun (and pray).

(1) (c) **Imperative** :—

रे धिया पुता ताहिर मियाँक हबेली देखाब. *rē dhiyā pūtā, tāhir miyāk habēlī dekhāb,* hulloa. girls and boys, show (me) Tāhir Miyā̃'s house.

चलह हो दादा धूनी उठाबह, *calah, hō dādā, dhunī uthābah,* come. O brother, lift up the brazier (of fire).

बहोरन ममा के लांबहोक बोलाय, *bahōran mamā kē lāb*[a]*hōk bolāy,* having called uncle Bahōran, bring him (here).

(b) (4) **Future** :—

(*Old forms*) :—

आठम भए हम अपनहिं आओब ।

जेहन बनत पुनु तेहन बनाओब ॥

āthama bhae hama apanahī āob ।
jehana banata punu tehana banāoba ॥

I myself will come, having become (incarnate as) the eighth (child). as it will become (necessary), so will I bring it to pass. (Man. i, 32).

गाए महिसि सरकार लगाओब ।

लुटब सकल ब्रज जत धन पाओब ॥

gāe mahisi sarakāra lugāoba ।
lutaba sakala braja jata dhana pāoba ॥

I will confiscate to government his cows and she-buffaloes, and plunder all Vraja of all the wealth I can find (in it). (Man. vi, 28).

नन्दी सँ रस रीति बचाओब, *nandī sā rasa rīti bacāoba.* thou wilt (*i.e.*, shouldest) conceal the way of love from (thy) sister-in-law. (Vid. xl, 12).

(*Modern forms*) :—

खूब अकड़ि अपन गहना कपड़ाक सुनरताई आओर मुंहक चमक-चिमक देखाएब, *khūb ak͎aṛⁱ apan gah͎anā kap͎aṛāk sunaṛatāⁱ āor mūhak camakcimak dekhāeb,* with much swagger I shall display the beauty of (my) ornaments and clothes, and the glory of my countenance.

हम अपनेक भल मानब आओर सदा गुन गाएब, *ham ap͎anek bhal mānab āor sadā gun g͎āeb.* I shall revere you, and ever sing your praises.

जलदी रुपेआ असूल करू। नहिं तँ पीछू पछताएब, *jal͎adī rupaiā asūl karū : nah͎ⁱ tā̃ pīchu pach͎atāeb.* realize (honorific) the money quickly ; otherwise you (honorific) will afterwards repent.

एकर उचित फल पैबह कालि, *ekara ucita phala paibaha* (for *paibáh*) *kāli,* on the morrow shalt thou obtain the fitting fruit of this. (Man. i. 38).

कहलक सोझ हमर जाँ आओत ।
जिबैत जाए एकौ नहिं पाओत ।

kahalaka sōjha hamara jā̃ āota |
jibaita jāe ekau nahī pāota |

said they, 'if they shall come before us, not one will obtain (permission) (*i.e.*, be able) to go away alive.' (Man. viii, 43).

चारू दीस बाट ताकथि जे कोन दीस साउ सलहेस आओतांह, *cāru dīs bāṭ tākath͎ⁱ jē kōn dīs saū sal͎ahēs autāh,* they watch the roads in the four directions, (to see) from what direction Salhēs will come.

(*c*) (5) **Past Conditional** :—

जनितहूँ तो बगहा में बरदी तमाकू लदबैतिऐ, *janit͎ahū̃ to bag͎ahā mē bar͎adī tamākū lad͎abaitiai,* if I had known, I should have loaded a bullock with tobacco in Baghā.

जौहरी एकरा पबैत तो अत्यन्त खुसी होइत, *jauh͎arī ek͎aṛā pabait. to atyant khusī hoit,* (if) a jeweller had found this, he would have been very happy.

आओतन्हि दुरागमन करैतैन्हि जमैया जाँजरि, *autanh͎ⁱ, durāgamau karaitainh͎ⁱ jamaiyā jā̃jaṛⁱ.* (if) they had come to Jā̃jari, his sons-in-law would have celebrated the *durāgamau* ceremony.

(c) (6) **Present Indicative** :—

माइ बापक नाम छिपबैत छी, *māi bāpak nām chip^abait chī.* we are concealing the names of our father and mother.

हम तोहरा प्रक कहिनी सुनबैछिञह, *ham toh^arā ek kahini sun^abai-chiah^u.* I am causing you to hear (telling you) a story.

कनौली में सात सै पट्ठा अखाढ़ा में खेलबैत अछि, *kanauli mē sāt sai paṭṭhā akhāṛhā mē khel^abait achⁱ,* in Kanauli he causes seven hundred athletes to play (*i.e.,* do gymnastics) on his arena.

But :—

प्रक सै प्रकैस उड्ड खेलाइत अछि अखाढ़ा पर, *ek sai ekais ḍaṇḍ khelāit achⁱ akhāṛhā par,* he *performs* one hundred and twenty exercises (*cognate accusation of an intransitive verb*) on the arena.

सदा भूंकि भूंकि कैं हमरा सभ कैं भड़कबैअछि, *sadā bhū̃kⁱ bhū̃kⁱ kai ham^arā sabh kē bhaṛ^akabai-achⁱ,* they make us quarrel by their continual barking.

तीनु गोंठे अबैत छथि *tinū gōṭē abait chathⁱ,* the three (respected people) are coming.

अबैति छौ *abaitⁱ chau,* she is coming to you. (See under Old Present).

पानि बिनु अबैत छौक तेजैत अबैत छौक परान, *pāni bin^u abait chauk, tejait abait chauk parān,* without water (*i.e.,* athirst) he is coming to you, he is coming to you giving up his life (*i.e.,* at the point of death).

(d) (8) **Past Indicative** :—

बिद्यापति प्रह गाश्रोल सजनी गे ।
ई थिक नब रस रीती ॥

bidyāpati eha gāola, sajani gē ।
ī thika naba rasa rītī ॥

(Saith) Vidyāpati, ' I sang this, O friend,
This is the way of young love.' (Vid. xxiii, 11).

चौदह कोस पकड़िआ चौकीदारी लिखाश्रोल चोरक बनार नहिं पाश्रोल, *caudah kōs pakaṛiā caukidārī likhāol, cōrak banār nahⁱ*

pāol. I caused (letters) to be written to the police of fourteen *kōs* (round) Pakariā, and I found no trace of the thief.

की कहि कै हमरा बन्ध खोलौलिहि, *kī kahi kai hamⁿrā bandh kholaulīhi,* saying what (on what pretext) did you (fem.) get me released (from my) bonds ?

एक दिन ओ अपना बेटा सभ कें बजौलक, *ek din ō apⁿnā bēṭā sabh kē̃ bajaulak,* one day he summoned his sons.

जत पौलन्हि खैलन्हि सभ बस्तु, *jata paulanhi khailanhi sabha bastu,* he (Kṛṣṇa) ate all the articles (of food) which he found. (Man. v. 30).

कथा सभ सँ बड़त बुझौलकै, *kathā subh sā̃ bahut bujhaulⁿkai,* he remonstrated much (with them) with many words.

(*a*) (9) **Perfect Indicative** :—

एक बकस पठाओल अछि से अहाँक हेतु, *ek bakas paṭhāol achⁱ, sē ahā̃k hētⁿ,* I have sent a box, it is for you.

तखन अहाँ कें खोलाओलि अछि, *takhun ahā̃ kē̃ kholāolⁱ achⁱ,* then I (fem.) have released you.

(*d*) (10) **Pluperfect Indicative** :—

हम तोहरा पहिले हस्सी में उड़ौने रहिअहु, *ham toharā pahilē hassī mē̃ uṛaunē* (for *uraulē*) *rahiahⁿ,* formerly I ridiculed you in sport.

Verbal Nouns :—

(1) (Obl.) आबए नहि पाबए से करब, *ābae nahī pābae sē karab* you will do that (by which) he will not get (power) to come (*i.e.* be able to come, *ābae* for *ābai,* obl. of *ābⁱ*). (Man. viii, 46).

(3) पछतौला सँ की भै सकैअछि, *pachⁿtaulā sā̃ kī bhai sakai-achⁱ,* what can happen from regretting ?

Participles :—

Present :—See Present Indicative.

Past :—सगरो बनल बनाओल घर बिगड़ि गेल, *sagⁿrō banal banāol ghar bigaṛⁱ gēl,* all (her) ready-made house (*i.e.,* castle in the air) went to pieces.

Conjunctive :—

भद्री आ{बि के कचॅत क{थि, *bhadri ābⁱ ke kahait chathⁱ*. Bhadri. having come, is saying.

सभ मिलाप्र कॅ तौनि में सं किच्छु ब{ढ़ जाप्रत, *sabh milāe kā̃ tīnⁱ sai sā̃ kicch^a barhⁱ jāet*, adding all together there will be something over three hundred.

चाथ घे के लॅलक उठाय, *hāth dhai ke lēlak uṭhāy*, seizing by the hand, raising (them) up, he took (them) (*i.e.*, he lifted them up).

Roots in इ *i* and ई *ī*.

285.　Roots in इ *i* and ई *ī* are conjugated exactly similarly, the only difference being that, according to the usual rule, the long ई *ī* is shortened to इ *i* when it falls in the antepenultimate.　Indeed the two most important roots of this class. पि *pi* or पी *pī*, drink. and जि *ji* or जी *jī*, live. may have the *i* either long or short.

As the model verb, I take the √सि *si*, sew.　It will be observed that in the case of the √सि *si* there are a number of optional forms. in which the letter ब *b* is inserted between two concurrent vowels.　In the case of the two verbs √पि *pi* or पी *pī*, drink, and √जि *ji* or जी *jī*, live, it is important to note that they almost invariably employ the forms with ब *b*.　Indeed. I may say, that I have never seen or heard the forms without the ब *b* in the case of these two verbs, though natives tell me they can be used.　The fact is that in these two verbs the ब is not inserted. but really belongs to the root, as will be seen when we compare the Sanskrit forms पिबति *pibati*, he drinks. and जीवति *jīvati*, he lives. It should also be noted that these verbs have their present participles पिबैत *pibait* and जिबैत *jibait* respectively, and insert ब *b* in other places, where they are not found in the case of √सि *si*. In order to illustrate the peculiarities of these two verbs, I give the conjugation of √पि *pi* or पी *pī* alongside of that of √सि *si*, to facilitate comparison. In the case of √पि *pi* or पी *pī*, when there are two forms, one with long ई *ī* and the other with short इ *i*, I only give the one with long ई *ī*, and it must be remembered that a form with short इ *i* can also be used. √जि *ji* or जी *jī*, live. is conjugated exactly like √पि *pi* or पी *pī*.

286. (1) (a) **Old Present.**

'I sew,' &c.   'I drink,' &c.

PERSON	'I sew,' &c. — SHORT FORM Group I	SHORT FORM Group II	LONG FORM Group I	LONG FORM Group II	'I drink,' &c. — SHORT FORM Group I	SHORT FORM Group II	LONG FORM Group I	LONG FORM Group II
(headers)	(Subject: non-honorific. Object: non-honorific.)	(Subject: honorific. Object: non-honorific.)	(Subject: non-honorific. Object: non-honorific.)	(Subject: honorific. Object: non-honorific.)	(Subject: non-honorific. Object: non-honorific.)	(Subject: honorific. Object: non-honorific.)	(Subj.: non-honorific. Object: non-honorific.)	(Subject: honorific. Object: non-honorific.)
1	सिऐ *sii.*	Same as 1st person.	सिबिइ *sibiai* Or (with object in 2nd person.) सिबिऔ *sibiau*	Same as 1st person, but no forms for object in 2nd person.	पीबी *pibī.*	Same as 1st person.	पिबिइ *pibiai* Or (with obj. in 2nd person.) पिबिऔ *pibiau*	Same as 1st pers., but no forms for object in 2nd person.
2	सि *si.*	सिबिथि *siathi,* सिबथि *sibathi*	सिऐ *siäh,* सिबह *sibäh*	GROUP I. सिऐ *siai,* सिब *sibai;* Or (with object in 2nd person.) सिऔ *siau,* सिबौ *sibau*	पी *pī.*	Same as 1st person.	पीबह *pibäh.*	GROUP I. पीब *pibai;* Or (with obj. in 2nd person.) पीबौ *pibau*
3	सिए *sie.*	—	—	—	पीबे *pibē.*	पीबिथि *pibathi.*	पीबिथि *pibathi.*	—

287. (b) (4) **Future Indicative. Second Form.**

'I shall sew,' &c.   .   .   .   .   'I shall drink,' &c.

'I shall sew,' &c. — सिअ *siab*

PERSON	SHORT FORM.		LONG FORM.	
	GROUP I. (Subject: non-honorific. Object: non-honorific.)	GROUP II. (Subject: honorific. Object: non-honorific.)	GROUP I. (Subject: non-honorific. Object: non-honorific.)	GROUP II. (Subject: honorific. Object: non-honorific.)
1	सिअब *siab*		सिअबौ *siabai*, सिब *sibai* — Or (with object in 2nd person.) सिअबौ *siabau*, सिबौ *sibau*.	
2	सिअबे *siabē*, सिबे *sibē.*	Same as 1st person.	सिअबाह *siabāh,* सिबह *sibāh.*	Same as 1st person, but no forms for object in 2nd person.
3	Wanting.	Wanting.	Wanting.	

'I shall drink,' &c. — पीअ *piab*

PERSON	SHORT FORM.		LONG FORM.	
	GROUP I. (Subject: non-honorific. Object: non-honorific.)	GROUP II. (Subject: honorific. Object: non-honorific.)	GROUP I. (Subject: non-honorific. Object: non-honorific.)	GROUP II. (Subject: honorific. Object: non-honorific.)
1	पीअब *piab*		पीअबौ *piubai*, पीब *pibai* — Or (with obj. in 2nd person.) पीअबौ *piubau*, पीबौ *pibau*.	
2	पीअबे *piubē,* पीब *pībē.*	Same as 1st person.	पीअबाह *piubāh* पीबह *pibāh.*	Same as 1st person, but no forms for object in 2nd person.
3	Wanting.	Wanting.	Wanting.	

288. (*b*) (4) Future Indicative. Third Form.

'I shall sew,' &c.   'I shall drink,' &c.

'I shall sew,' &c.

PERSON	SHORT FORM — GROUP I. (Subject: non-honorific. Object: non-honorific.)	SHORT FORM — GROUP II. (Subject: honorific. Object: non-honorific.)	LONG FORM — GROUP I. (Subject: non-honorific. Object: non-honorific.)	LONG FORM — GROUP II. (Subject: honorific. Object: non-honorific.)
1	सिअतहुँ *siatahŭ*, सिबहुँ *sitahŭ*.	Wanting.	सिअलिऐ *siatai*, सिलिऐ *sitai*. Or (with object in 2nd person.) सिअलिऔ *siatiau*, सिलिऔ *sitiau*.	Same as 1st person.
2	Wanting.	Same as 1st person.	Wanting.	Same as 1st person, but no forms for object in 2nd person.
3	सिअत *siat*, सिअत *siut*.	सिअतथि *siataithi*, सिलथि *sitathi*.	सिअतऐ *siatai*, सिअत *sitai*. Or (with object in 2nd person.) सिअतौ *siatiau*, सिलौ *sitiau*.	

'I shall drink,' &c.

PERSON	SHORT FORM — GROUP I. (Subject: non-honorific. Object: non-honorific.)	SHORT FORM — GROUP II. (Subject: honorific. Object: non-honorific.)	LONG FORM — GROUP I. (Subject: non-honorific. Object: non-honorific.)	LONG FORM — GROUP II. (Subject: honorific. Object: non-honorific.)
1	पिबितहुँ *pibitahŭ*, पिअलहुँ *piutahŭ*.	Wanting.	पिअलिऐ *piutai*. Or (with obj. in 2nd person.) पिअलिऔ *piutiau*.	Same as 1st person, but no forms for object in 2nd person.
2	Wanting.	Same as 1st person.	Wanting.	Same as 1st person, no forms for object in 2nd person.
3	पिअब *piut*.	पिअतथि *piutathi*.	पिअतऐ *piutai*. Or (with obj. in 2nd person.) पिअतौ *piutiau*.	

289. (c) (5) Past Conditional.

'Had I sewn, &c.; 'I should have sewn, &c.   'Had I drunk, &c.; 'I should have drunk, &c.

PERSON.	SHORT FORM.		LONG FORM.		SHORT FORM.		LONG FORM.	
	GROUP I. (Subject: non-honorific. Object: non-honorific.)	GROUP II. (Subject: honorific. Object: non-honorific.)	GROUP I. (Subject: non-honorific. Object: non-honorific.)	GROUP II. (Subject: honorific. Object: non-honorific.)	GROUP I. (Subject: non-honorific. Object: non-honorific.)	GROUP II. (Subject: honorific. Object: non-honorific.)	GROUP I. (Subj.: non-honorific. Object: non-honorific.)	GROUP II. (Subject: honorific. Object: non-honorific.)
1	सिइतहुँ *siitahũ*, सिइतुँ *sitũ*.	Same as 1st person.	सिइतिहुँ *siittai*, सिइतुँ *sittai* Or (with object in 2nd person.) सिइतिख्ओ *siittau*, सिइतिब्ओ *sittiau*.	(Subject: honorific. Object: non-honorific.) *sittai*	पिबिलॅ *pibitẽ*.	Same as 1st person.	पिबिलिहुँ *pibitai* Or (with obj. in 2nd person.) पिबिलिब्ओ *pibitiau*.	(Subject: honorific. Object: non-honorific.) *pibitai*
2	सिइदॅ *sitdẽ*, सिइतॅ *sitẽ*.	सिइतबि *siitathi*, सिइनुबि *sitathi*.	सिइदतेहु *siidãh*, सिइतॅहु *sitãh*. Same as 1st person, but no forms for object in 2nd person.		पिबिल *pibait*.	Same as 1st person.	पिबिबॅहु *pibitãh*, पिबिबॉ *pibitãh*. Same as 1st person, but no forms for object in 2nd person	
3	सिइटेन *siit*.	सिइदबि *siitathi*, सिइनुबि *sitathi*.	GROUP I सिइदतु *sittai*, सिइतॅ *sitai* Or (with object in 2nd person.) सिइतॉ *siittau*, सिइतॉ *sitau*.		पिबिल *pibait*.	पिबिलबि *pibitathi*.	GROUP I. पिबिब *pibitai* Or (with obj. in 2nd person.) पिबिबॉ *pibitau*.	

290. (8) Past Indicative.

'I sewed,' &c. (Intransitive).   'I drank,' &c. (Transitive).

PERSON	SHORT FORM — GROUP I. (Subject: non-honorific. Object: non-honorific.)	SHORT FORM — GROUP II. (Subject: honorific. Object: non-honorific.)	LONG FORM — GROUP I. (Subject: non-honorific. Object: non-honorific.)	LONG FORM — GROUP II. (Subject: honorific. Object: non-honorific.)	SHORT FORM — GROUP I. (Subject: non-honorific. Object: non-honorific.)	SHORT FORM — GROUP II. (Subject: honorific. Object: non-honorific.)	LONG FORM — GROUP I. (Subj.: non-honorific. Obj.: non-honorific.)	LONG FORM — GROUP II. (Subject: honorific. Obj.: non-honorific.)
1	सिचलहुँ *sialahũ*, सिउलहुँ *siulahũ*.	Same as 1st person.	सिचलिऎ *sialiai*, सिचलिऎ *sialiai*. Or (with object in 2nd person.) सिचलिऔ *sialiau*, सिचलिऔ *sialiau*.		पीउलें *piulẽ*.	Same as 1st person.	पीउलहुँ *piulāh*. Or (with obj. in 2nd person.) पीउलौं *piulau*.	पीउलौ *piulai*. Or (with obj. in 2nd person.) पीउलौ *piulau*.
2	सिचलें *sialẽ*, सिउलें *siulẽ*.	सिचलह *sialah*, सिउलह *siulah*.	सिचलह *siulāh*, सिउलह *siulāh*. Or (with object in 2nd person.) सिचला *siulau*.	Same as 1st person, but no forms for object in 2nd person.	पीउलहु *piulahũ*.	Same as 1st person.	Same as 1st person, but no forms for object in 2nd person.	
3	सिचल *sial*, सिउल *siul*.		*GROUP I.* सिचलिऎ *sialai*, सिउलिऎ *siulai*. Or (with object in 2nd person.) सिचला *sialau*, सिउलो *siulau*.		पीउलक *piulak*.		*GROUP I.* पीउलक *piulākut*. Or (with obj. in 2nd person.) पीउलको *piulakau*.	

291. Verbal Nouns.

(1) सि *si* ; obl. सिऔ *siai* or सिबै *sibai* ; the act of sewing.

(2) सिअब *siab* ; obl. सिअबा *siabā*. सिबा *sibā* ; the act of sewing, to sew.

(3) सिअल *sial* ; obl. सिअला *sialā*, सिला *silā* ; the act of sewing.

(1) पीबि *pībi* ; obl. पीबै *pibai* ; the act of drinking.

(2) पीउब *piub* ; obl. पीउबा *piubā* ; the act of drinking, to drink.

(3) पीउल *piul* : obl. पीउला *piulā* ; the act of drinking.

292. Participles.

Present.

सिउत *siut*, सिइत *siit*, सिऔत *siait*, sewing.

पिबैत *pibait*, drinking.

Past.

सिअल *sial*, सिउल *siul*, sewn.

पिउल *piul*, drunk.

---

293. It must be added that the root सि *si* also sometimes takes the forms of √ पि *pi* or पी *pī* (compare Sanskrit सीव्यति *sivyati*, he sews), but those given above are the usual ones. These three roots (सि *si*, पि *pi*, जि *ji*) are the only roots in र *i* which I have come across.

294. I have met no examples of √ सि *si* in literature, but the following are examples of the two others :—

(a) (I) **Old Present :—**

भनहिं बिद्यापति तौ पय जीबे ।

अधर सुधा-रस जौं पय पीबे ॥

bhanahi bidyāpati taü paya jībe ।

adhara sudhā-rasa jaü paya pibē ॥

Saith Vidyāpati, ‘it (the bee) will live, so long as it drinketh the nectar of (your) lower lip.’ (Vid. ii, 5).

लोभित मधुकर कौसल अनुसर ।

नब रस पिबु अबगाही ॥

lōbhita madhukara kausala anusara ।
naba rasu pibu abagāhī ॥

The bee, tempted (by its sweetness), cleverly searcheth for it, and, diving (into the lotus) sips the fresh honey. (Vid. xxix, 2).

जाइ पिश्राबिष्टे अधर सुध्रा रस ।

तौं पय जीबथि जीबे ॥

jāi piābiui adhara sudhā rasa ।
tau paya jībathi jībē ॥

Having gone (to her), cause her to drink (*causal verb*) the nectar of thy lower lip; then may she indeed live (present conditional) (*lit.*, live with life). (Vid. x. 10).

जमुना ह्रद बिखबत कै जानि ।

पसू पच्छि क्यो पिबै न पानि ॥

jamunā hrada bikhabnta kai jāni ।
pasū pacchi kyō pibai na pāni ॥

Knowing the pool (in) the Jamunā (to be) like poison, no beast (or) bird drinks (its) water. (Man. iv, 20).

ता पर भमर पिबय रस मजनी गे ।

बैसल पंख पसारि ॥

tā para bhamara pibaya (for *pibai*) *rasa, sajani gē ।*
baisala pankha pasāri ॥

On it, O friend, a bee drinks nectar, seated with outspread wings. (Vid. xv, 6).

(*a*) (3) **Imperative** :—

खाह पिर्बह चैन करह, *khāh, pibáh, cain karah*, eat, drink, be happy.

जुग जुग जिबथु बसथु लख कोस :

हमर अभाग इनक कोन दोस ?

juga juga jibathu, basathu lakha kōsa ।
hamara abhāga hunaka kona dōsa ॥

May he live for ages (even though) he dwell a hundred
thousand *kōs* (away from me). It is my misfortune. What
fault is it of his ? (Vid. lviii, 2).

(*b*) (4) **Future** :—

तौं हमरा गाइक दूध पीबें । मुंह भेलौक पिबेक । नहिं रे अहिरा
दूध पीबें देबें तो एक जुम तमाकू दे, '*tŏ hamᵃrā gāik dūdh pibḗ! mūh
bhelauk pibaik!*' '*nah̃, rē ahirā, dūdh pībai dēbḗ, to ek jum
tamākū dē,*' 'you will drink the milk of my cow! you have made
(*lit.*, to you there is become) a mouth for (*lit.* of) drinking!' 'If
you will not, O cowherd, give me milk to drink, then give me
one mouthful of tobacco.' (Also example of 1st Verbal noun).

माधब आब न जीउति राही, *mādhaba āba, na jiuti rāhi*, O Mādhava, come. The fair one (*fem.*) will live no (longer) (Vid. x, 1).

(*c*) (6) **Present Indicative** :—

सीना गाइक दूध ले पिबैत अहि गुलामी जट, *sinā gāik dūdh lai
pibait achᵢ gulāmī jaṭ*, Gulāmī Jaṭ takes and drinks the milk of the
cow Sīnā.

(*c*) (7) **Imperfect Indicative** :—

दीना भद्री जिबैत कल उहे गबैत रहै, *dinā bhadrī jibait chal uhē
gabait rahai*, when Dīnā and Bhadrī were living, they used to
sing that (song).

जां जिबैत कलाह दीना भद्री जोगिया नगर कौनो मुसहरनी नहिं
कैलक सिंगार, *jŏ jibait chalāh dīnā bhadrī jogiyā nagar, kauno
musaharᵃni nahᵢ kailak sīgār*, if Dīnā and Bhadrī were living in
Jogiyā town, not one Musahar's wife would (have dared to) adorn
herself. (Here the Past Indicative is employed in the sense of
the Past Conditional).

(*d*) (8) **Past Indicative** :—

प्रहन धप्रस तेजि पड़ परदेस गेल ।
कुसुम पिउल मकरंदा ॥

31

> *ehana baesa teji pahu paradesa gela* |
> *kusuma piula* (for *piulak*) *makarandā* ॥

At such (a tender) age my lord left me and went to a far country. (There) drank he the nectar of the flower. (Vid. lxvi, 8).

हरि भरि पेट पिउल दुध हरखि, *hari bhari pēṭa piula* (for *piulak*) *dudha harakhi*, Hari joyfully drank his bellyful of milk. (Man. ii, 51).

Verbal Nouns :—

(1) For पीबै *pibai* (obl.) and पिबेक *pibaik* (genitive), see example of future. So also किच्छु दूध देति अछि । नेना सभ कें पिबेक भरि भे जाइत छेक, *kicch^u dūdh dait^i ach^i ? nēnā sabh kẽ pibaik bhar^i bhai jāit chaik*, does she give any milk ? There becomes the fill of drinking for the children (*i.e.*, she gives all that is wanted for the children).

जिबए दिखथो बरु बालक लेब, *jibae* (for *jibai*) *diao baru bālaka lēb*, allow (her) to live, but, rather take the child. (Man. ii, 8).

आबह बैसह पिबि लह पानि, *ābaha* (for *ābah*) *baisaha* (for *baisáh*) *pibi laha* (for *láh*) *pāni*, come, sit down, take a drink of water (*pib^i láh* is an intensive compound, see § 342). (Vid. lxxx, 4).

Present Participle :—

जिबइत जाए एको नहिं पाओत, *jibaita jāe ekau nahī pāota*, not one will be able to go away living. (Man. viii, 43).

जिबैत रहैत तो जोगिया अबैत पलटि, *jibait rahait to jogiyā abait palaṭ^i*, (if) they had remained living, then they would have returned back to Jogiyā.

देखलि सलहेस कें कलालक भट्ठी पर दारू पिबैत, *dēkhal^i sal^hēs kẽ kalālak bhaṭṭhī par dārū pibait*, I (fem.) saw Salhēs drinking spirits at a grog-maker's still.

Conjunctive Participle :—

बौरम नदी में पानि पीबि कें ऊपर होए, *bauram nadī mẽ pāni pib^i ke ūpar hōai*, he is (coming) up, having drunk water in the river Bauram.

Roots in ए ē.

295.   Only two roots end in ए ē, *viz.* √दे dē, give, and ले lē, take.   They are irregular throughout, and their conjugation will be given in chapter VI (§§ 314 ff).

Roots in ऊ ū and ओ ō.

296.   These are conjugated as follows.   It will be seen that, as in the case of verbs in इ i, a ब b is often optionally inserted. Sometimes we find य y instead of ब b.   This is practically the only irregularity.

The model verbs are √चू cū, drip (intransitive) and √धो dhō, wash (transitive).

The most important of the roots in ओ ō is the √ रो hō, become.   This is very irregular, and will be conjugated in chapter VI (§§ 322 ff).

297. (1) (a) Old Present.

'I drip,' &c.

'I wash,' &c.

PERSON	SHORT FORM — GROUP I (Subject: non-honorific. Object: non-honorific.)	GROUP II (Subject: honorific. Object: non-honorific.)	LONG FORM — GROUP I (Subject: non-honorific. Object: non-honorific.)	GROUP II (Subject: honorific. Object: non-honorific.)	SHORT FORM — GROUP I (Subject: non-honorific. Object: non-honorific.)	GROUP II (Subject: honorific. Object: non-honorific.)	LONG FORM — GROUP I (Subj.: non-honorific. Obj.: non-honorific.)	GROUP II (Subject: honorific. Obj.: non-honorific.)
1	चुऎँ cũĩ, चुबी cūbī.		चुऎइ cuiai, चुबिइ cubiai.		धोऎँ dhõĩ, धोबी dhōbī.		धोऎइ dhōiai, धोबिइ dhōbiai.	
2	चु cū. { Same as 1st person. }		चुऎह cũăh, चुबह cūbăh. { Same as 1st person, but no forms for object in 2nd person. }		धो dhō. { Same as 1st person. }		धोऎह dhõăh, धोबह dhōbăh. { Same as 1st person, but no forms for object in 2nd person. }	
3	चुऎँ cũẽ, चुबे cūbē.	चुऎथि cũathĩ, चुबथि cũbathĩ.	चुऎि cũni, चुब cūb cũni. (GROUP I)		धोऎ dhōĕ, धोबे dhōbĕ, धोये dhōyĕ, धोय dhōy.	धोबथि dhōbathĩ, धोबथि dhōbathĩ.	धोबे dhōni, धोब dhōbai. (GROUP I)	

298. (b) (4) **Future Indicative.** Second form.

'I shall drip,' &c. — 'I shall wash,' &c.

PERSON.	SHORT FORM.		LONG FORM.		SHORT FORM.		LONG FORM.	
	GROUP I. (Subject: non-honorific. Object: non-honorific.)	GROUP II. (Subject: honorific. Object: non-honorific.)	GROUP I. (Subject: non-honorific. Object: non-honorific.)	GROUP II. (Subject: honorific. Object: non-honorific.)	GROUP I. (Subject: non-honorific. Object: non-honorific.)	GROUP II. (Subject: honorific. Object: non-honorific.)	GROUP I. (Subj.: non-honorific. Object: non-honorific.)	GROUP II. (Subject: honorific. Object: non-honorific.)
1	चूइब *cũib*, चूइव *cũib*.		चूइब *cũabui*, चूइव *cũibui*, चू *cũbai*.	(Same as 1st person, but no forms for object in 2nd person.)	धोइब *dhõib*, धोइव *dhõeb*.	(Same as 1st person.)	धोइबुइ *dhõibui*, धोइ *dhõbui*, धोइ *dhõebui*, धोव *dhõbai*.	(Same as 1st person, but no forms for object in 2nd person.)
2	चूइबे *cũabẽ*, चूइवे *cũibẽ*, चूव *cũbẽ*.	Same as 1st person.	चूइबाह *cũabãh*, चूइवाह *cũibãh*, चू *cũbãh*.		धोइबे *dhõibẽ*, धोइवे *dhõebẽ*, धोवें *dhõbẽ*.	Same as 1st person.	धोइबाह *dhõebãh*, धोइवाह *dhõebãh*, धोव *dhõbãh*.	
3	Wanting.	Wanting.	Wanting.		Wanting.	Wanting.	Wanting.	

299. (b) (4) Future Indicative. Third Form.

PERSON.	'I shall drip,' &c.				'I shall wash,' &c.			
	SHORT FORM.		**LONG FORM.**		**SHORT FORM.**		**LONG FORM.**	
	GROUP I. (Subject: non-honorific. Object: non-honorific.)	GROUP II. (Subject: honorific. Object: non-honorific.)	GROUP I. (Subject: non-honorific. Object: non-honorific.)	GROUP II. (Subject: honorific. Object: non-honorific.)	GROUP I. (Subject: non-honorific. Object: non-honorific.)	GROUP II. (Subject: honorific. Object: non-honorific.)	GROUP I. (Subj.: non-honorific. Object: non-honorific.)	GROUP II. (Subject: honorific. Object: non-honorific.)
1	चुचलहुँ *cūatahũ,** चूदल्हुँ *cūtalhũ,* चूह्लुँ *cūhlũ.*		चुचिऐ *cuatiai,* चुतिऐ *cutiai,*	चुतिऐ *cutiai,*	धोअतहुँ *dhŏatahũ,* धोएतहुँ *dhŏetahũ,*	धोतहुँ *dhŏtahũ.*	धोअतिऐ *dhoatiai,* &c.	
2	Wanting.	Same as 1st person.	Wanting.	Same as 1st person, but no forms for object in 2nd person.	Wanting.	Same as 1st person.	Wanting.	Same as 1st person, but no forms for object in 2nd person.
3	चुचत *cūat,* चूह्ल *cūl.*	चुचतथि *cūatath,* चूदलथि *cūtalath,* चूह्लथि *cūhlath.*	चुचतऐ *cuatai,* चुत *cutai,* चूत *cūtai,*	चुतिऐ *cutiai,*	धोअत *dhŏat,* धोएत *dhŏet.*	धोअतथि *dhŏata,* त्हि *ti,* धोएतथि *dhŏitath,* धोतथि *dhŏtath.*	धोअतऐ *dhoatai,* धोत्त *dhŏtai,* धोत *dhŏtai.*	

* Or चुचित्लुँ *cuitalhũ,* and so throughout.

* Or चुतिऐ *cuitiai,* and so throughout.

* Or चुचितथि *cuitath,* and so throughout.

300. (c) (5) Past Conditional.

'(If) I had dripped,' &c.; 'I should have dripped,' &c.   '(If) I had washed,' &c.; 'I should have washed,' &c.

PERSON.	SHORT FORM. GROUP I. (Subject: non-honorific. Object: non-honorific.)	SHORT FORM. GROUP II. (Subject: honorific. Object: non-honorific.)	LONG FORM. GROUP I. (Subject: non-honorific. Object: non-honorific.)	LONG FORM. GROUP II. (Subject: honorific. Object: non-honorific.)	SHORT FORM. GROUP I. (Subject: non-honorific. Object: non-honorific.)	SHORT FORM. GROUP II. (Subject: honorific. Object: non-honorific.)	LONG FORM. GROUP I. (Subj.: non-honorific. Object: non-honorific.)	LONG FORM. GROUP II. (Subject: honorific. Object: non-honorific.)
1	चूअलँ *cūitalã,** चूलैक *cūitalak.*	चूलैक *cūitalak.*	चूलतैक *cūitai,* चूलैक *cūitai.*	Same as 1st person.	चोअतलँ *dhoetalã,* धोतै *dhotah.*	चोतथ *dhotah.*	चोअतैक *dhoetai,* धोतै *dhotai.*	Same as 1st person, but no forms for object in 2nd person.
2	चूलै *cūile,* चूँ *cūtẽ.*	Same as 1st person.	चूलाह *cūitāh,* चूँ *cūtāh.*	Same as 1st person, but no forms for object in 2nd person.	चोलै *dhoet,* चोलै *dhoet.*	Same as 1st person.	चोलाह *dhōetāh,* चोलाह *dhōtāh.*	Same as 1st person, but no forms for object in 2nd person.
3	चूअत *cūat,* चूल *cūit,* चूअत *cūait.*	चूलथि *cūitathi,* चूथि *cūtathi.*	GROUP I. चूतै *cūtai,* चूँ *cūtai.*		चोअत *dhōat,* चोलत *dhōet,* चोइत *dhōuit.*	चोअतथि *dhōetathẽ,* चोतथि *dhōtathẽ.*	GROUP I. चोअत *dhoetai,* धोतै *dhōtai.*	

* Or चूबिनलस *cūbitalã,* and so throughout.

301. (*d*) (8) **Past Indicative.**

'I dripped,' &c. (Intransitive).   'I washed,' &c. (Transitive).

PERSON	Intransitive — SHORT FORM — GROUP I (Subject: non-honorific. Object: non-honorific.)	Intransitive — SHORT FORM — GROUP II (Subject: honorific. Object: non-honorific.)	Intransitive — LONG FORM — GROUP I (Subject: non-honorifio. Object: non-honorifio.)	Intransitive — LONG FORM — GROUP II (Subject: honorific. Object: non-honorific.)	Transitive — SHORT FORM — GROUP I (Subject: non-honorific. Object: non-honorific.)	Transitive — SHORT FORM — GROUP II (Subject: honorific. Object: non-honorific.)	Transitive — LONG FORM — GROUP I (Subj.: non-honorific. Object: non-honorific.)	Transitive — LONG FORM — GROUP II (Subject: honorific. Object: non-honorific.)
1	चूअलहुँ *cūalahũ*, चूरलहुँ *cūilahũ*.	*(Same as Group I)*	चूअलिऐ *cūalaiũ*, चूरलिऐ *cūilaiũ*.	*(Same as Group I)*	धोअलहुँ *dhŏalahũ*, धोएलहुँ *dhŏelahũ*.	*(Same as Group I)*	धोअलिऐ *dhŏaliai*, धोएलिऐ *dhŏeliai*.	*(Same as Group I)*
2	चूअलह *cūalăh*, चूरलह *cūilăh*.	Same as 1st person	चूअलह *cūalăh*, चूरलह *cūilăh*.	Same as 1st person, but no forms for object in 2nd person.	धोअलॅ *dhŏalĕ*, धोएलॅ *dhŏelĕ*.	Same as 1st person.	धोअलाह *dhŏalāh*, धोएलिइह *dhŏeliih*.	Same as 1st person, but no forms for object in 2nd person.
3	*(GROUP 1)* चूअल *cūul*, चूरल *cūil*.		*(GROUP 1)* चूअलइ *cūalai*, चूरलइ *cūilai*.		*(GROUP 1)* धोअलक *dhŏalak*, धोएलक *dhŏelak*.		*(GROUP 1)* धोअलकइ *dhŏalakai*, धोएलकइ *dhŏelakai*.	

302. Verbal Noun.

(1) चूबि *cūb*[i] ; obl. चूबै *cūbai*, (1) धो *dhō*, धोर *dhōi*, धोबि
चूऐ *cūai ;* the act of dripping.   *dhōb*[i] ; obl. धोबै *dhōai*, धोबे
  dhōbai ; the act of washing.

303. Participles.

Present.

चूबत *cūat,* चूरत *cūit,* चूऐत *cūait* | धोबत *dhōat,* धोएत *dhōet,* धोऐत
dripping. | *dhōait,* washing.

Past.

चूबल *cūal,* चूरल *cūil,* dripped. | धोबल *dhōal,* धोएल *dhōel,* washed.

Probably ब *b* can be inserted in many more forms than are given above, but I have not met them. In conversation. a good deal depends on the personal equation of the speaker.

304. The only example of the use of a root in क *ū* which I have noted in literature is the following :—

देखलक जे अंगूर एहन गुच्छ सभ पाकल टट्टी में लटकि रहल अछि कि जकरा सँ रस चूबि रहल अछि, *dekh*[a]*lak jē āgūr ehan gucch sabh pākal ṭaṭṭī mē̃ laṭak*[i] *rahal ach*[i]*, ki jak*[a]*rā sã̄ ras cūb*[i] *rahal ach*[i]*,* he saw that such bunches of grapes were hanging ripe from the trellis. that from them (*lit.* from which) the juice kept dripping (Intensive compound, see § 342).

Examples of roots in धो *ō* are more common. Such are :—

(a) (1) Old Present :—

एक रोये अमाँ दोसर रोबे चन्ना हाइ हाय ।
तेसर रोबै दूध छाड़ि बलकवा रे हाइ हाय ॥

ek rōyē amā̃ ; dōsar rōbē cannā, hāe hāy ;
tēsar rōbai dūdh chār[i] *balak*[a]*wā, rē, hāe hāy.*

One (person), the mother, weeps; a second, Cannā weeps, alas, alas ! A third, a child leaving (its mother's) milk, weeps. ah ! alas, alas !

32

(*a*) (3) **Imperative** :—

बाबू गोड़ चाँय धोञ, *bābū gōṛ hāth dhōü*, gentlemen, wash your feet and hands.

जौड़ि जनू फोर्षद आष्ठोर काठी सवहि कें तोड़ि दैच, *jauṛi janu phōāh, āor kāṭhī sabahi kē tōṛi daih*, do not open the string, and break the sticks.

(*d*) (8) **Past Indicative** :—

मारि लोभ सँ मुँच फोप्रलक, *māri lōbh sã muh phōelak*, by reason of greed he opened his mouth.

1. **Verbal Noun** (oblique) :—

लगलाँच कानै रोप्रे, *lagᵃlāh kānai rōai*, they began to wail (and) weep.

Past Participle :—

धोप्रल धाप्रल भेँड़ी पाँका लागे चाहे अछि, *dhōal dhāel bhēṛi pākā lāgai cāhai-achi*, the well-washed sheep is about to fall into the slough. (Proverb= there's many a slip, etc.)

Conjunctive Participle :—

रोय रोय कजलि दहाय गेल ना, *rōya* (for *rōi*) *rōya kajali dahāya gela* (m.c. for *gēla*) *nā*, lo, weeping, weeping the collyrium was washed away (from her eyes). (Vid. xxvi, 4).

बान्ह फोप्र दरि हिदप्र लगाप्रोलि, *bānha phōe* (for *phōi*) *hari hridae lagāoli*, unloosing (his) bonds, she took Hari to her heart.

फेरि गट्स्थ फो कें प्रक प्रक काठी देलकै, *phēri gṛhasth phō kã ek ek kāṭhī delᵃkai*, then the farmer, having opened (the bundle), gave (them) the sticks one by one.

CHAPTER VI.

Irregular Verbs.

305. The following verbs are irregular :—

√कर *kar*, do, make.

√धर *dhar*, seize, place.

√मर *mar*, die.

√जा *jā*, go.

√आब *āb*, come.

√दे *dē*, give.

√ले *lē*, take.

√हो *hō*, become.

306. The roots कर *kar* and धर *dhar* are irregular in the formation of the past participle and of the tenses derived from it and also in the formation of the first and third verbal nouns. The two are conjugated on exactly parallel lines.

The past participle of the √कर *kar*, do, make, is केल *kail*, often written कयल *kayal*, करल (*i.e.*, कएल) *kael*, or कैल *kail*. From this the past tense is formed as follows. As before, only the most commonly used forms of Groups I and II are given :—

(*d*) (8) **Past Indicative.** 'I did,' 'I made,' &c.

PERSON.	SHORT FORM.		LONG FORM.	
	GROUP I. (Subject: non-honorific. Object: non-honorific.)	GROUP II. (Subject: honorific. Object: non-honorific.)	GROUP I. (Subject: non-honorific. Object: non-honorific.)	GROUP II. (Subject: honorific. Object: non-honorific.)
1	केलहुँ *kailahŭ*, केल *kail.*		केलिऐ *kailiai.*	
2	केले *kailē.*	Same as 1st person.	केलह *kailăh.*	Same as 1st person, but no forms for object in 2nd person.
3	केलक *kailak.*	केलन्हि *kailanhĭ.*	GROUP I. केलकै *kailăkai.*	

Similarly the Perfect is केलहुँ अछि *kailahŭ achĭ* or केले छी *kailē chī*, and the Pluperfect is केले छलहुँ *kailē chalalŭ*.

The first **verbal noun** is regularly करि *kari*, but usually takes the form कै *kai*, कय *kay*, or कँ *kãi̐*.

The third verbal noun, like the past participle is कैल *kail*, not करल *karal*, oblique कैला *kailā*.

The √धर *dhar*, seize, place, is conjugated exactly like the √कर *kar*, the ध *dh* being substituted for the क *k*.

307. The following are examples of the use of the irregular forms of these verbs.

जखनहिं लेल हरि कंचु अछोरि ।
कत परजुगुति कयल आंग मोरि ॥

jakhanahĩ lela hari kañcu achōri ।
kata parajuguti kayala ā̃ga mōri ॥

when Hari snatched away my bodice, how many devices did I make, as I twisted my limbs. (Vid. xxxi, 1).

हम अपराध कैल, *ham apᵃrādh kail*, I committed a fault.

कहिओ जनम भरि चोरी नहिं कैली, *kahiō janam bhar*ⁱ *cōri nah*ⁱ *kailī*, never in my whole life did I commit a theft.

लाख अपराध कैलौक, *lākh apᵃrādh kailauk*, a hundred thousand faults I committed against you.

मारि केना कैलैं फोटरा के, *mār*ⁱ *kenā kailẽ phōṭᵃrā kē*, how did you kill Phoṭrā ?

जेहि मुँहैं धैलैं कटैया ओहि मुँहैं धर अपना बाप के, *jeh*ⁱ *mũhẽ dhailẽ kaṭaiyā, oh*ⁱ *mũhẽ dhar apᵃnā bāp kē*, with the mouth with which you seized (me) in Kaṭaiyā, with the same mouth seize your own father.

तों हो ददा कैल गुलामीक साथ बैर, *tõ, hō dadā, kail gulāmīk sāth bair*, you, O brother, made enmity with Gulāmī.

तों एहि कथा पर भरोसा कैलाह, *tõ eh*ⁱ *kathā par bharōsā kailāh*. you made belief on (*i.e.*, you believed) this statement.

जेंह कइलकें से केलक, *jaih kahal^akai. sē kailak,* as he said, so he did.

अंगूरक टाट पर जाल लगाय कैं ओकरा घेलक, *āgūrak ṭāṭ par jāl lagāy kai ok^arā dhailak,* having put a net on a vine trellis, he caught it (the bird).

ओकरा में कोन गुण छैक जे दाता ओकरा नेहाल केलुन्हि आओर हमरा कंगाल केलुन्हि, *ok^arā mē kōn guṇ chaik, je dātā ok^arā nehāl kailanhⁱ āor ham^arā kāgāl kailanhⁱ,* what are his virtues that the Giver made blessings for him, and made me a beggar ?

तीनू मामा भगिना घेलुन्हि कटैया पन्थक बाट, *tīnū māmā bhaginā dhailanhⁱ kaṭaiyā panthak bāt,* the three, uncle and nephews, took the path of the road (to) Kaṭaiyā.

केवल राहड़ि बाओग कैल अछि, *kēbal rāharⁱ bāog kail achⁱ,* I have sown (*lit.* done sowing) only rāhar.

हम एकरा मारबा में बहुत दौड़-धूप कैलें छी । आओर तेसर खंड ई घेल अछि, *ham ek^arā mār^abā mē bahut daur-dhūp kailē chī, āor tēsar khaṇḍ ī dhail achⁱ,* in killing this (deer) I have done much exertion. And this third portion I have placed (here).

क्यों करुना करि अभरन तेज, *kyō karunā kari abharana tēja,* some full of woe (*lit.* doing woe) cast aside their ornaments (Man. vii. 40).

हरि हरि कय पुनि उठति धरणि धरि ।
रैनि गमाबय जागी ॥

hari hari kaya (for kai) puni uṭhati dharaṇi dhari ।
raini gamābaya (for gamābai) jāgī ॥

crying (*lit.* doing) ' Hari, Hari,' again she (is) rising, having lain upon (*lit.* having seized) the ground ; so waking passeth she the night (Vid. x, 7).

एकरा सभ कें किच्छु कें दखाबी, *ek^arā sabh kē kicch^u kai dekhābī,* having done something, let me show it to all these (boys).

धैरज धै रह मिलत मुरारि, *dhairaja dhai rahu, milata murāri,* having seized patience (*i.e.,* being patient), remain. Murāri will meet you (Vid. lxii, 6).

दौड़-धूप केला सँ किछु नहिं हैत, *dauṛ-dhūp kailā sã kicch^u nahⁱ* *hait*, nothing will occur (*i.e.*, you will get no benefit) from running about.

In one instance Vidyāpati (lxvi, 1) has a kind of long form of the conjunctive participle, *viz.*, करिए *karie* for करि *kari* (poetical for करि *karⁱ*).

The verse runs:—

अवधि करिए पऊ गेलाह, *abadhi karie pahu gēlãh*, my husband went, having fixed a date for his return. Compare टुटिए *ṭuṭiē* in § 344.

308. The conjugation of the √मर *mar*, die, closely resembles that of √कर *kar* and √धर *dhar*, allowance being made for the fact that it is an intransitive verb. It is only irregular in the fact that its present participle is मरैत *marait* or मुऐत *muait*, and that its past participle is मरल *maral* or मुइल *muil*. Its past conditional is therefore मरितहुँ *maritah^u* or मुइतहुँ *muitah^u*, and its past indicative is मरलहुँ *maralah^u* or मुइलहुँ *muilah^v*. The 3rd verbal noun is the same as the past participle. The oblique form of the first verbal noun is vulgarly मुऐ *muai* for मरै *marai*. See § 350.

309. I have not come across any forms of the irregular present participle in literature. The following are examples of tenses derived from the past participle:—

घन घन जे ऐलाह से मरल, *ghana ghana jē ailãha sē marala*, every troop that came (with him) died. (Man. x, 55).

ठामहि घूमि मुइल कै गोट, *ṭhāmahi ghūmi muila kai gōṭa*, several turned round and died on the spot. (Man. v, 41).

मुइल अरिष्ट भेल उपकार, *muila ariṣṭa bhēla upakāra*, the dead bull became a blessing. (Man. vi, 14).

मुइला पूतक बहुत नाओँ, *muilā* (oblique) *pūtak bahut nāõ*, a dead son has many names (*i.e.*, is always spoken of affectionately). (Proverb).

हमरा मुइनैं एक तरसी उद्धार, *ham^orā muinẽ* (for *muilẽ*, instr. of

3rd verb. noun) *ek ur^asī udgār*, from our death joy has arisen only in (the village of) Ursi.

310. The ✓जा *jā*, go, is conjugated like an intransitive verb in बा *ā* (see §§ 270 ff.), but is irregular in its past participle, and in the tenses derived from it. The past participle is गेल *gel*, fem. गेलि *gelī*. On the other hand, the third verbal noun (that in ल *l*) is regular, and does not follow the past participle. It is जाएल *jāel*, obl. जैला *jailā*, not गेल *gel*.

The following are the more usual forms of the tenses derived from the past participle :—

(d) (S). Past Indicative. ' I went,' &c.

PERSON.	SHORT FORM.		LONG FORM.	
	GROUP I. (Subject : non-honorific. Object : non-honorific.)	GROUP II. (Subject : honorific. Object : non-honorific.)	GROUP I. (Subject : non-honorific. Object : non-honorific.)	GROUP II. (Subject : honorific. Object : non-honorific.)
1	गेलहुँ *gelah^u*.		गेलिऐ *geliai*.	
2	गेलें *gelē*.	Same as 1st person.	गेलाह *gelāh*.	Same as 1st person, but no forms for object in 2nd person.
3	गेल *gel*.	गेलाह *gelāh*.	GROUP I. गेलै *gelai*.	

The Perfect is गेलहुँ बछि *gelah^u achi* or गेल छी *gel chī*, I have gone, I am gone. The Pluperfect is गेल छलहुँ *gel chalah^u* or गेलें छलहुँ *gelē chalah^u*, I had gone, I went a long time ago.

311. The following are examples of the use of the irregular forms of this verb :—

हम तोहरा हाथ सँ निकसि गेलहुँ *ham toh^aⁿrā hāth sã nikas^i gēlah^ū*, having emerged from your hand, I went, *i.e.*, I escaped from your clutches.

नान्हिटा कली गे तिरिया हम रमिता भै गेली *nānhiṭā chalī, ge tiriyā ham ramitā bhai gēlī*, I was very young, O ladies, (when) I having become a wanderer went, *i.e.*, when I became a wanderer (see § 342 regarding the intensive compound भै गेली *bhai gēlī*).

तौं हमर तीनू कथा एखनहि बिसरि गेलें, *tõ hamar tīnū kathā ekha-nah^i bisar^i gēlē*, you went having forgotten (*i.e.*, you have entirely forgotten) already the three words of mine (§ 342).

एतबहि मे गेलाह खिसियाय, *etabah^i mē gēlāh khisiyāy*, at only this much did you go into a rage (§ 342).

कहाँ गेल किय भेल थारू दोनबार, *kahā̃ gēl kia bhēl thārū don^abār*, where has Tharū Donbār gone, what has become of him ?

एक कोस गेलाह, हो बहोरन, दुइ कोस गेलाह, *ek kōs gēlāh, hō bahō-ran, dui kōs gelāh*. O Bahōran, they went one *kōs*, they went two *kōs*.

माछी बैसलि दूध पर, पाँखि गेलइ लपटाय, *māchī baisal^i dūdh par, pākh^i gelai* (m.c. for *gēlai*) *lap^aṭāy*, a fly sat on milk, (and) his wings went entangled (in it) (§ 342).

मटकुरी माथ सँ खसि टुकरी टुकरी भै गेलैक, *maṭ^akurī māth sã khas^i ṭuk^arī ṭuk^arī bhai gelaik*. the pitcher having fallen from her head became (*i.e.*, was broken to) fragments (§ 342).

एक पैघ लोकक घर में रातिक समय आगि लागि गेलैन्हि, *ek paigh lōkak ghar mē rātik samay āg^i lāg^i gelainh^i*, fire seized at night time the house of a rich man (§ 342).

हुनक बाप मरि गेलथौन्हि, *hunak bāp mar^i gel^athīnh^i*, their (respected) father died (§ 342).

दुनू भाइ मारल गेलथुन्हि कटैया खाप, *dunū bhāi māral gel^athūnh^i kaṭaiya khāp*, the two (respected) brothers were killed in Kaṭaiyā Khāp (Passive § 331).

कथी लय ओतय गेल कलहुँ । ओतय हमर खेत अछि ओकरा देखे गेल
कलहुँ, *kathī lay otay gēl chalah^i ? otay hamar khēt ach^i, ok^arā dēkhai gēl chalah^v*, why had you gone there ?   My field is there, I had
gone to see it.

It will be observed that this root is frequently used with the
conjunctive participles of other verbs, to form what are called
'Intensive Compounds.' These will be fully explained in § 342.
It is also used to form the passive voice as will be explained in
§ 331.

312.   The √आब *āb,* come. is in most of its tenses conjugated
like an intransitive verb in आब *āb,* see §§ 270 ff.   Its past participle is, however, formed as if the root ended in आ *ā,* so that it is
आएल *āel* (आयल *āyal* or आइल *āil*), not आओल *āol.*   The following
is therefore the conjugation of the past tense.   Examples of the
present. future, etc., will be found under the head of roots in
आब *āb.*

(*d*) (8) **Past Indicative** ' I came.' &c.

PERSON.	SHORT FORM.		LONG FORM.	
	GROUP I.	GROUP II.	GROUP I.	GROUP II.
	(Subject : non-honorific. Object : non-honorific.)	(Subject: honorific. Object: non-honorific.)	(Subject : non-honorific. Object: non-honorific.)	(Subject : honorific. Object: non-honorific.)
1	प्रेलहुँ *ailah^ū.*		प्रेलिप्र *ailiai.*	
2	प्रेलें *ailē.*	Same as 1st person.	प्रेलाह *ailāh.*	Same as 1st person, but no forms for object in 2nd person.
3	आएल *āel.*	प्रेलाह *ailāh.*	GROUP I. प्रेले *ailai.*	

Similarly for the Perfect and Pluperfect.

The Present Participle is (regularly) अबैत *abait* (अवयित *abayit*). The 3rd singular Old Present is आबै *ābai* or आय *āē*, honorific आबथि *ābathⁱ*, etc. The 1st singular future is आएब *āeb* (poetical also आओब *āob*). The Conjunctive Participle is आबि *abⁱ*, and also आइ *āi* (आय *āy*, etc.).

313. The following are examples of the use of this verb :—

खन परितज खन आबए पास, *khana paritaja khana āboi pāsu*, sometimes she retreats and sometimes comes near him (Vid. viii, 3).

राङु दूरि बसु निआरो न आबथि, *rāhu dūri basu niaro na ābathi*, Rāhu dwelleth afar, (and) doth not approach her (Vid. xiv, 8).

फेरि पलटि मोरंग नहिं आएब, *phērⁱ palaṭⁱ mōraṅg nahⁱ āeb*, again I will not come back to Mōraṅg.

गौरी आओत ना, *gaurī āot nā*, O Gaurī, will he not come ?

जिबैत रहैत तो जोगिया अबैत पलटि, *jibait rahait, to jogiyā abait palaṭⁱ*, if they had been living, then they would have come back to Jogiyā.

आेतन्हि दुरागमन करैतैन्हि, *autanhⁱ durāgaman karaitainhⁱ*, if they had come they would have performed the *durāgaman*-ceremony.

दुर चारि पैसा खातिर हम ऐलहुँ दरबाजा पर, *dui carⁱ paisā khātir ham ailahⁱ darᵃbājū par*, for the sake of two or four pice I came to your doorway.

तीनू मिलि गेलाह हे बहोरन अकसर ऐलाह, *tinū milⁱ gēlāh, hē bahōran, akᵃsar ailāh*, the three went together, O Bahōran, (but) you came (back) alone.

कथी ला ऐलीह दरबाजा पर, *kathī lā ailīh darᵃbājā par*, for what did you (fem.) come to the doorway ?

एक बिदेशी आएल, *ek bidēsī āel*, a foreigner came.

सखि सभ देलि भबन के सजनी गे ।
घुरि आएलि सभ नारी ॥
sakhi sabha dēli bhaban kai, sajᵃnⁱ gē
ghuri āeli sabha nāri ॥

O friend, the bridesmaids brought me to the chamber, and then all the women (left me and) went back home (Vid. xxiii, 7).

निष पड़ परिहरि आइलि कमल मुखि । *nia pahu parihari āili kamala-mukhi*, the lotus-faced girl came, having left her own husband (Vid. vii, 7).

अब ऐलाह दीनाक पास भद्री, *ab ailāh dīnāk pās bhadrī*, now Bhadrī came near to Dinā.

ई देखि ओकरा मुंह में पानि भरि ऐलै, *ī dēkhi oka rā mūh mē pāni bhari ailai*, seeing this, water came into and filled his mouth (*i.e.*, his mouth watered).

कालू सदा कनैत कनैत ऐलैक जोगियाक गाम, *kālū sadā kanait kanait ailaik jogiyāk gām*, Kālū Sadā, weeping weeping, came to the village of Jogiyā.

An example of the present participle will be found under the head of roots in आब *āb* (§ 284).

314. The roots दे *dē*, give, and ले *lē*, take, are conjugated exactly alike. It is sufficient to give the conjugation of the √दे *dē*. That of √ले *lē* can be ascertained by simply substituting ल *l* for द *d* throughout.

These two verbs present many irregularities. These are partly due to the combination of the final vowel of the root with the terminations, but are also due to the fact that there are really two pairs of roots, *viz.*, √दे *dē* and √दि *di*, and √ले *lē* and √लि *li*. Sometimes one of the pair is used, and sometimes the other. Moreover, owing to दि *di* and लि *li* having short vowels, the long *ē* of दे *dē* and ले *lē* is often shortened by analogy, so that, although I have, as a rule, only written a long *ē* in the paradigms, a short *e* can always be substituted. This is shown from the use of these forms in poetry, where pairs like देब *dēb* and देब *deb*, लेब *lēb* and लेब *leb*, देल *dēl* and देल *del*, लेल *lēl* and लेल *lel* are of frequent occurrence. Numerous instances will be found in the examples given below.

Note that, as in the conjugation of the Old Present of the regular verb (see § 176), when a dissyllabic form ends in ऐ *ai* derived from अहि *ahi* the long ए *ē* is not shortened on that account (though of course it may be shortened as above explained). Thus the long *ē* of देब *dēb* is not shortened in the form देबै *dēbai* (for *देबहि *dēbah^i*). In the redundant form देबैक *debaik* (for *देबहिक *deb^ahik*) it is. of course, shortened under the usual ante-penultimate rule.

I give the conjugation of the √ दे *dē* in Groups I and II pretty fully, as there are numerous irregular forms. The forms for Groups III and IV can easily be derived from these, and instances of them will be found among the examples.

315. (*a*) (1) **Old Present.** · I give,' &c. **Future (First Form).** ‘ I shall give,' &c.

PERSON.	SHORT FORM.		LONG FORM.	
	GROUP I. (Subject: non-honorific. Object: non-honorific.)	GROUP II. (Subject: honorific. Object: non-honorific.)	GROUP I. (Subject: non-honorific. Object: non-honorific.)	GROUP II. (Subject: honorific. Object: non-honorific.)
I	दी *dī*.		दिऐ *diai* (poetical, दिअ *dia*). Or (with object in 2nd person). दिऔ *diau*, दिअङ्ङ *diah^u*.	
2	दे *dē*, देसि *dēsi* (poetical).	Same as 1st person.	दिअँह *didh*, दँइ *dâh*, दिअङ्ङ *diah^u* दिङ्ङ *dih^u*, देङ्ङ *deh^u*, देइ *daih*, दएइ *daeh*.	Same as 1st person, but no forms for object in 2nd person.
3	दे *dē*, दिअ *dia*, देअ *dea*, देओ *deo*, देए *dēē*.	देथि *dēth^i*.	GROUP I. देइ *dēai*, Or (with object in 2nd person). देओ *dēau*.	

Similarly, *mutatis mutandis*, the Present Conditional and the Imperative. See the examples of these tenses below.

Second Form.   Third Form.

316. (b) (4) Future.   'I shall give.'

PERSON	Second Form — SHORT FORM, GROUP I (Subject: non-honorific. Object: non-honorific.)	Second Form — SHORT FORM, GROUP II (Subject: honorific. Object: non-honorific.)	Second Form — LONG FORM, GROUP I (Subject: non-honorific. Object: non-honorific.)	Second Form — LONG FORM, GROUP II (Subject: honorific. Object: non-honorific.)	Third Form — SHORT FORM, GROUP I (Subject: non-honorific. Object: non-honorific.)	Third Form — SHORT FORM, GROUP II (Subject: honorific. Object: non-honorific.)	Third Form — LONG FORM, GROUP 1 (Subject: non-honorific. Object: non-honorific.)	Third Form — LONG FORM, GROUP II (Subject: honorific. Object: non-honorific.)
1	देब *dĕbē.*	देब *dĕb*, देबों *dĕbõ*, देबइ *dĕbaik.*	देबै *dĕbai* Or (with object in 2nd person.) देबौ *dĕbau*, देबक् *dĕbak* (देमन *dĕman*, vulgar.)	Same as 1st person, but no forms for object in 2nd person.	देतह *dĕtahū.*	Same as 1st person.	देतिइ *dĕtiai,* Or (with obj. in 2nd pers.) देतिओ *dĕtiau.*	देतिअ *dĕtiau.*
2	Wanting.	Same as 1st person.	देबह *dĕbāh.*		Wanting.	Same as 1st person.	Same as 1st person, but no forms for object in 2nd person.	Same as 1st person, but no forms for object in 2nd person.
3	Wanting.	Wanting.	Wanting.		देत *dēt*, देत *dait.*	देतथ *dētathi.*	देत *dētai,* Or (with obj. in 2nd pers.) देतौ *dētau.*	देत *dētau.*

317. (c) (5) Past Conditional: '(If) I had given,' &c.

PERSON	SHORT FORM		LONG FORM	
	GROUP I. (Subject: non-honorific. Object: non-honorific).	GROUP II. (Subject: honorific. Object: non-honorific.)	GROUP I. (Subject: non-honorific. Object: non-honorific)	GROUP II. (Subject: honorific. Object: non-honorific.)
1	दित्तहुँ *ditahů*	*(see Group I)*	दितिऐ *ditiai*, Or (with object in 2nd person). दितिऔ *ditiau*.	Same as 1st person, but no forms for object in 2nd person.
2	दित् *dite.*	Same as 1st person.	दितैह *ditaih.*	
3	दैत *dait*, दैत *deit.*	दितथि *ditathi.*	GROUP I. दित् *ditai*, Or (with object in 2nd person). दितौ *ditau.*	

318. (d) (8) Past Indicative: 'I gave,' &c.

SHORT FORM.		LONG FORM.	
GROUP I. (Subject: non-honorific. Object: non-honorific)	GROUP II. (Subject: honorific. Object: non-honorific).	GROUP I. (Subj.; non-honorific. Object; non-honorific.)	GROUP II. (Subject: honorific. Object; non-honorific.)
देलिअहँ *deliahẽ*, देलौ *deliẽ*, देलि *deiẽ* (fem. देलि *deiẽ*).	*(see Group I)*	देलिऐ *delai*, Or (with obj. in 2nd person.) देलौ *delau.*	Same as 1st person, but no forms for object in 2nd person.
देलँ *deliẽ.*	Same as 1st person.	GROUP I. देलह *delah*, Or (with obj. in 2nd person.) देलौ *delau.*	
देलक *delink.*	देलनि *delanhi*, देलथि *delathi.*	देलकै *delakai*, Or (with obj. in 2nd person.) देलकौ *delakau.*	

319. Verbal Nouns.

1. दे *dē*, देइ *dēi*, दँ *dá*, दै *dai*, दय *day*, दए *dae*, देए *dee*: the
   act of giving: obl. देमै *dēmai* or दीयँ *dīá*.

2. देब *dēb*, the act of giving, to give ; obl. देबा *dēbā*.

3. देल *dēl*, the act of giving ; obl. देला *dēlā*. Its instrumental
   is देलँ *dēlẽ*, or देनँ *dēnẽ*. Similarly, for √ ले *lē*, we have लेलँ
   lēlẽ, लेनँ *lēnẽ*, or (a common corruption) नेनँ *nēnẽ*.

320. Participles.

Present.

देत *dēt*, देइत *dēit*, or दैत *dait*, fem. देति *dēt^i*, दैति *dait^i*, giving.

Past.

देल *dēl*, fem. देलि *dēl^i*, given.

321. The following are examples of the use of these two
verbs. In several of the instances given these verbs form intensive compounds with the first verbal nouns of other verbs. In
such cases the root meaning of 'giving' or 'taking' has almost
disappeared. See § 342.

Old Present and First Form of Future :— कहिअ तँ सभ अभरन
दिअ काढ़ि, *kahia tā sabha abharana dia kāṛhi*, if you say (the word)
I will tear off the ornaments from my body (intensive compound,
§ 342) (Man. vii, 43).

तोंहरा कंएक कथा सभ सिखाय दिअङ्, *toh^{a}rā kaiek kathā sabh sikhāy diah^u*. I will teach you (§ 342, and so elsewhere below)
several matters.

किच्छ सीखि लेय तँ पठाय दिऐक । बेस हमरा बालकक संग पठाय दिऔक,
*kicch^u sikh^i lēē. tā paṭhāy diaik. Bēs, ham^{a}rā bālakak saṅg paṭhāy
diauk*, let him learn a little, then I will send him. Good, send
him with my son.

मदन बेदन दे मानस अन्त, *madana bedana dē mānasa anta*, Love
gives pangs in the inmost recesses of my soul (Vid. lxi, 2).

तेल सिन्दुर सभ देलन्हि आओरि ।
चरि चरि चुर देश (r. l. देओ) मथा गोआरि ।

tela sindura sabha dēlanhi āori ।
cari cari cura dea (or deo) mathā goāri ॥

Other herd-maidens all gave oil and vermilion, and going
here and there put (*lit.* give) handfuls (of the same on each
others') heads (Man. ii, 43).

आ घरि दाओ कृष्ण देथि आड, *ā dhari dāo kṛṣṇa dethi* (for *dēthi*)
āṛa, adopting that trick Kṛṣṇa wards him off (*lit.* gives warding
off) (Man. ix, 36).

राम भरोखा बैसि कँ   सबचिक मोजरा लेथि ।
जेहन जनिकर चाकरी   तेहनें सन भरि देथि ॥

Rāma jharōkhā baisi kã   sabahika mojarā lēthi ।
Jēhana janikara cākarī   tehanẽ sana bhari dēthi ॥

Rām sitteth at an upper window and taketh cognizance of all.
As each one's service is, so in full He payeth him.

उपर में सुगा देइ चक भाउर, *upar mẽ sugā dēai cak-bhāur,* above
(them) the parrot flies in (*lit.* gives) circles.

Imperative : फेरि अपना में बाँटि ली, *phēri apanā mẽ bãṭi li.*
afterwards, let us divide (it) amongst ourselves.

एक चुरुक दे पियाय, *ek curuk dē piyāy,* give one sip (of water)
to drink.

ले गे गिरथाइनि हरवा ले, *lē, ge girathāini. harawā lē,* take, O
mistress, take (my) strings of beads.

धोबिनि कहए मुख उक दे लगाए, *dhobini kahae mukhu uka de lagāe,* he says to the Dhōbin ' thrust a torch in (their) faces ' (Man.
viii, 10).

तोरित केसि कँ देसि बजाए, *torita kēsi kẽ dēsi bajāe.* quickly
summon Kēsi (Man. vi, 22).

से इनाम दाह हमरा तब तोहरा मन पुराएब, *sē inām dāh hamarā,*
tab tohrā man purāeb, give me that reward, (and) I will fulfil for
you (your) heart's (desire).

प्रक बेरि द्दा ङ्कुम दिङ्, *ek bēr^i, dadā, hukum dih^u,* give, O brother, the order but once.

सूपत बेंचा देलौक सौदा देङ् पुराय, *sūpat bēcā delauk, saudā deh^u purāy,* I have given you barter-price of full weight, give me (therefore) the full weight in commodities.

दुनू सेर बेंचा जोखि लेङ्, *dunū sēr bēcā jōkh^i leh^u,* take and weigh these two seers of grain as barter-price.

भनहिं बिद्यापति देइ सुमति मति, *bhanah^i bidyāpati daiha, sumati, mati,* saith Vidyāpati, O Wise One, give heed (Vid. xxvii, 5).

ब्राह्मण कें द्प्रइ, *brāhman kē daeh,* give to the Brāhman (from a private letter written to the author).

दुनू चार दुनू हाँथ दे बेठाय द्हँक, *dunū cār dunū hāth dai baithāy dahak,* set down the two thatches with (*see below*) (your) two hands.

ओतहि रहथु द्र्रह फेरि हे सखि ।   द्रसन देथु प्रक बेरि ॥

otahi rahathu drrh phēri, hē sakhi ǀ darasana dethu eka bēri ǁ

Let him dwell there permanently, but, O friend, let him give us a sight (of him) but once (in a way) (Vid. lxviii, 4).

Honorific Imperatives :—

प्रक बेरि ङ्कुम दिअ, *ek bēr^i hukum diā,* be pleased to give thy order but once.

नहिं खलीफा प्रक बेरि ठाढ़ में कें कुस्ती लिअ, *nah^i khalīphā ek bēr^i thārh bhai ke kustī liā,* nay, Your Highness, once more stand up and wrestle a fall (*lit.* take a wrestle) (with me).

माधब जनि दीअङ्ड मोर दोस, *mādhaba jani diahu mora dōsa,* O Mādhava, do not give my blame (*i.e.,* blame me) (Vid. lxvii, 4).

सरन दिअओ सरनागत जानि, *sarana diao saranāgata jāni,* (addressed to Viṣṇu) grant (me) protection, considering (me) as one who has taken refuge (with thee) (Man. i, 18).

आजुक दिन दिअओक कमाय, *ājuk din diauk kamāy,* be pleased to work for this day (only).

हमरो नमस्कार लिखि दिअओन्हि, *hamarō namaskār likh^i diaunh^i.* please write down (*lit.* having written give) my compliments also.

34

एक सेर अन घटि नहिं देबहीन्हि, *ek sēr an ghaṭi nahi debᵃhinhⁱ,* please do not give (even) one seer too little.

Future :—

प्रातहिं आध देस देब बाँटि, *prātahī ādha dēsa deba bā̃ṭi,* at dawn, having divided the country I will give (you) half (Man. vi, 31).

सिसु दुह्रु मारि नन्द लेब दाँड़ि, *sisu duhu māri nanda lebu dā̃ṛi,* having killed the two children, I will take a fine from Nand (Man. vi, 27).

मारब धनुखा देब खसाय, *mārab dhanukhā, dēb khasāy,* I will kill him (with an arrow) from my bow, and will fell him.

तन्हिका भवन जनम हम लेब, *tanhikā bhabana janama hama lēba,* in his house I will take birth (Man. i, 21).

सभ के देबौं हम चारि सेर बोनि, *subh kē dēbõ ham cārⁱ sēr bonⁱ,* to all (others) I will give four seers (of grain) as wages.

देबहुँ गोआही गुजराय, *dēbahⁿ goāhī gujᵃray,* I will bear testimony.

धरती देबै लोटाय, *dharᵃtī dēbai loṭāy,* I will throw (him) on the ground.

तोरा देबौ मोती-चूरक लड्डु, *tōrā dēbau mōtī-cūrak laḍḍū,* I will give you sweetmeats of fried pulse-grains.

तखन तोहरा फुरसति देबहु बीच में नहिं देबहु, *takhan tohᵃrā phurᵃsatⁱ dēbᵃhu, bīc mē nahⁱ dēbᵃhu,* then I will give you leave to depart : in the meantime I will not give you (leave).

हम तोहरा बचा लेबहु, *ham tohᵃrā bacā lēbahu,* I will take care of you.

नाहि ठाम देबैक धूनी खसाय, *tāhⁱ ṭhām debaik dhūnī khasāy,* there will we set down our fire.

जौ लागि हाजिर करबै नहिं तो लागि फुरसति नहिं देबौक, *jau lāgⁱ hājir karᵃbai nahⁱ, tau lāgⁱ phurᵃsatⁱ nahⁱ debauk,* as long as you do not produce (the thief), so long will I not give (Salhēs) leave to depart for you (*i.e.,* as you request).

नहिं रे अहिरा दूध पीबै देबें, *nahⁱ, rē ahirā. dūdh pībai dēbẽ,* (if) you will not, O cowherd, give (me) milk to drink.

बेरि बेरि देबकि गभं देब सब्य, *beri beri debaki garbha deba sabya,* turn and turn about shalt thou place all of them in Dēvaki's womb (Man. i. 29).

सातम संकरखित कै लेब । देबकि सों रोहिनि कें देब ॥ . *sātama saṅkarakhita kai lēb ǀ dēbaki sõ rōhini kē dēb ǁ*

The seventh (child) thou shalt take, having withdrawn it from Dēvaki's (womb), and shalt give it to Rōhinī (Man. i, 30).

परल अनाइत तें चथि अंतय ! बालमु दोस न देबा । *parala anāita tē chathi antaya ǀ bālamu dōsa na dēbā* (m.c. for *dēb*),

He is elsewhere unwillingly, thou shalt not (*i.e.,* do not) give blame to thy beloved (Vid. lxiv, 12).

जखन तौं हमरा छाड़ि देबह तखन कहबङ्, *jakhan tō hamᵃrā chāṛⁱ dēbáh, takhan kahabahᵘ,* when you will let me go, I will tell you.

से बकस खोलि दुइ-टा रुपैआ ओ आधा आधा सभ मसाला लछमी दाइ कें अपनें चुप्पे देबैन्हि, *sē bakus khōlⁱ dui-tā rupaiā ō ādhā ādhā sabh masālā lachᵃmī dāi kē apᵃne cuppē debainhⁱ,* having opened the box you will please give to the respected Lakṣmī Dēvī two rupees and half of each of the dainties.

नारद देत-गए उकठी लारि. *nārada deta-gae ukaṭhī lārī.* Nārada will stir up some evil deed (Man. ii, 19).

हमरो काज भंग कें देत, *hamᵃrō kāja bhaṅga kai dēta,* will he interrupt even my business (Man. v. 33)?

हमहूँ हेठ होएब तो हमरो धै लेत, *hamahuᵘ hēṭh hōeb, to hamᵃrō dhai lēt,* if I also shall descend, then he will seize me also.

देतौ लाख गारि ने अपराध, *dētau lākh gārⁱ bē apᵃrādh,* for no fault she will give you a hundred thousand abuses.

घर घर जोगियाक देतैक पुराय, *ghar ghar jogiyāk detaik purāy,* from house to house the (people) of Jogiyā will fulfil (our order).

Past Conditional :— एहि नहिं जनली अहाँ भद्री छी । हम सीना गाइक दूध दितहुँ पियाय, *ehⁱ nahⁱ janᵃlī ahā bhadrī chī : ham sīnā gāik dūdh ditahᵘ piyāy,* I did not know that you are Bhadrī (or) I should have given you the milk of the cow Sīnā to drink.

जाँ ताँ हमरा नहिं छाड़িতहুঁ আঝোर मारি দিতहुঁ তখन ও মোতী
তোহরা হাথ লগैत, *jõ tõ hamᵃrā nahⁱ chāṛitâh, āor mārⁱ ditâh, takhan
õ mõtī tohᵃrā hāth lagait,* if you had not let me go, and had killed
me. then that pearl would have come into your possession.

Present Indicative :—सलহेसक पहরা সौঁ সে তোরা इनाম দैत ची,
salᵃhēsak pahᵃrā saũ sē tõrā inām dait chī. (what I stole) from
Salhēs's guard, that give I thee as a reward.

মাঁরैত अछि হাঁक গাइ দैत अছি भড়কाয, *mắrait achⁱ hắk, gāi dēit
achⁱ bhaṛᵃkāy,* they utter a howl, and throw the cows into dis-
order.

आलस্য এহনে কীরा अছি জে धन কें धূরা কে দैত अছি, *ālasya ehᵃnē
kīrā ahⁱ, jē dhan kē dhūrā kai dait achⁱ,* idleness is in such a manner a worm that it turns wealth to dust.

धিया পুতা ভদ্রী কে লैत চैन্হি ডाঁটि, *dhiyā putā bhadrī kē lēit
chainhⁱ ḍā̃ṭⁱ,* the girls and boys scold Bhadrī.

किच্ছু দূध দैত अছি, *kicchᵘ dūdh daitⁱ achⁱ,* is she (a cow)
giving any milk ?

Past Indicative :—

> पथ अपराध पिশुन পরচারল ।
> তথিহূঁ উতর হম দেলা ॥
>
> *patha aparādha piśuna paracārala ।
> tathihũ utara hamu dēlā* (m.c. for *dēl*) ।

On the way the slanderers cast reproaches at me, and I an-
swered them on the spot (Vid. xl, 9).

सूपत বेচা দেলौক, *sūpat bēcā delauk,* I gave you barter-price
in full.

লাখ अপराধ কैলौक লাখ গারি দেলैঁ, *lākh apᵃrādh kailauk, lākh
gārⁱ dēlȇ,* a hundred thousand faults I committed against you. a
hundred thousand abuses you gave me.

ফোটরা গীদর কথী লা মরদ ঔতার লেলैঁ, *phoṭᵃrā gīdar kathī lā mu-
rad autār lēlȇ,* O Phoṭrā jackal, why did you take human form ?

মেলি ন মিলয দেলहूঁ হিম কোটি, *meli na milaya delahũ hima
kōṭi,* even after bringing them together they do not unite. (though)
thou didst give ten millions of gold (Vid. xxx, 3).

सेहो देल कोन काजे, *sēhō dela kona kājē*, even (if) you gave that, what good is it (Vid. lxiii, 2) ?

> पहिल बचन उतरो नहिं देलि ।
>
> नैन कटाक्ष सैं जिब हरि लेलि ॥

> *pahila bacana utar-ō nahī dēli*
> *naina kaṭāchu sā* (m.c. for *sã*) *jiba hari lēli* ॥

Thou (*fem.*) gavest not even a reply to my first words, but with a glance of your eye you took away my life (Vid. xlix, 2).

> बिध मोर परसन भेल ।   रघुपति दरसन देल ।

> *biha mora parasana bhēla* ।
> *raghupati darsana dēla* (poet. for *dēlanh*ⁱ) ॥

The Creator was pleased with me. Raghupati gave (me) a vision (of himself) (Vid. xi. 1).

> रानी कें उठाय कै भीमसेनक खटिया पर देल, ओ सोनाक पलंग मथा पर

राखि लेल, *rānī kē uthāy kai bhīm-sainak khaṭiyā par dēl* (vulgar for *dēlak*), *ō sōnāk palaṅg mathā par rākh*ⁱ *lēl* (vulgar for *lēlak*), he lifted the queen and put her upon Bhīm Sēn's cot, while he took the golden bed and placed it upon (his own) head.

> तोहर बदन सन चांद होअथि नहिं ।
>
> जैओ जतन बिध देला ॥

> *tohara badana sana cãda hoathi nahī* ।
> *jaio jatana bihu dēlā* (m.c. for *dēl*, poetical
>   for *dēlanh*ⁱ).

The moon doth not equal thy face, however great efforts the Creator made (*lit.* gave) (Vid. vi, 3).

गमार भेंड़ा सभ एहि कपटी झंड़ार सभक कथा मानि लेलक । आओर कुकुर सभ कें झंड़ारक ओतय पठाय देलक, *gamār bhēṛā sabh eh*ⁱ *kapaṭī hūṛār sabhak kathā mān*ⁱ *lēlak, āor kukur sabh kē hūṛārak otay pathāy dēlak*, the silly sheep believed the words of these deceitful wolves, and sent the dogs to where the wolves (were staying).

उमड़ि चलल कै लेलक सलाम, *umaṛi calala kai lelaka salāma*, he took leave to go and departed swaggering (Man. v, 36).

तिरिया देलन्हि सपना जोगिया गाम, *tiriyā dēlanh[i] sap[a]nā jogiyā gām.* he gave (*i.e.*, showed) his wife a dream in Jogiyā village.

सबुज कमान लेलन्हि दीना भद्री हाथ के, *sabuj kamān lēlanh[i] dīnā bhadrī hāth-kē.* Dīnā and Bhadrī took up into their hands their green bows.

देहि दुनू भाइ कोंड़ि देलथि, *dēh[i] dunū bhāi chōr[i] dēlath[i].* the two brothers abandoned their bodies.

कतहुँ सँ दुद सै रुपैआक चांनी ओहि रसायनी कें आनि दलकै, *katah[u] sā dui sai rupaiāk cānī oh[i] rasāy[a]nī kē ān[i] del[a]kai.* having brought from somewhere two rupees' worth of silver he gave it to that alchemist.

सुनू रन्द्रासन छपन कोटि देबता जे इन्द्र जनम देलन्हि, *sunū indrāsan chapan kōt[i] dēb[a]tā jē indra janam delainh[i]* (vulgar for *Jel[a]kainh[i]*) hear, ye fifty-six times ten million gods of heaven, (and) the Indra who gave me birth.

इं सुनि कें अतीथि उत्तर देलथीन्हि, *i sun[i] kē atīth[i] uttar del[a]thīn-h[i],* having heard this the respected ascetic gave answer politely.

Perfect Indicative :—

रूपत बेचि कें देली अहि, *rūpat bēch[i] ke dēlī ah[i],* having sold I have given the full weight.

जोराबर सिंघ राजपूत डोला कें देलक अछि घेरि, *jorābar singh rāj[a]pūt ḍōlā kē dēlak ach[i] ghēr[i].* Jorāwar Singh, the Rajput, has stopped the (brides') litters.

Pluperfect Indicative :—

जखन धै लेलें (or लेनें or लेनें or नेनें) चलें तखन छाड़ब की रहौ, *jakhan dhai lēlē* (or *lēnē* or *lēnē, or nēnē*) *chalē, takhan chār̤ab kī rahau,* when you had caught me. why did you let me go? (Literally, ' what letting go was there to you ' ?)

जतवा जनिकर लेनें चलि सुन्दरि ।
से सभ सोपलक ताही ॥

jatawā janikara lenē chali sundari
sē sabha sopalaka tāhi

The fair one made over everything to everyone from whom she had taken them (Vid. x, 2).

Verbal Nouns:—

(1) See Conjunctive Participle: (Obl.) हमरा एक बकरी लेमैक अछि, *hamᵃrā ek bakᵃri lemaik achⁱ*, there is to me (necessity) of taking a goat, *i.e.*, I want to get a goat.

देखाय देमै जाइत छी, *dekhāy dēmai jāit chī*, I am going for (*i.e.*, in order to) showing you.

(2) कंगालक पूरब आओर अतीथिक उत्तर देब, *kāgālak pūchab āor atithik uttar dēb*, the question of the beggar, and the answer-giving of the holy man. (This is the title of a story).

(3) हाथ लेलें बाढ़नि चलि भेलि, *hā̃th lēlē̃ bāṛhanⁱ calⁱ bhēlⁱ*, taking (*lit.* by taking) in her hand a broom she went away.

हमर समाद लेनें जाउ जाँजरि, *hamar samād lēnē̃ jāū jā̃jarⁱ*, having taken my message go to Jānjari.

अहिरा गोआर समाद नेनें अबैत छैक, *ahirā goār samād nēnē̃ abait chaik*, Ahirā, the cowherd, is coming with (*lit.* on taking) the message.

Participles:—

*Present:—*See Present Indicative.

*Past:—*Compare Past Indicative.

The Past Participle, or possibly the 3rd verbal noun, of लेब *lēb*, is often used as a postposition meaning 'on account of,' 'for the sake of,' as in Man. ii, 38 :—

लाजक लेल मुख हेरिओ न होअ, *lājaka lela mukha herio na hōa*, on account of shame, even looking you in the face does not take place.

*Conjunctive:—*चटि दे घैलक पटि दे मारलक, *caṭⁱ dē dhailak, paṭⁱ dē mārᵃlak*, giving abruptness (*i.e.*, suddenly) he seized (him), giving instantaneous (*i.e.*, instantly) he struck (him).

मोर समाद जोगिया ले जाह, *mōr samād jogiyā lē jāh*, having taken my message, go to Jogiyā.

बाज सभ ले कं भेल तैयार, *bāj subh lē kĕ bhēl taiyār*, taking his horses he became ready.

.

आस दैइ फेरि करु न निरासे, *āsa dēi pheri karu na nirāsē*, having given hope, do not again make hopelessness (Vid. xlix, 4, corrected reading).

ककर सक अछि जे हमरा सोझा सँ उठा लँ जाएत, *kakar sak achⁱ jē hamᵃrā sōjhā sằ uṭhā lá jāet*. who has (sufficient) strength that he will lift (it) up from before me and take it away?

कतेक भूमि पर दे दे पटकलक, *katek bhūmⁱ par dai dai paṭakᵃlak*, how often placing it again and again on the ground she dashed it (*i.e.,* how often she dashed it on the ground. but without result).

डौंका कँ लँ कँ उड़लि, *ḍõkā kẽ lai kẫ uⁱⁱ*, taking the shell she flew (up in the air).

सीना बेना लँ के चरबैत अछि बरा डीहक बथान, *sīnā bēnā lai ke carᵃbait achⁱ barā dīhak bathān*, he is herding (the cows) Sinā and Bēnā at the cowshed of Barā Dih.

अपनहूँ मन दय बुझु अबगाहे, *apanahū̃ mana daya bujhu abagāhē*, having applied (*lit.* given) your mind consider deeply (Vid. ii. 4).

जानि असक्य बक्क दए चार, *jānⁱ asakya bakka dae chāra*, knowing him to be invincible he suddenly (*lit.* giving suddenness) let him go (Man. ix. 36).

हरि अनुमति लए ई मति भेल, *hari anumati lae ī mati bhēla*, having taken Hari's permission. this was (their) determination (Man. i, 26).

पहिरि माल बर देइ हरि राम ।   कैल प्रबेस नरेसक गाम ॥

pahiri māla. bara dee, hari rāma ǀ kaila prabēsa narēsᵃka gāma ǁ

Having put on the garlands, having given the boon. Hari and Balarāma entered the king's village (Man. viii, 19).

The Conjunctive Participles are often used as postpositions. दे *dē*, etc., in the meaning of 'through,' 'by means of.' and लै *lē*, etc., meaning 'for.'

बड़ेरिक उपर दे निकसि चलह, *baṛērik upar dē nikasⁱ calắh*, come out by means of (going) over the ridge-pole (of the thatch).

दुनू चार दुनू हाथ दे बैठाय दहह, *dunū cār dunū hẫth dai baiṭhāy dahắk*. set down the two thatches with (*or* by means of) (your) two hands.

तकरा दे के भेजब समाद, *tak*ⁱrā dē ke bhējab samād*, by means of him we will send the message.

जाहि मरद ले जोबन सेबलें, *jāhⁱ marad lai jōban seb*ⁱlē*, the man for whose sake you have kept your virginity.

322. The ✓हो *hō*. become, is also used to supply the missing tenses of the verb substantive (see § 226). Its past participle is भेल *bhēl*, which is conjugated as the same principle as देल *dēl* and लेल *lēl*, that is to say the vowel may always be shortened *ad libitum*, so that we may always have either भेल *bhēl* or भेल *bhel*.

It has for its first verbal noun होइ *hōi* or भे *bhai*, with an oblique form होमे *hōmai*.

The tenses not formed from the past participle may all be regularly formed from हो *hō*, which, as in the case of ✓दे *dē* and ✓ले *lē*, may always be shortened to हो *ho*. Moreover, instead of हो *hō* or हो *ho*, we often have a base ह्व *hwa* or ह *ha*, so that the third person of the future may be होएत *hōet* or होएत *hoet* (or contracted होत *hōt* or होत *hot*). or ह्वैत *hwait* or हैत *hait*. There are also the usual varieties of spelling. Thus होएत *hōet* is often found written होयत *hōyat*, होइत *hōit*, or होयित *hōyit*.

The optional shortening of the vowels and these various spellings are not shown in the paradigms, but numerous instances will be found in the examples which follow.

35

323. (a) (1) Old Present. 'I become,' 'I am,' &c. (Including Present Conditional, Imperative, and first form of the Future).

324. (b) (4) Future. 'I shall become,' 'I shall be,' &c. (1st & 2nd persons in 2nd form, and 3rd person in 3rd form).

323. (a) (1) Old Present

PERSON	SHORT FORM — GROUP I. (Subject: non-honorific. Object: non-honorific.)	SHORT FORM — GROUP II. (Subject: honorific. Object: non-honorific.)	LONG FORM — GROUP I. (Subject: non-honorific. Object: non-honorific.)	LONG FORM — GROUP II. (Subject: honorific. Object: non-honorific.)
1	होइ *hōĭ,*	होिँ *hōī̃,* (Imper.t. होिक *hōŭ.*)	होइछ *hōĭh,* होिछ *hōĭ,*	होइए *hōĭai,* Or (with object in 2nd person.) होिखी *hōĭau.*
2		Same as 1st person.		Same as 1st person, but no forms for object in 2nd person.
3	होिए *hōĕ* (poetical), होिप *hōĕ,* होिख *hōĕy, hōĕu, hōĕy*	चाँिछिप *hōãthĭ,* (Pros. Cond. and Imperat.) चाँिछख *hōãthŭ.*	होिछ *hōĕh,* होिछ *hōh.ʳ*	होिछए *hōĩai,* Or (with object in 2nd person.) होिखी *hōĩau.*

324. (b) (4) Future

PERSON	SHORT FORM — GROUP I. (Subject: non-honorific. Object: non-honorific.)	SHORT FORM — GROUP II. (Subject: honorific. Object: non-honorific.)	LONG FORM — GROUP I. (Subject: non-honorific. Object: non-honorific.)	LONG FORM — GROUP II. (Subject: honorific. Object: non-honorific.)
1	हैब *haib,* चाँिप्प *hōĕb,* चाँिप्पँ *hōĕbā̃, hōĕ.*	चाँिप्प *hōĕb,* चाँिप्पँ *hōĕbā̃, hōbā.*	हैब *laibai,* चाँिप्प *hōbai,* Or (with obj. in 2nd pers.) हैब *haibau,* चाँिबी *hōbau.*	चाँिप्प *hōĕbai,* चाँिप्प *hōbai,* चाँिबी *hōbau.*
2	हैबँ *haibā̃,* चाँिप्प *hōĕ, hōĕdē, hōĕ.*	Same as 1st person.	हैब *haibah,* चाँिप्प *hōĕbh*	Same as 1st person, but no forms for object in 2nd person.
3	हैत *hait,* हैत *hwai,* चाँिप्प *hōĕt, hōĕ, hōt.*	हैछिप *haituthĭ,* चाँिप्पिप *hōĕtathĭ.*	हैत *haitai,* चाँिप्प *hōĕtai,* Or (with obj in 2nd pers.) हैत *haitau,* चाँिप्पी *hōĕtau.*	चाँिप्प *hōĕtai,* चाँिप्पी *hōĕtau.*

325. (c) (5) **Past Conditional.** '(If) I had become,' &c. | 326. (d) (8) **Past Indicative.** 'I became,' &c.

PERSON	Past Conditional — SHORT FORM — GROUP I (Subject: non-honorific. Object: non-honorific.)	SHORT FORM — GROUP II (Subject: honorific. Object: non-honorific.)	LONG FORM — GROUP I (Subject: non-honorific. Object: non-honorific.)	LONG FORM — GROUP II (Subject: honorific. Object: non-honorific.)	Past Indicative — SHORT FORM — GROUP I (Subject: non-honorific. Object: non-honorific.)	SHORT FORM — GROUP II (Subject: honorific. Object: non-honorific.)	LONG FORM — GROUP I (Subject: non-honorific. Object: non-honorific.)	LONG FORM — GROUP II (Subject: honorific. Object: non-honorific.)
1	होइलूँ *hŏilõ.*	होइतलाँ *hŏitalaû.*	होइतलँ *hŏitlah.*	होइतिऎ *hŏitiai.*	भेलूँ *bhĕlũ.*	भेलहूँ *bhĕlahũ.*	भेलिउ *bhĕliũ.*	भेलिऎ *bhĕliai.*
2	होइलैं *hŏilê.*	Same as 1st person.	होइतलह *hŏitlah.*	Same as 1st person, but no forms for object in 2nd person.	भेल *bhĕl.*	Same as 1st person.	भेलाह *bhĕilah.*	Same as 1st person, but no forms for object in 2nd person.
3	होइत *hŏit.*	होइतथि *hŏitathi.*	GROUP I — होइतइ *hŏitai.*		भेल *bhĕl.*	भेलइ *bhĕlai.*	GROUP I — भेलइ *bhĕlai.*	

327. Verbal Nouns.

(1) होइ *hōi* or भै *bhai* (भए *bhae.* etc.). the state of becoming. Obl. होमै *hōmai.*

(2) होएब *hōeb* (होयब *hōyab.* etc.). or हेब *haib* (हयब *hayab,* etc.), the state of becoming. to become. Obl. होबा *hōbā* or हेबा *haibā.*

(3) भेल *bhēl,* the state of becoming. Obl. भेला *bhēlā.*

328. Participles.

Present, होएत *hōet* (होइत *hōit.* होयित *hōyit.* होयत *hōyat,* etc.) or ह्वैत *hwait.*

Past, भेल *bhēl.*

329. NOTE.—In the Southern Maithili tract we commonly hear the regular form होल *hōl,* or होअल *hōal,* instead of भेल *bhēl* for the past participle (with the tenses formed from it) and for the third verbal noun.

———

330. The following are examples of the use of this verb. Several instances will be noted of spellings different from those given in the paradigms :—

Old Present (and First form of Future).

भनहिं विद्यापति अपरुप नेह ।　जेहन विरह हो तेहन सिनेह ॥

bhanahī bidyāpati aparupa nēha ǀ jehana biraha hō tehana sinēha ǁ

Saith Vidyāpati, 'O wondrous love, according to the length, of the separation so (more groweth) the passion' (Vid. lxxx, 7).

अरि मन होप लोप भेल सृष्टि, *ari mana hōe lōpa bhela sṛṣṭi.* to the enemies the mind becomes (*i.e.,* they imagine) (that) the universe has come to an end (Man. x. 45).

से हरखित मुंह हेरि न होए, *sē harakhita mūha hēri na hōē* (m.c. for *hōe*), therefore joyfully looking at (my) face (in a mirror) does not take place (*i.e.,* I no longer care to look at a mirror) (Vid. lxiii, 8.)

चलु चलु मुंदरि सुभ करि आज ।
तततत करद्रुति नहिं होए काज ॥

calu (m.c. for *calū*) *calu sundari subha kari āja ।*
tatamata karaiti nahĩ hoe kāja ॥

Depart. depart, fair one, considering to-day to be propitious. If thou make delay, thine object will not be accomplished (Vid. xxv, 1).

गगन मगन दोश्र तारा *gagana magana hoa tārā*, the stars have become sunken in the sky (*i.e.*, it is dawn) (Vid. xxvi, 1).

दू पुनि तीनि न दोइं, *dū puni tīni na hōī*, two, however, cannot become three (Vid. xxix. 7). Here and elsewhere in Vid. *hōī* is m.c. for *hōy*, which is again for *hōe*. See under Imperative.

उपर दोश्रथि तॉ ठामहि ठाम, *upara hoathi tō ṭhāmahi ṭhāma*, as he comes up (*i.e.*, when he came to the surface of the water) then (they were) there as before (Man. viii, 4).

बौरम नदी में पानि पीबि कें उपर दोइ, *bauram nadī mẽ pāni pībi ke ūpar hōai*, having drunk water in the Bauram river, he is becoming up (*i.e.*, is ascending the bank).

से सुनि दोश्रए निपति मन दरद, *sē suni hoae* (for *hōai*) *nripati mana darada*, hearing that (noise) there became in the mind of the king a pain (*i.e.*, he got a headache) (Man. x, 15).

Present Conditional :—

बुध जन दो से कहें बिसेख, *budha jana hō sē kahē bisēkha*, if a man be wise he tells the meaning (Vid. lxvii, 5).

जदि सन्सए दोश्र जनमक काल ।
बान्हि धरिश्र बर बन्दी साल ॥

jadi sansae hoa janamaka kāla।
bānhi dharia baru bandī-sāla ॥

If there be doubt, then at the time of the child's birth bind her, yea, cast her into prison (Man. ii, 10).

जोड़हिं जोड़ लागि गेल जूधि ।
जे नें दोए किछु धरम बिरूधि ॥

jōrahī jōra lāgi gela jūdhi।
jē nē hoe kichu dharama birūdhi ॥

Equal with equal began the fight, in order that nothing might be done contrary to fair play (Man. x. 32).

जेहि सौं ओकर परबरस होइक से अबस्य॰ कर्तव्य॰ थीक, *jehi saũ ūkar parᵃburaś hōik* (for *hōᵘik*) *sē abasya kartabya thĩk*, in order that there may be support for it (the child), the necessary action must certainly be taken.

Imperative :—

तौं हेठ होअह, *tō hẽth hōâh*, do thou become below (*i.e.*, descend from the tree).

हरि कह हलधर होउ समधान, *Hari kaha,* 'Haladhara, hou samadhāna.' Hari says, 'Haladhar, be of good courage' (Man. v, 17).

होउ परसन हे पुरउ मोर आसे, *hohu parasana he purahu mora āsē*, be gracious, (and) O fulfil my hope (Vid. xlix, 4).

जे कल होअओ मञु कां तेहन, *jē chala, houo satru kā̃ tehana*, what (day) that was,—may such be for my enemies (Man. vii. 60).

पुनु दरसन होअ पुनमति गंगे, *punu darasana hoa punamati Gaṅgē*, Holy Ganges, may I see thee once again (Vid. lxxviii, 2).

मांगि लाएब बित से जदि होय नित ।
अपन करब कौन काजे ॥

māgi lāeba bita, sē jadi hoya nita ।
ᵘpana karaba kona kājē ॥

You will get wealth by begging. If that become everlasting, what will you do with that which is your own (Vid. li, 8) ?

Hoya is for *hōe*, as explained above.

नन्दी सँ रस रीति बचाओब । गुपुत बेकत नहिं होइ ॥
nandī sā̃ rasa rīti bacāoba । guputa bekata nahĩ hōi ॥

Daily you will conceal the way of love from your sister-in-law, (and therefore see thou that) that which is concealed be not revealed (Vid. xl, 12).

*Future Indicative :—*हम हैब मगन रसातल फेरि, *hama haiba magana rasātala phēri*, I shall again become plunged into the infernal regions (Man. i, 14).

हमहूँ हेठ होएब तो हमरो भँ लेत, *hamah^u hēṭh hōeb,* to *ham^arō dhai lēt,* (if) I also shall descend (*lit.* become below), then he will seize me also.

नहिं हेठ होएबौं *nahĩ hēṭh hōebõ,* I will not descend.

जिब जाएत परान बचत तैयो नै परसा गाछ पर से हेठ होबौं, *jib j̃et parān bacat taio nē par^asā gāch par sē hēṭh hōbõ,* whether I lose my life or save it, still I will not descend from the *parsā* tree.

परसाक गाछ पर से हेठ होबहो, *par^asāk gāch par sē hēṭh hob^ahō* (for *hōbah^u*). you will descend (*i.e.,* please descend) from the *parsā* tree.

दौड़-धूप कैला सँ किच्छु नहिं हैत, *daur-dhūp kailā sã kichh^u nah^i hait,* from running and fussing nothing will result.

से अब हैत तीनि दिन मध्य, *sē ab^a hwaita tīni dina madhya,* that will now occur within three days (Man. vii, 32).

ओ बालक घर घालक होएत, *ō bālaka ghara-ghālaka hōeta,* that child will become the destroyer of (your) house (Man. vi, 20).

होएत अमोघ मोघ कए जानि, *hoita* (for *hōet*) *amōgha mōgha kae jāni.* knowing that success will be non-success (Man. x. 35).

बनहिं गमन करु होएति दोसर मति ।
बिसरि जाएब पति मोरा ॥

banahĩ gamana karu (m.c. for *karū*) *hoeti dosara mati ।*
bisari jāeba (m.c. for *jāeb*) *pati mōrā ॥*

Thou wilt make thy way to the forest, and thy mind will become changed : thou wilt. my Lord, forget me (Vid. lv, 3).

तोहरा सभक केसो टेढ़ नहिं हैतउ, *toh^arā sabhak kēs-ō ṭerh nah^i haitah^u,* to you not a hair even will become crooked.

एह बेकूफ कें कहाँ तक नीक अकिल हैतैक, *eh bēkūph kẽ kahã̄ tak nik akil haitaik,* how far will there be decent wisdom to this fool.

Past Conditional :—जौहरी एकरा पबैत तँ अत्यन्त खुसी होइत, *jauh^arī ek^arā pabait. tã̄ atyant khusī hōit,* if a jeweller had got this, he would have been extremely happy (*lit.* happiness would have been).

Present Indicative :—किएक सबङ दोरबिष मति मूढ़, *kieka sabahu hoi-chia* (for *chiai*) *mati mūrha.* why are ye all of foolish mind. (Man. v, 22).

कोनो मुसहर ने घर से दोइत अछि बाहिर, *kauno musahar nē ghar sē hōit ach[i] bāhir,* not one Musahar comes out (*lit.* becomes outside) of his house.

दोइछि (*v.l.* ह्वइछि) उपद्रब बारंबार, *hoich[i]* (v. l., *hwaiachi*) *upadraba bārambāra,* attacks are being continually made (upon us) (Man. iv. 4).

स्वामि-धन वृथा नष्ट दोइछ, *swāmi-dhan vrtha nast hōich.* (my) master's wealth is being wasted in vain. (*Purush-Parīkṣā,* p. 51).

Imperfect Indicative :—माक सबरि में लाही लागि गेलैक । नहिं तं बङत दोइत चल, *gāch sabah[i] mē lāhī lāg[i] gelaik. nah[i] tā bahut hōit chal,* the trees were attacked by blight, otherwise there would have been much (fruit). (Here the imperfect is, as sometimes occurs, employed in the sense of the past conditional.)

Past Indicative :—कोन तप चुकल भेलहुँ जननी, *kona tapa cukala bhelahū janani,* what penance was omitted, that I became his mother (Vid. lxxix, 2).

अहाँ सभक कुसल-केम बूभल मन आनंद भेल, *ahā sabhak kusal-chēm būjhal, man ānand bhēl,* I learned the news of your good health, (and) in my heart there became joy.

संग देब बरह्मा भेल आगु, *sanga dēba barahmā bhela āgu.* Brahmā became (*i.e.,* stood) in front of the gods who were with him (Man. i, 9).

धरनी भार बेआकुलि भेलि । सुरभि रूप धै सुरपुर गेलि ॥
किछु नहिं ततहु काहु सों भेल । धरनिक संग सबहु जन गेल ॥

dharanī bhār beākuli bhēli । surabhi rūpa dhai surapura gēli ॥
kichu nahī tatahū kāhu sō bhēla। dharanika sanga sabahu jana gēla ॥

The earth (fem.) became distressed with the burden, and, taking the form of a cow, went to Indra's paradise ; but thence no assistance came to her from any one, and with the earth all its inhabitants went away (to Brahmā) (Man. i, 6).

ओहि अवसर धरनी भेलि आगू, *ohi abasara dharanī bhelī āgū*, at that moment the earth came forward (Man. i, 12).

कै बेरि काटि बनाओल नव कय ।

तैओ तुलित नहिं भेला ॥

kai beri kāṭi banāola naba kayu ।

taio tulitu nahi bhēlā (m.c. for *bhēla*) ॥

Many times he cut it and fashioned it anew, but still it could not equal (thy beauty) (Vid. vi, 4).

दीना भद्री ठाढ़ भेलाह, *dīnā bhadrī ṭhāṛh bhēlāh*, Dinā and Bhadrī became erect (*i.e.*, stood up).

भेलिह निसंक, *bhelihu nisanku*, she became free from care (Man. iii, 9).

ठाढ़ि भेलिचि धनि आँगो न डोले, *ṭhāṛhi bhelihi dhani ā̃go na ḍōlē*, the lady became motionless, not even do her limbs move (Vid. xxvii, 2).

एक दिन ब्रज मझ खेड़ि भल भेलइ, *eka dinu braja mahā̃ kheṛi bhala bhelai*, one day there was an excellent game in Braj (Man. v, 12).

तोहरा सँ इ चूकि भेलहु, *tohᵃrā sā̃ i cūkⁱ bhēlahᵘ*, from you this mistake has happened (*i.e.*, you have made this mistake).

कै मास सँ गाभिनि अचि । भेलैक तँ आठ मास, *kai mās sā̃ gābhinⁱ achⁱ ? bhelaik tā̃ āṭh mās*, from how many months is she in calf? Eight months, indeed, were (*i.e.*, have passed).

फोटरा के देखि अजगुत भेलौक, *phoṭᵃrā kē dēkhⁱ ajᵃgut bhelauk*, the seeing Photrā was wonderful to you.

बहुत दिन भेलैन्हि अहाँ लोकनि तकाजा नहिं करैछिऐन्हि, *bahut din bhelainhⁱ ahā̃ lokᵃni takājā nahⁱ karaichiainhⁱ*, it is a long time since you pressed (him for the money).

Perfect Indicative :—चीज बस्तु सभ अहाँक नोकसान भेल अचि, *cij bastᵘ sabh ahā̃k nokᵃsān bhēl achⁱ*, your property has been damaged.

Verbal Nouns :—

(1) Obl. होमए लागल अकासक बानि, *hōmae lāgala* (m.c. for *lāgala*) *akāsaku bāni*, there began to be a voice of (*i.e.*, from) the sky (Man. x, 35).

36

(2) मुर्गीक अंडा सभ सँ पैघ मोती हमरा पेट में हैब कहिआ ध्यान में आबि सकैअछि, *murgīk aṇḍā sabh sẵ paigh mōtī hamᵃrā pēṭ mẽ haib kahiā dhyān mẽ āb^i sakai-ach^i*, can the existence of a pearl bigger than a hen's eggs in my belly come within (the realm of) thought ?

अन्धक नेत्र॰ हयबाक औखध अछि, *andhak nētra hayᵃbāk* (for *haibāk*) *aukhadh ach^i*, there is a medicine for the becoming of eyes of a blind man (*i.e.*, which gives sight to the blind).

Participles :—

Present :—हैत प्रात भेल नग्र हकार, *hwaita prāta bhela nagra hakāra*, on dawn becoming, there arose a cry in the town (Man. ii, 42).

होइत भिनसरवा भागि चलल, *hōit bhinᵃsarᵃwā bhāg^i calal*, as morning dawned he ran away.

जनिका जनम होइत हम गेलहुँ ।

ऐलहुँ तनिकर अंते ॥

janikā janama hoita, hama gēlahū̃ |
ailahū̃ tanikara antē ǁ

I returned at the death of him, at whose birth I went out (Vid. xxxix, 2).

मुक्तबन्ध होयित भेलाह, *mukta-bandh hōyit bhēlāh,* he became becoming released from his bonds (*i.e.*, he gradually got free).

Past : See Past Indicative.

Conjunctive :—बिमुखि सुतलि धनि सुमुखि न होइ, *bimukhi sutali dhani sumukhi na hōi*, the damsel, not having become sweet-faced (*i.e.*, refusing to smile), slept with her face turned away (Vid. xxx, 2).

ब्याकुल भै सभ पहुँचल धाए, *byākula bhai sabha pahū̃cala dhāe*, all becoming distressed ran up (Man. iv, 32).

भद्रीक आगू सल्हेस भै गेलाह ठाढ़ि, *bhadrīk āgū salhēs bhai gēlāh* (Hindi *hō gayā*) *ṭhāṛh^i*, Salhēs became erect (*i.e.*, stood up) before Bhadrī.

प्रक बेरि ठाढ़ भे कं कुस्ती लिष्रं, *ek bēr*[i] *ṭhāṛh bhai ke kustī liā,* just once, having stood up, wrestle a fall (with me).

च्राठम भप्र इम च्रपनर्हिं च्राञ्ग्रोब, *āṭhamu bhae hama apanahī āoba,* having become the eighth (child), I shall come myself (Man. i, 32).

———o———

CHAPTER VII.

THE PASSIVE VOICE.

331. As in Hindi, the passive is usually formed by conjugating the past participle with the √जा *jā*, go. The participle is liable to inflection as to gender, in which respect it agrees with the subject of the verb, but in other respects it remains unaltered. Thus देखल जाप्रब, *dēkhal jāeb,* means 'to be seen' देखल जाइत च्रछि, *dēkhal jāit ach*[i], he is being seen; देखल गेल, *dēkhal gēl,* he was seen; देखलि गेलि, *dēkhal*[i] *gēl*[i], she was seen. Examples of this form of the passive are the following :—

बड़ सुकुमार हमर खामी सल्हेस । मारि सहल नहिं जाइकेन्हि, *baṛ sukumār hamar swāmī sal*[a]*hēs; mār*[i] *sahal nuh*[ī] *jāichainh*[i], very tender is my lord Salhēs, a beating is not (*i.e.,* cannot be) borne by him. (Regarding the inanimate feminine मारि *mār*[i], see § 186.)

भाइ जेठ हलङ्ड से मारल गेल कटैया, *bhāi jēṭh chalah*[u], *sē māral gēl kaṭaiyā,* he (who) was your elder brother has been killed in Kaṭaiyā.

अखन च्रपने मन चाही तखन तोड़बा लेल जाय, *jakhan ap*[a]*ne man cāhī, takhan toṛ*[a]*bā lēl jāy,* when your soul desires, then having caused (the fruit) to be plucked, let it be taken away.

In old Maithilī poetry we sometimes find the passive participle put into a strong form in च्रा *ā,* as if we said देखला *dekh*[a]*lā* for देखल *dēkhal.*

Thus, Man. vii, 12 :—

मुइल च्रसुर गोट हुइला गेल, *muila asura goṭa chuilā gēla,* a dead Asura had been touched (by him, and he was consequently unclean).

332. Another form of the passive is formed by conjugating the first verbal noun with the verb पड़ब *paṛab* or परब *parab,* to

fall. Thus देखि पड़ब *dēkh* *parab*, to be seen; देखि पड़ल *dēkh* *paral*, he was seen. The first verbal noun remained unchanged throughout. The whole is an intensive compound (see § 342), and the final र *i* is often omitted.

Examples of the use of this form of the passive are :—

इं तँ केओ अपूर्ब ढंगक लोक देख पड़ैअछि, *i tã keo apūrb dhaṅgak lōk dēkh parai-achi*, this, indeed, is seen (to be) (*i.e.*, is evidently) a person of some extraordinary kind.

कुमरबैनि अछि बा एखन नहिं । हँ किछु किछु बूझि पड़ैअछि, *kumara-baiti achi bā ekhan nahi? hã kichu kichu būjhi parai-achi*, is she showing signs of being in calf or not? Yes, a little is becoming manifested.

333. A **Potential Passive** is formed for some verbs by adding आ *ā* to the root. Thus √देख *dēkh*, see, √देखा *dēkhā*, to be able to be seen, to be visible. This root *dēkhā* is conjugated exactly like any other intransitive root in आ *ā* (see §§ 270 ff). The potential passive indicates not so much that a thing *is* done, as that it *can be* done. Thus इं पोथी पढ़ाइअछि, *i pōthī parhāi-achi*, this book *can be* read, but इं पोथी पढ़ल जाइअछि, *i pōthī parhal jāi-achi*, this book *is being* read. Similarly (√मीझ *mĩjh*, extinguish) we have हमरा पेटक आगि एहि सँ नहिं मिंझाएत, *hamarā pēṭak āgi ehi sã nahi mĩjhāet*, the fire of my belly will not be able to be extinguished by this.

———o———

CHAPTER VIII.

The Formation of Transitive and Causal Verbs.

334. As in other Indo-Aryan languages the intransitive verb in Maithilī can be made transitive and the transitive verb causal.

The transitive verb is generally formed by adding आब *āb* to the root, and the causal by adding अबाब *abāb*, but there are many exceptions. The roots thus formed are conjugated like transitive verbs in आब *āb* (see §§ 270 ff). We often find व *w* written instead of ब *b*, as in स्राव *āw*, स्वाव *ᵃwāw*, and this pronunciation is usually heard in Southern Maithilī, but in the northern or standard dialect the sound is always that of ब *b*, no matter what is written.

In Hindī grammars we have rules about shortening the root vowel of certain causal verbs. These rules are not necessary in Maithilī. The root vowels are shortened according to the regular rule of the short ante-penultimate vowel (see §§ 32 ff).

It thus follows that in forms which consist of only two syllables, the root vowel is not shortened. Thus from √जाग *jāg*, 'be awake,' the transitive root जागाब *jāgāb*, which is also the shortest form of the 2nd person imperative, meaning 'awaken thou.' But the first person future of the transitive is जगाएब *jagāeb*, with the *ā* shortened, as it is now in the ante-penultimate.

335. The following are examples of intransitive verbs becoming transitive, and causal. All verbs are given in the form of the infinitive, so as to show the shortening of the ante-penultimate vowel. It will be remembered that roots in स्राब *āb* form their infinitives in स्राएब *āeb* :—

INTRANSITIVE.	TRANSITIVE.	CAUSAL.
गिरब *girab*, to fall.	गिराएब *girāeb*, to fell.	गिरबाएब *girᵃbāeb*, to cause to fell.
चढ़ब *caṛhab*, to ascend,	चढ़ाएब *caṛhāeb*,	चढ़बाएब *caṛhᵃbāeb*.
पिघलब *pighᵃlab*, to melt.	पिघलाएब *pighᵃlāeb*,	पिघलबाएब *pighalᵃbāeb*.
लटकब *laṭᵃkab*, to hang,	लटकाएब *laṭᵃkāeb*,	लटकबाएब *laṭakᵃbāeb*.
जागब *jāgab*, to awake.	जगाएब *jᵃgāeb*,	जगबाएब *jagᵃbāeb*.
पाकब *pākab*, to ripen,	पकाएब *pakāeb*,	पकबाएब *pakᵃbāeb*.
बाजब *bājab*. to speak,	बजाएब *bajāeb*. to call, summon.	बजबाएब *bujᵃbāeb*.
लागब *lāgab*, to be applied, to begin.	लगाएब *lagāeb*.	लगबाएब *lagᵃbāeb*.
भीजब *bhījab*, to be wet.	भिजाएब *bhijāeb*,	भिजबाएब *bhijᵃbāeb*.

INTRANSITIVE.	TRANSITIVE.	CAUSAL.
घूमब *ghūmab*, to go round.	घुमाप्रब *ghumāeb*,	घुमबाप्रब *ghumᵃbāeb*.
डोलब *ḍōlab*, to be shaken.	डोलाप्रब *ḍolāeb*,	डोलबाप्रब *ḍolᵃbāeb*.
लेटब *leṭab*, to lie down,	लेटाप्रब *leṭāeb*,	लेटबाप्रब *leṭᵃbāeb*.

In the above, note that the √बाज *bāj*, like the Hindi √बोल *bōl*, is intransitive.

Note also that no verbs insert ल *l* as sometimes occurs in Hindi. Thus :—

INTRANSITIVE.	TRANSITIVE.	CAUSAL.
जीअब *jīab*, to live,	जिआप्रब *jiāeb*, to make alive.	जिअबाप्रब *jiabāeb*, to cause to make alive.

336. In the same way transitive verbs form causal and double causals. Thus :—

TRANSITIVE.	CAUSAL.	DOUBLE CAUSAL.
सुनब *sunab*, to hear,	सुनाप्रब *sunāeb*, to cause to hear.	सुनबाप्रब *sunᵃbāeb*, to cause to be heard.
देखब *dēkhab*, to see,	देखाप्रब *dekhāeb*, to show.	देखबाप्रब *dekhᵃbāeb*, to cause to show.
देब *dēb*, to give,	देआप्रब *dēāeb* or दिआप्रब *diāeb*, to cause to give.	देअबाप्रब *deabāeb* or दिअबाप्रब *diabāeb*, to cause to be given.
धोअब *dhōab*, to wash,	धोआप्रब *dhōāeb* or धोबाप्रब *dhōbāeb*.	धोअबाप्रब *dhoabāeb*.
पीअब *piab*, to drink,	पीआप्रब *piāeb* or पीबाप्रब *pībāeb*, to give to drink.	पिअबाप्रब *piabāeb*.
सीखब *sikhab*, to learn,	सिखाप्रब *sikhāeb*,	सिखबाप्रब *sikhᵃbāeb*.

337. Many intransitive verbs with a short vowel in the root simply lengthen it to form the transitive, and form the causal regularly with अबाब *ᵃbāb*; thus :—

INTRANSITIVE.	TRANSITIVE.	CAUSAL.
কটব *kaṭab*, to be cut,	কাটব *kāṭab*, to cut,	কটবাপ্ৰ *kaṭ*ᵃ*bāeb*.
গড়ব *gaṛab*, to be buried.	গাড়ব *gāṛab*, to bury,	গড়বাপ্ৰ *gaṛ*ᵃ*bāeb*.
মরব *marab*, to die.	মারব *mārab*, to kill,	মরবাপ্ৰ *mar*ᵃ*bāeb*.
পলব *palab*, to be reared.	পালব *pālab*, to rear,	পলবাপ্ৰ *pal*ᵃ*bāeb*.
লদব *ladab*, to be loaded.	লাদব *lādab*, to load,	লদবাপ্ৰ *lad*ᵃ*bāeb*.
নিকসব *nikasab*, to come out.	নিকাসব *nikāsab*, to bring out.	নিকসবাপ্ৰ *nikas*ᵃ*bāeb*.

338.　The following are irregular :—

INTRANSITIVE.	TRANSITIVE.	CAUSAL.
খুলব *khulab*, to be open.	খোলব *khōlab*,	খোলবাপ্ৰ *khol*ᵃ*bāeb*.
চূটব *chūṭab*, to go off,	চাড়ব *chāṛab* or চোড়ব *chōṛab*.	চড়বাপ্ৰ *char*ᵃ*bāeb* or চোড়বাপ্ৰ *chor*ᵃ*bāeb*.
টূটব *tūṭab*, to be broken.	তোড়ব *tōṛab* or তোরব *tōrab*.	তোড়বাপ্ৰ *tor*ᵃ*bāeb* or তোরবাপ্ৰ *tor*ᵃ*bāeb*.
ফটব *phaṭab*, to be rent.	ফাড়ব *phōṛab*,	ফড়বাপ্ৰ *phar*ᵃ*bāeb*.
অটব *aṭab*, to be stopped.	অড়াপ্ৰ *aṛāeb* or আড়ব *āṛab*.	অড়বাপ্ৰ *ar*ᵃ*bāeb*.
বিকব *bikab* or বিকাপ্ৰ *bikāeb*, to be sold.	বেচব *bēcab*, or বেচব *bēcab*.	বেচবাপ্ৰ *bec*ᵃ*bāeb*.
রহব *rahab*, to remain,	রাখব *rākhab*,	রখবাপ্ৰ *rakh*ᵃ*bāeb*.
খা *khā*, to eat,	খিষাপ্ৰ *khiāeb*, to feed, give to eat.	খিষবাপ্ৰ *khiabāeb*.

Amongst others, the following verb takes the causal form, but does not use it in a causal, but only in a transitive sense; the causal form thus becomes an optional form of the transitive.

SIMPLE VERB.   TRANSITIVE.

कहब *kahab,* to say,   कहाएब *kahāeb* or कहबाएब *kah^a-bāeb,* to say.

339. A few examples of the Transitive and Causal verbs in literature may be given. Many more will be found under verbs in आब *āb* in § 284.

हीरा हीरा मति बाजू, *hīrā hīrā mat^i bājū,* say not 'diamonds diamonds.'

एक दिन ओ अपना बेटा सभ कें बजौलकै, *ek din ō ap^anā bētā sabh kẽ bajaul^akai,* one day he summoned his sons.

आगि लागल, *āg^i lāgal,* fire was attached (to the house, *i.e.,* the house took fire).

स्वामी में लय किऐ नहि लगबैछह, *swāmī mẽ lay kiai nah^i lag^abai-chah,* why do you not apply your mind in (*i.e.,* on the contemplation of) the Lord ?

सूपत बेंचि कें देली अहि दियाय, *sūpat bẽc^i ke dēlī ah^i diyāy,* I, having sold, have given the full weight, having caused (him) to give (tobacco in exchange).

अनाथ लोक काँ इच्छा भोजन देआबथि, *anāth lōk kā̃ icchā bhōjan deābath^i,* to the destitute people he causes food to be given (according to) their desires (*Puruṣa Parikṣā,* p. 49).

बस्तु देअबयित छथि, *hast^u deabayit chath^i,* he is causing goods to be given (Ib., p. 51).

जाइ पिआबिऐ अधर सुधारस, *jāi piābiai adhara sudhārasa,* having gone, give her the nectar of your lower lip to drink (Vid. x, 10).

हम की की निकासू ! आगि लागल झोंपड़ी जे निकसे से लाभ *ham kī kī nikāsū ? āg^i lāgal jhōp^a^rī, je nikase, se lābh,* what shall we bring out ? When a hut is afire, whatever comes out, that is gain.

बहुत उपर जाइ कें छाड़ि देलक, *bahut ūpar jāe kã̊ chāṛ^i dēlak,* going up very high, he let it go.

धाबाक डारि तोरि मांछी चौंक, *dhābāk ḍār̐ tōr̐ mā̃chī haũk,* having broken off a branch of the *dhābā* tree, drive away the flies.

दुनू भाइ के खियौलक, *dunū bhāi kē khiaulak,* she fed the two brothers.

————o————

CHAPTER IX.

COMPOUND VERBS.

340. Compound verbs may be classed as—(1) those formed with a verbal noun, and (2) those formed with a participle.

 I. Those formed with a verbal noun are—

    (*a*) Intensives.
    (*b*) Potentials.
    (*c*) Completives.
    (*d*) Permissives.
    (*e*) Acquisitives.
    (*f*) Inceptives.
    (*g*) Desideratives.
    (*h*) Frequentatives.

 II. Those formed from the participles are—

    (*a*) Continuatives.
    (*b*) Staticals.

Class I.—**Compounds formed with the Verbal Noun.**

341. As explained in §§ 178 ff., there are three verbal nouns, *viz.* :—

  (1) देखि *dēkh̐* ; obl. देखै *dēkhai* or देखा *dēkhā*.

  (2) देखब *dēkhab*; obl. देखबा *dekhªbā*.

  (3) देखल, *dēkhal*; obl. देखला *dekhªlā*.

The following are made with the direct form of the first verbal noun :—

 (*a*) Intensives.
 (*b*) Potentials.
 (*c*) Completives.

 37

The following are made with the oblique form of the first verbal noun :—

(*d*) Permissives.

(*e*) Acquisitives.

(*f*) Inceptives.

(*g*) Desideratives are sometimes made with the genitive of the second verbal noun, but more usually with the oblique form of the first verbal noun.

(*h*) Frequentatives are made with the direct form of the third verbal noun.

342. (*a*) **Intensive** compounds intensify, or otherwise modify, the meaning of the verb whose root stands first in the compound. They are made by adding to the direct form of the first verbal noun one of certain auxiliary verbs. The verbal noun remains unchanged, and the auxiliary verb is conjugated throughout as usual. This second auxiliary conjugated member does not, however, retain its separate character and significance, but only modifies, in accordance with the general idea which it embodies, the meaning of the unconjugated verbal noun to which it is attached.

The first verbal noun ends in ₹ *i* (देखि *dĕkhⁱ*). This final vowel is only half-pronounced, and, in these compounds, it is often dropped both in writing and in pronunciation ; so that, *in these compounds*, we may have either देखि *dĕkhⁱ* or देख *dĕkh*. This elision of *i* (or *y*, etc., see § 281) most frequently occurs in the case of verbs whose roots ends in vowels.

The auxiliary verbs usually employed to form intensives are :—

देब *dĕb*, to give, implying in these compounds *intensity.*

डारब *ḍārab*, to throw,	,,	*violence.*
आएब *āeb*, to come, ⎱	,,	*completion.*
जाएब *jāeb*, to go, ⎰		
पड़ब *paṛab* or परब *parab*, to fall.	,,	*chance.*
उठब *uṭhab*, to rise,	,,	*suddenness.*
रहब *rahab*, to remain,	,,	*continuation.*
लेब *lĕb*, to take,	,,	*reflexiveness.*

Note that पड़ब *paṛab*, to fall, is also used to make passives. See § 332.

Examples of such intensive compounds are :—

भरब *bharab*, to fill. | भरि देब *bhar^i dēb*, to fill up.
उड़ाएब *uṛāeb*, to cause to fly. | उड़ाइ or (उड़ा) देब *uṛāi (or uṛā) dēb*, to squander.
हेड़ाएब *heṛāeb*, to lose. | हेड़ा देब *hēṛā dēb*, to lose out and out.
खसाएब *khasāeb*, to cause to fall. | खसाय देब *khasāy dēb*, to throw down.
काटब *kāṭab*, to cut. | कािट डारब *kāṭ^i ḍārab*, to cut off.
बनब *banab*, to be made. | बनि आएब *ban^i āeb* or बनि जाएब *ban^i jāeb*, to be completely made.
चलब *calab*, to go. | चलि जाएब *cal^i jāeb*, to go away.
खाएब *khāeb*, to eat. | खा जाएब *khā jāeb*, to eat up.
पीअब *pīab*, to drink. | पी जाएब *pī jāeb* or पिबि जाएब *pib^i jāeb*, to drink up.
होएब *hōeb*, to be, to become. | हो जाएब *hō jāeb*, भे जाएब *bhai jāeb*, to become (definitely).
जाएब *jāeb*, to go. | जाए पड़ब *jāe paṛab*, to happen to go.
पुकारब *pukārab*, to call out. | पुकारि उठब *pukār^i uṭhab*, to call out suddenly, give a scream.
होएब *hōeb*, to be, become. | हो रहब *hō rahab*, to be.
सूतब *sūtab*, to sleep. | सूति रहब *sūt^i rahab*, to sleep on.
पीअब *pīab*, to drink. | पी लेब *pī lēb* or पिबि लेब *pib^i lēb*, to drink, take to drink.
राखब *rākhab*, to place. | रािख लेब *rākh^i lēb*, to lay by (for one's own use).
लेब *lēb*, to take. | ले लेब *lai lēb*, to take for oneself.

343. It will be remembered that the conjunctive participle may be the same in form as the verbal noun. Phrases in which this form of the conjunctive participle occurs are not intensive compounds. Thus ले जाएब *lai jāeb*, 'having taken to go,' 'to take away,' is not an intensive compound. If it were an intensive compound, it would mean ' to take completely,' which it does not

mean. On the other hand दे आएब *dai jāeb* is an intensive compound and means 'to give out and out.' Again, while बनि आएब *bani āeb* is an intensive compound, and means 'to be completely made,' निकसि आएब *nikasi āeb* is 'having emerged to come,' *i.e.*, 'to come out,' and is not an intensive compound, but is simply a phrase with the conjunctive participle. The essence of an intensive compound is that the auxiliary verb loses all or some of its proper meaning, which is not in the case in निकसि आएब *nikasi āeb*.

344. These intensive compounds are extremely common in Maithili. Dozens of instances will be found on every page of any book in the language. The following are a few typical examples :—

काठी सबहि कें तोड़ि दे, *kāṭhī sabahi kē tōṛi dē*, break the sticks.

हमरा लग पठाय दैह, *hamᵃrā lag paṭhāy daih*, send (them) to us.

सभ भेंड़ड़ खाय गेल, *sabh bhẽ̄rahᵘ khāy gēl*, they ate up all the sheep also.

तीनि सै सँ किच्छु बढ़ि जाएत, *tīni sai sẫ kicchᵘ baṛhi jāet*, they somewhat exceed three hundred.

सभ बस्तुजात जरि कें छाउर भे गेल, *sabh bastujāt jari kẫ chāur bhai gēl*, all the property being burnt became ashes.

एक खिखिरि कोनो फुलबारी में जाय परलि, *ek khikhiri kōnō phulᵃbārī mē̃ jāy parali*, a she-fox happened to go into a certain garden.

अम्माक सबद सुनि दीना भद्री उठल चिह्राय, *ammāk sabad suni dīnā bhadrī uṭhal cihrāy* (for *cihrāy uṭhal*), hearing their mother's words Dīnā and Bhadrī started up.

एक मुर्गा गोबरक ढेरी कें चाँगुर सँ उकटि रहल चल, *ek murgā gobᵃrak ḍhērī kẽ cā̃gur sẫ ukaṭi rahal chal*, a cock was scratching (going along scratching) a dunghill with his claw.

किच्छु सीखि लेए, *kicchᵘ sīkhi lēē*, let him learn (for himself).

अपना में बाँटि ली, *apᵃnā mē̃ bā̃ṭi lī*, let us divide (it) among ourselves.

আবহ বৈসহ পিবি লহ পানি, *ābaha* (m.c. for *ābáh*), *baisaha* (*baisáh*), *pibi laha* (for *láh*) *pāni*, come, sit down, take a drink of water (Vid. lxxx, 4).

In one place Vidyāpati employs a sort of long form of the first verbal noun.

জৈতহিঁ হার টুটিপ গেল না, *jaitahĩ hāra tuṭie* (for *ṭuṭi*) *gela nā*, as I went my necklace broke in pieces (না *nā* is expletive) (Vid. xxvi, ૦). Compare Vidyāpati's conjunctive participle করিপ *karie* at the end of § 307.

345. (*b*) **Potential** compounds are formed by conjugating the verb সকব, *sakab*, 'to be able,' with the direct form of the first verbal noun of the principal verb. As in intensives, the final ই *i* is sometimes omitted. Thus:—

চলি সকব *chali sakab*, to be able to move.

বাজি সকব *bāji sakab*, to be able to speak.

লিখি সকব *likhi sakab*, to be able to write.

দে সকব *dai sakab*, to be able to give.

লে সকব *lai sakab*, to be able to take.

জাএ সকব *jāe sakab*, to be able to go.

ভেট সকব *bhēṭ sakab*, to be able to meet.

Examples from literature are—

ধ্যান মে আবি সকৈঅছি, *dhyān mē ābi sakai-achi*, it can come into thought, it is conceivable.

পছতৌলা সঁ কী মে সকৈঅছি, *pachᵃtaulā sã̄ kī bhai sakai-achi*, from regretting what can happen?

অঁগূর সভক গুচ্ছ লগ নহিঁ পড়ঁচ সকলি, *ãgūr sabhak guchch lag nahĩ pahū̃c sakali*, she could not reach the bunch of grapes.

346. (*c*) **Completive** compounds are similarly formed with the verb চুকব *cukab*, to be finished. The ই *i* is here also sometimes dropped. Thus:—

मारि चुकब, *mār^i cukab,* to have finished beating.

खा चुकब, *khā cukab,* to have finished eating.

दै चुकब, *dai cukab,* to have finished giving.

Curiously enough, I have not noted any occurrence of this compound in literature.

347. (*d*) **Permissive** compounds are made by conjugating the verb देब *dēb,* to give, with the oblique form of the first verbal noun. Thus :—

कहे देब, *kahai dēb,* or कहाँ देब *kahā́ dēb,* to allow to speak.

जाए देब, *jāe dēb,* to allow to go.

ओ ओकरा खाए देलकैक, *ō ok^{a}rā khāe del^{a}kaik,* he allowed him to eat.

कालू सदा दीना भद्री के बैसे देलथीन्हि, *kālū sadā dīnā bhadrī kē baisai del^{a}thīnh^i,* Kālū Sadā allowed Dinā and Bhadri to sit down.

नहिं दूध पीबै देबे, *nah^i dūdh pībai dēbē,* (if) you will not allow us to drink milk.

348. (*e*) **Acquisitive** compounds are similarly formed with the verb पाएब *pāeb,* to get. Thus :—

ओ उठे नहिं पाबथि, *ō uṭhai nah^i pābath^i,* let him not get (permission) to rise.

जिबैत जाए एकौ नहिं पाओत, *jibaita jāe ekau nah^i pāota,* not one will get leave (*i.e.*, be able) to depart alive (Man. viii, 43).

349. (*f*) **Inceptive** compounds are similarly formed with the verb लागब *lāgab,* to begin. Thus :—

कहाँ लागब, *kahā́ lāgab,* to begin to speak.

दीआँ लागब, *dīā́ lāgab,* to begin to give.

मारै लागल, *mārai lāgal,* he began to beat.

बाघ खाए लागल, *bāgh khāe lāgal,* the tiger began to eat.

बुढ़िआ कहे लागलि, *buṛhiā kahai lāgal^i,* the old woman began to say.

चारि जन आलसी पुरुख ततहिं असंक सूतल परस्पर कथा करय लगलाह,
cārⁱ jan āl^asī purukh tatahⁱ asaṅk sūtal paraspar kathā karay lag^a-lăh, four lazy men, lying there without anxiety, began to talk to each other (Puruṣa Parikṣā, p. 51).

In one instance Manbōdh (i, 12) uses the oblique form of the second verbal noun in an inceptive compound, as follows :—

कमलासन किछु कहबाँ लागु, *kamalāsana kichu kahabā̃ lāgu*, (Brahmā) whose seat is on the lotus begins to say something.

350. (*y*) **Desiderative** compounds, as in Hindī, often indicate that something is on the point of occurrence. They are formed in two ways :—

(i) By the phrase इच्छा अछि *icchā achhⁱ*, meaning "there is a desire," following the genitive of the second verbal noun in ब *b*.

(ii) By the accusative, genitive, or simple oblique form of the first or second verbal noun with the verb चाहब *cāhab*, to wish :—
Examples —

(i) देखबाक इच्छा अछि, *dekh^abāk icchā achhⁱ*, there is a desire of seeing, *i.e.*, I wish to see.

(ii) हम देखैं कें चहैंछी, *ham dekhẵ kẽ cahai-chī*, I wish to see.

ओ बाजा चहैअछि, *ō bājă cahai-achⁱ*, he wishes to speak.

मारै चाहलक, *mărai căh^alak*, he wanted to kill (him).

धरै चाह फेरि साँपे, *dharai cāha pheri sẵpē*, a snake again wishes to seize it (Vid. xxii, 6).

घड़ी बाजै चहैचलि, *gharī bājai cahai-chalⁱ*, the clock was about to strike:

हमहूँ अपना बालक कें स्कूल में पठाबै चाहैछी, *hamah^ū ap^anā bālak kẽ skūl mẽ paṭhābai căhai-chī*, I also want to send my boy to school.

ओ जाए चहैछथि, *ō jāe cahai-chathⁱ*, he wishes to go.

ओ मरै (vulgarly मुऐ) चहैत अछि, *ō marai* (vulgarly *muai*)· *cahait achⁱ*, he is at the point of death.

धोअल धाप्रल मेंड़ी पाँका लागे चा॑ंदृ॓ब्कि, *dhōal ăhăel bhēṛī pākā lāgai căhai-ach^i*, the sheep washed (for sale) is about to fall into the slough. (Proverb.)

प्रदि पोथी कें पढ़ंक चा॑ही, *eh^i pōthi kē puṛhăk cāhī*, one should read this book.

तो॑दरा ओ॑तय जा॑प्रक (or जा॑प्र or जा॑प्र कें) चा॑ही, *toh^arā otay jāek (or jāe or jāe kē) cāhī*, you should go there.

बड़त सोच बिचा॑रि कें करैक चा॑ही . . . पछ॑तैबाक नहिं चा॑ही, *bahut sōc bicār^i kai karaik cāhī . . . . pach^ataibāk nah^i cāhī*, one should act after much thought and consideration . . . . one should not regret.

In the above, note the use of चा॑ही *cāhī*, equivalent to the Hindi चा॑हिये *cāhiyē*.

Class II.—Compounds formed with Participles.

351. (*a*). **Continuative** compounds are formed with the direct form of the masculine Present Participle. Thus :—

लिखैत जा॑प्रब, *likhait jāeb*, to continue writing.

पढ़ैत जा॑प्रब, *puṛhait jāeb*, to continue reading.

बजैत जा॑प्रब, *bajait jāeb*, to continue speaking.

जा॑इत र॑ख़ब, *jāit rahab*, to continue going

प॑बैत आ॑प्रब, *pabait āeb*, to go on finding.

पा॑नि ब॑दैत जा॑द्रब्कि, *pāni bahait jāi-ach^i*, the water keeps flowing away.

नदी क॑र धार ब॑दैत र॑द्रब्कि, *nadī kēr dhār bahait rahai-ach^i*, the stream of the river keeps flowing on.

352. (*b*) **Statical** compounds are similarly made except that the participle agrees in gender with the subject of the verb. Thus :—

कनैत च॑लब, *kanait calab*, to go along crying.

गबैत आ॑प्रब, *gabait āeb*, to come singing.

प्रक स्त्री गबैति अबैक॑लि, *ek strī gabait^i abai-chal^i*, a woman was coming singing.

रसायनी ओहि राति कँ कतहूँ चलैत भेल, *rasāyᵃnī ohⁱ rātⁱ kằ katahᵘ calait bhēl*, the alchemist that night became going somewhere (*i.e.*, took to his heels).

Quasi continuative or statical compounds are also formed with the third verbal noun or past participle, as in :—

पानि बहल जाइत अछि, *pāni bahal jāit achⁱ*, the water keeps flowing away.

एक बाघ पड़ल फिरैछल, *ek bāgh paṛal phirai-chal*, a tiger was prowling about.

हमरा संग लागल चलँह *hamᵃrā saṅg lāgal calằh*, come along with me.

अढ़ाइ सै तँ बचले रहत। आओर ओहि मैं सँ जे बाँचल निकसत, ओहि सभक नीक दाम भेंटत, *aṛhāi sai tã bacᵃlē rahat, āor ohⁱ mẽ sã jē bằcal nikᵃsat, ohⁱ sabhak nīk dām bhẽṭat*, at any rate a hundred will remain over and above, and from those that will remain over and above, I will get a good price for them. Note in this case that the locative of the verbal noun and the direct form of the participle are quite synonymous.

353. The equivalent of the Hindī चला जाना *calā jānā* is the intensive compound चलि जाएब *calⁱ jāeb* or चलि होएब *calⁱ hōeb*. Thus :—

चलि गेल जोगिया जाँजरि, *calⁱ gēl jogiyā-jãjarⁱ*, they went away to Jogiyā-Jānjari

हाँथ लेलैं बाढ़नि चलि भेलि सिंघ दरबाज, *hãth lēlẽ bāṛhanⁱ calⁱ bhēlⁱ siṅgh darᵃbāj*, taking the broom in her hand she went to the main door of the house.

कुंज भबन सँ चलि भेलि हे, *kuñja bhabana sã cali bhelⁱ hē*, (as) she came out of the arbour (Vid. xxi, 1).

चलि जाएब *calⁱ jāeb* means 'to go away,' चलि होएब *calⁱ hōeb* is simply 'to go.'

354. Attention has also been called in § 180 to the use of the instrumental or locative of the third verbal noun or past

participle to indicate continued action, especially to the phrases लेलें जाप्रब *lēlē jāeb*, to take away with one, and लेलें स्राप्रब *lēlē āeb*, to bring with one, equivalent to the Hindī लिये जाना *liyē jānā* and लिये स्राना *liyē ānā*, respectively. Equivalent to the Hindī ले स्राना *lē ānā* or लाना *lānā* is लें स्राप्रब *lai āeb*, or लाप्रब *lāeb*, to bring. Varieties of लें स्राप्रब *lai āeb* are लिस्राप्रब *liāeb*, लय स्राप्रब *lay āeb*, and लँ स्राप्रब *lå̄ āeb*. Equivalent to the Hindī ले जाना *lē jānā* is लें (लय or लँ) जाप्रब *lai* (*lay* or *lå̄*) *jāeb*, to take away. Thus:—

किच्छु चाँनी दमरा स्रोतय लें स्राबँद, *kicch^u cāni ham^arā otay lai ābåh*, bring some silver to my house.

स्रामी सलदेस लाप्रब जादू सौं लोभाप्र, *swāmī sal^hēs lāeb jādū saŭ lobhāe*, I will bring my lord Salhēs, having enticed him by enchantment.

दमरा सौं की लेबें स्रोजद दनाम, *ham^arā saŭ ki laibai ojah inām*, what reward or present will you bring from me?

दम चोरी कै लेलहुँ, *ham cōri kai lailah^u*, having done theft, I have brought (it).

लें जाद, *lai jāh*, take away, as in § 180.

दमरा सोभा सँ उठा लँ जाप्रत, *ham^arā sōjhā så̄ uṭhā lå̄ jāet*, he will take it away from before me.

दमरो रंग रभस लय जेबद ।
लेबद कोन सनेसे ।

hamarō ranya rabhasa laya jaibaha (for *jaibåh*) ।
laibaha (for *laibåh*) *kōna sanēsē* ॥

Thou wilt also take away also all my joy and passion. What present will you bring (in return) (Vid. lv, 2).

More usual than लाप्रब *lāeb* is the verb स्रानब *ānab*, to bring, as in दुर सै रुपैस्राक चाँनी स्रोद्दि रसायनी कें स्रानि देलकं, *dui sai rupai-āk cāni oh^i rasāy^anī kē ān^i del^akai*, having brought silver (to the value) of two hundred rupees, he gave it to that alchemist.

PART IV.

Indeclinables.

A. Adverbs.

355. Henceforth I shall not transliterate.

The following lists have been collected :—

I. Adverbs of Time.

এখন, আব	Now.	পহিলে	At first.
তখন তদ্দিন	} Then.	সবের সবেরক অত্যুষ ভোর	} Early, at dawn.
কখন কদ্দিন	} When?		
যখন অদ্দিন	} When.	কদাচিত কদাপি কচিক্রো	} Perhaps, some-times.
আজ	To-day.		
কালি	Yesterday, to-mor-row.	এতবা মেঁ	In the meantime.
আজ কালি	Now-a-days.	নিদান অন্ত অন্তকাল	} At last.
পরশু	The day before yes-terday, or the day after to-morrow.		
		বেরিবেরি বারংবার	} Often.
প্রতিদিন অনুদিন সবদিন	} Every day.	শীঘ্র	Quickly.
		লগলে	Instantly.
সদা সর্বদা	} Always.	পশ্চাত্ পাছা	} Afterwards.
		ফেরি	Again.
নিনি	Continually.	একবেরি	Once.

356.   II. Adverbs of Place.

प्रतय	*Here.*	सगपास	*On all sides.*
ओतय	*There.*	समीप	*Near.*
कतय, कहाँ	*Where ?*	प्रद्दिकात	*On this side.*
जतय, जहाँ	*Where.*	ओद्दिकात	*On that side.*
ततय, तहाँ	*There.*	सर्बत्र	}*Everywhere.*
एम्हर	*Hither.*	सभठाम	
ओम्हर	*Thither.*	उपर	*Above.*
केम्हर	*Whither ?*	नीचें	*Below.*
जेम्हर	*Whither.*	पार	*Across.*
तेम्हर	*Thither.*	निकट	}*Near.*
कतहुँ	*Somewhere.*	नगीच	

357.   III. Adverbs of Manner.

अचानक	*Suddenly.*	मिथ्या or व्या	}*In vain.*
अकस्मात्	}*Accidentally.*	ब्यर्थ	
अचक में		नाहक	
चुप्पे	*Privately.*	एना	*Thus.*
अति	*Very.*	किप्रे	*Why ?*
प्रथक	}*Separately.*	किप्रेक तं	*Because.*
फराक		कोना, कोन तरहें	*How ?*
भटपट	}*At once.*	जेना, जैं तरहें	*As.*
भटट्		तेना, तैं तरहें	*So.*
तथापि	}*Nevertheless.*	नीक	*Well.*
तैओ		सत्य	*Truly.*
यद्यपि	}*Although.*	सद्दज, सद्दजें,	}*Gratis.*
जद्पि		सद्दज·में	
अैओ		रत्यादि, र्आदि,	*Etcetera.*

358.   IV.   ADVERBS OF AFFIRMATION AND NEGATION.

हँ, *Yes.*	बस, *Enough !*
निश्चय, *Certainly.*	नहिं, ने, नै, न, *No, not.*
निस्सन्देह, *Doubtlessly.*	जनु, मति. *No, do not* (with im-
अवश्य, *Necessarily.*	perative).

359. The following are further examples of COMPOUND ADVERBS :—

एक बेरि, *Once upon a time.*	और कतहुँ, *Elsewhere.*
कहिआ कहिआ, *Sometimes.*	कतहुँ नहिं, *Nowhere.*
नहुँ नहुँ, सुस्ते सुस्ते, *Gently.*	एतय धरि, *Hitherto.*
एखन धरि, *Till now, yet.*	नहिं तँ, *If not, else.*
कहिआ धरि, कखन धरि, कहाँ तक, *Till when ? How long ?*	कहिओ न कहिओ, *Some time or other.*
कहिओ नहिं, *Never.*	कतहुँ न कतहुँ, *Somewhere or other.*
दुनु दिग्, *On both sides, all round.*	
एहम अोेहन, *Indifferently.*	जखन न तखन, *Now and then.*
जौं कहिओ, *Whenever.*	एना नें एना, *Somehow or other.*

360. The following are examples in which adverbs take the signs of cases after them :—

एखनुक बेरि नीक छक, *Now is the best time.* (Lit. *The time of now is good*).

तहिआ सँ आइ भेट भेल अछि, *I have not seen you since then till to-day.* (Lit. *From that time to-day a (first) meeting has occurred*).

निदान कँ ऐलाह, *At last he came.*

अन्तकाल में ग्यान भेलन्हि, *At length he came to his senses.*

अो आइ कँ काल्हि कहैत छथि, *He puts off from to-day to to-morrow.* (Lit. *He calls to-day to-morrow*).

PARTICLES OF EMPHASIS.

361. These are इ and चि or हिं, *only, even,* and ओ and उ or हुँ, *also, even.* They are always used enclitically, and when any

of them is added to a word ending in आ, that आ is omitted.
Examples : हमरी, *mine only* (हमर + ई), or *me only* (हमरा + ई); प्रखनहिं,
even now, already ; हमरो or हमरहुँ, *mine also*, or *me also* ; उतर,
a reply, उतरो, *even a reply* ; अपनहुँ, *even one's own*.

B. Postpositions.

362. The following is a list of the more usual Postpositions:—

आगू, आगां, *Before.*	संमुख, सोभां, *Facing.*
पीछु, पाछु, पाछां, *Behind.*	साढान, *Before.*
बाढ़ि, *Except.*	लेल, *For, on account of.*
अपर, *Above.*	बिनु, बिना, *Without, except.*
नीचां, *Beneath.*	बाहिर, *Out.*
पर, पै, *On, upon.*	संग, *With.* [(of).
भीतर, *Within.*	बदला, *In exchange (for), instead*
तक, *Up to.*	जकां, *Like.*

The above all govern either the simple oblique form or else
the genitive case, saving बाढ़ि, *except*, and बिनु or बिना, *without.*
The latter governs either the Instrumental or the Dative,
as in :—

बिना पुरुख सौं कोना दिबस गमाप्रब, *how shall I pass my days
without a husband ?*

बिना पुरुख कें चिष्रा प्रतेक बेरि सूतलि, *did a woman sleep so long
without (her) husband.*

बाढ़ि takes the accusative. खुंदचा बाढ़ि किच्छु नहिं, *nothing but
the husk.*

C. Conjunction.

363. The following are the more useful :—

आखोर, औ, or ओ *And.*	की...की, *Either...or.*
के or कि, *That.*	परंतु, *But.*
चो. *Else, even.*	नौं, *If.*
नं, *Then,*	

यौं is often idiomatically omitted.   Thus :—

ओहरी प्रकरा पबैत तॅ अत्यंत खुस चोदस, *if a jeweller had got this then he would have been much pleased.*

364. D. **Interjections**, see § 93.   Others as in Hindi.

ERRATA.

A few of these are important.

Page 5. line 19, *for* see *read* obtain
,, 6, ,, 7, ,, देखइ ,, देखइत
,, 7, ,, 1 and 3 of footnote, *for* dipthongal *read* diphthongal
,, 9, ,, 9, *for* ढ   *read* द्
,, ,, ,, 17, ,, ष   ,, ए्
,, 10, ,, 19, ,, म लौवा   ,, मांलौवा
,, 11, ,, 2, ,, *aū*   ,, *au*
,, 12, ,, 1 of footnote, *for* on ,, in
,, 13, ,, 10, *for* ∽ *ṛh*   ,, ~ *ṛh*
,, ,, ,, 15, ,, खाँभ *bhā̃bh* ,, खाँभ *khā̃bh*
,, 14, ,, 7, ,, देखलङ्   ,, देखलहुँ
,, 15, ,, 2, *for* indicate by the sign, *read* indicate by the sign ,
,, 16, ,, 13, ,, ष a   *read* ष a
,, 21, ,, 8, ,, पोथ   ,, पोथी
,, ,, ,, 12, ,, *wā̃* or *wē̃*   ,, *wā̃* or *wē̃* व *wē̃*
,, 25, ,, 5, ,, *ūnā*   ,, *sūnā*
,, 27, ,, 8, ,, rower   ,, rower ;
,, 29, ,, 5, ,, § 10,   ,, (§ 10,
,, ,, ,, 6; ,, बङ   ,, बङ्
,, 36, ,, 10, ,, करौनी   ,, कँरौनी
,, ,, ,, 14, ,, डंगौनी   ,, डंगौनी
,, 39, last line, *for* the   ,, by the
,, 44, line 1, *for* रि   ,, रि
,, 46, ,, 14, ,, ल   ,, ले
,, ,, ,, 17, ,, a *a* ब   ,, a ब
,, 49, ,, 9, ,, वदिरा   ,, बदिरा
,, 52, ,, 7, ,, al   ,, all
,, ,, last line, ,, t   ,, it
,, 53, line 16, ,, कथँ   ,, कथँ

Page 55, line 18, *for* o   *read* of

 ,, ,, ,, 21, ,, *carhābai*   ,, *carhā̃bai*

 ,, 59, ,,   2, from bottom, *for* म   ,, में

 ,, 60, ,,   4, ,,   ,,   ,, मैं   ,, में

 ,, 86, ,,   11, *for* एचि   ,, प्रचि

 ,, 90, ,,   13, ,,   क   ,, कें

,. 95, ,,   23, ,,   केस... *kēśu*   ,, केस... *kesa*

 ,, 109, ,,   3, ,,   *dekhau*   ,, *dēkhau*

 ,, ,, ,,   4, ,,   *dekhah^u*   ,, *dēkhah^u*.

 ,, ,, ,,   6, ,,   औ   ,, औ   *au*

 ,, 120, ,,   2, from bottom, *for* कौ *read* कौ

 ,, 127, ,,   1, and heading.   This page should commence with § 197.

 ,, 133, line 18, *for* कर-गं *read* करें-गं

 ,, 139, ,,   9, ,,   देव   ,, देब

 ,, 155, ,,   7, from bottom, for *lagal^a thinh^i* read *lagal^athīnh^i*

 ,, 216, ,,   9, *for* sees   *read* is visible

 ,, 270, ,,   10, ,,   two   ,, two hundred

 ,, 302, ,,   2, from bottom, *for* नों   ,, जों

 ,, ,,   last line, *for* नं   ,, तं

 ,, 303, line 1,   ,, यों   ,, जों

Table shewing the various alphabets used in Mithilā.

Dēva Nāgarī	Kaithī	Maithilī	English Transliteration	Dēva Nāgarī	Kaithī	Maithilī	English Transliteration
			a				ñ
			ā				ṭ
			i				ṭh
			ī				ḍ
			u				ḍh
			ū				ṇ
			r̥				t
			r̥̄				th
			l̥				d
			ē				dh
			ai				n
			o				p
			au				ph
			aṁ				b
			ah				bh
			k				m
			kh				y
			g				r
			gh				l
			ṅ				v or w
			c				ś
			ch				s
			j				s
			jh				h

The semi-vowel व is not used by Kāyasths in writing Maithilī the vowel इ being substituted for it.

See § 4 APPENDIX

A Sanskrit Slóka written in the three characters of Mithilā.

उद्द स्माख्यात्मीय तांविद् मिद मेवास्म द्द ष्यन्ते ·॥

दयाल्लुरपियन्क्क शेानास्मद्दु : र्व्वजिह्हींनि ॥१॥

श्वस्मास्वात्मीश्र्श मील् मीद् मेवासीश्र कींशींस्रि ·।

द्द स्श्ाहन पील त्क्की रेानास्मद्दुऽव्यंदी द्दीर्व्यंनी ·॥१॥

The Kayathi character is not adapted for writing Sanshrit. It has no form for short medial i, and has no semivowel ya.

अग्मा स्वाम्मेर्यतां ठिक्दु मिद मेरास्पद्दुज्यते ·॥

दयान्तु रपियक्केक्केोना स्माद्दु : र्व्जिद्वींर्षठि ·॥१॥